Creative Arts Marketing

To our children and god-children

Creative Arts Marketing

Elizabeth Hill, Catherine O'Sullivan and
Terry O'Sullivan

Butterworth-Heinemann Ltd
Linacre House, Jordan Hill, Oxford OX2 8DP

ℛ A member of the Reed Elsevier plc group

OXFORD   LONDON   BOSTON
MUNICH   NEW DELHI   SINGAPORE   SYDNEY
TOKYO   TORONTO   WELLINGTON

First published 1995

British Library Cataloguing in Publication Data
Hill, Elizabeth
    Creative Arts Marketing
    I. Title
    700.688

ISBN 0 7506 2237 7

Printed in Great Britain by Scotprint Ltd, Musselburgh, Scotland

Contents

Acknowledgements

We would like to take this opportunity to thank those individuals and organizations who have given us permission to use and adapt material for this book. Every effort has been made to trace the owners of copyright material, though in a few cases this has proved impossible and we apologize to any copyright holders whose rights may have been unwittingly infringed. We trust that in the event of any accidental infringement, the owners of the material will contact us directly.

Our warm thanks are also due to the following people, for their help with this book, or for the example of good practice they set us by their work in the arts:
Mike Bettison, Michael Birch, Clare Brennan, Mike Brown, Annie Castledine, David Charters, Padraig Cusack, David Edwards, Sarah Finlay, Fiona Gasper, Tomas Hardiman, Deborah Hindley, Chris Honer, Jenny Houghton, Andy Iredale, Philip Jones, Jude Kelly, Maureen Lawrence, Emer McNamara, Suzi Morse, Jonathan Petherbridge, Liza Stevens, Dominic Tinner, Stephen Walton, Will Weston, Lisa Williams, Julian Woolford and Tom, Isabelle, Oliver, Ruari and Ned.

Introduction

A brief history of marketing

Marketing is one of the big ideas of the twentieth century. And, at least in the last twenty years, it has been one of the biggest ideas in the arts. But in a sense there is nothing new about it. It is simply the active recognition by organizations that without customers they have nothing but costs. Peter Drucker, a leading thinker and writer on management, once described it simply as 'creating and keeping customers'. It is this focus on customers that distinguishes successful organizations from their less successful counterparts. In an increasingly competitive economic environment, marketing offers organizations of whatever size or purpose a lifeline not only to success but to survival itself.

Marketing as a recognized management discipline first emerged in post-war America, when the supply of goods began to grow more rapidly than consumer demand for them. Manufacturers found that in the face of increased competition they had to rethink their attitudes to business. The old ways of operating were no longer working. These included 'production-led' and 'sales-led' approaches.

Production-led businesses maintained that if a product was of sufficiently high quality, people would flock to buy it without any further effort. It's an attitude rather like that of Ralph Waldo Emerson in his famous dictum that 'If a man but make a better mousetrap than his neighbour, tho' he build his house in the woods, the world will make a beaten path to his door.' Certainly, as we shall stress in this book, quality is essential to marketing success. In the arts a central part of a customer's experience is the sense of excellence itself – the deftness of a painter, the grace of a dancer, the 'rightness' of a theatrical moment, the welcome extended by a venue. But in an environment where there are so many other claims on people's attention and energies, the arts cannot afford to hide their light, however bright, under a bushel.

Sales-led businesses maintained that the key to success lay in the energy an organization put into selling its goods to customers. High-pressure sales techniques offered a way for businesses to browbeat their way to prosperity. It's probably true that, given energy and application, you can sell anything. But you will probably only be able to sell it once. Where the sales approach falls down is in establishing long-term business relationships. It's interesting to reflect that businesses which rely heavily on selling, such as encyclopedias, double glazing and life assurance, all involve purchases which tend to be one-offs. The principles of selling, as we shall see, have an essential role in the way that arts organizations service their customers. And arts marketers need to be as evangelistic about their product as the most fervent 'foot in the door' sales rep. But genuine success in the arts, as elsewhere, lies not in isolated transactions but in long-term relationships with customers.

The marketing approach allows you to establish such relationships. In the words of the Chartered Institute of Marketing it is 'The management process which identifies, anticipates, and supplies customer requirements efficiently and profitably.' By moving the focus of an organization's planning and decision making on to a consideration of its customers' requirements, what the organization produces can be made more appropriate to their needs. This in turn should lead to their choice of it above the alternatives available in the marketplace, guaranteeing an organization's success and growth.

Marketing, then, is a total approach to the way a business operates. It is, to quote the definition, a 'management process' . This has two implications. The first is that it should imbue every aspect of the way an organization is run. Marketing is too important to be left to the marketing department alone. It will not work unless the organization as a whole adopts it. The second implication, stemming from the fact that it is a 'process', means that the job of marketing never ends. It needs to be finding new ways of improvement, new areas where an organization can develop its approach to customers to the long-term benefit of each party.

Marketing is more than just a philosophy, of course. It involves the practical application of techniques which we will be examining in depth in the following chapters. Together they provide the route by which an organization 'identifies, anticipates and supplies' what its customers need and want. In this analysis, the 'hidden' areas of research and planning are every bit as important as promotion or distribution as marketing functions. For example, the serious adoption of market research by an arts organization does not mean that it abdicates its responsibility for programming choice. Being customer-centred does not necessarily mean what is sometimes called 'populism', or pandering to the lowest common denominator. Instead, a systematic approach to finding out about its customers allows an organization to gauge how relevant its offering is to their needs. Marketing input needs to be at a senior level. Marketing is not a veneer that can be applied to existing decisions to make them successful. It needs to be involved from the earliest stages of planning to connect the organization with its customers.

Marketing grows up into the non-profit sector

A large number of firms adopted the marketing approach in the late 1950s and 1960s because they found that it worked. At first most of the expertise resided in advertising agencies, where marketing specialists acted as 'consultants' to external clients. But gradually manufacturing companies began to recruit their own in-house marketing departments. Like the American firms of the 1950s who had started the marketing ball rolling, these companies were almost exclusively involved in the manufacture and sale of packaged goods.

Box 0.1

How deep is your marketing?

Lancaster and Massingham (1993) suggest five areas from which an organization's commitment to marketing can be assessed. How does yours measure up?

- Company philosophy/business definition: check your mission statement. How would you define what you do? How do customers fit into that definition?
- Managerial/workforce attitudes: do you share a concept of who your customers are? How does this manifest itself in your internal and external relationships?
- Organizational structure: do you have senior marketing personnel, or senior management committed to the philosophy of marketing?
- Planning and information gathering: how much research do you do? How is information on sales or attendances shared and used in the organization? What are your planning cycles, and who is involved?
- Processes and procedures for decision making: does the 'customer' feature in each level of decision making?

Marketing for the 'service' sector began to take off in the 1970s. Industries in this sector, such as tourism, transport and financial services, offer an intangible service rather than a product which can be handled and examined. As we shall see in Chapter 4, this presents problems and opportunities which make their marketing particularly interesting. At first, service providers such as banks were sceptical about the need to market themselves. But as the industry in which they operate became increasingly competitive (due to deregulation and increased customer expectations), they embraced marketing and promotion to the point where they are now seen as innovators in the areas of customer care and customer retention programmes. The arts are part of the service sector and their marketing offers many parallels with practice in the sector as a whole.

But arts organizations are often also in the non-profit sector. Even commercial arts organizations will have objectives which include more than just a return for the shareholders – important as that is. Marketing began to be applied to the non-profit sector increasingly in the late 1970s and 1980s, leading the Chartered Institute of Marketing to acknowledge the goal of satisfying customer requirements 'efficiently' as well as 'profitably' in the definition of marketing cited earlier. Just as the marketing of services is problematical compared to the relative simplicity of tangible goods, so non-profit organizations offer a further tier of potential marketing complexity. They often have ambiguous goals and objectives, and there is frequently internal disagreement on how these are to be achieved most effectively. The situation is further complicated by the difficulty of measuring outputs meaningfully. At least profit-led companies have a 'bottom line'. As we shall see, the 'bottom line' in the arts is complicated not only by the varying objectives of different organizations, but by the difficulty of measuring the impact and 'added value' of the activities they generate.

In the late 1970s and 1980s marketing literature started to recognize the wider scope of marketing capability across areas like health, education and the arts. The pioneering literature on arts marketing, though limited in quantity, includes some excellent accounts of good practice from both sides of the Atlantic. We are indebted to it, as the many references throughout this book suggest. But up to now the focus in writing about arts marketing has tended to be tactical, concentrating on particular areas of marketing technique (such as pricing and promotion) rather than on a holistic account.

This book aims to be not only practical but also strategic in its approach, reflecting the background and interests of its authors in attempting to marry the realities of working in the arts with a comprehensive approach to marketing theory. What we hope will emerge from it for the reader (whether student, arts worker, artist or manager) is not only a rigorous treatment of the principles of marketing as applied to the arts, but also a sense of the specialness of the arts themselves as something to market.

Marketing in the arts: the same but different

As a working environment, the arts are hardly ideal. Even compared to the turbulent milieu of business life in the 1990s, the arts as an industry offer little in the way of career development, job security or financial reward. Yet they remain an oversub-scribed area for job hunters. To market the arts in a professional environment, you have to want very much to do so. Motivation and belief in their product set arts marketers apart, but there is also a sense in which the process of marketing itself in the arts is singular. David Mercer (1992) discusses 'conviction marketing', drawing attention to the way that global brands such as McDonald's, IBM and Coca-Cola are driven forward with a sense of missionary zeal by organizations who have a very definite and confident style. The conviction and values of an arts organization are similarly involved in its marketing style. Successful arts marketing presses the techniques and technology of modern marketing practice into the service of a burning ideal. It's the same as any other kind of marketing, but it is rendered different by its commitment and the kind of engagement it seeks with customers.

What makes arts marketing different is the special nature of the arts experience, and the centrality of the customer in creating that experience. The emerging perspective of 'relationship marketing' in the 1990s offers a relevant new model on which to base marketing thinking in the arts. Rather than limiting itself to tactical selling or promotional activity to increase or maintain a pattern of purchase, arts marketing towards the millenium needs to address the issue of forming and nurturing long-term relationships with customers. Such relationships are not only essential to

There's a beauty in candlelight

Jude Kelly, artistic director of the West Yorkshire Playhouse, puts her vision of marketing as follows:

> The arts release things in people: like courage, flair, skills. It's like finding your own personality. And the kind of people who work in the arts have a sense of Utopia. They are ambitious to share what they have got with others, but there is often a kind of fear that holds them back. It's as if you have a secret knowledge that what you actually need to do is grapple with humanity at the most ordinary level – but don't because there is a kind of marketing 'industry' approach backing up reasons for not doing it. Arts marketing is about loving *people*. You have this sense that you've got something that matters and you want them to have it too. Real evangelists get a lot back from dealing directly with customers. But that kind of marketing is called nonsense because it's not sufficiently 'technical'. Yet repeat bookings come from customer loyalty. People respond to the place because they like the *people* there.
>
> Word of Mouth is the best kind of marketing because it's leading to a personal encounter with the art. But there's the temptation never to leave the office, never to cut yourself free from the computer or the telephone, never to get out and *see* the public, but take refuge in talking about C1s and C2s, instead of human beings. Or worse still, calling customers 'punters', as if they were being conned into parting with their money on a gamble. We do a lot of mouthing off about 'communities', but we lack the courage to go out and meet them as we should. Arts marketers need to believe in their own power as *people*. Even something as simple as giving out leaflets, talking to people, telling them direct that they'll love it when they come: they'll remember you, and you build up a greater 'evangelism' yourself through it.
>
> For a while the vocabulary of arts marketing was redolent with the kind of language you would expect from Littlewoods catalogues. It didn't contain the generosity of the language of art itself. You almost need an 'event' culture – a sense that every performance, every encounter with art, is unique and special. But being open 52 weeks of the year means you fall into thinking of it not as one event, even though that is how the customer sees it. There needs to be a phenomenal amount of attention to the personal; but unless you take that attitude as your ideal in all your marketing you are not reflecting the character of what you are talking about. You need to harness the technology, but you must get the balance right. Nobody is saying electricity should never have been invented, but there is a beauty in candlelight.

the financial security of arts organizations, but also to their missions. The arts are essentially about personal encounter, so is marketing: an encounter where an exchange takes place between customer and supplier. For all the sophistication of technology and planning which it involves, the vision of marketing we are advocating in this book never loses sight of the intensely personal nature of this exchange.

Reference

Lancaster, G. and Massingham, L. (1993) *Essentials of Marketing*, (2nd edn), McGraw-Hill.
Mercer, D. (1992) *Marketing*, Blackwell Business.

1 The arts: the market and the environment

Introduction

This chapter is a general introduction to the nature of the arts industry and the marketplace in which it operates. It will cover:

- The nature of the market.
- The role of public subsidy.
- The infrastructure of the subsidized sector.
- The international dimension.
- Marketing problems specific to the arts.

The arts environment, in common with other areas of society, is changing at an ever increasing pace. This can in part be attributed to overt political will, but is in part the reflection of broader changes in the environment which are impacting on the world of the arts in an uncontrolled and unplanned way. Time will test whether or not these changes are for the better or, indeed, whether they prove to be of significance at all.

What are the arts ?

A comprehensive definition of the arts was provided by the 89th US Congress, and later endorsed by the Education, Science and Art Committee of the House of Commons:

> The term 'the arts' includes, but is not limited to, music (instrumental and vocal), dance, drama, folk art, creative writing, architecture and allied fields, painting, sculpture, photography, graphic and craft arts, industrial design, costume and fashion design, motion pictures, television, radio, tape and sound recording, the arts related to the presentation, performance, execution and exhibition of such major arts forms, and the study and application of the arts to the human environment.
>
> (ACGB, 1993)

Comprehensive as this definition of the arts is, marketing the arts presents its own definition problems, depending on the artform concerned. For the performing arts, these include:

Box 1.1

Popular pastimes in Britain in the 1990s

1	Walking	45%
2	Crafts	26%
3	Swimming	22%
4	Photography	19%
5	Dancing	16%
6	Snooker/billiards/pool	14%
7	Keep fit/yoga/aerobics	13%
8	Music	12%
9	Painting and drawing	8%
9	Darts	8%
10	Golf	8%

Problems with defining the product. Is it:
- The event, i.e. a performance of The Messiah.
- The company, i.e. Birmingham Royal Ballet.
- The performer, i.e. Jeremy Irons in . . .
- The evening out, i.e. a family night out supporting Dad's band.

Problems with identifying the customers. Are they:
- The traditional attenders/fans/audiences.
- People who need 'converting'.
- Occasional attenders who might come more often.

Problems with identifying the marketplace. Does it include:
- Televised live performances.
- Recordings of performances.
- Teaching and learning through the medium of performance.

Similarly with the visual arts:

- Product – the exhibition or the paintings?
- Customer – someone who looks or someone who buys?
- Marketplace – individuals, galleries or publications?

The arts tend to spread outwards and, as with many activities with a strong social dimension, they cross-fertilize with other areas and programmes. This was well illustrated in the Voluntary Arts Network (VAN) report *Strengthening Foundations* (1994), which considers the case for local arts provision; 'People go out "to sing", "to paint" or "to play football". They do not go out "to participate in local cultural activity".' In support of this, VAN produced a table of the 'Top Ten' sports and arts activities in the country (Box 1.1). As the compilers of the statistics themselves point out, it is easy to criticize data of this sort by arguing about definitions, or by faulting something in the research method-ology. Nonetheless, they feel able to draw the conclusion that the figures they cite lay

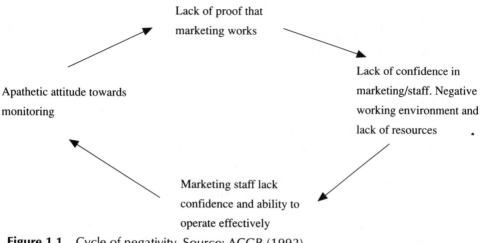

Figure 1.1   Cycle of negativity. Source: ACGB (1992)

to rest the stereotype of popular, mass and socially egalitarian sport set against the elitist arts.

Why do the arts need marketing?

As part of the consultation and discussion that went into the process of considering *A National Strategy for the Arts* (1992), a group of marketing officers drawn largely from the subsidized sector formed a consortium called MANAR – Marketing the arts nationally and regionally.

Among the problems they identified was a lack of faith in marketing within the sector. This is illustrated in Figure 1.1.

This is consistent with a more general perception of marketing in the not-for-profit sector, identified by Kotler and Andreasen (1991):

> Over the years, marketing has had difficulty in gaining acceptance in a number of non-profit organizations. One hindrance was the view that marketing really wasn't necessary. It was argued, for example, that good health does not need to be sold, that hospitals don't need to be marketed . . .

He further identifies that not-for-profit organizations may see marketing as a waste of public money, an unnecessary overhead, that market research may be perceived as intrusive and that marketing is seen as manipulative.

In addition to these, in the arts there is a further perception that marketing can lead to a 'lowest common denominator' approach, i.e. by promoting only that which the marketplace demands rather than seeking to develop new taste, or to raise standards: 'there is certainly nothing in economic theory which tells us that a competitive market will bring about an optimal level of investment in the formation of tastes' (Blaug, 1976).

Box 1.2

Goals for arts marketers

1 To become more scientific:
   'We need to improve our understanding of marketing tools; to prove what works and what doesn't.'
2 To develop a more consistent approach to market intelligence:
   'to improve our knowledge of audiences, current and potential.'
3 To rethink the way audiences are seen and addressed:
   'arts organizations really need to focus on the customer in:
   i Communications (print, copy, our whole attitude)
   ii Customer care.'
4 To see an improvement in the infrastructure and resources for marketing – financial, human and technical.

Source: ACGB (1992)

The Minister's mission

The National Heritage for which I am responsible brings together all those activities which shape our sense of national identity. Some have thought to relabel the new department as a 'ministry of culture' – but that makes it sound limited and exclusive when a department of National Heritage must speak to the whole community. Others have dubbed it the 'ministry of fun' – but that undervalues the commitment to excellence which must lie at the heart of everything we do.

Stephen Dorrell, The National Heritage Secretary, 1994

MANAR identified the priorities in Box 1.2 as the way forward to improve marketing in the arts.

For arts organizations to succeed – in both artistic and financial terms – a market-centred ethos should permeate the organization. An awareness of marketing issues and techniques should extend well beyond the team directly charged with the primary marketing responsibility. Increased professionalism will assist in helping shape this organizational culture.

The nature of the market: a mixed economy

The Department of National Heritage was created by the Conservative Government upon their return to power in April 1992. It brought together a number of activities that had previously been funded by departments ranging from the Home Office, the Department of Education and the Department of the Environment to the Department of Employment and the Department of Trade and Industry. Previously, only the

Box 1.3

Organizations sponsored by the Department of National Heritage

- Arts Council of Great Britain
- British Film Institute
- British Library
- British Tourism Authority
- Crafts Council
- Football Licensing Authority
- Museums and Galleries Commission
- National Film and TV School
- Royal Armouries

- The Royal Commission on Historical Manuscripts
- The Royal Commission on the Historical Monuments of England
- Royal Fine Arts Commission
- Royal Household Works
- Royal Parks
- The Sports Council

performing arts, museums and galleries had been funded by the Office of Arts and Libraries.

An examination of the activities funded by the DNH (Box 1.3) shows the size of this area in the public sector. The arts are closely allied to some of the larger industries of modern Britain: the broadcast media, publishing and recording, sport and leisure, and tourism. Many private sector companies rely on products developed in the public sector for their profit-making activity, e.g. the recently hugely successful commercial exploitation of Luciano Pavarotti, who has developed his talent in subsidized opera houses all over the world.

The workforce moves freely between the profit and the not-for-profit sector. Actors, in particular, may work variously in the theatre, in film, in television and in advertising, but would argue that they are exercising the same profession in all these arenas.

In addition, profit and not-for-profit organizations can exist quite happily alongside each other. The commercial theatres run, for example, by the Apollo Group will put on performances by both commercial and subsidized theatre companies.

It is therefore difficult to define precisely 'the arts industry' or to attempt to put a value on the sector. Box 1.4 lists the strengths of the sector from the perspective of the Association of Metropolitan Authorities. However, some doubt has been cast on the claims made by advocates of the arts for valuing the sector as they do, by the many detractors from the case for public funding.

The arguments for and against public subsidy are examined in more detail later in this chapter. The various cases are based on either socio-economic arguments or, perhaps more cogently, on philosophical and aesthetic grounds. Interestingly, all political parties debate the question with equal ferocity, and find little consensus within party ranks. Sir Alan Peacock and Dr Samuel Cameron examined the question in one of the discussion documents prepared as part of the consultation work for *The National Strategy for the Arts* (1992) and concluded:

Box 1.4

Socio-economic value of arts industry in local community

- Annual turnover of sector – £10 billion.
- Employment 496,000: 2.1% of total employment population, per Office of Population Census and Surveys.
- Provides spin-off into other industries.
- Generate growth in ancillary industries.
- Stimulate tourism.
- Sustain employment.
- Job creation.
- Urban renewal.
- Improve image of region as a place to live and work.
- Business asset to regions where there is strong cultural infrastructure.

Source: Arts and Cultural Policy AMA (1990)

A number of our comments concern over-estimation of beneficial effects. This should not be misconstrued as meaning that the arts are not important in economic terms. One of the main drawbacks of impact studies is their focus on measurement in terms of money without reference to value. The sums which have been computed fail to put a value on many of the socio-economic effects of the arts which are not directly registered in the marketplace.

(ACGB 1992)

The debate on subsidy should not prevent our recognition that the industry is essentially mixed. Successful profit-making companies are wholly committed to the idea of artistic excellence. All sectors of the industry share the common challenge of marketing the experience of the arts.

Outline of the subsidized sector

It is difficult to quantify the value of the subsidized sector, in much the same way as it is difficult to talk about the whole industry. However, a brave attempt to do that very thing was made in the report cited above *Strengthening Foundations* (1994), which compared the level of public subsidy per head spent by local government in the UK on sports (£24) and on the arts (£7). At national levels, they found the Sports Council received only £66m compared to the Arts Council's £230m. However, this ignores the hidden subsidy into both industries by various sports and arts related businesses, as well as the contribution to the public purse arising out of the subsidy (what economists call the multiplier effect).

Statistics of this sort leave the reader confused with both the problems of attempting to compare like with like when we are talking about large amounts of

---

Box 1.5

National public funding of the arts

1 Arts Council of Great Britain 1993/4 grant: £225.63m
   Major clients:

Royal Opera, Royal Ballet and Birmingham Royal Ballet	£19.5m
The South Bank Centre	£13.4m
English National Opera	£11.7m
Royal National Theatre	£11.2m
Royal Shakespeare Theatre	£8.5m

2 Regional Arts Boards (10) 1993/4 grants: £44.4m
3 National Sponsorship 1991: £57.2m

The Arts Council of England grant for 1995/6 is expected to be £186.9m.

Source: ACGB (1993).

For 1993, the budget of The Arts Council – An Chomhairle Ealaión was £11.5m.

Source: Art matters 14 (produced by the Council)

---

money, used in complex ways, and also with the hidden agendas of the people compiling the statistics. Imperfect as they are, the attempt to quantify through statistics draws attention to the importance of the debate.

The shape of the subsidized sector in both the arts and sport has been subject to recent change: and policy makers are considering the impact of unknowns such as the National Lottery on leisure provision over the rest of this century. The desire of all those involved in setting such policies at both national and local level to match resources to what the population wants, is matched by the difficulty of getting reliable data to describe leisure demand, and how it is currently being met.

For the latter half of this century, it has largely been the role of the Arts Council to answer on behalf of the nation's art lovers. Some commentators would argue that it has been failing to do so with any accuracy for the last few years: 'the Council [has] not only abandoned a claim to "speak for" the arts in Britain, but [has] fallen so far into the pit of political expediency, that never again can its wider credibility be restored' (Pick, 1986). Nonetheless, an organization with hundreds of millions of pounds of public money to distribute must be seen as a significant influence in the subsidized sector, so it is with the Arts Council that any discussion of the public sector funders must start.

The Arts Council of Great Britain was founded in 1946, one of the first national organizations of its kind in the world. Its aims are:

- To develop and improve the knowledge, understanding and practice of the arts.
- To increase the accessibility of the arts to the public throughout Britain.
- To advise and co-operate with departments of government, local authorities and other bodies.

Following on from the Wilding Report in 1989, much of the responsibility for funding was devolved to ten local Regional Arts Bodies (RABs) which replace the Regional Arts Associations (RAAs) that previously funded the smaller regional clients, particularly in the local community. This was a gradual process over several years, and suffered several sea changes during the process, largely because of changes at ministerial level. Finally, on 1 April 1994, the functions and responsibilities of the Arts Council of Great Britain (ACGB) were transferred to three successor bodies: the Arts Council of England, the Scottish Arts Council and the Arts Council of Wales. Most of the references in this book refer to the ACGB, because the real impact of the changes will not be felt in the sector for some time. It is worth noting in this context that The Arts Council – An Chomhairle Ealaion, which is referred to on several occasions in this book, is the Arts Council of the Republic of Ireland and is, and always has been, totally unrelated to the Arts Council of Great Britain.

The objectives of the Arts Council of England are very much the same as those of the ACGB, except there is an increased liaison role because of the many councils and boards resulting from devolution. The criteria for assessment for awarding grants set by the new Council for its first full year of operation post-change (1995/6) are as follows:

- Artistic performance and standards (which includes developing standards, enterprise in programming, and commitment to new work).
- Strategic role (which includes education work, audience development and training).
- Organizational effectiveness (which includes marketing, success in generating earned income, and value-for-money).

The Crafts Council is the national organization for promoting contemporary craft. It funds individuals and organizations directly, as well as funding the RABs and the Scottish and Welsh Arts Councils. The Museums and Galleries Commission, the body with national responsibility for promoting museums and galleries, was incorporated in 1987 to reflect its altered status from an advisory to a grant-giving body.

There are ten Regional Arts Boards in England whose purpose is to provide funding, information and advice to artists and arts bodies. The remit of all of these is broadly the same, but each may express its mission in somewhat different language. The aims and objectives of the Eastern Arts Board, for example, are reproduced in Chapter 8 and focus on both short-term and longer-term strategies for increasing the range and participation in arts activities in their area of influence.

Commentators, in looking at the roles of the Regional Arts Associations which preceded the RABs, have tended to look to them to offer a more localized, and therefore more responsive, provision, and have found them wanting:

> On the whole, despite a host of democratic intentions, RAAs and local authorities tend to spend most of their money on much the same kinds of activity as the Arts Council . . . the audience for the more 'community based' initiatives they support tends to be, once again, highly educated and middle class.
>
> (Lewis, 1990)

It will fall to the new bodies to reverse this perception.

The other major sources of public funding are the local authorities. Taken together, they are the largest source of public funds for the arts. Although the major player in this area, the many local authorities take very different views on cultural policy, and it is therefore harder to analyse the aims and objectives of this very important source of funds.

> To take one simple example of something never mentioned in descriptions of 'the' political economy of the arts, that of conferences. Many local authorities (Birmingham, Brighton, Harrogate and Bournemouth among the most prominent) have invested in huge amenities which are termed conference centres, and which thus fall outside the description of Arts provision, yet the music, the dancing, the films, the exhibitions, the dramas that are presented within them each year would make an impressive list.
>
> (Pick, 1986)

The funding implications of these bodies are considered again in the section on income generation (Chapter 5). The concern of this chapter is to examine the reasons for public funding in a political and social context and to give a snapshot of the funding structure.

Objectives of public funders

The recent priorities of the Arts Council (identified in 1993) are:

- Quality: it supports both the creation of original work and the preservation and renewal of arts of the past.
- Access: it is committed to increasing the number and range of people experiencing and participating in the arts.
- Growth of the arts economy: to increase the total funds available to the arts and ensure that arts organizations provide value for money.
- Efficiency and quality as service providers: the ACGB aims to provide high quality cost-effective service to both the public and the arts community.

Some of the marketing challenges that arise from the dynamic tensions created by attempting to satisfy all these objectives are examined later in this chapter. It is likely that local authority funders would offer a similar list of priorities.

> Local authorities must ensure that they market the cultural services which they provide efficiently to ensure that provision is delivered as effectively as possible. Marketing can be addressed in a more general sense in that local authorities can also be seen to be marketing life choices and the possibilities for participation.
>
> (AMA, 1990)

Arguments for and against a subsidized arts sector

Practitioners in the subsidised sector, particularly in the marketing department, are often asked to justify the use of public funding in the arts.

The arguments split broadly between the belief that market forces alone should

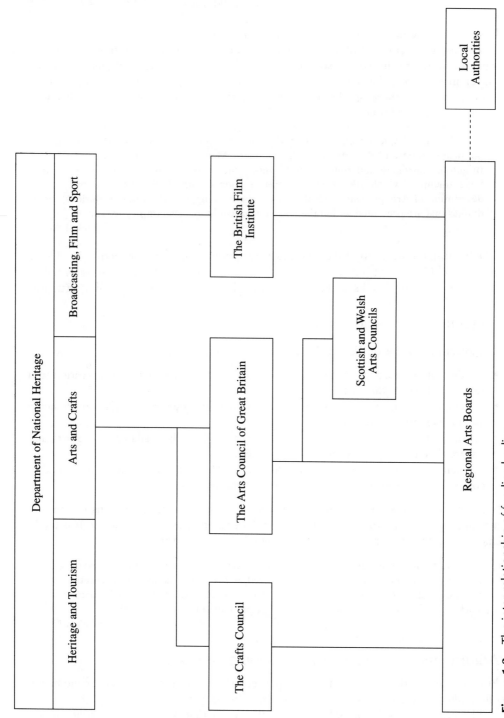

Figure 1.2 The inter-relationship of funding bodies

Aesthetic worth under-valued?
Concerning the 1988 publication: *The Economic Importance of the Arts in Britain:*

> After all, they were investigating economic values, and not aesthetic, or spiritual, or educational values. But it would have been much more honest if they had elaborated a little upon two important facts. The first is that nearly all art has no direct economic cause and no direct economic consequences. The second is that there is absolutely no proven relationship between the artistic value of a work of art and its economic value. (There are certain market conditions which are necessary for art to meet its public, but those market conditions don't create art, or make it worthwhile.)
>
> John Pick, *MAILOUT* June/July 1994

determine the product and level of funds needed to support the arts (i.e. through entrance fees and ticket prices) and the counter argument that the arts are a fundamental right of the individual akin to education or health, and are therefore too important to leave to the marketplace. This latter argument is strengthened by socio-economic arguments that the sector is a major employer, and provides wealth to the nation through direct and indirect taxation. This argument was cogently put forward by Myerscough in 1988 in *The Economic Importance of the Arts in Britain.* This book argued the value of the subsidized sector as a means of wealth generation. However, as we have seen, such statistics are open to question.

The market forces line can be summed up in what Sir Alan Peacock (1992) described as the doctrine of 'consumer sovereignty':

• The individual should be free to buy whatever services he or she wants at a competitive market price, which implies no subsidy.
• The individual is the best judge of what he wants, and there is no hierarchy of tastes or preferences.

This argument 'explicitly rejects the idea that the creative artist, the performing artist, or the informed aesthetes can have ... any special status in the community when it comes to the allocation of resources to the arts'.

• Even if the individual is not a good judge, no one else is necessarily better. People should be allowed to make up their own minds.

Sir Alan Peacock acknowledges that this 'free market' attitude does not allow for inequalities in the distribution of provision hence restricting choice; inequalities in income; and inequalities in education in the broadest sense.

On the other hand, the arguments for subsidy of the arts are based on the belief that they are life enhancing and that therefore nobody should, because of inequalities in provision or income, be refused access to them: 'The arts have become indivisible

---

Box 1.6

Public attitudes to the arts

- 69% of all adults support public funding of the arts and cultural activities.
- 55% of all adults support the funding of new and experimental work.
- 79% consider that arts and cultural activities help to bring people together in local communities.
- 71% consider that arts and cultural activities help to enrich the quality of our lives.
- 54% of all adults claim to be interested in arts or cultural activities.

Source: Research Surveys of Great Britain, 1991, commissioned by the Arts Council.

---

from the objectives of a humane, democratic society in which personal fulfilment enhances public success' (National Campaign for the Arts, 1990).

To the fact that they add meaning and colour to life, arts advocates would also adduce the following benefits (and there are many powerful and persuasive advocates to do so):

- Education.
  Children not only need to know the isolated facts; they need to see connections that bridge the disciplines and discover how ideas are connected. Without a comprehension of larger patterns, we prepare our students not for wisdom but for a game of Trivial Pursuit.' Ernest L. Boyer, President Carnegie Foundation (ACA, 1989)

- Urban regeneration, employment and community growth.
  There has also been, from the outset, recognition that the arts would help to assure the total rebirth of this community – making it a better place to live and work by refreshing the spirit, in addition to serving as a stimulus for economic growth.' CEO Johnson & Johnson (ACA, 1989)

- It is the hallmark of a civilized nation.
  Our place in the community of nations is enhanced by permitting the creative energies of our artists to touch the lives of people throughout the world.' Independent Commission on Arts Policy, USA (ACA, 1989)

The main problem with arguments both for and against public subsidy of the arts (as we have seen) is finding data to substantiate either case. For the reasons discussed above, the exact boundaries of the subsidized part of the sector are far from clear. Statistical evidence can always be criticized on the grounds of methodology of collection or the validity of interpretation, but never more so than when the arena of interest is so hard to define.

Box 1.6 gives some Arts Council consumer research on this subject, and Box 1.7 contrasts some opinions of two creative artists.

Box 1.7

Artist opinions on subsidy

The function of the arts is to bring order out of chaos, coherence out of the endless static, the gibberish of the stars, and to render people capable of thinking metaphorically. The arts are an essential part of public education.

Edward Albee

For the motion: J. B. Priestley

People in general should have the opportunity to experience good art ... the more people have this chance, the more natural understanders and appreciators we shall discover.

Art is like yeast in the doughy stuff of life ... life without art is life already turning sour. Something must take the place of that leaven.

I do not believe the state should maintain its artists so long as they are able to work and maintain themselves. All that the state should do is to create the conditions most favourable for the self-maintenance of artists.

Good taste and judgement in these matters of fine art will not be miraculously bestowed on the leaders of collectivist society.

We English are beginning to cry in the darkness for the colour and grace and glory of the arts.

Fabian Society, 1947

Source: The Arts Under Socialism, Turnstile Press. Courtesy of the Peters, Fraser and Dunlop Group Ltd

Against the motion: Kingsley Amis

The trouble with bringing art to the people is that it tends to become fatally damaged in transit.

If you really are interested in quality, one way of allowing it to improve would be to withdraw public money from the arts.

If you're paid in advance or have your losses underwritten, the temptation to self indulgence is extreme. If you have to please to live, you'll do your best to please.

We'll supply the finance, you'd better supply the interest; a very clear example of the Socialists' habit of giving the public not what it wants but what they think it ought to want.

The Victorians bought a pre-Raphaelite picture because they liked it, not because some interfering git called Ruskin said they should.

Conservative Party Conference, 1979

Source: An Art Policy? Centre for Policy Studies

> **Cynicism about the National Lottery**
> What's sad about the Lottery is that it's likely to be used to prop up the sagging infrastructure of an elitist, decaying and largely nineteenth century arts practice. In doing so it will fail to address the needs and interests of the mass of Lottery ticket buyers by investing in the local, the participatory, the relevant and the socially useful.
> Comment by F. Gleens, 'Mail-in', *MAILOUT* Dec/Jan 1994/5, following the launch of the National Lottery in November 1994

International arts marketing

Space does not allow an exhaustive examination of the very varied international scene, but some illuminating contrasts can be drawn between certain countries' practice and that which pertains in Great Britain. In fact, most countries do concur with the British model of the mixed arts economy (with private and public organizations existing side by side), and many have explicitly based their Arts Council on the ACGB: 'In 1984, a Special Committee on the Arts in Ontario found that the principle of arms-length funding offered the best means so far devised for government support of the arts' (Sullivan, 1988).

The arms-length principle is defined and discussed later in this chapter. It is one of the founding principles of the Arts Council of Great Britain, and of the British pluralist funding model, and it has been widely copied internationally.

Some of the differences between the British and other nations' experience listed below will disappear over the next few years, as the UK Government is seeking to learn from good practice elsewhere. The most obvious of these are:

Lotteries

Lotteries have raised substantial monies for the arts in many nations. On their introduction, arts companies usually have concerns that subsidy will be cut, and replaced by a variable and unpredictable source of income. In practice, most lotteries have proved successful and the Arts Council will distribute funds from a National Lottery from 1995. In a similar way, concern has been expressed in the UK about the impact this will have on the subsidized arts sector.

Taxation

Taxation regimes can vary enormously, and therefore the pattern of arts funding varies according to tax incentives offered by different countries. In the US, for example, charities are exempt from federal, state and income tax, as they are in the UK. In addition, they are usually exempt from local property tax whereas the norm in Great Britain is 80 per cent relief. The rates burden of a sizeable city centre property can be significant.

More importantly, in the US there are a range of other exemptions. These include major incentives for individuals who give to the arts; lower bulk postage rates; reduced charges for federal services; some exemptions from Employer National Insurance and access to donated space and air time from media (Kotler and Andreason, 1991).

Merchandising

Among the industrial nations, Britain has been relatively slow to develop full commercial exploitation of its arts products. The Metropolitan Museum of Art, for example, sells goods directly and licenses its name to line manufacturers. In 1987–8 this resulted in $25.9m turnover.

Market research

In 1988, the Ministry of Culture in France initiated a major survey into data and information in the arts sector. This resulted in a national on-line database (3615 SICI: Interpreters and Creators Information Service) which holds detailed information on the arts under fifteen section heads. Holland is another country that has taken evaluation and research very seriously.

Level of subsidy

This obviously varies enormously from country to country. However, in some respects, our level of subsidy is less.

Box 1.8

Public subsidy of European opera

Percentage of total income from public subsidy
International opera houses 1987/1988

London	Hamburg	Vienna	Berlin	Paris	Munich
46%	73%	73%	81%	72%	72%

International examples in the following chapters can illuminate an effective marketing strategy, or contrasting practice show how different marketing decisions are in different marketplaces. The award-winning 'Shakespeare on the Saskatchewan' festival, for example, consistently achieves 80 per cent box office for its main productions. This is attributed to its market-centred focus:

> ... Here was a belief and an enthusiasm for the product, in this case a belief in a 'Canadian Shakespeare'. But this belief was founded upon a strong appreciation of the character of Saskatchewan communities – in short, the product was crafted for its market. The productions were populist; the context of the productions was readily understandable to a Canadian population that did not all share an Anglo-Saxon heritage which included Shakespeare.'
>
> (Meidan and Moutinho, 1993)

> ## Arts funders challenged
> The claims for the subsidized arts world in Britain become ever larger as its audience shrinks and its bureaucracy swells, until one has a nightmare vision of the whole structure being reduced to a chain of tightly-guarded Georgian dwellings, into which secretive armies of arts bureaucrats daily shuffle, a network which swallows up most of the available funds in its own running costs and gives the rest to other organizations who exist largely to have meetings with it [and to issue strategies] 'Fertilising the Pansies', 'Grobags for the Regions', 'Pruning and Shredding', and, to maintain continuity with the past, every ten years or so a report on the problems of the Four London Orchestras.
>
> John Pick, *MAILOUT* (1986)

The generic marketing principle here, that the product itself is framed within the context of its market, and that consequent marketing activity should be consistent with the product concept, is of universal significance.

Marketing problems

This chapter has considered the UK marketing environment, and the multiplicity of forms of arts activities carried out within the public and the private sector. It has looked at some issues of cultural policy, including in particular the case of public subsidy of the arts.

This mixed model economy gives rise to some dynamic tensions which can act as a restraint or as an opportunity for the marketing teams of arts organizations. A general awareness of some of the principal areas of tension will facilitate an understanding of how marketing techniques and general principles are specifically applied within the arts sector.

The arm's-length principle

The arm's-length principle is fundamental to the funding of the arts by political bodies. It states that the organizations which distribute the funds remain independent of local or central government and do not seek to bend creativity or artistic interpretation to party politics.

It has its roots in the creation of the Arts Council in 1946, after the end of the Second World War. At that time, the horrors perpetrated by Fascism were starting to emerge, and the effects of Communist ideology on freedom of expression were beginning to be manifested. Later governments, more removed from ideological conflict, have strained the arm's-length principle by their power to grant or withhold funds.

Central to the operation of the arm's-length philosophy is the use of peer appraisal in funding allocations. Groups of practitioners and specialists in an artform assess the work of their fellow artists and this is fed, over time, into the decision-making process. Arising from this is the freedom of the funding bodies to take on new clients and to recognize new forms of expression. Finally, and most importantly, freedom of expression is assured to clients while the funding body assumes the burden of financial accountability to central government.

All countries which operate a system of arm's-length funding find the principle can become severely strained on occasions by political pressure. In Australia, for example, serious political concern about the inequalities in distribution of opportunities throughout the regions has caused enormous pressure on the Council's independence in their distribution of arts funds.

For marketing staff, the arm's-length principle has implications about the quality of the product. Peer appraisal requires a generally high standard and this may be at odds with the marketing imperative to 'give the customer what he or she wants'. The ACGB or RAB will itself be a significant customer, and this is considered at greater length in the chapter on income generation.

Some commentators recently have argued that the arm's-length principle will become less important as the economy continues to become more mixed; with arts organizations becoming less dependent on one source of income and the Arts Council itself moving to a role it describes as 'a co-ordinator and planning authority for the whole system', with largely delegated funding responsibility.

Excellence v accessibility

As outlined above, peer-group appraisal places a high value on 'excellence'. This involves both innovation in the use of new forms, and the preservation and renewal of art forms from either minority cultures or the past.

An equally important imperative is 'access' – the sector-wide commitment to increase the number and range of people who enjoy and participate in the arts. More difficult or unusual expressions of artistic creativity may prove a barrier to building big audiences or increasing the number of visitors to an attraction, particularly to those sectors of the community who traditionally are non-attenders.

Modern technology is shaping audiences' expectations of a live performance, e.g. the widespread existence of video recorders, which allow the viewer to go forwards, backwards and pause, may have an increasing impact on the attention span of audiences. In museums, traditional display methods which depend on written explanations may be seen as too inaccessible; both in terms of difficulties in understanding and also problems with getting close enough to read the text.

> The shift towards greater spending on cultural hardware ... as opposed to services has also meant that entertainment is increasingly located in the home ... The privatization of pleasure – driven by basic economics – has become a fundamental issue, whilst traditions of civic, municipal, and public cultures are being swept away.
>
> Mulgan and Worpole (1986)

It is the marketing staff who are likely to be most aware of, and responsive to, the needs of customers. The artistic director or exhibition curator and their teams will tend to be production-centred in that they will always hope to challenge and stimulate their audience by giving them something beyond their expectations. At its best, this tension is dynamic and challenging. Often in practice it is difficult to achieve the correct balance between 'excellence and access'.

Sympathetic funders will look at the provision over a period of time, but it is necessary to develop explicit strategies that explain how these two aims are being achieved. In a multi-funder situation, there may be different emphasis given, with the more local sources of income perhaps more interested in wider access opportunities.

> As major deliverers of service to the local community, it would be appropriate for authorities to give greater consideration to activities people find most attractive, and which have, perhaps, a greater personal relevance. This is not to lessen the importance of existing provision, but to recognize that diversity of content and presentation are arguably some of the most important factors in making the arts central to people's lives.
>
> (AMA, 1990)

Sir Kenneth Clark, Chair of ACGB, 1958, summarized this debate as 'raise or spread'. It will be looked at again in several later chapters, particularly in that on product.

Professional versus amateur arts

The dichotomy between performance standards of professional orchestras, companies and performers and those of amateur groups is another manifestation of the 'excellence versus access' debate. It stems in part from the highly-unionized musicians and actors workforce, and from the limited resources available to producers, which may tempt them to use non-union or untrained staff. In part too it has its roots in a belief that perhaps stems from Matthew Arnold, and other Victorian thinkers, that there is a divide between 'high' art and 'popular' culture, and that the first is preferable to the second. This suggests that professional practitioners have a mission to educate and enlighten the non-professional: 'The men of culture are the true apostles of equality' (Arnold, 1869 *Culture and Anarchy*).

The growing and powerful community arts movement seeks to break down this divide by fusing the trained skills of professional workers with the commitment of local and community groups, to produce often large-scale works whose value lies as much in the process of developing the piece as in its final performance. However, there are certain restraining forces on the growth of the community arts movement.

The first of these is finance; and in particular, a hostility among community arts workers to the whole funding system. Community arts work tends to be fairly small, informally organized and fast changing. This makes systematic funding more difficult than the funding of comparatively stable building-based or larger companies. Perhaps as a result of this, community arts workers believe they have historically been underfunded for the value of the contribution their work makes. If salaries are an indication of the funding coming into arts companies, there certainly appears to be truth in this claim. An examination of the salaries offered in community arts work as opposed to larger building-based companies certainly shows a significant differential, as can be seen by scanning the jobs pages in *The Guardian* any Monday morning.

> The community arts movement has let the elitist aesthetics of the dominant subsidized culture off the hook. Most community artists [are] opposed to this cultural elitism, and yet, by forming a separate entity, 'community arts', they allow themselves to be appropriated by it.
>
> (Lewis, 1990)

The tendency of art workers in the community is to perceive these larger organizations as highly bureaucratic. This perception extends inevitably to the even more remote funding organizations:

> European arts bureaucrats have never lived so high on the hog. Community arts organizations have never been so bureaucratically harassed, nor so starved of money. Is it not time to organize an Underground Arts Resistance movement, with the aim of destroying the Flying Circus of European Freeloaders and all their supporting bureaucrats?
>
> John Pick, *MAILOUT* (June/July, 1993)

A second, related area is political activity. The nature of community-based art work lends itself to work with the socially disadvantaged in order to develop individual potential, revitalize local communities and encourage urban regeneration. Often, the projects take place in areas of particular political tension, poverty, unemployment or high crime.

> It is in precisely those areas that community-based arts activities are flourishing. Most especially drama, the art form that tackles human conflicts, human dilemmas, human emotions, head on. Community drama groups are offering local people an opportunity to reassert and re-define their personal and cultural identity, to tell their own stories in their own way.
>
> Gerri Moriarty, Irish arts worker, *MAILOUT* (June/July, 1993)

Out of this type of work can arise a strong articulation of injustice, division and lack of opportunities in certain sectors of our society. This type of message is unpalatable for some.

The third area is that of control. Community arts work is structured, and is targeted at particular sections of the community, or may be funded to have a particular geographical focus. Some critics feel that this should exclude the traditional arts attender, i.e. the white middle-class pottery-maker who has other opportunities to enjoy arts activity. The counter argument is that community arts offers a unique chance to participate, and should be open to all enthusiasts. Debates over control also concern the role of paid professional leaders/facilitators; the community remit of building-based companies who are funded by the whole community, not just the attender at their building; and the lack of structured follow-up activity.

All these problems lead to a perceived gap in provision filled by the continued flourishing existence of amateur arts. An amateur group will usually be self-financing, have no paid workers (though frequently amateur companies consist in part of people who have worked or trained professionally) and no restrictions on membership, other than group consensus. They may not seek to broaden their member base, or to strengthen their skills in areas of weakness. Their primary motive for coming together is to have fun, and this may lead to an avoidance of 'issue-based' material.

The Voluntary Arts Network (1994) argues that amateur arts have suffered at the hands of the Arts Council and other funders who chose to concentrate on professional work, and therefore left the funding of amateur activity to the Department of Education. This led to the anomalous situation of the English Folk Dance and Song Society receiving its only public support from the Sports Council, who 'inherited' them as a client. They go on to discuss the particular disdain for amateur dramatics, which is the dominant art form in the public sector. This can be epitomized in the comment of Lord Goodman in the House of Lords: 'My lords, I speak for the arts, not for amateur theatricals.'

VAN contrast this attitude with:

- Amateur choirs, or amateur lace makers, who have a far more positive image.
- The attitude in other countries, including Wales, Scotland and Ireland.
- Other cultures, such as the place of Carnival in some communities.
- The positive image of amateurs in sport, all the way to the Olympics.

Their examination of the distinctions our cultural tradition imposes on arts activity paves the way for a re-examination of national preconceptions, if any one is brave enough to grasp the nettle in the turmoil of new priorities and structures. Such preconceptions form an important part of the background against which arts marketing activity takes place.

Nonetheless, many fruitful partnerships at local level belie such general tendencies. Increasingly, the barriers between the organizations are blurring or being challenged. In the West Yorkshire Playhouse, for example, every Wednesday, the theatre is filled with older members of the community under the umbrella of 'Heydays'. The theatre provides some activity directly, most notably a special early matinee; other activities are arranged by specialist workers from the local arts community, and other activities are organized, formally or informally, by the attenders themselves. Such activity is becoming increasingly common.

Although there are some conflicts between professional/community/amateur groups, the strengths and cross-fertilizations outweigh these. The variety of the types of organization are a sign of the continued interest in the arts in Britain; and arts funders are recognizing this by ensuring that all three types of company are eligible for funding.

All three sectors have marketing needs. Community groups will perhaps have a particular focus on 'place' – that element of the marketing mix which considers in particular how a product is made available/accessible to its customers. Amateur groups in contrast may find their hardest decision is 'product' – they know their audiences and the best way to reach them, the difficulty is to choose a piece that the group wishes to perform and that family, friends and the local community will want to attend.

Traditional versus new arts forms

This is the area which most feels the impact of new technology. Audiences' expectations are changing as a result of improvements in telecommunications and the mass media. We live in the age of the 'sound-bite' and this may alter the attention span of a captive audience. Digital sound may increase expectations in the PA systems, for example, of a rock concert audience, and they are becoming used to big screens at stadium performances. The technology is available for this, and the audiences are more used to watching videos of the band than being able to attend live performances.

There are considerable opportunities for cross-fertilization across art forms arising from new developments in technology. Some of these are incorporated into the production values of a performed piece of work, and others might arise in ancillary activity around the main performance. Examples of these might be lighting and sound technology, the use of music, video links, photography and audio recordings. New art forms are being recognized in their own right, involving new technology, or multi-media fertilizations (such as animation integrated into traditional film). New times can lead to new ways of working; our current concern with the environment has developed 'living sculptures' and pieces of work in which decay is part of the lifecycle of the artwork.

Participative theatre is also breaking down barriers between art forms and, in particular, is fusing minority and folk art with the mainstream European arts tradition. Particularly successful examples of this might include reggae musicals, dance drama and the use of 'artists-in-residence' such as sculptors working for a period with dance groups. Commercial considerations may encourage companies to mount co-productions such as the Opera North/Royal Shakespeare Company collaboration on Showboat (1990).

New work is often exciting and highly visible, and thus can present a great opportunity for marketing staff. On the other hand, the unfamiliar can challenge or threaten core audiences and thus offer particular problems with promotional or pricing decisions.

Special constituencies

The marketing department cannot carry alone the task of new audience development. For those organizations who most believe in equality of opportunity for all, a market-centred philosophy must be developed in the culture of the whole company so that particular groups can be identified at a strategic level, and a systematic approach taken to encouraging their attendance.

Nonetheless, it is the marketing department who will carry out much of the day-to-day work of audience development with targeted groups: e.g. lesbians, women, ethnic minority groups, gay men and the disabled. In these areas, market research will play a significant part in avoiding the charge of tokenism or patronage.

> Nor is it about making mainstream arts – the ones which use spoken language – accessible to deaf people. I'm not knocking interpreted performance ... [but] for many deaf people the initial impulse is to create art which makes a statement about the integrity of the deaf community ... an exploration and celebration of difference.
>
> John Wilson, Shape London, *MAILOUT* (June/July, 1993)

It is a very difficult task to offer the appropriate opportunities and experiences to such varied and disparate groups. In some cases, there are increasingly radical and politicized organizations with whom a dialogue can be established, if the initial approach is correctly handled. In these cases, it is important to recognize that these groups may be justifiably angry because of the lack of understanding of their needs that they have experienced from the wider community. In other cases, one of the first difficulties can be to identify a way of reaching the particular targeted group. All too often, marketing to Asian women can begin and end with leaflets sent in Urdu to community groups.

Marketing practitioners in arts organizations will want to build new audiences to create new markets for their product. However, for a given piece of work, received marketing wisdom might be to address existing customers, the repeat business. The strategic objectives of the organization, which might include addressing particular constituencies, need to be held in balance with the general objective of maximizing attendance.

> People should not be discouraged from attendance at arts events by either true or false expectations that they will find the atmosphere and conventions alienating or intimidating. Their attendance or otherwise should be determined by the events or activities that are on offer.
>
> (ACGB, 1993)

Summary

This chapter has discussed the organization of the arts industry in Great Britain, some of the elements that inform cultural policy formation and some of the marketing problems that may concern an arts organization. These can be summarized as follows:

Political

- There is a changing political context, leading to a more pluralist funding system.
- The 'arms-length' principle strives to remove political pressure from arts performance, but it is a political decision to give or withhold funds.
- Ultimately, all money in the public sector comes from the people: and this imposes a need to maximize the range and opportunities available for enjoyment or participation.

Sociological

- The arts seeks to encourage cultural diversity, and to develop or retain new or disappearing art forms.
- The arts seeks to address issues of social concern as part of a wider process of integration and community building.
- Individuals enjoy the arts, and opportunities should be available for non-professional performance and participation.

Economic

- There is a thriving profit-making industry, that exists alongside the subsidized sector.
- There is a close relationship between the arts and other industries, such as broadcasting, publishing, leisure and tourism.
- The arts provides employment and training for a mobile workforce.

Technological

- Advances in technology are changing audiences' needs and expectations.
- New and existing art forms are using technology as a creative input.
- The sector lacks the systematic research and recording of data that modern technology allows, and this should be an objective of arts marketing staff.

Key concepts

accessibility	excellence
amateur arts	local government
arms-length principle	international environment
Arts Councils	MANAR
community arts	National Lottery
Crafts Council	public subsidy
definitions of art	technology
Department of National Heritage	

Discussion questions

1 What are the key features of the national funding structures, and how are they changing?
2 Give arguments for and against public subsidy of the arts. What is your own opinion?
3 To what extent do you think there is a difference between the arts industry, and other industries such as broadcasting or leisure?

4 Discuss the problems involved in estimating the size and scope of the arts industry?
5 What changes are affecting the arts industry, and what opportunities do they offer?

Action problems

1 Examine the public funders of your arts organization. How will changes in the funding structure affect you? How can you ensure you benefit from these changes?
2 Consider the connections between your organization and other local professional/building-based/community/amateur organizations with whom you are familiar. What opportunities do you see to forge working partnerships with them?
3 Prepare a brief justification for local taxpayers for the public subsidy you enjoy.
4 Obtain details of the National Lottery awards and prepare an outline of a possible bid for funding.
5 Analyse your current season in terms of excellence and accessibility to new attenders. How can the balance be improved in future seasons?

References

American Council for the Arts (1989). *Why We Need the Arts*. ACA Books.
Arts Council of Great Britain (1992). *45 Consultation Papers and Draft Towards a National Arts and Media Strategy*. ACGB.
Arts Council of Great Britain (1993). *A Creative Future: The Way Forward for the Arts, Crafts and Media in England*. HMSO.
The Arts Council/An Chomhairle Ealaion (1989). *Art and the Ordinary: the ACE Report*. Arts Community Education Committee.
Association of Metropolitan Authorities (1990). *Arts and Cultural Policy: A Discussion Document*. AMA.
Blaug M. (1976). *The Economics of the Arts*. Martin Robertson.
Gleens, F. (1995). Mail-In. *MAILOUT*, December/January, 4.
Kotler, P. and Andreasen, A. (1991). *Strategic Marketing for Non-Profit Organisations*. Prentice-Hall.
Lewis, J. (1990). *Art, Culture and Enterprise*. Routledge.
Meidan, A. and Moutinho, L. (1993). *Cases in Marketing of Services*. Addison-Wesley.
Moriarty, G. (1993). A safe place to dream. *MAILOUT*, June/July, 10–11.
Mulgan, G. and Worpole, K. (1986). *Saturday Night and Sunday Morning*. Routledge.
Myerscough, J. (1988). *The Economic Importance of the Arts in Britain*. Policy Studies Institute.
Pick, J. (1986). *Managing the Arts? The British Experience*. Rhinegold.
Pick, J. (1988). *The Arts in a State*. Bristol Classical Press.
Pick, J. (1993). A pick up the arts. *MAILOUT*, June/July, 5.
Pick, J. (1994). Arts and Economics. *MAILOUT*, June/July, 5.
Shaw R. (1987). *The Arts and the People*. Cape.
Sullivan, M. (1988). *Arts Councils in Conflict*. The Canada Council, Ottawa.
The Voluntary Arts Network (1994). *Strengthening Foundations*. VAN.
Wilson, J. (1993). Signs of definitions. *MAILOUT*, August/September, 6–8.

2 Audiences

Introduction

Whilst there are philosophical arguments which support the view that art can exist in a vacuum, for most artists the audience is an integral part of an artistic experience. Only when the public experiences what the artist wishes to communicate is the creative process complete. The audience is vital for more practical purposes too. Art which does not generate audiences will seldom generate revenues, whether from box office receipts or funding bodies and sponsors. The development of audiences is therefore a fundamental responsibility of the marketing function. In practice, this means that the main task of arts marketing is to motivate people to attend performances and exhibitions or purchase art works or crafts, encouraging them to share in the artistic experience being provided.

To do this effectively, arts organizations must understand the needs, desires and motivations of all these people who are, or could be, attenders at their events or venues. This chapter aims to shed some light on the characteristics of audiences, and then goes on to look at how this information can be used and applied in practice. The chapter includes sections on:

- The nature of audiences.
- Influences on audience decision making.
- Target marketing.
- Marketing information systems.

What is an audience?

The term audience can take on a variety of meanings in a variety of contexts:

Audiences as 'arts receptors'

Lamos (1983) sees the audience as 'a sounding board for the artistic impulse ... The artist is the communicator, the audience is his other self.' He implies that an audience consists simply of those who experience art.

From a marketing point of view, this definition is of limited value as it excludes the notion of intention. It may, though, be useful in considering the audience for, say, public art. Public art may or may not be actively sought by those who see it. It may simply be an expression by the artist which exists in peoples' lives, thereby making

---

Box 2.1

Sponsorship as partnership at AT&T

The American telecommunications firm, AT&T, are active sponsors of the arts in the UK, who unlike many sponsors, are interested in supporting more adventurous stage works. The company feels that one of its core strengths is in innovation and risk-taking. For them to be associated with new work or revivals of old work is more appropriate than being involved in '"white gloves, private box and champagne" types of sponsorship.'

Their sponsorship of 'Chatsky', an 1890s Russian satire at the Almeida theatre in Islington, well away from traditional West End venues, was a case in point. When it subsequently toured at five regional theatres it was used as a means of communicating with employees in the subsidiaries around the country. The aim was to create some sense of identity with the holding company for these employees, who were invited to 'meet the cast' and get involved in a way that would generate talk and interest back in the work-place.

Source: Business Marketing Digest (1993)

---

them members of its audience even in the absence of any intention on their part to view it.

Audiences as associates

An audience can also be thought of as comprising all those with whom an individual or organization has some form of communication. For an arts organization, this may include all those who support the arts in any way, or who have an interest in their development. Attenders of arts events are obviously central to this, but the definition also refers to those with less direct contact with the organization, such as:

- Central government funding bodies.
- Regional arts boards.
- Local authorities.
- Charitable trusts.
- Primary, secondary and tertiary educational establishments.
- The local/national/regional press and media.
- Potential customers for ancillary services, such as catering, space hire or costumes.
- Local, regional or national business sponsors.
- Friends or members, trustees or governors of arts organizations.

Audiences as customers

This approach views the audience as being involved in a transaction with an artist or arts organization. 'The theatre invests money, time and artistic commitment to give the audience pleasure. The audience invests money and time in support of the theatre. It also invests emotional commitment' (Schlosser, 1983).

This definition sees audiences as being those with whom the arts organization is trying to exchange something of value. For marketers it is the most useful definition, as it implies that people make choices about the art forms or events that they wish to be involved with and are willing to offer something in return for that participation. Marketing activity can be undertaken in an attempt to enhance the value of the exchange process to both parties. Schlosser sees it as activity which 'directs the traffic on this two-way street that connects theatre and audience, and keeps the movement going in both directions.'

This definition sees primary audiences as those who attend (or could attend) arts events, including audiences at a play or concert, customers at a gallery looking at pictures and even collectors buying pictures from a selling exhibition, and indeed this will be the emphasis of the rest of this chapter. The concept of exchange, though, can also be seen as having relevance to secondary audiences such as funding bodies, sponsors and members, who are also looking to exchange value with arts organizations. Marketing activity can also be used effectively in developing these relationships.

Audience development

If we view the objective of marketing activity as enhancing the value of exchange processes between arts organizations and audiences, we can view the task of building audiences as being more than just increasing the numbers of attenders (though this is often a priority in the short-term, usually for financial reasons). Total value can certainly be enhanced if the same people enjoy the arts more often, but equally this goal can be achieved by enabling people who don't usually attend to enjoy the experience. Audience development is as much about increasing the range of audiences as it is about the size of audiences.

In the long term, the task of audience development is one of improving access to the arts for a wide range of people, not just those who are already committed attenders. It requires that the arts are made more accessible in variety of ways – physically and geographically, but also socially and psychologically, breaking down traditional elitism which threaten to devalue the arts for sizeable proportions of the population. To achieve this, arts organizations need to understand people's relationships with the arts and to identify the range of influences on the decision to participate. Only then can the needs of potential audiences be identified and catered for and techniques designed to help them to get the most out of the arts.

The decision to attend

The overall profile of UK arts attendance can be drawn from the data gathered in the Target Group Index, discussed further in Chapter 3. Patterns of arts attendance are not uniform throughout the population. The wide variety of definitions of arts activities makes measures of participation in the arts problematic, but the general

> Box 2.2
> ## Festival audiences
> Festivals reported an increase in attendance between 1986 and 1991, but these audiences continue to be disproportionately middle-class and middle-aged. This class profile was particularly strong for traditional arts festivals, particularly those featuring classical music, but also for folk festivals. Festivals in rural areas and small towns attracted predominantly middle-aged or retired people.
>
> Many festival organizers identified the main obstacle to achieving a more even spread of attenders from throughout the population as being the perception of arts venues as being only for the wealthy and artistically inclined. Ticket prices were found to discourage attendance amongst the less well off. Therefore, in attempts to change the social composition of their audiences, they have altered their programming to include events more likely to attract younger and working-class people, including jazz and film events. They have also staged a higher proportion of outdoor and free events.
>
> *Source:* Policy Studies Institute (1992)

conclusion that emerges is that although attendance patterns vary across art forms, arts audiences are most likely to emerge from particular age groups, social classes and educational backgrounds (Verwey, 1991).

The reason arts attendance is not uniformly spread throughout the population is because, as in most buying decisions, people are influenced by a wide variety of social, personal and psychological factors which either predispose them towards the arts or serve to alienate them. The better arts organizations understand these factors, the better placed they are to find ways of breaking down the physical and mental barriers which restrict access to the arts and hinder the development of wide-ranging audiences.

Influences on arts attendance

Social factors, especially the influence of culture, reference groups and social class can affect patterns of arts attendance considerably.

Cultural factors

A culture comprises everything in society, both tangible and intangible, that is created by its people. This includes the values and behaviours which are acceptable, and these values and behaviours are learned and passed on from one generation to the next. Societies which value cultural features such as education, creativity and leisure are the ones most likely to support a strong arts infrastructure and place importance on the development of the arts and audiences.

Subcultures can be found within cultures, where there are groups of people

Box 2.3

Black arts audiences

Following her qualitative attitudinal study into the current status of and problems associated with 'Black Arts', Jenni Francis concluded that the social aspect of entertainment activities is an important key to attendance. She cites the success of loosely-structured music events such as carnivals and the role of family celebrations as continuing to sustain the visible minority communities, despite their lack of mainstream recognition. She emphasizes, however, that black audiences are keen to participate in a wider range of activities, provided that consideration is given to addressing their particular needs. The decision criterion of 'will I have a good time?' is of major importance to the Afro-Caribbean and Asian communities, and this needs to be faced by arts marketers if they genuinely wish to meet the needs of this sector of the population.

Source: Francis (1991)

displaying even closer similarities of attitudes, actions and values than in the culture as a whole. These subcultural groups are usually separated by geographical regions or ethnic background. Culture-specific events may be appropriate if subcultural groups are sizeable, but other factors may be influential in encouraging or discouraging arts attendance. For example, Marplan (1988) found that 'the welcoming atmosphere and entertaining nature of the performance were much more important than other factors' for Asian, African and Caribbean live arts attenders in the UK.

Reference groups

A reference group is any group, including family, friends and work associates, with whom an individual identifies so closely that he or she adopts many of their values, attitudes and behaviour patterns. Parental influences are particularly strong, more so than the influences of school. Children whose parents support the arts, particularly those involved at the amateur level, are more likely to participate and to continue to do so as adults, than those from homes with little interest in the arts (Waters, 1989).

Reference groups encourage individuals to build up pictures of themselves which include 'what people like me do in their spare time' or 'how people like me behave'. If arts attendance is seen as irrelevant or alien to a person's reference groups, it is likely to be rejected. This is particularly so in the case of the performing arts, where only a small proportion of attenders are likely to be alone and having a companion will be a deciding factor in participation for most people. Arts organizations can turn this situation to their advantage by making special efforts to target the social secretaries of clubs and organizations, who can be relied upon to make party bookings and bring in groups of individuals who might not otherwise have been interested in attending.

Box 2.4

Definitions of social class

A   Higher managerial, administrative or professional.

B   Intermediate managerial, administrative or professional.

C1   Supervisory or clerical, and junior managerial, administrative or professional.

C2   Skilled manual workers.

D   Semi and unskilled manual workers.

E   State pensioner or widows, casual or lowest grade workers, or long-term unemployed.

Note: Students living away from home are usually classified as C1. Retired people with personal pensions retain their former social grade.

Social class

A social class is a group of individuals who are seen to have a similar rank in society. It is usually based on the occupation of the head of the household.

Those within the same social class tend to develop similar attitudes, values and behaviour patterns, and this is evident in arts participation. Audience surveys from across the UK continue to demonstrate that members of the ABC1 social grades are more active in almost all types of arts participation than those in the C2DE grades. In 1989/90, 63 per cent of ABC1s were attending at least one of the arts activities measured by the TGI, as opposed to 33 per cent of C2DEs. Some argue that practical difficulties such as low income levels and lower car ownership amongst the lower grades are responsible for the disparities, but evidence suggests that mental barriers are more influential than these. The gap between the classes becomes even more apparent when different art forms are considered, with opera and ballet being almost exclusively the domain of the higher social groups. This in itself is likely to alienate those who are not familiar with the established social conventions.

Personal factors, including age, gender, income and education levels, appear to influence an individual's pre-disposition towards arts, though the latter two are the stronger predictors of arts attendance.

Age

As a rule, arts attendance is greatest in the 35–54 age band, but there are notable departures from this across the different art forms, and different patterns emerge within certain ethnic minority groups, so generalizations are difficult and can be unhelpful. Audiences for contemporary dance, for example, are far younger than audiences for ballet, and a survey of Asian, African and Caribbean live arts attenders (Marplan, 1988) recorded 85 per cent of attenders as under 35, whereas the average for the UK population as a whole was only 33 per cent. Even within an art form, the

Over the hurdles . . .

Stark (1985) sympathizes with art-phobia by explaining his own fear of betting shops:

> I've always wanted to place a bet on a horse, but I've never done so – why? I look at those painted doors of betting shops, and I know that beyond that portal, that threshold, is an alien environment in which I would feel vulnerable. One in which I would run the risk of making a fool of myself because I don't know the language. I wouldn't know where to walk first, I wouldn't know what to say. I mean, do you walk in and say: 'I want to put a bet on a horse?' People might collapse in laughter or just look pitying. Everyone in there looks so self assured and confident.

Source: Stark (1985)

age of attenders will vary. An audience survey for English National Opera at the Coliseum showed that over half the audience for *Akhnaten* (Philip Glass) were under 35 whilst 60 per cent of the audience for *The Bartered Bride* were over 45.

Gender

Patterns of arts attendance are related to gender, but this varies widely across art forms. Women buy more theatre tickets than men and dance audiences record very high proportions of females, but more men than women attend jazz.

Income

A close relationship has been demonstrated between income levels and attendance at arts events (Verwey, 1988) though it is not clear whether this relationship is primarily due to social class, as the higher social groups tend to earn higher incomes. If income is a strong influence on attendance, then ticket prices or admission fees could be expected to have a major impact on attendance, though there is conflicting evidence on this point. For example, a survey of London concert audiences revealed that the proportion of C2DE social groups was much larger for light music than for symphony concerts, though ticket prices were comparable. On the other hand, the introduction of even voluntary admissions charges at national museums has been shown to reduce attendance. Undoubtedly there is a relationship between arts attendance and income levels, particularly amongst the unwaged and those on the lowest income levels, but the picture becomes less clear at the higher income levels.

Education

There is consistent evidence to show that attendance at an arts event is closely related to the age at which full-time education was completed. The 1989/90 TGI survey showed that 77 per cent of those who took their education to 19 or over were currently attending arts activities as opposed to 58 per cent and 28 per cent of those

Box 2.5

Young people and theatre going

Different approaches are likely to be required for building audiences in different age groups. Amongst some young people, theatre has a serious image problem, and there is a lack of awareness about what theatre offers. Memories of the positive experience of pantomime as a child are seldom carried over into later attitudes, which seem to be shaped more by the experience of theatre being used as part of the education process: 'It gets rammed down your throat . . . at school when you're forced to go and watch Shakespeare your teacher's expectations of what you're supposed to get out of it are unreasonable.'

Overcoming such negative attitudes is a difficult though not insurmountable problem, but it does require an understanding of the tastes, interests and motivations of this key target audience. Further to their qualitative research into young people and theatre going, Young Direction suggest a variety of innovative approaches which may prove quite controversial amongst those with traditionalist leanings, including:

Programming
- More music to act as a 'hook': 'we all travel really long distances to see bands . . . you'll go to see any old crap . . . I mean people are so desperate for music they'll travel 30 miles to hear something they don't really like.'
- More revues, comedies, real life, participatory and subversive programmes ('stuff that takes the piss').

Young persons night
- No people over 30 allowed, late night shows and a relaxed atmosphere: 'It's going to be more lively . . . it's a laugh, sort of "ha ha look at that" instead of it's all quiet and hush hush before the performance starts.'

Print
- Programmes with a brasher content with jazzed-up front covers and information and reviews of relevance to young people: 'They are appealing to the arty sort of people . . . people who already know . . . they should give it to someone who has never heard of it, tell them the basic story and say design something.'

Venue
- Photographs of the interior outside to show that it isn't intimidating.
- Publicize the facilities of the bar and focus on its qualities as a meeting place, subtly divorced from theatre.
- Run special bus services for young people.

The conclusion that emerges is that young peoples' leisure time is concerned with relaxation and escape: theatre is failing to match their expectations of leisure.

Source: Young Direction (1990)

who left education at 17/18 and 16 respectively (Verwey, 1991). Differences can be seen though between different types of performance and/or venue. For example, about half the visitors to the Victoria and Albert Museum have been in full-time education until at least 20 years of age but six out of ten visitors to the National Railway Museum have completed their full-time education by the age of 16.

Jenny Haughton, the director of Artworking, a Dublin-based visual arts agency, comments: 'We need to develop the way the visual arts are in Germany. They are a compulsory element of the curriculum throughout the education system. As a result the Germans are serious purchasers. They see pictures as important in the home.'

Psychological factors, especially perception, beliefs and attitudes personality and motivation are also influences on the decision to attend arts events.

Perception

This is the process by which people make sense of the world. Each of us selects, organizes and interprets information to produce meaning. Because we are unable to be conscious of all the messages which surround us every day, we select information that will help us to satisfy our needs, and screen out messages which are of no use to us (known as selective perception). Then we interpret that information based on the attitudes and beliefs we have stored in our memories (which may or may not be accurate) and only if the information is deemed important will we remember it (selective retention).

This explains why arts organizations find it difficult to attract groups who have traditionally shown little interest in the arts. First of all, these groups ignore the messages about the arts – they are unlikely to notice the adverts or critical reviews. If they do notice them, they may interpret them negatively if they hold negative attitudes towards the arts. Promotional activity has to break through selective perception before it can communicate its messages, and the messages must attempt to break down any negative attitudes or override any previous experiences before they will be retained and interest generated.

This may mean that sizeable proportions of the total potential market for the arts are effectively unavailable to individual arts organizations (Diggle, 1994). The process of breaking through selective perception, distortion and retention is likely to be one that takes time as well as money, and education rather than promotion is the most likely means of achieving this breakthrough.

The emergence of arts marketing consortia offers an opportunity to tackle this problem collectively. Liza Stevens of Leeds Arts Marketing comments:

> The idea behind Leeds Arts Marketing is to try to do things together that none of the members can afford to do separately. We need an infrastructure to build new audiences – we are trying to put the machinery in place. Now we feel we are ready to grow into an audience development agency.

Beliefs and attitudes

A belief is a descriptive thought that a person holds about something, which may be based on knowledge, but also on faith or opinion. Beliefs lead to the formation of attitudes, which are an emotionally charged reaction to a set of beliefs, and lead to

Box 2.6

Barriers to arts attendance

Resistance to the arts by non-attenders has been shown to be underpinned by a variety of beliefs and attitudes towards participation in the arts. Those who rarely or never participate gave some practical reasons why they don't go, such as the availability of transport and the costs involved and cultural reasons included lack of interest amongst family and friends and lack of education in the arts. However, reasons were also given which reflect underlying beliefs and attitudes towards the arts rather than any physical or social barriers to attendance.

Class distinction: a general belief exists that the arts are for the wealthy and the upper classes and not for the working classes.

Inferiority: fear of not understanding the point of a play, piece of music or painting makes people feel inadequate about their intellectual abilities.

Displacement: feelings of being overawed and out of place detract from enjoyment.

Conformity: people fear ridicule if they show an interest in activities which are considered to be out of their class or in groups where supporting the arts is considered 'unmanly'.

Effort: attending the arts is more like work than leisure.

Risk: unfamiliar events are too risky as there is a danger of spending money without guarantee of enjoyment.

Source: NOP (1991)

behaviour patterns which are very slow to change. For example, if a person believes that 'only intellectuals and tourists go to art galleries' then they may conclude that they would feel uncomfortable in such an environment and form negative attitudes which will deter them from attending.

Personality

This includes all the internal traits and behaviours that make a person unique and arises from both heredity and personal experiences. Personalities are described by characteristics such as compulsiveness, gregariousness, authoritarianism, extroversion, introversion, aggressiveness and dogmatism. Because these traits are generally difficult to measure, links between personality and arts attendance are difficult to measure, though stereotypical images exist as to the types of people who, for example, are most likely to participate in amateur productions or to frequent museums. These images may need to be dispelled to avoid other personality types being alienated.

Motivation

Reasons for involvement with the arts are wide ranging, but people can be seen as satisfying needs at all levels in a spectrum.

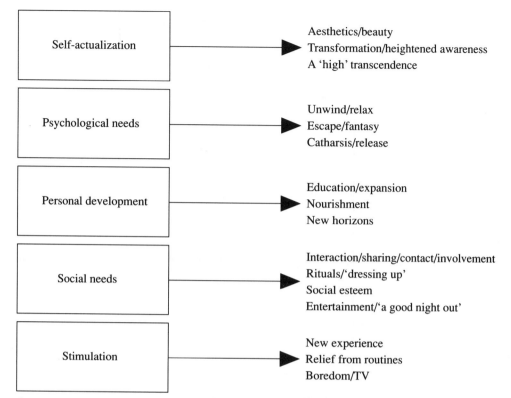

Figure 2.1   Motivations for arts attendance. Adapted from Cooper and Tower (1992)

People with similar motivations can be identified and grouped together. They will often need to be offered different types of arts experience, services and facilities to satisfy their wide-ranging needs. In the performing arts, these groups have been characterized as follows (NOP, 1991), and it is interesting to note that several of the motivations identified have little, if anything, to do with the arts event itself:

- Entertainment seekers: motivated by the need for amusement and the arousal of curiosity.
- Self-improvers: driven by a need for personal development.
- Trendsetters: wish to be identified with an elite intellectual minority.
- Status seekers: wish to be identified with a socially superior minority.
- Lonely escapists: motivated by an opportunity to be in the company of others.
- Inspiration/sensation seekers: looking for sensory and emotional stimulation.
- Extroverts/performers: motivated by a forum for self-expression.
- Social attenders: anticipate that a social setting will add to their enjoyment of the arts.

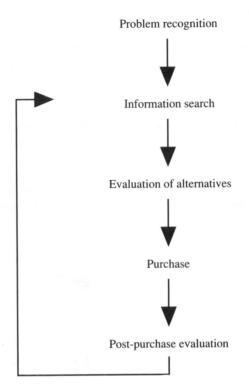

Figure 2.2   The audience decision-making process

How is that choice made?

If arts organizations are to develop audiences, they need not only to understand the factors that influence the decision to attend, but also the way in which people make choices and come to decisions about attending arts events.

Arts organizations face competition from a wide range of sources (discussed further in Chapters 5 and 8). Potential audiences start off with the choice as to whether to attend an arts event at all (maybe they could choose a sports event, a shopping expedition or an evening in front of the TV instead), and those who decide in favour of the arts will be faced with the dilemma of choosing between a wide range of both similar and different artistic experiences.

Audiences generally pass through five distinct stages in making these choices.

Problem recognition
This can occur when individuals become aware of a desire or need. Sometimes it is a stimulus from the environment which can prompt the desire. A person may read a critical review in the newspaper which sparks an interest, or receive a leaflet which

announces the tour of a famous artist or favourite play. On other occasions the awareness of a need stem from unrelated factors. For example:

'It's Saturday afternoon and I haven't got anything to do.'
'It's my birthday and I want to mark the occasion.'
'I want to have a good time with my friends.'
'I need some ideas for my English homework.'

Although the needs expressed here are wide ranging (in these cases for pastime, celebration, entertainment and education) each of them could potentially be satisfied by attending an arts event. It is problem recognition which turns the public into potential attenders.

Information search

Next, a search is undertaken for information to help these potential attenders solve their problems and satisfy their desires. They will first of all search their memories for previous experience of solving similar problems (e.g. 'Did I enjoy my last visit to an art gallery?' or 'Was my last theatre trip good value for money?'), but if this is insufficient to convince them as to a course of action, they will look externally. Common sources of information include the opinions of friends and relatives, advertisements and leaflets and editorial comment.

As a result of this information search, potential attenders focus on a much narrower group of alternative ways to satisfy the problem identified – known as the evoked set.

Evaluation of alternatives

Each potential attender will then identify criteria for comparing the options in the evoked set. For an arts event, the comparisons will be made as much between expectations of the event than any tangible features. Expectations have to be the basis for the evaluation of aspects such as the quality of performance, or the ambience, as it is not until the show or exhibition is actually produced that such features are realized. Thus the prices of events can be compared at this stage, but their value for money cannot.

Purchase

When the alternatives have been evaluated, choices are made as to

- What to attend.
- When to attend.

And the transaction is made when

- The tickets are purchased.
- The event is attended.

The potential attenders are converted into members of the audience.

Box 2.7
Ringing the wrong number?
Pre-show expectations can affect sponsors too. A shadow was cast over the Cable and Wireless sponsorship of 'Die Walkure' at the Royal Opera House when an unconventional production of 'Das Rheingold' the previous evening, provoked the outrage of Lord Young, the Cable and Wireless chairman. £65,000 had been pledged for the forthcoming performance of 'Die Walkure', but the evidence of 'Das Rheingold' (which was booed by the audience and described as 'awful, abysmal, disastrous' by Young) radically altered last-minute expectations. Nonetheless, the sponsorship was not withdrawn at the eleventh hour, and Lord Young declared the performance of 'Die Walkure' as excellent, but he admitted that as a sponsor he had heaved a sigh of relief!

Source: Jamieson (1994)

Post-purchase evaluation

After the event, members of the audience will evaluate the experience to see if it met expectations. This evaluation will be used in the information search for the next arts-related decision process. If expectations are not met, the disappointment is likely to lead to considerable negative word-of-mouth publicity. 'Whereas, on average, a satisfied customer tells three people about a good product experience, a dissatisfied customer gripes to eleven people' (Kotler and Armstrong, 1991).

This process of choice has some important implications for arts organizations, who must ask themselves a number of questions:

- What problems are we solving for our audiences?
  Identifying why people attend is fundamental to satisfying their needs and attracting others with similar needs. It is the underlying principle behind the whole concept of target marketing, discussed later in this chapter.
- Where do our audiences find their information?
  Efforts must be made to ensure that audiences store positive impressions in their memories, and research must also be done to identify the most effective form of publicity materials.
- Which are the most influential evaluative criteria?
  Organizations need to identify the most important factors that potential attenders take into consideration in deciding between alternatives. The knowledge of this should influence a whole range of factors from pricing policy to programming schedules. They can also be highlighted in promotional materials to attract audiences.
- How easy is it for potential customers to complete the transaction?
  If galleries have limited opening hours or box offices have continually busy phone lines, unhelpful staff or limited payment options, a decision to attend or purchase can be reversed even at a very late stage.

- Are expectations met and exceeded?
  Customer satisfaction needs to be continually assessed, as the consequences of dissatisfaction for the reputation of the organization can be very serious. The causes must be identified as soon as possible. They may be quite easy to remedy, for example, in the case of misleading promotional material, but there may be fundamental problems related to corporate image, customer care or target markets which need to be addressed to bring the arts experience in line with expectations; either this or the customers must be educated into appropriate levels of expectation (discussed in Chapter 4).

The process of marketing research is the means by which answers to these questions can be revealed. This is covered in the next chapter.

Who makes the choice?

Not every member of an arts audience will have played the same role in the decision to attend. Indeed, the whole decision-making process may have been divided up between a group of individuals, who collectively are known as the decision-making unit.

The **initiator** is the one who first suggests a visit to a gallery or museum, or a trip to the theatre (e.g. a friend suggests you go to a particular concert on Wednesday).
The **influencer's** advice carries weight in the evaluation of alternatives and whose opinion is valued by other members of the group (e.g. a colleague of yours went to the previous night's performance but wasn't very impressed, and recommended an alternative).
The **decider** makes the final choice as to where and/or when to go (e.g. you decide that you'd like to go to this recommended concert on Tuesday, rather than the one your friend suggested).
The **buyer** performs the transaction (e.g. your friend agrees with you and buys the tickets).
The **attender** experiences the event (e.g. you both go to the concert).

If a person chooses to attend an arts event alone, he or she may take all of these roles and be responsible for all the stages of the choice process. Normally though, a range of people are involved, so the arts organization needs to be aware of all who participate in the decision process and the ways in which they affect the choice. Influencers are particularly important, and the importance of critics as opinion leaders should not be underestimated.

Target marketing

The study of audience behaviour leads us to the conclusion that potential audiences consist of subgroups of individuals with similar needs, characteristics, motivations and buying practices. For arts organizations to attempt to attract members of all of these groups at the same time for the same events is unrealistic. Target marketing is the process by which the specific needs of different parts of the total potential audience are matched with the artistic product being produced. This process has two distinct steps: firstly market segmentation, whereby marketers identify the nature of the relevant subgroups for their organizations, and secondly market targeting, when different activities are aimed at different groups using different marketing techniques.

Market segmentation

A market segment simply consists of buyers with similar needs and wants, and markets can be usefully divided up according to those buyer needs. Different groupings will be appropriate in different markets and one of the most important task of the marketing function in an arts organization is to identify the most appropriate ways to divide up their potential audience.

Key criteria for market segmentation

In dividing up a potential audience, two important constraints have to be borne in mind.

Size   Is the group big enough for it to be worth treating it separately?
The ultimate form of market segmentation is customization, whereby each person's differences are recognized and each individual is offered something different to match their needs exactly. Clearly this is unrealistic and unnecessary for arts organizations operating with scarce resources. One of the key criteria for dividing up their potential audiences has to be the size of the group identified. The numbers of people in each group have to be quantified so that decisions can be made as to whether the effort of reaching them can be cost effective (or at least justifiable in educational or social terms).

Accessibility   How easy is it to communicate with this group?
As the purpose of market segmentation is to enable potential audiences to be targeted more appropriately, unless the subgroups in that potential audience can be extracted from the overall market and exposed to separate marketing offers, the segment is of no practical use.

The bases for market segmentation

With these constraints in mind, there are four broad bases from which to start the process of market segmentation:

Geographic segmentation   Audiences can be divided up according to where they live. First of all, arts organizations have to identify their geographical catchment area, which will normally consist of those living within a certain drive-time of a venue. Within this catchment area, certain postcodes are more likely than others to be the homes of arts attenders (for more information see the discussion of ACORN and the

TGI in Chapter 3). In targeting these homes, for example with direct mail or leaflets, arts organizations can be more certain of appealing to those who are positively disposed towards the arts and who are more likely to at least evaluate the possibility of attending rather than rejecting it outright.

Certain postcodes are also more likely than others to house young people, families, the elderly, the unemployed, students or the ethnic minorities. This is useful if a production or exhibition is of special interest to one or more of these groups; by using direct mail or a leaflet drop they can be reached with relative accuracy and a minimum of waste of promotional expenditure.

Tourists may form another discrete geographic segment. Their needs may be quite different from local people. They may, for example, be available for matinee performances at a theatre or concert and may require language translations at galleries and museums. They are more likely to be attracted through posters and literature in hotels and tourist offices than direct mail or newspaper advertising.

Demographic segmentation   As we have seen when looking at influences on arts attendance, some demographic factors are good predictors of audience preferences. The benefits sought by attenders in different age, sex, income, education and racial groups may vary widely and different productions and approaches may be required to attract them and satisfy their needs. Demographic segmentation can be useful, but it is often an incomplete means of segmenting arts audiences. Closer and more effective target marketing can sometimes be undertaken if the attitudes and behaviour of audiences are considered alongside their demographic characteristics.

> All we know about non-goers is who they are rather than why they never visit galleries and what might it take to induce them to do so. Even so, this offers a starting point for future policy direction. Non-goers tend to be disproportionately concentrated in the following sectors of the population:
>   the elderly
>   children
>   homemakers
>   tourists
>   rural dwellers
>   men
>   members of low-income households
>   non-English speakers
>   those with primary or secondary education.
>
> (Bennett and Frow, 1992)

Psychographic segmentation   Audiences can be segmented according to their psychological characteristics, as discussed earlier. Perhaps the most important of these psychographic segments are attitude groupings.

Diggle (1984) suggests that potential audiences comprise:

Attenders: those with very positive attitudes towards the arts and whose attitudes are translated into attendance, either just from time to time or on a regular basis.

Box 2.8

Aesthetic attitudes of arts attenders

In a study of South Australian art galleries and history museums, it was found that arts attenders tend to be exceptionally well educated. They are likely to be professionals or students from households with above average incomes and are usually in the young or lower-middle age groups.

There are some differences between galleries and museums though. Museum visitors are generally slightly less educated and less affluent, and fewer are professionals and students. Museums are more successful than art galleries at attracting the over-50s, housewives and visitors with children.

Whilst statistics such as these are of interest, more useful still is an analysis of these demographic characteristics in conjunction with the behaviour patterns of attenders. In the study of art galleries, six relevant market segments were identified on the basis of the attitudes, behaviour, and demographics of their members.

Art enthusiasts: those who consistently display the highest rates of involvement in art institutions and activities. They tend to be progressive in their views about new art and are generally highly qualified, middle-aged, and have had a high level of practical or professional involvement in the arts.

Apprentice enthusiasts: those who are involved with arts institutions and activities, but who display slightly less progressive attitudes than 'art enthusiasts'. They also tend to be younger, to have lower incomes and are less likely to be in professional occupations than their older counterparts.

Moderate progressives: those who have only a more moderate involvement in the arts but whose attitudes towards art have a lot in common with arts enthusiasts. The age structure, occupations and levels of education of this group are mixed, but it is likely to be relatively affluent.

Progressive traditionalists: those who display some strong tendencies towards traditional arts whilst agreeing with the arts enthusiasts about the importance of the role of education in galleries. Their own levels of education are lower than other groups and they are less likely to be in professional occupations or to be high income earners.

Older conservatives: those who feel most at home with the more traditional conception of an art gallery and resist new developments. Demographically this group is older than the others, with a lower percentage of professionals and lower educational achievements.

Conservatives: those who hold a traditionalist view similar to the 'Old conservatives' but are younger, more likely to be highly educated and likely to have relatively high incomes.

It is clear from this study that aesthetic attitudes are not solely determined by demographic variables such as age, education, income and occupation.

Source: Bennett and Frow (1992)

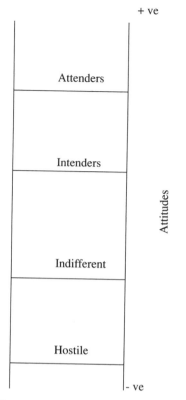

Figure 2.3   The attitude ladder

Intenders: those who think the arts are a 'good thing' and like the idea of attending, but never seem to get around to it.

The indifferent: those who have no strong opinions on the arts and no strong desire to attend either.

The hostile: those who dislike the idea of the arts altogether and have no intention of participating.

The extent of marketing activity (and resources) required to encourage arts participation by attenders at the top of the attitudinal ladder is far lower than that required to change the attitudes and motivate behaviour amongst the indifferent and the hostile. The further down the scale people are, the greater the efforts required to get them to attend.

For arts organizations with limited resources, this form of segmentation creates a dilemma. Attenders and intenders are undoubtedly the most cost-effective groups to target if their objectives are simply to increase audience numbers. However, as attenders and intenders normally come from similar social and educational backgrounds, to expend effort solely in this way is likely to mean ignoring those from

---

Box 2.9

Opening times in the visual arts

The Liverpool branch of the Tate gallery found that Sunday opening was very popular amongst visitors and closed its doors on Mondays instead, in line with most European museums. This offered the additional benefit of being able to undertake work in the gallery on a week-day, without spoiling the public's enjoyment (Tait, 1990).

Another view on opening times is that galleries and exhibitions in a particular catchment area should close on different days of the week to ensure that potential audiences who are only available, say, on a Monday, are not denied access altogether to the visual arts. This may be particularly important in tourist centres. Local consortia can be influential in determining such a policy.

---

other socio-economic groups, the ethnic minorities and other sectors who have traditionally eschewed any involvement with certain art forms. This may not sit very comfortably with a prevailing mission statement which espouses access for all, but may be the only practical solution to audience development for arts organizations under severe financial constraints, for whom 'bums on seats' makes the difference between survival and extinction. Funding bodies, however, may take a different view.

Attitude change is a process which often takes years, or even generations. Education and public relations through appropriate media can speed up the process, but for most arts organizations this will not take place quickly enough to stimulate seat sales and admissions amongst those less well disposed to the arts. The attitudinal segments most important and accessible to arts organizations are likely to remain the attenders and intenders, at least in the medium term. The task of converting the indifferent and the hostile is likely to require the resources of the funding bodies and a positive attitude from both government and the media.

Behavioural segmentation   This involves dividing buyers into groups based on their responses to the arts product and, for arts organizations, can be usefully examined in the following five ways:

When do they attend?
Audiences can be grouped according to those who prefer to attend matinees as opposed to evening performances, and weekends as opposed to weekdays. A number of galleries are finding that there is a sizeable segment wishing to attend on Sundays and are moving towards seven-day opening or shifting their weekly closing day to either Mondays or Tuesdays.

Why do they attend?
We have already looked at the different motivations people may have for attending

the arts, and these groupings can be useful when planning programmes and designing promotional activity. People may attend because they want to:

- Celebrate (events such as birthdays).
- Socialize (with friends or colleagues).
- Do business (entertaining clients).
- Learn (either for self-development or linked with formal education).
- Purchase (art work for their own collection or for a present, for example).

Under what circumstances do they attend?
Some people will attend when there's nothing good on the TV; others will combine a theatre or gallery visit with a shopping trip, or only attend when they're on holiday. If an associated activity can be identified, then this may be used as a basis for the promotional message in particular, and influence the distribution of literature.

How knowledgeable are they?
Different programmes will attract those with different levels of expertise, or indeed confidence, in the art form being presented. Classical music programmes, for example, can be broadly divided into the popular and the high-brow, with certain works being accessible to relatively wide audiences with little or no music education, whilst others are enjoyed more by those who are able to appreciate the subtleties of technique and form. Failing to segment the market in this way can lead to disappointments for both groups, and may alienate them from future events. For some there's nothing worse than the embarrassment of clapping in the wrong place amongst an audience who knows the music better than you do; others may be equally horrified at the rustling of sweet wrappers in the midst of a piano recital!

How often do they attend?
Those who are frequent and committed attenders need to be approached in a different way from those who attend occasionally. Season tickets, subscription schemes, friends and members clubs and similar activities may be appropriate for those who see the arts as a central part of their lives and who are looking for involvement as well as the pleasures of attendance. Little inducement is required to encourage them to attend, so the marketing emphasis to this group should be on providing information to make it easy to plan ahead and book tickets. The irregular attenders are far more challenging as a promotional target. The promotional campaigns need to be more intrusive, as this group is not actively seeking information about arts events.

Market targeting

Market segmentation is a critical step in the matching process between the arts product and its potential audience. Market targeting is the process by which those subgroups are approached with appropriate offers. Most arts organizations are faced with a choice between a concentration strategy and a multi-segment marketing strategy.

Concentration strategy   Some arts organizations have a specific mission which requires them to focus their activities on a single market segment, such as young people, the disabled, an ethnic minority group, inner city communities. These organizations will follow what is known as a concentration strategy, whereby they target their product and promotional efforts at just one fairly homogeneous group, and will attempt to build an audience by putting out a single clear message to this target audience. Credibility needs to be built up within the target market so that all members of that market know that 'people like me attend this arts organization.' In many ways, this is quite a straightforward task. The organization is in a good position to build its reputation as it will have a good understanding of the needs of its audiences – vital if the matching process is to be effective.

Multi-segment marketing   Other arts organizations need to attract a diverse audience and typically their task is more difficult. Local authority venues, for example, which may be attempting to serve a wide range of people within their boundaries, will need to put out diverse messages about their activities and aim these messages at different parts of their total potential primary audience. This is known as a multi-segment marketing strategy. Organizations following this strategy often find it difficult to position themselves in the minds of their potential audiences. People can be unsure as to whether that organization is 'for them' as they may, on occasions, investigate what is on offer and find that it doesn't appeal to them at all. They may then exclude that organization from consideration in the future.

Communicating with a number of different segments can be costly and is likely to require considerable marketing expertise. Information technology which enables a direct marketing approach to be followed is serving to make the task easier and more cost effective. Public relations is also a useful tool for addressing a number of segments. These are discussed further in Chapters 6 and 7.

Information systems for target marketing

To implement the concept of target marketing, arts organizations need to:

- Separate their audiences into discrete groups.
- Gather information from the different groups.
- Use this information to present appropriate programmes to the different groups in an effective way.

Computerized systems offer one of the best ways of managing this interaction with audiences. Indeed, the researching and analysis of potential audiences and information retrieval and statistical analysis related to these audiences may only be possible with help from the computer. Prochak (1993) asserts that most of the information collection and storage needs of arts marketers can be satisfied by computer systems which are currently available on the market, and that these systems can be effectively used for processing and analysing data in most arts organizations, whether or not they are involved with ticket sales.

A great deal of commercially available software is dedicated to marketing applications. Market research software can help with questionnaire construction and survey analysis; databases help with the formation of mailing lists and the effective targeting of promotional literature; telephone marketing packages can be used to help generate sales; and geo-demographic systems enable customer records to be mapped and compared with national data. For many organizations though, a dedicated application in the form of a box office system will be the most useful of all.

Box office systems

Tomlinson (1993) describes box office systems as 'systems which integrate ticketing and marketing functions, compile a "patron" or customer database as central function and offer additional opportunities to record information.'

As the database is the central feature of the box office system, it is essential that relevant and up-to-date information is fed in. The responsibility for gathering this information usually lies with the box office, so it is important that the system is user friendly. As the primary function of box office staff is to sell tickets, the task of information collection will receive scant attention if it slows down ticket processing and creates queues at the box office window.

The customer record

In a computerized box office system, information about attenders is stored in the form of customer records. In most systems, the basic information to be collected in an individual's record is pre-programmed, but many also offer scope for organizations to add other types of information which might be of specific relevance to them alone.

The software is able to search through all the records held and select all those carrying the same text, numbers, or dates and times, or some combination of these (some systems can handle multiple combinations while others are more restricted in their flexibility). Groups of people with similar characteristics (e.g. those who attend matinees, those of similar age, those from the same postal districts, those who paid the same ticket prices) can be identified and linked with their choice of performance.

Using box office data

Box office data can be used in many ways, but some very useful applications are as follows:

Direct marketing

The box office system is commonly used to create mailing lists. As the box office captures data on all those who ever purchase a ticket, it enables mail to be sent to the whole potential audience – not just those who have bothered to put their names on the mailing list. As a result, direct marketing is undoubtedly one of the most common and effective uses of box office data. It is discussed in more detail in Chapter 7.

Box 2.10
Useful data for customer records
In addition to basic customer information relating to names and home addresses which are quite easily obtained (particularly from those who pay by credit card), arts organizations may attempt to include the following data on their customer records:

- Title.
- Gender.
- Initials, first name and familiar name (if different).
- Qualification (as a suffix).
- Employment.
- Posts in voluntary organizations.
- Business address.
- Temporary address (such as holiday homes).
- Phone number(s).
- Date of birth/age.
- Socio-economic group.
- Ethnic origin.
- Geo-demographic classification (based on ACORN or other coding).
- Performance(s) attended.
- Source(s) of information about the performance.
- Other links with the organization (e.g. member, sponsor).
- Number and types of tickets bought.
- Prices paid.
- Payment methods.
- Time of booking.

In theory these data should be quite easy to obtain, but new procedures may have to be set up and rehearsed by the box office staff who will be required to input them accurately and consistently into the system.

Source: Tomlinson (1993)

It is estimated that 25 per cent of current attenders obtained their information about what was on from a mailing in the post. By using a box office system, marketers are in a position to mail information specifically to groups of people who are most likely to attend particular performances or events (based on the fact that they have attended this type of performance or event before). This avoids the scatter-gun effect for which direct mail is often criticized. Not only does poorly directed promotional literature offend the recipient (hence being dubbed junk mail), but also it is a waste of an arts organization's limited resources.

In addition, the more that is known about the recipient of the mailed message, the better that message can be formulated to interest the potential reader. Frequent attenders, for example, are likely to need different messages from occasional attenders. Those who see the arts as an integral part of their social life need information to help them to decide which events to attend, whereas less committed customers will need to be convinced that the arts event in question is an appropriate leisure choice. The content of the message needs to be different for these two groups.

Analysis of booking patterns

Box office data provide a history of booking patterns over time. This enables:

- Booking patterns for previous events to be used for forecasting similar current events (e.g. how far in advance did people book? did they come in groups or alone? which were the most popular seats? what was the average ticket price?).
- Current patterns which depart significantly from forecast patterns can be flagged up and remedial action taken (e.g. if advance ticket sales are very slow, more efforts can be put into promotion or price promotions introduced; if an event is quickly sold out, efforts can be made to switch-sell the disappointed customers).

Audience profiling

A box office system can capture data which provide a statistical overview of the audience for a particular venue. Catchment areas, demographic customer profiles, ACORN classifications, attendance patterns and the character of attenders can all be collected and stored. This information is particularly useful for touring companies

The MapEast project

A particularly large-scale profiling project called the MapEast Project was undertaken by Eastern Touring Agency in conjunction with Select Ticketing, one of the leading producers of computerized box office systems. Information was extracted from fourteen venues with computerized box office systems across the east of England, leading to the profiling of 395,000 arts attenders.

The findings were instrumental in knocking down two traditionally held assumptions: that the average arts attender in the region travelled a long distance to arts events, which led to the second assumption that there was significant competition between venues.

By examining the behaviour of those who had attended more than twice in the previous 12 months, mapping showed that the majority lived within 30 minutes' drive time. Hence there was relatively little competition between venues, limited to just a few postcodes. The research also enabled the frequency of attendance for different postcodes to be identified, and indicated those which were below average, presenting an opportunity for attracting new attenders.

Source: Stockton (1994)

and events, who will be trying to include areas where the profile of local attenders is similar to the profile of attenders for their own art form.

Ad hoc research

Box office data can be used to provide answers to specific marketing problems. This can avoid the necessity for primary data to be collected through a survey, and therefore can be a very cost-effective way of generating useful marketing information (discussed further in Chapter 3).

Conclusion

Audiences are an important element of the artistic experience. They are the customers for the arts form and the raison d'être of the arts organization. But audiences are not homogeneous. They comprise subgroups of individuals who display similar characteristics, behaviour, motivations and attitudes. To satisfy the different subgroups, the marketing function in an arts organization must know their composition and their needs, so that the art being produced can be targeted most appropriately at those who will appreciate the experience on offer and return for more as a result. The mechanism for gathering such information is known as marketing research, which is the subject of the next chapter.

Key concepts

Age   Gender
Audience development   Income
Beliefs and attitudes   Market segmentation
Box office systems   Motivation
Concentration strategy   Multi-segment strategy
Culture   Perception
Customer records   Personality
Decision-making process   Psychographics
Decision-making unit   Reference groups
Demographics   Social class
Education   Target marketing

Discussion questions

1 Imagine that you are a visitor from the planet Mars and you have been invited to attend a production of *Aida* at the Royal Opera House. What social conventions might you be in danger of breaking?

Subscription pricing at Northern Sinfonia

Whilst revenue from subscriptions to Northern Sinfonia's Newcastle City Hall series had risen by 3 per cent between 1989 and 1991, the number of individuals subscribing was down by 7 per cent. Marketing manager, Stephen Cashman, used box office data to compare customers' booking behaviour in 1990 with that in 1989 so that the underlying behavioural trends could be quantified and mapped, and decisions made as to pricing policy.

The conclusions drawn from the research were:

- That most re-subscribers either did not change their booking or changed the type of package they booked but did not change their seating area or number of visits.
- That subscribers would reduce their number of visits rather than move seats to a lower price.
- That top price bookers were an increasingly significant proportion of all bookers.
- That those seated in area C would rather not come at all than trade-down to area D.
- That 'rover' subscribers comprised either new subscribers or those trading down from full season subscriptions.

As a result of this, decisions were taken to:

- Increase the top price.
- Increase the range of packages on offer to create a spectrum with more gradations (to reduce the impact of individuals who chose to trade down whilst retaining their seating position).
- Reduce the relative price of area C.
- Decrease the differential between the 'rover' and fixed package by increasing the price of the 'rover'.

Source: Stockton (1994)

2 Is there anything that a mixed programme venue could do to increase the number of men who attend their ballet performances? Should they bother to try? If so, why?

3 What type of negative attitudes do you think people hold about art museums? Are they justified? What could be done to correct any distortions?

4 How could a visual arts organization better cater for the needs of the 'lonely escapist'?

5 Do tourists form a single market segment, or are they simply parts of other geographic, demographic, psychographic or behavioural segments?

6 What criteria should a concert hall take into account in deciding whether or not to invest in a computerized box office system?

7 'Elitism in the arts is perpetuated by the need to break-even'. Discuss.

Action questions

1 How effectively does your organization communicate with educational establishments? With whom do you try to communicate: the initiators, influencers, deciders and/or potential attenders?

2 How do you obtain information for the customer records in your box office system? What could you do to improve the effectiveness of the database?

3 Is your venue welcoming? How much effort do you put into satisfying the needs of the 'social attenders'? What else could you do to improve the sociability of an event at your venue?

References

Bennett, A. and Frow, J. (1992). Art galleries: who goes? In *Marketing the Arts* (S. Blackall and J. Meek eds) 137–151, The International Council of Museums.

Business Marketing Digest (1993). AT&T's offbeat approach to theatre backing, **18**, 11–16 (no author given).

Cooper, P. and Tower, R. (1992). Inside the consumer mind: consumer attitudes to the arts. *Journal of the Market Research Society*, **34**, 4, 299–311.

Diggle, K. (1984). *Guide to Arts Marketing*. Rhinegold Publishing.

Diggle, K. (1994). *Arts Marketing*. Rhinegold Publishing.

Francis, J. (1991). What are we waiting for? *The Insider*, **10**, spring 1991.

Jamieson, B. (1994). Opera rides out sponsors' ring of no confidence. *The Sunday Telegraph*, 16 October, 1.

Kotler, P. and Armstrong, G. (1991). *Principles of Marketing*. Prentice Hall.

Lamos, M. and Stewart, S. (1983). Theater: the vital relationship. In *Market the Arts!* (J.V. Mello, ed.) 17–21, Foundation for the Extension and Development of the American Professional Theatre.

Marplan (1988) *Survey of Asian, African and Caribbean Live Arts Attenders*. Marplan Ltd.

NOP Market Research (1991). *Report on Qualitative Research into the Public's Attitudes to the Arts.* Commissioned by The Arts Council of Great Britain.

Policy Studies Institute (1992). Arts festivals. In *Cultural Trends*, 15.

Prochak, M. (1993). *Computers for Arts Marketing*. Commissioned by The Arts Council of Great Britain.

Research Surveys of Great Britain (1991). *Report on a Survey on Arts and Cultural Activities in G.B.* Commissioned by the Arts Council of Great Britain.

Schlosser, R.J. (1983). Audiences. In *Market the Arts!* (J.V. Mello, ed.) 87–98, Foundation for the Extension and Development of the American Professional Theatre.

Stark, P. (1985). Can the arts do anything about unemployment? In *Arts and Unemployment* (A. Battram and C. Segal, eds) 24, Research Training Initiatives.

Stockton, S. (1994). *Using Box Office Data for Marketing.* Administration Research Training Services, commissioned by the Arts Council of Great Britain.

Tait, S. (1990). V&A considers fee and Monday closing. *The Times*, 12 October, 3.

Taylor, C. (1990). *Research into methods of attracting an 'Ethnic Audience' to the West Yorkshire Playhouse, Leeds.* Taylors.

Tomlinson, R. (1993). *Boxing Clever.* Administration Research Training Services, commissioned by The Arts Council of Great Britain.

Verwey, P. (1988). *Target Group Index 1987/88: Summary of Results.* The Arts Council of Great Britain.

Verwey, P. (1991). Ever increasing circles. *The Insider*, **10**, Spring 1991.

Waters, I. (1989). *Entertainment, Arts and Cultural Services.* Longman.

Young Direction (1990). *Young People and Theatre Going: a Qualitative Research Investigation.* Connexions Group Ltd, commissioned by The Arts Council of Great Britain.

Recommended further reading

Tomlinson, R. (1993). *Boxing Clever.* Administration Research Training Services, commissioned by The Arts Council of Great Britain.

3 Marketing research

Introduction

Marketing research[1] can be defined as the process of collecting, analysing and interpreting information to help managers make better marketing decisions. This chapter will introduce a number of techniques of marketing research which can help arts organizations to gather and use information more efficiently and effectively. This will include sections on:

- The benefits and scope of marketing research.
- Setting research objectives.
- Types of research.
- Sources of secondary data.
- Methods for collecting primary data.
- Conducting a survey.

This chapter is more than just a step-by-step guide to the process of research. It encourages the consideration of both the information needs of an organization and the way in which information can be used, as well as examining the variety of techniques for gathering that information.

The benefits of marketing research

Organizations that have taken marketing research seriously report significant benefits. At the South Bank Centre in London (which includes both visual and performing arts venues), marketing research is seen to be at the heart of their planning and has driven the centre's development. Programming and marketing decisions, merchandising policy, advance booking systems and sponsorship strategy have all been influenced by the results of a number of marketing research projects (McCart, 1992).

Benefits are not restricted to large organizations. Many small-scale organizations on quite restricted budgets have recognized the importance of marketing research.

---

[1] The term 'marketing' research is often shortened to 'market' research, though strictly speaking this is incorrect. Marketing research is a wide-ranging discipline which seeks to gather information about any aspect of an organization and its environment, whilst market research is concerned only with trends in customer or audience behaviour, and is usually known as 'audience research' in an arts context.

Audience surveys at Phoenix Arts Centre

Leicester-based Phoenix Arts Centre reports a diverse array of benefits from research carried out in collaboration with De Montfort University:

It goes without saying that one of the most important benefits of regular audience research relates to knowing your audience. Our annual audience survey provides us with an understanding of our existing audiences and of audiences for other venues, and therefore helps us to identify the most appropriate market segments for development. The survey data inform the development of future marketing campaigns through an understanding of which product types are of interest to which types of customer and which promotional tools are most effective at reaching them. Tracking the development of our audiences through the annual survey helps us to measure our success in achieving our marketing objectives. The survey is also a means of testing audience opinion on practical issues relating to our service delivery.

Information about the demography of our audiences is also invaluable for dealing with funding bodies, sponsors and local authorities as it gives us real evidence to convince them of the importance of our organization and of the arts in general. The results of the survey are presented annually to the Phoenix board which is made up solely of City Council members and senior staff from De Montfort University. The survey is vital for indicating to both the board members and the organizations that they represent that Phoenix is an organization well worth the support it receives from them.

There is also a benefit associated with the physical process of surveying our audience. Many of our attenders have commented on how pleased they are that we are taking the time and effort to find out about them, their needs and wants. The audience survey is, in more than one way, a central part of our customer orientated approach to marketing. It helps show our audiences that we care about them and fosters a feeling of belonging and a sense of ownership. A copy of the results of the survey is made available at the box office should customers wish to read it.

Source: Hinds & Waters (1992)

Objections to marketing research

Arts organizations who choose not to undertake marketing research may give a number of reasons, but the following are perhaps the most common:

'**It's too expensive**'   A popular misconception is that marketing research is a highly technical discipline which can only be successfully pursued by experts (and normally at great expense). Certainly it is a systematic and orderly process, and it is possible to use sophisticated information technology to interpret large quantities of data. There are some industries and organizations for whom vast consumer surveys and detailed statistical analysis can be extremely cost effective, but there are many more organizations who reap significant rewards from a whole host of far less expensive methods of gathering the information that they need to help them better serve their customers. Even the smallest arts organization can benefit from a more rigorous analysis of its box office takings, informal discussions with its regular attenders and a closer examination of the impact of press comment and publicity material, all of which can be done at very little cost. Arts centres such as Phoenix have demonstrated that much can be achieved with very limited budgets.

To say that marketing research is too expensive implies that an organization may not have fully considered the range of marketing data available and the very limited costs involved in the majority of data collection. Perhaps also it hasn't considered the cost of poor decision making which could lead to marketing mistakes and consequently lost audiences.

Marketing research is certainly not the exclusive property of large, wealthy private-sector commercial organizations; neither is it such a complex discipline that it must be left to professional market research agencies, whose fees may be beyond the reach of all but the central arts funding bodies.

'We don't want to be popular'   It is sometimes feared that marketing research will identify demand for a programme of events which would be popular but not worthy. The research may be resisted on the grounds that its findings would not be implemented for cultural or artistic reasons. (The Barbican Centre came under fire for planning a series of events which were specifically included to entice a segment of the market that may not have previously attended the venue, by producing shows such as *Godspell* and Son et Lumières instead of traditional concerts. Moves such as this are supported in some circles, and seen as a commitment by more progressive venue directors to reaching as wide an audience as possible; by others they are condemned as an insult to the serious performers and a betrayal of the classical culture that the funding bodies intend to be served.) Again this is a flimsy reason for ignoring marketing research, which can be a very useful tool for identifying the most appropriate programmes, facilities and services within the ruling artistic policy, and without alienating existing interest groups and audiences.

'We know what our audiences want'   Service providers in the not-for-profit sector are renowned for their over-confidence in knowing instinctively what their customers want. Cushioned by funding bodies and sponsors, some arts organizations are not required to be as sensitive to the acid test of financial viability as some of their commercial competitors. Faced with an overriding profit motive, commercial arts are keenly aware of their customers' opinions, which are critical to their survival. In the subsidized sector, marketing research is often the only tool available to arts organizations to assess the extent to which their own non-profit objectives are being met. To ignore it is to ignore the core of the marketing concept, which places the needs of the customer at the heart of the organization.

> **No smoking?**
> At Phoenix Arts Centre in Leicester, it was decided that there was a need for a specific policy on smoking in the centre. The management team agreed that it was impossible to enforce a no-smoking policy in the bar but the cafe area was a source of contention for both staff and customers. The audience survey found that 59 per cent of those surveyed wanted the cafe to be no smoking while 34 per cent wanted to be able to smoke there. A further 7 per cent expressed no preference. In true democratic style, the management designated two-thirds of the cafe to be non-smoking areas.
>
> *Source:* Hinds & Waters (1992)

The scope of marketing research

The definition given of marketing research is deliberately broad in scope. It refers to any attempt to gather information from the environment which may be useful in the planning of marketing activity. However, marketing research can be subdivided into a number of categories, according to its purpose:

Audience research

This is primarily concerned with identifying the nature, composition and preferences of current and potential audiences. It is commonly used to help organizations identify audience groupings (or market segments) with similar characteristics and arts preferences, enabling visitor or audience profiles to be constructed for different types of exhibitions or performances. An audience survey will typically ask for details of demographic characteristics including age and sex, but also income, occupation, education, and perhaps means of transport and distance travelled to the venue. This type of information helps galleries and theatres to target their future programmes, events, promotional literature, fund-raising and advertising more precisely, and it can provide useful quantified information when negotiating sponsorship.

Customer satisfaction research

This aims to measure the extent to which an arts event has met its audiences' expectations. Word-of-mouth recommendation has been found to be the most influential factor in the choice of leisure services, so it is important for organizations to understand and respond to their customers' perceptions of both the artistic product and the environment in which it is produced.

Motivation research

This attempts to get to the bottom of audiences' reasons for attending a particular event or venue, again to enable better market segmentation and improved targeting of potential audiences. It has also been successfully used in developing an understanding of reasons for non-attendance and hostility towards the arts. At its simplest, motivation research involves asking direct questions of visitors as to why they chose a particular event in a particular venue on a particular day and time: but as many people are unable to describe exactly why they act as they do, some motivation research involves a variety of less conventional techniques in seeking a deeper understanding of the more covert or even unconscious reasons for attendance.

Competitor research

It is often argued that arts events do not face direct competition, as it is difficult to imagine two venues within close geographical proximity of each other offering identical programmes at the same time. Nonetheless, audiences do have choices as to how, when and where to spend their money, and different venues and programmes will be competing for a share of that money over a longer period of time. For this reason it is important for arts organizations to understand how their audiences perceive them in comparison with other similar organizations. Competitor research can help organizations to understand these perceptions and then to differentiate themselves positively from other providers of similar arts services. Failing to do so can lead to an ill-defined image and consequent rejection by key target audiences. This was a trend which was identified and rectified at an early stage by the South Bank Centre.

Product research

This is quite a difficult area in the arts. Commercial and industrial organizations conduct product research to help them improve the products and services that they offer to their customers and to identify demand for new developments. This reflects the overall objectives of most firms in the private sector, which are related to profitable trading activity. If demand exists which can be supplied, then there is an opportunity to make money.

In the subsidized arts sector, though, a balance must be achieved which recognizes that the organization's objectives may not be purely financial, and may be equally related to the serving of minority interests and the continued development of art forms which may or may not hold popular appeal. The policy of arts organizations in the subsidized sector may therefore be to influence demand, as well as to respond to it. Marketing research can help organizations achieve this balance.

Product research in the more tangible areas of facilities, such as retailing and catering, can be equally as valuable. This type of research can help to identify both inadequacies in existing provision and demand for new facilities and services which may improve audience perceptions of a venue, encourage new attenders and consolidate customer loyalty.

Pricing research

For commercial arts organizations, this can help in the setting of entrance fees or ticket prices. Revenue from the box office or entrance fees can be maximized if the

The South Bank Centre: traditional or trendy?

As part of a wider research programme, the management at the South Bank Centre wanted to gain a better understanding of the public's current awareness of the centre and where it fitted into their perceptions of the major London arts venues. Their survey included potential customers who were attenders at other London arts venues, including people who went to the:

- Barbican but not concerts of the South Bank.
- Royal Academy but not exhibitions at the Hayward Gallery.
- English National Opera but not opera on the South Bank.
- Riverside but not dance on the South Bank.
- Festival Hall foyers, but not a paid performance.

The survey findings indicated that the 'traditionalist', enthusiast and classical concert-goer saw the South Bank as becoming fringe, contemporary and innovative, whilst 'modernist', fringe and experimentalist audiences saw it as too predictable, safe and popular.

Further research led to some strategic changes in artistic programming. Programmers developed a number of regular classical music strands across all three halls to provide regulars with predictable and reassuring programmes. In addition, the centre's country and concept festivals and living composers, contemporary and multi-cultural series all received a regular slot. 'This facilitates audiences' understanding and expectation of the Centre's season as a whole. The changes in programming policy together with a better understanding by the Centre of the size, shape and strike rate of series has led to a significant increase in attendances.'

Source: McCart (1992)

organization has done some pricing research to help it understand the monetary value that their audiences will place on the experience they are expecting to enjoy (there is more discussion on this point in Chapter 5). In the non-profit sector, pricing research can also be used to help the formulation of pricing policies that will promote wider access to the arts. An understanding of the key influences on audience price sensitivity can be gained by experimenting with different price levels and monitoring the associated attendance figures.

Promotional research

This is normally undertaken to assess the effectiveness of different media, messages and promotional techniques in attracting audiences. It is generally retrospective. If money has been spent on promoting an event, it is important to be able to gauge the cost-effectiveness of the chosen methods and media of promotion. Promotional research attempts to gather information which will identify the most persuasive

Brochure copy research at the Derby Playhouse

Qualitative research was used to refine brochure copy approaches at the Derby Playhouse in the mid 1980s. Focus groups, drawn from a sample of regular and occasional attenders, revealed a desire for more explicit descriptions of the content of plays rather than the kind of subjective generalizations which marketing departments sometimes favour. The result was to make brochure copy a great deal more direct.

promotional techniques by linking them to attendance figures. Under some circumstances it may also be of use to pre-test advertising campaigns, to identify the most effective visual or verbal creative concept, and to identify the target audiences to whom a particular campaign appeals.

Policy research

Organizations such as the Arts Council use marketing research to help them make recommendations about the levels of arts provision and the allocation of resources. Information about national and regional public attitudes towards the arts, as well as attendance and participation figures, is invaluable in creating a strong case for public funding of the arts. Research can demonstrate economic benefits from the arts, such as spending in restaurants or attraction of tourists. It could indicate the effect of arts facilities on the image of a town, or on local or national pride. Marketing research can also be used to detect audience trends and attitudes in other countries which may have domestic implications or simply provide early warning of likely developments at home.

Conducting marketing research

If marketing research is to be an effective tool for improving the quality of marketing decisions, it needs systematically to address three key questions:

What do we want to know?   The first stage of marketing research should be to examine the marketing problem or opportunity which requires further investigation and this should lead to a set of specific objectives for the research. Having set clear, unambiguous objectives it is possible to pinpoint the nature of the information that must be obtained to help solve the problem or develop the opportunity.

Where can the information be obtained?   Secondly it is essential to identify who can provide the information and what is the best method for collecting it. The most visible aspect of marketing research is the collecting of information using surveys. Whilst surveys are very important, they are but one mechanism for finding out about people, and may be neither the most appropriate nor the most cost-effective method of data collection.

Box 3.1

Marketing research in the visual arts

Market research can tackle a range of different issues and be used in different ways:

- It can be used to reach a better understanding of who is using your gallery. This information can be vital both for extending the types of users of your gallery and for deepening the relationship of all users with the gallery.
- The information about your audiences you gain through market research can then be used for lobbying or leverage purposes with funders or for local authority galleries in discussions over budgets.
- It can tell you about your visitors' attitudes to the overall programme or to individual exhibitions, and their perception of the cultural profile of the gallery. This will let you know whether the programming policy of the gallery is clearly understood by users.
- It can be helpful in reviewing the physical layout of the gallery, its signposting and labelling. It can examine the levels of knowledge visitors bring to the work so that labelling is neither patronizing nor too complex. At a practical level, you can discover whether the visitor found it easy to get round. At a conceptual level, you can find out whether the way the work is presented helps visitors interpret it to their own satisfaction.
- It is able to pinpoint other factors affecting the way the gallery is viewed and used, like physical and emotional access, street safety, transport and parking, child care and opening hours. These factors will frequently not be within the gallery's control but the information will allow you to lobby those who do control them.

Source: Boyden Southwood Associates (1993)

How do we use the findings?   Marketing research provides facts, but information is created when the facts are interpreted in the context of the original problem. The final stage, therefore, is for managers to make sense of the findings and ensure that they influence decision making in the organization. Without intelligent interpretation, research is at best worthless, and at worst it can be misleading and dangerous.

The rest of this chapter explores the techniques and research methods which will help managers to answer these three questions for themselves in their own organizations.

The Pegram Walters theory of research

Figure 3.1   Never underestimate the importance of the interpretation stage.

Research objectives

Why set objectives?

Research objectives are explicit statements of what the organization wants to know. They are important for two main reasons:

1 They are a constant reminder to managers of what they are trying to find out. This can prevent time and energy being wasted on the collection of information which will not ultimately be of use in solving the marketing problem facing the organization.
2 They can provide a benchmark or target against which the results of the research can be measured. This enables managers to assess whether the research was effective, which can be a crucial activity for arts organizations, particularly in the subsidized sector. If money is scarce, marketing research may be viewed as a luxury, and marketing managers are likely to be required to justify their expenditure in this area.

Categories of objectives

Broadly speaking, research objectives can be divided into three categories:

Exploratory objectives

These tend to be quite broad in scope, and are normally specified when an organization feels that it needs a better insight into the nature of certain marketing issues. For example, a lot of exploratory research is conducted by funding bodies to help them make policy decisions and set planning priorities, as well as to give guidance to those they subsidize.

Descriptive objectives

These are usually set when an organization needs more concrete evidence to support specific marketing decisions. Audience research reports are normally descriptive. In other words, they describe an audience or potential audience by their characteristics and preferences, so that the relationships between different characteristics and preferences can be examined. For example, it would be possible to design a survey which investigates the age, sex and socio-economic profile of a regional opera audience, as well as their musical preferences. It could then be determined whether opera-goers are also interested in orchestral concerts, pop concerts or ballet, and whether any particular age group, social class or sex is more likely to prefer one of those art forms to another. This type of information could be very helpful in promotional campaigns.

Box 3.2
Public attitudes towards the arts

Background

The Arts Council of Great Britain intended to formulate a national arts strategy based on a clear understanding of the ways in which the arts are perceived by the population. In order to gain a better understanding of the attitudes of various sections of the public to the arts, they undertook a qualitative research programme to elicit the views of people whose practice and commitment to the arts ranged from strongly involved and favourably disposed, to those who expressed antipathy. Views from different areas of England and Scotland, covering urban to rural communities, were gathered to provide an overview of the situation. The primary purpose of the research was exploratory, seeking to identify aspects of the current attitudinal climate. It was anticipated that the findings from this research would be used in subsequent descriptive research, which would be repeated over time to enable changes in public attitudes to be monitored.

Research objectives

1 The broad objectives of the overall research programme were:

- To gain a better understanding of overall attitudes towards the arts held by different sectors of the public:
  Regular attenders   people who already attend arts events at least once every two months.
  Occasional attenders   people who already attend arts events occasionally – two or three times a year.
  Active amateurs   people who actively engage in art activities as amateurs, e.g. music – play an instrument or sing; produce craft work; take classes; engage in community arts.
  Passive/interested   people who do not attend arts events but who are (a) supportive of, or (b) interested and make a point of watching or listening to arts programmes on radio or TV.
  Apathetic or hostile   people who neither enjoy nor support the arts, or who have no interest in the arts.
- To identify particular issues and attitudes which should be validated quantitatively'
- To obtain indicators of public attitudes to the arts which could be monitored over time to show changes/improvements resulting from the operation of a National Arts Strategy.

2 The specific objectives of the qualitative research were:

- To establish what people understand to be encompassed by the terms 'the arts' and 'culture'.
- To examine the value of the arts in terms of
  - Entertainment
  - Social interaction
  - Education
  - Enhancement of the quality of life.
- To look at the aesthetic benefits of the arts, now and in the future:
  - The development of creative thinking, critical and aesthetic standards and national culture, and parochial benefits such as adding value to an area, civic pride and providing jobs.
- To understand the role of broadcast media in shaping the arts.
- To gauge perceptions of the accessibility of the arts.
- To ascertain the role of non-European art forms in the development of the arts in Britain.

Source: NOP Consumer Market Research (1991)

Causal objectives

Research can be undertaken with a view to identifying cause-and-effect relationships, in an attempt to explain why things happen. Experiments are widely conducted to test alternative prices or concessions by monitoring their impact on audience size and composition. This type of research could be used for developing access policies, or simply for assessing audience price sensitivity. Similar exercises can be performed to assess the impact of different advertising media, programme design or even interval length, thus providing information to help with promotion and programming decisions.

In practice, a major marketing research project may require all three types of objectives to be set. Exploratory research could lead to the design of a survey which would enable an audience to be defined and described. The significant relationships between the different characteristics and preferences of this audience could then be further investigated in a causal study. Nonetheless, the distinction between these types of objectives is very useful in helping managers to focus systematically on the purposes of the research.

Types of research

Having set research objectives, it is possible to identify the *style* of research which should be undertaken.

Qualitative research

If the research objectives require information to be generated about why people act as they do, or how they think and feel about the experiences that the arts are offering them, then the research is described as being qualitative. Conducting qualitative research usually requires interviews to be conducted with small numbers of people, though other techniques such as observation and experimentation may also be useful in getting to the root of audience behaviour. In the arts, qualitative research is particularly useful as it is able to explore the subtleties of people's reactions to the aesthetic experience. It may seek to explore issues such as:

- Motivations and inhibitions for participating in the arts.
- What people are looking for from the arts.
- Perceptions of different art forms.
- Reactions to specific productions, titles and artists.
- Reasons for success or failure of productions or events.
- Appropriate types of promotion.
- Sources of influence over audiences (reviews, advertising, word-of-mouth).
- The perceptions of sponsoring organizations.

Quantitative research

If the research objectives require information to be generated about how many people hold certain views or fit into certain categories, then the research is described as being quantitative. Conducting quantitative research usually requires a survey to be undertaken amongst a sample of the population of interest to the researcher. The findings can then be interpreted with the help of statistical techniques, and assumptions can be made about the whole population from the information generated amongst the sample. This is a very common form of research in the arts, and is a popular method for investigating the nature of audiences.

The necessary *duration* of research is also implied by the research objectives:

Continuous research

Continuous research examines an issue or problem on a regular basis in order to monitor changes that are occurring over a period of time. For example, funding bodies may be interested in changes in public attitudes towards the arts, or theatres may like to know whether audiences are more or less satisfied with offerings and facilities than they were six months, a year, or five years ago.

Ad hoc research

Ad hoc research is a term given to a one-off piece of research, undertaken to obtain information relating to a particular issue or problem. The findings of this type of research are reported in such a way as to help a specific marketing decision to be made.

Finally, the objectives will determine the *process* by which the marketing data should be collected. Generating marketing information requires the collection of marketing data, the term data referring to the facts and figures that must be gathered to achieve the research objectives.

Secondary research

Secondary research, also known as desk research, involves the gathering together of relevant data that exist prior to the start of a marketing research programme. The researcher is therefore a secondary user of already existing data. This accounts for its name. Internal secondary data are data which already exist within the organization conducting the research; external data have been collected outside the organization, for example by the government, by funding bodies or by commercial market research houses. It is possible that both these types of data have originally been collected for a purpose other than marketing research, but nonetheless they can be valuable to the researcher. If secondary data are adequate to satisfy the objectives of the research, then the more costly processes of primary research can be avoided.

Primary research

Primary research involves the generation and collection of original data. The organization determines exactly what information is necessary and from whom it needs the information and then sets about acquiring it. The data are thus specific to the purpose for which they have been acquired. It is quite likely that primary research will be undertaken after secondary research, to provide a more complete set of answers to the researcher's questions.

Sources of secondary data

Internal sources

This refers to data which already exist within an organization. Arts organizations frequently own a lot of data which can potentially be used for marketing research: the accounting system, for example, may be able to identify the relative popularity of catering and retail outlets during specific exhibitions or performance programmes; staff may be able to report on customer reactions to ticket prices at the box office. However, the most important sources of internal data for arts organizations are invariably their databases storing details of attenders. Performing arts organizations, as sellers of tickets to specific performances, are best placed to make the most of this type of data.

Those who maintain a comprehensive database through their box office systems have immediate access to information which can help answer both strategic and tactical questions. For example:

- At whom should we direct mail shots for contemporary dance productions?

Customer analysis at the Brewhouse

At the Brewhouse Theatre and Arts Centre in Taunton a detailed analysis of the types of customer and their characteristics enabled the allocation of customers into a series of discrete groupings to enable tailored and personalized direct mailings for each season brochure. A complex hierarchical selection and sort was necessary to analyse the 13 000 names and addresses and then enable the production of the direct mail letters with tailored content and personalized salutations and booking forms, all in the Post Office Mailsort order. As well as being personalized, the booking forms contained a tracking code to identify the specific mailing details being responded to. There was a 15 per cent increase in sales and a 20 per cent increase in membership.

Source: Tomlinson (1992)

- What price concessions should be offered on which days of the week?
- At what point should action be taken to improve ticket sales for a low-selling event?
- Who should I include in a sample for conducting primary research into attendance at productions of Shakespeare?
- What type of person prefers to attend exhibitions on a Sunday as opposed to a weekday?

Even manual box offices are in a position to gather basic transaction data for all attenders. Computerized box office systems simply extend the range of details that can be stored. Data can be recorded automatically by the system as part of processing the ticket sale – name and address, ticket prices and concessions, details of event attended, time of performance or exhibition etc. Additional data can be added to this by simple questioning – how did the customer hear of the event? What was the main influence on attending? Finally, observations can be added, to give more data still, perhaps indicating the approximate age of the ticket purchaser, or any relevant comments made during the transaction. (There is more discussion of computerized box office systems in Chapters 2 and 7.)

External sources

Published data are widely available for use by arts organizations, through libraries, through Regional Tourist Boards and in particular through funding bodies such as the Arts Council and the Regional Arts Boards.

Published surveys

The Arts Council carries a database of individual surveys carried out both by itself and by a wide range of arts organizations. These can be of considerable help in the investigation of similar problems in different organizations, or simply in planning a methodology for

Box 3.3
Interpreting survey research results

A survey was conducted amongst 1000 18–65-year-olds nationwide to investigate attendance at arts events. The first question asked whether respondents had attended any arts event in the last month.

The findings were reported as follows:

Attenders at arts events

	Total	London	Midlands	North	South
	1000	300	300	200	200
Attended any arts event last month					
Yes (%)	17	20	15	25	10
No (%)	83	80	85	75	90

BASE: All respondents (1000)

For these data to be useful, the first thing that needs to be known is what constitutes an arts event? Which categories of the arts were included? The regional split needs to be clarified too and, within each region, were the interviews conducted in just a few towns or cities or from both rural and urban communities?

The survey went on to ask those who had attended about the nature of the performance, and the findings were presented as follows:

Arts events attended last month

	Total	London	Midlands	North	South
	170	60	45	45	20
Ballet %	5	8	2	6	0
Opera %	5	5	11	0	0
Other dance %	10	12	4	6	25
Classical music %	20	28	13	10	30
Other %	80	72	72	90	70

BASE: All who attended any arts event last month (170)

Note here that the question was not asked of all respondents, only 170 people. The base for each region was very small, only 20 people in the South. The table totals more than 100 per cent – it totals 120 per cent, because some respondents may have been to more than one arts event in the last month. Some re-percentaging is presented. In fact, only 5 per cent of those who attended any arts event in the last month attended the ballet or, expressed another way, only 1 per cent of all respondents went to the ballet in the last month.

The only real conclusion that can be drawn from this table is that amongst those who have attended arts events in the last month, a very wide range of events were attended, as evidenced by the 80 per cent who had attended some 'other' arts event.

Source: Oakden (1992)

the implementation of a piece of primary research. Care must be taken in their use though. It is important, for example, to check who the original client was and their reasons for conducting the research. This will indicate whether a particular slant has been taken in the interpretation of the findings. The nature and size of the sample is also relevant. Findings should be treated with caution if the number of respondents in any subgroup is small, particularly if comparisons are made between different groups of people.

ACORN and the TGI

Two additional sources of secondary data available through the Arts Council include the ACORN classification system and the Target Group Index (TGI).

ACORN This is a consumer classification system based on 'Geodemographics'. Designed by CACI, it combines the geographic and demographic information contained in census data to classify consumers into groups of distinct types who are likely to have similar characteristics and behaviour patterns. The residential postcodes of these groups have been identified and arts organizations can have their own database postcodes compared with the ACORN groups to help them identify the profile of their current audiences (CACI, 1994). This information is valuable to arts organizations in helping them to quantify market penetration for each category of performance but, perhaps more importantly, it enables them to identify all postcodes in their catchment area where similar types of people are likely to live and target their promotional campaigns accordingly.

The British population is divided into primary categories, according to lifestyle. For example, category A consists of those described as thriving – people who are established at the top of the social ladder, who tend to be healthy, wealthy and confident consumers. Each category is then broken down into groups, with category A, for example, being subdivided into three groups, namely the wealthy achievers in suburban areas, affluent greys in rural communities and prosperous pensioners in

ACORN categories	ACORN groups	ACORN types
A:THRIVING	1 Wealthy achievers, suburban areas	1.1 Wealthy suburbs, large detached houses 1.2 Villages with wealthy commuters 1.3 Mature affluent home-owning areas 1.4 Affluent suburbs, older families 1.5 Mature, well-off suburbs
	2 Affluent greys, rural communities	2.6 Agricultural villages, home-based workers 2.7 Holiday retreats, older people, home-based workers
	3 Prosperous pensioners, retirement areas	3.8 Home-owning areas, well-off older residents 3.9 Private flats, elderly people
B:EXPANDING	4 Affluent executives, family areas	4.10 Affluent working families with mortgages 4.11 Affluent working couples with mortgages, new homes 4.12 Transient workforces, living at their place of work
	5 Well-off workers, family areas	5.13 Home-owning family areas 5.14 Home-owning family areas, older children 5.15 Families with mortgages, younger children
C:RISING	6 Affluent urbanites, town and city areas	6.16 Well-off town and city areas 6.17 Flats and mortgages, singles and young working couples 6.18 Furnished flats and bedsits, younger single people
	7 Prosperous professionals, metropolitan areas	7.19 Apartments, young professional singles and couples 7.20 Gentrified multi-ethnic areas
	8 Better-off executives, inner city areas	8.21 Prosperous enclaves, highly qualified executives 8.22 Academic centres, students and young professionals 8.23 Affluent city-centre areas, tenements and flats 8.24 Partially gentrified multi-ethnic areas 8.25 Converted flats and bedsits, single people
D:SETTLING	9 Comfortable middle-agers, mature home-owning areas	9.26 Mature established home-owning areas 9.27 Rural areas, mixed occupations 9.28 Established home-owning areas 9.29 Home-owning areas, council tenants, retired people
	10 Skilled workers, home-owning areas	10.30 Established home-owning areas, skilled workers 10.31 Home owners in older properties, younger workers 10.32 Home-owning areas with skilled workers
E:ASPIRING	11 New home owners, mature communities	11.33 Council areas, some new home owners 11.34 Mature home-owning areas, skilled workers 11.35 Low rise estates, older workers, new home owners
	12 White collar workers, better-off multi-ethnic areas	12.36 Home-owning multi-ethnic areas, young families 12.37 Multi-occupied town centres, mixed occupations 12.38 Multi-ethnic areas, white collar workers
F:STRIVING	13 Older people, less prosperous areas	13.39 Home owners, small council flats, single pensioners 13.40 Council areas, older people, health problems
	14 Council estate residents, better-off houses	14.41 Better-off council areas, new home owners 14.42 Council areas, young families, some new home owners 14.43 Council areas, young families, many lone parents 14.44 Multi-occupied terraces, multi-ethnic areas 14.45 Low rise council housing, less well-off families 14.46 Council areas, residents with health problems
	15 Council estate residents, high unemployment	15.47 Estates with high unemployment 15.48 Council flats, elderly people, health problems 15.49 Council flats, very high unemployment, singles
	16 Council estate residents, greatest hardships	16.50 Council areas, high unemployment, lone parents 16.51 Council flats, greatest hardship, many lone parents
	17 People in multi-ethnic, low income areas	17.52 Multi-ethnic, large families, overcrowding 17.53 Multi-ethnic, severe unemployment, lone parents 17.54 Multi-ethnic, high unemployment, overcrowding

Figure 3.2   The ACORN targeting classification. *Source*: CACI Information Services.

Figure 3.3   ACORN Group 8

retirement areas. Finally, each of these groups is broken down further into types, according to any distinctive differences within the group. In total there are six primary categories, 17 groups and a total of 54 types, all of which can be identified by postcode.

Nationally, certain groups are more likely to be the most frequent arts attenders. Group 8, for example, comprises better-off executives, inner city areas, who are well qualified people, over a third of whom are single with no dependants. The age profile of this group is relatively young and there is a high proportion of students, professionals and executives. They tend to read quality newspapers, in particular *The Guardian*, eat out regularly and are much more likely than average to attend theatres, cinemas and art galleries.

Figure 3.4   ACORN group 1

	Any performance in a theatre	Plays	Opera	Ballet	Contemporary dance	Classical music concerts	Jazz concerts	Popular or rock concerts	Art galleries or exhibitions

1 About how often these days do you go to the following...?

Once a month or more often

Once every 2 or 3 months

Once a year

Less often

I never go out these days

2 How long ago was the last occasion you went to the following?

Within the last 4 weeks

Over 4 weeks ago (up to and including 3 months ago)

Over 3 months ago (up to and including 6 months ago

Over 6 months ago (up to and including 12 months ago)

Over 12 months ago/can't remember

3 Which of these do you like to watch on TV if it's shown or like to read about in the papers or magazines if it's reported?

Watch on TV

Read about it in the papers/magazines

Figure 3.5   The Target Group Index: questions used to quantify arts attendance and interest

Another group which tends to support the arts more than average is group 1. The majority of people in this group live in large detached houses and have access to two or more cars. They are typically well-educated professional people with the money to enjoy very comfortable lifestyles.

Overall, groups 1, 3, 6, 7 and 8 tend to be the most frequent arts attenders, while groups 11, 14, 15 and 16 attend at a rate below average. However, there are clear differences in attendance pattern according to art form. For example, group 2, the affluent greys in rural communities, are above average attenders at the opera but below average at contemporary dance. Group 15 attend jazz concerts with average frequency but are well below average attenders at classical music concerts.

The TGI   This is a survey conducted by BMRB International which asks questions about consumer habits and attitudes. Based on an annual sample of around 24000 adults, data are gathered through a detailed self-completion questionnaire which is placed via the BMRB weekly survey. The survey includes three questions on nine types of arts events, namely plays, opera, ballet, contemporary dance, classic music, jazz concerts, popular or rock concerts and art galleries or exhibitions (see Figure 3.5).

Annual summaries of national findings are available, and regional findings, broken down by age group, by sex, by social class, and by ACORN group or type, can be compared with national averages.

An interesting feature of the TGI data is its scope. It is possible to relate theatre attendance to all other consumer information contained in the survey, including information about the products people buy, the newspapers that they read and their exposure to various media. For the art forms covered, this can help in planning marketing activities to reach potential audiences, but also to identify appropriate products or services which offer sponsorship opportunities.

Collecting primary data

Audience or visitor surveys are very useful and effective ways of collecting certain types of primary data and the final part of this chapter is dedicated to the planning and implementation of such surveys. However, they are not the only methods of collecting primary data. Neither are they necessarily the best methods for collecting certain types of data, in particular qualitative data. Decisions about the best method or methods to use for collecting primary data should always be made by considering first of all the objectives of the research.

There are four methods commonly used to collect primary data:

Observation

Quite simply, this is a technique which involves watching people, their behaviour and their actions. It is particularly useful when people are unable to give accurate verbal accounts of their behaviour, perhaps because they cannot remember it in

Audience research at Madame Tussauds

A research exercise at the internationally famous Madame Tussauds London waxworks revealed some interesting features of the audiences and their experiences. The combination of a comprehensive visitor survey and the systematic observation of visitor behaviour revealed that it was not so much the wax figures themselves that were of interest to the visitors, but rather the relationship between the figure and visitor. The physical presence of the wax figures was providing a forum for interaction, with heroes, heroines and villains, and it was this interaction which was providing the pleasure from the visit. Having identified this, the management rescinded the long held policy of banning photography at Tussauds, so that visitors could take home with them a reminder of the occasion when they finally came face to face with their idols.

Reported in *The Marketing Mix*, (1984), Yorkshire TV in association with The Institute of Marketing

sufficient detail; for example, if you wished to know what path an individual had taken around an exhibition, which exhibits he or she stopped to look at and for how long. Observation may be overt, whereby the subject of research is aware of the observation taking place, but, commonly, the observation is covert, so that the true relationship between the audience and an art form can be studied without interference from the researcher.

Galleries and museums have benefited greatly from this type of research:

> The real issue is understanding audiences and their experiences. I think closeness of staff to visitors is key. They should sit where they can actually see people, and be encouraged to spend more time in the gallery to observe the nature of participation. This applies to curators, exhibition and education staff as well as to marketing staff.
>
> (Macgregor, 1990)

Experimentation

Primary data can be gathered by experimentation, which is a particularly useful technique when some decision is under consideration and the results cannot be predicted from existing experience either of the organization itself, or from the experience of other organizations. In an experiment, the researcher tries out some marketing action on a small scale, observing and measuring the results, whilst controlling as far as possible the effects of factors other than the marketing action being taken. The key advantage of experimentation is that the researcher chooses which factors (or variables) are going to be tested. This enables conclusions to be drawn as to the nature of causal relationships between variables.

Suppose, for example, a theatre wished to assess the price sensitivity of audiences for Shakespearean productions. Assuming that attendance profiles at previous productions have been compiled, they can be used as a benchmark (or control) for assessing the impact of a different pricing structure on attendance profiles. Statistics can be compiled to indicate any significant differences in attendance profiles between the production in which the experiment is taking place and previous productions, and these differences can be attributed to the pricing structure.

It is important that extraneous variables (i.e. those factors which are not the subject of the research) are as similar to the control situation as possible. One disadvantage of experimentation stems from the extent to which the extraneous factors can be controlled. Factors such as the weather, the economic climate, the promotional campaign, critics' reviews and the style of production may have an equal, if not stronger, impact on audience profiles than the price of a ticket, and if these vary greatly between the experiment and the control situation, it will not be possible to identify the true cause of changing attendance patterns.

Interviews

A high proportion of qualitative data is collected using the technique of loosely structured interviews. Qualitative research does not demand that a formal structure is imposed on the data collected. Indeed, a formal structure may so constrain responses to questions which require the articulation of attitudes and motivations that the findings may be of little real value. The interview is an approach to data collection which is highly sensitive to the views of the individual being questioned. It attempts to probe beneath the surface of the responses which can be obtained to a formal question, the like of which are normally included in survey questionnaires. Two specific techniques are commonly used, namely the depth interview and the focus group.

Depth interviews   These are usually prolonged one-to-one interview, during which the interviewer will ask questions on a series of topics, but has the freedom to phrase the questions as seems most appropriate and to order them and probe them according to the responses. The interviewer only has a checklist of points to cover and will be using mainly open questions to encourage full and explanatory responses from the interviewee. The interviewer will attempt to move from the general to the specific and from topic to topic in a logical manner and will also try to monitor the non-verbal behaviour of the respondent. The abilities of the interviewer are of paramount importance in gaining the deepest insight into the behaviour, attitudes and motivations of the research subject.

Focus groups (also known as group discussions)   These are interviews in which one interviewer, know as a moderator, asks questions of a group of respondents, usually six to eight persons. The essence of a focus group is that group dynamics are used to draw out individual beliefs which might not be so freely expressed in a one-to-one interview situation. The role of the moderator is simply to act as a catalyst to the generation of appropriate conversation between members of the group, intervening as little as possible except to keep the conversation on the right lines and to ensure that all the required topics are covered. The discussion is tape recorded and can be transcribed. Quotations should be used to support the interpretation.

Conducting a group discussion requires that due consideration is given to the ambience of the occasion and the dynamics of the interaction between group members. The less assertive individuals may feel group pressure to conform to the norms of attitudes expressed in the group and dominant individuals can discourage a full discussion of topics about which they feel strongly. Again, it is the role of the moderator to attempt to control excessive behaviours within the group 'shy members will have to be encouraged to speak out, the "angry silent" types to abandon their self-imposed Siberia and the dominators to keep quiet for a while to give others a chance to voice their views!' (Webb, 1993).

A successful focus group has three major advantages:

- It is quicker and cheaper than interviewing respondents individually.
- Groups can provide a social background which reflects the fact that many of the decisions made by an individual are taken in a group context, particularly decisions on participation in leisure activities such as the arts – depth interviews do not provide the restraining influence of others' opinions.
- The range of opinions being expressed in a group discussion helps to stimulate an individual to articulate his or her own beliefs, attitudes, opinions and feelings – this stimulus is absent from other forms of research.

As a research approach the interview can stand alone, though it must be recognized that, as the size of the sample is generally small and no explicit attempts are made to ensure that the sample is representative, difficulties may arise if the findings from the research are used to generalize about whole audiences or segments. Such information does not give the statistical significance of the larger samples used in surveys. The interpretation of the data, as well as the conducting of the interviews and discussions themselves, is usually the responsibility of the interviewer or moderator, who has observed the data collection first-hand and is therefore in the best position to interpret its meaning. The role of the moderator needs tact and detachment. A good moderator can make all the difference to the success of a piece of research, so it may be worth the investment to hire an experienced agency to do the job for you rather than attempting it yourself.

Used in conjunction with quantitative surveys though, this method has few drawbacks. Interviews can be of immense value in exploratory research or to further illuminate the results of a survey.

Survey

If the objectives of the research require that quantitative data are generated, then a survey must be undertaken. A survey is a method of data collection which involves identical questions being asked of a large number of individuals and a systematic record being made of their responses. This process is usually conducted by means of a questionnaire. The rest of this chapter will take a closer look at the whole issue of survey design, implementation, analysis and interpretation and the way in which surveys should be conducted.

Box 3.4

Infrequent attenders

The Arts Council wished to examine the potential effectiveness of various schemes for increasing the frequency with which less frequent attenders went to performing arts events.

Objectives

The objectives of the research were:

- To assess reactions to and interest in various schemes.
- To examine the effectiveness of different styles of communication both in terms of sample letters and a wide variety of scheme brochures.
- To make recommendations as to the type(s) of scheme which might be successful in encouraging the infrequent attender to make greater use of performing arts events.

Methodology

Literature describing different types of schemes was gathered and analysed, and examples chosen for use in focus group interviews. The research was conducted using group discussions among a homogeneous sample of four groups, two held in Leeds and two in Manchester on 1 and 2 April 1992. Each group comprised men and women aged 35 to 54 from socio-economic groups B and C1. All of these people attended performing arts events between four and eight times per year. They had easy access to city centres, were mobile and willing to go out in the evenings. No current or recent users of the types of scheme under discussion were included in the groups.

Source: Moseley (1992)

Conducting a survey

Arts organizations most commonly use surveys in ad hoc research relating to specific marketing decisions, and in particular to find out more about audiences. If you wish to conduct an ad hoc survey there are a number of stages to consider, as shown in Figure 3.6:

These stages will now be examined in more detail.

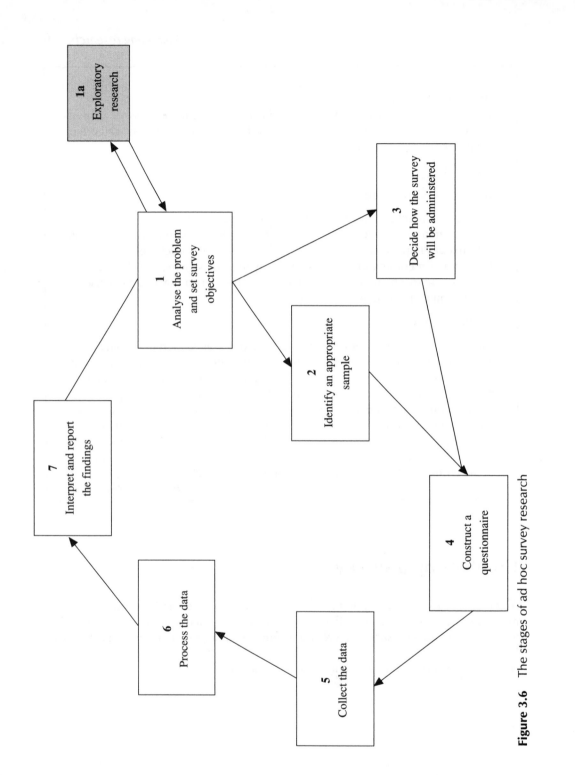

Figure 3.6 The stages of ad hoc survey research

Stage 1   Identify the precise nature of the problem to be solved and set specific objectives for the survey

The researcher should begin by analysing the problem or problems that the research is to address. It is not enough to have a vague notion that you would like to know more about your audience or believe that you could attract more visitors if you changed your promotions. Since the purpose of a survey is to get answers to important questions, a crucial first step must be to state those questions very explicitly in the form of objectives for the survey – when the survey has been completed, precisely what do you want to know the answer to? It may be wise, if not essential, to undertake some exploratory research at this stage to help define the questions more clearly.

The next two stages need to be considered in tandem. Decisions have to be made as to who should be asked to respond to a survey and this may affect the way in which it is administered.

Stage 2   Identify an appropriate sample

The individuals chosen to respond to a survey dictate its findings, so it is important for the target audience of the survey to be clearly defined so that the questions can be asked of appropriate individuals.

Surveys rely upon the mathematical fact that the views expressed by a relatively small number of individuals, known as the sample, will be representative of the views of a much larger group, known as the population, if that sample is chosen in a particular way and is of a particular size. These laws of probability mean that the larger the sample, the more representative it will be of the population from which it was drawn. A random[2] sample will be most representative of all, and you can be far more confident in assuming that the views of the sample reflect the views of the whole population with a random sample than with any other method. In practice, of course, it costs far more to interview and interpret the findings from large samples than it does from small samples. Also, the logistics of identifying each member of your population and ensuring that those you select to be in the sample do in fact respond to your survey can be too time consuming for most arts organizations. As a result, rules of thumb may be more appropriate to guide the process of sampling in arts organizations than pure statistical techniques.

A number of questions commonly arise in sampling, and the answers to these are useful in designing a sampling mechanism:

1 *When should I take my sample?*
If the research objectives relate to a specific play or exhibition, the sample needs to

---

[2] Random does not mean haphazard. In survey terminology it means that each person in the population studied has the same chance of being chosen as any other member, and that this probability can be numerically calculated.

take into account the variations in audience profile caused by season (e.g. school holidays), day of the week, time of day and perhaps weather conditions. A gallery or museum may have access to historical data relating to attendance figures. In this case it is possible for a weighting to be calculated and applied so that more respondents are questioned during busier times. If this information is not available, as is usually the case for a specific theatrical programme, the best method is simply to make an estimate of when the busier periods will occur, plan the data collection accordingly, but then, before analysing the survey, weight the results to reflect the actual variations in audience profile recorded during the period of the survey.

In the performing arts, unless a single long-running play is the focus for the research, the sample will have to recognize the effects of variations in programme, as well as time of day, day of week, and time of year. In this case, the sampling procedure will depend upon the objectives of the survey. If the objective is to compare audience profiles of different plays, all the other factors, such as day of the week, should initially be held constant to allow as direct a comparison as possible to take place. This comparison can be repeated under different levels of the factors concerned (e.g. different days of the week) to be more representative of the total audience.

Box 3.5

Sampling: the accuracy of response data

Depending on the sample size, the responses given by a random sample will represent the views of the population to a greater or lesser extent. In 95 per cent of cases, the population's response can be calculated from the sample's response by adding or subtracting the percentages in the following table:

Sample size	Response from sample				
	10%	20%	30%	40%	50%
2000	1.3%	1.8%	2.0%	2.1%	2.2%
1000	2.0%	2.0%	3.0%	3.0%	3.0%
500	3.0%	4.0%	4.0%	4.0%	4.0%
200	4.0%	6.0%	6.0%	7.0%	7.0%
100	6.0%	8.0%	9.0%	10.0%	10.0%

Example: With a random sample of 500, a response from the sample of 20 per cent implies that the response for the whole population lies between 16 per cent and 24 per cent in 95 per cent of cases.

---

2 Who should be in my sample?

The important issue here is how to obtain a good cross-section of responses which will be representative of most of the audience. In some cases it is possible for an exhaustive survey (known as a census) to be undertaken, whereby all visitors or audience members at a venue at the selected time are asked to complete the

Audience profiling of West End theatre

The Society of West End Theatres set a research objective of profiling the audience to West End theatre. This demanded a pragmatic and iterative approach. Pilot surveys of a range of plays and shows used to test questionnaire design and research method also yielded information on the relative effects on audience profile of performance type, compared with those of day of the week. They showed that in key aspects of audience profile (age, gender, place of residence, frequency of theatre-going) the type of production was the dominant factor: variations in profile for the same show across different days of the week were comparatively small. The research programme then went on to look in more detail at the effects of production type, comparing ten different types (modern drama, traditional musical, classical play and so on). Audiences to each type were profiled only on Tuesday, Wednesday and Thursday – the limit to which day of the week could be held constant – and the exercise was repeated at intervals through the year in order to take account of seasonal effects. In parallel, more information on seasonality was obtained by monitoring the audiences to two long-running shows over the year, showing that the major influence was on the proportion of overseas visitors. Similarly, more information on the effects of day of week was sought by profiling the audiences to the same play on at least four performances in a single week, repeated at intervals, confirming that the effects were small. Detailed box office returns by show type then allowed a weighted composite to be derived from the ten separate exercises profiling audiences to each type. Finally, the returns also allowed for some validity checks, for example of ticket source, on the weighted survey data.

Source: Gardiner and Collins (1992)

questionnaire. The mechanism used for this is usually a self-completion questionnaire, discussed further at stage 3, either left on the seats in an auditorium or available to be picked up. The latter will almost always lead to serious bias in the survey results as the visitors themselves select whether to take the questionnaire and frequently only those with a higher than average interest in the event will take the trouble to complete them. Similar problems can arise with questionnaires left on seats or placed in programme though, for practical reasons, these may be the best methods to use.

A smaller, but carefully controlled sample can produce more accurate results than an uncontrolled attempt at a census, so it may be worth devoting time and money to ensuring that questionnaires are handed out individually, rather than left for collection. This enables the potential respondent to be reassured as to the purpose of the survey and encouraged to take part (most people enjoy having their opinions sought and will generally be happy to co-operate provided they know what you are trying to do).

To approach a representative sample, an objective selection rule is needed to protect the survey from the bias which can arise if interviewers are allowed to choose whom they approach. Inexperienced researchers may unwittingly favour those who make themselves more accessible and avoid those who are less forthcoming. One method would be to approach, say, every tenth person through the door, or to use a quota system, whereby the interviewer or questionnaire distributor is asked to approach a target number of males and females within certain age ranges (though this may have to be based on a judgement which may ultimately prove to be incorrect!). However, as most people attend arts events in groups a good method is to give out one questionnaire to each group of people and one to each person who comes alone. In the case of the group, one person in a party is more likely to fill in a questionnaire than every person in a party. All entrances to the building need to be covered to ensure that all visitors have an equal chance of participating.

3 *How many people should be in my sample?*

The more questionnaires that are completed, the more confident one can be that the responses obtained are representative of the whole population and not just the individuals who answered the questions. In total, a figure of 500 completed question-naires should be plenty to provide results which are statistically valid, though a minimum of 300 is acceptable under severe resource constraints. If the sample is any smaller than this, comparisons cannot be made between sub-sections within the population, such as differences between responses by males and females, different age groups, those attending on different days of the week or those who are regular as opposed to infrequent attenders.

These 500 however should be spread across the whole time period of the research and, in the case of performances, at least three performances should be sampled to improve the cross-section, even if it is possible to obtain all 500 responses at one performance.

It must be recognized that more than 500 questionnaires will have to be given out to obtain 500 responses. Response rates vary according to the way that the question-naire is administered (see stage 3), but will be significantly reduced if the survey is not well explained, the questionnaire is poorly laid out or worded, or if there is nowhere obvious to return it.

Stage 3   Decide how the survey will be implemented

Methods of questionnaire administration fall into four main categories:

Interview surveys

These are conducted face-to-face with respondents and have several advantages:

- Interviewers can be involved in the sampling process by selecting an appropriate range of respondents using a quota system, described above, and eliminating those who are not in the target audience for the research.
- The interviewer can encourage respondents to answer as fully as possible and check, where appropriate, that the question has been fully understood.

Box 3.6
How to make sure you get a good response
To get the results you can view with confidence and to make sure the survey is cost-effective, you must aim to maximize the return of the question-naires.

Here are the main ways of achieving this aim:

- Make sure the questionnaire looks smart and short.
- Put up large notices drawing attention to the survey and explaining about what you are doing.
- Offer a prize draw – it will encourage people to complete a questionnaire. Cash is the best incentive (say five to ten prizes).
- Provide pens for people to write with.
- Have a table near the return boxes in the foyer so people can write easily.
- Have clearly marked large return boxes 'Post your questionnaire here'.
- Have enough boxes to cover all exits, bars and foyers.
- Make sure the people handing out the questionnaires are smart, friendly and polite.

Source: Walshe (1992)

- Any materials, such as publicity items, that need to be shown to the respondents can be properly presented.
- Interviewers can usually persuade respondents to complete the interview and response rates are consistently higher than for other types of questionnaire administration.

These advantages mean that the quality of the data derived from interview surveys is generally superior to other methods but, to some extent, this depends upon the skill of the interviewer. As Kent (1993) explains, 'The interviewer is, on the one hand trying to be "standard" in all his or her approaches to respondents, but, on the other hand, may need to react to individual circumstances for the successful completion of the interview – in short, the interviewer needs to act like a robot but retain the appearance of a human being.' It must be recognized that the interview itself is a highly artificial process of social interaction and there are dangers of bias arising simply due to the age, sex, social class, dress, accent and personality of both the interviewer and the respondent. The key to removing interviewer bias is good training. For this reason, most commercial organizations rely on market research agencies to supply well-trained interviewers, though this is too costly for many arts organizations. If this is the case, organizations should ensure that they arrange some form of interview training for their own (usually volunteer) researchers, and ensure that they are thoroughly briefed as to the objectives of the survey and the instructions for sampling.

Self-completion surveys

These are distributed and collected on site, either by placing questionnaires on seats, in programmes, or in prominent places in the building. As they dispense with the need for an interviewer, both the costs of interviewing and interviewer bias are entirely avoided. However, as respondents are self-selecting, bias is more likely to creep in through the nature of the sample.

The best way to avoid this is to construct a visually appealing, concise and self-explanatory questionnaire which attracts the attention and appeals even to those with no particular interest in responding.

Mail surveys

Postal surveys are extremely cost effective, requiring neither interviewers nor telephone systems. Their usefulness in market research has increased as arts organizations have improved their databases and more accurate sampling has become possible. A major advantage of mail surveys is that respondents can devote more time to filling in the questionnaire, so longer questionnaires are possible. Respondents can fill them in at a time convenient to them and consult with other members of their household if necessary.

Several disadvantages of postal questionnaires restrict their use however. Firstly, the person who fills in the questionnaire may not be the one selected in the sample. In addition, there is no interviewer to assist and encourage questionnaire completion, and therefore certain types of questioning techniques cannot be used. It is often argued, though, that the main disadvantage of mail surveys is the very low response rate usually achieved. This can be overcome to a certain extent by well constructed questionnaires and in particular by the use of a covering letter which 'sells' the value of the research to the respondent and encourages him or her to respond. The letter should at minimum explain:

- Who is carrying out the research.
- What is the purpose of the research.
- How the respondent was selected.
- That responses will be confidential.
- How to complete and return the questionnaire.

Enclosing an incentive with the letter (such as ticket discounts, or restaurant vouchers) is known to improve response rates slightly, but the cost of this needs to be weighed against the value of extra responses. It is normal to enclose a pre-paid reply envelope.

It can be useful to send out reminders after two to three weeks, encouraging those who haven't responded to do so. If this is the intention, it is important that the original questionnaires are numbered and lists maintained relating named respondents to numbered questionnaires, so that those who have replied are excluded from the follow-up letter. The only problem here is that respondents cannot then be assured of the anonymity of their responses, simply the confidentiality with which they will be treated.

> Box 3.7
>
> ## A questionable question
>
> Leading questions often come about because you are trying to supply a context for the question. For example, consider the question:
>
> 'Most people are willing to pay a small entrance fee to a museum. To what extent do you agree with this statement?'
>
> There are three flaws in this:
>
> - The phrase 'most people' makes it difficult for respondents to do anything other than agree – who knows what the rest of the population thinks?
> - What is meant by 'a small entrance fee'? Small is a relative term which different people will interpret in different ways.
> - The question itself asks the extent to which the respondent agrees – it doesn't suggest that people might disagree.

Telephone surveys

Whilst this technique is very common in some industries, and particularly in the USA, the major problem for a telephone arts survey is how to get the phone numbers of members of the arts audience unless these have been gathered on a database. Systematic sampling, therefore, becomes a very difficult task, and there is a serious danger of bias. Those who have volunteered their telephone numbers are likely to be those most supportive of a particular theatre, museum or gallery, and are unlikely to be representative of the whole population. Also, telephone ownership is by no means universal and parts of the audience, including less affluent, yet quite sizeable, groups such as students will be under-represented.

If a telephone survey is the preferred method, questions must be relatively straightforward because it can be quite difficult to comprehend complex questions heard over the phone. Interviewers need to be even more skilled than in face-to-face situations, as non-verbal messages can be neither sent nor interpreted by interviewer or respondent. It is not a suitable task for amateurs, so the cost of employing professionals plus the telephone bill are likely to put this method beyond the budget of most arts organizations.

Stage 4   Design the questionnaire

A couple of points need to be taken into account before starting to construct a questionnaire. Firstly, the way in which the data will be collected will affect the questionnaire length and layout, as well as the style of question. Another consideration is the way in which the data will be analysed. There are a number of quite simple and affordable computer packages which are ideal for the analysis of small surveys. The package to be used must be identified at the stage of questionnaire design as

---

Box 3.8

Examples of open-ended questions

Overall, what did you like best about tonight's performance? Please write your answer below.

_____

_____

_____

And what did you like least?

_____

_____

_____

---

each package places different constraints on the way in which questions are worded. These are seldom constraints which will affect the quality of questioning, but they must be recognized if data collected is to be successfully fed into the system.

Criteria for effective questions

As each question is written, it should be evaluated against the following criteria:

Relevance   Does it help reach the objectives of the survey? If the only questions asked are those of direct relevance to the objectives, the questionnaire length can be kept to a minimum.

Clarity   Will respondents understand every word in the question? Complex terminology and ambiguity must be avoided at all costs. If respondents fail to understand a question, they will either miss it out altogether or, worse still, guess at its meaning and give a response to the question they think you are asking, which may be very different from what you intended.

Brevity   In general, a question should consist of no more than 20 words, otherwise it becomes too difficult to comprehend quickly

Impartiality   The wording of the question should not influence the respondents' answers. This is more difficult than it sounds. It is quite easy unwittingly to introduce leading questions by failing to recognize the overtones of certain words.

Precision   Each question should only deal with one issue at a time. If two issues are introduced, the respondent may have opposing views on different parts of the question and may not be able to express these within the response mechanism provided.

Inoffensiveness   Questions relating to sensitive issues, in particular salary, age, ethnicity and social class, can be construed as offensive unless worded very carefully. They should also be placed at the end of the questionnaire so that the respondent has built up a relationship with the interviewer (if any) and committed him- or herself to completing the questionnaire and is less likely to be put off at this stage.

The form of survey questions

There are two basic ways to ask questions in a survey. Open-ended questions allow respondents to provide answers using their own words, while closed questions (also known as closed-ended, fixed-response or forced choice questions) provide a limited number of possible responses which the respondents must choose between.

Open-ended questions   These collect information with minimum direction to respondents, and are very useful questions if the possible range of responses is very broad. Another advantage of this type of question is that it uses the respondent's own words and therefore allows them to vent strong opinions and helps the researcher to understand the way that people really think about an issue.

Probing questions and clarifying questions may be used to gain more complete answers to open-ended questions, especially if interviewing is being used to collect the data. Interviewers can build upon subjects offered by the respondents, following up any vague or general terms given in their answers, though they should offer no prompts or suggestions for clarification, as this will introduce bias. It is important too that sufficient space is allowed on the questionnaire for full responses to be filled in as any curtailment or paraphrasing of an answer can also introduce bias.

The main disadvantage of open-ended questions arises in their interpretation. All responses have to be read and coded. This means devising a set of categories that covers the range of all open-ended responses. Inevitably some answers will be ambiguous and difficult to code precisely and, even under the best circumstances, coding is a very time-consuming activity. Bias can creep in simply from poor coding.

Closed questions   As these types of question offer more limited scope for response, respondents tend to find them easier and less time consuming to complete, so most surveys use a high proportion of closed questions to encourage high response rates. Closed questions also avoid the difficulties of coding, as the code is written into the question in the form of a response mechanism which prevents respondents producing ambiguous answers.

Despite the limitations on response, closed questions can be used to investigate a range of issues, including facts, behaviour, attitudes and opinions.

Closed questions tend to be one of three types:

Multiple response questions   These offer a series of possible responses and can allow response in just one, or in a number of categories. Sometimes, a category will be included for those who are unable to respond (the 'don't know' box) and if there is some doubt as to whether all possible responses have been identified in advance, space is provided for respondents to write in their own answer (the 'other' box) and the answers are coded when the results are analysed. For example:

What type of admission ticket do you have? (tick one)

student ☐	group or party ☐
season subscription ☐	senior citizen ☐
single performance ☐	don't know ☐
free pass ☐	other (please explain) ☐

_____

Box 3.9

Examples of closed questions:

. . . revealing facts

Is your age . . . ? (tick one)
- under 18 ☐
- 18–25 ☐
- 26–35 ☐
- 36–45 ☐
- 46–55 ☐
- 56–65 ☐
- over 65 ☐

. . . revealing behaviour

How much time did you spend in the gallery today? (tick one)
- less than one hour ☐
- one to two hours ☐
- two to four hours ☐
- more than four hours ☐

. . . revealing attitudes

How interested are you in the following types of activities?

	very interested	quite interested	slightly interested	not at all interested
amateur dramatics				
playing an instrument				
studio art classes				
dance classes				

. . . revealing opinions

Compared with what you expected, how would you rate tonight's performance? (tick one)
- much better than I expected ☐
- better than I expected ☐
- as I expected ☐
- not as good as I expected ☐
- much worse than I expected ☐

Dichotomous questions are particular types of multiple response questions, where there are only two possible answers, such as 'true/false', 'yes/no' or 'male/female'. In practice, these questions should be used infrequently, partly because of their very limited scope but also because a 'don't know' or 'other' category is nearly always needed for some respondents.

Scaled questions   These provide a scale on which respondents can express the strength of their attitudes or opinions. This enables different attributes of performances, venues and exhibitions to be compared. Bipolar questions put forward widely differing opinions of a particular attribute and ask respondents to place their own opinion somewhere between the polarized views suggested. For example:

Compared to what you expected, how would you rate tonight's performance? (tick one)
    much better than I expected   ☐
    better than I expected   ☐
    as I expected   ☐
    not as good as I expected   ☐
    much worse than I expected   ☐

Agree/disagree questions ask people to indicate the extent to which they agree or disagree with a particular statement. They are useful for measuring attitudes. For example:

To what extent do you agree or disagree with the following statement: (tick one)
'Most people who go to the opera are only there to impress their friends.'
    agree strongly   ☐
    agree slightly   ☐
    neither agree nor disagree   ☐
    disagree slightly   ☐
    disagree strongly   ☐

Semantic differential questions use words of opposite meaning to suggest descriptions of attributes of, for example, a venue or performance. Respondents are asked to indicate their own perceptions along this scale. For example:

Compared with other theatres I have been to, the bar here is:

very small						very large
1	2	3	4	5	6	7

very cheap						very expensive
1	2	3	4	5	6	7

very comfortable						very uncomfortable
1	2	3	4	5	6	7

The only problem with scaled questions is that people are reluctant to express very strong opinions and therefore tend to avoid the first and last categories in any list. This reduces the sensitivity of the question as a tool for capturing true attitudes and opinions, which is why qualitative research is so useful for this task.

Ordering questions These enable respondents to express preferences, and if appropriate, to state these preferences in terms of priorities.

Preference questions will ask for one or more issues or attributes to be identified as being of more importance than others. They are frequently asked as closed questions, whereby respondents will be asked to choose from a list of possible options and given an 'other' box for responses which are not identified, and a 'no preference' box for those who are unable or unwilling to make a selection. For example:

Which three benefits do you feel are the most important benefits of belonging to the 'friends' of the theatre: (please tick)
    regular information about events   ☐
    cost savings on tickets   ☐
    cost savings on other purchases   ☐
    priority booking   ☐
    attendance at members' activities   ☐
    involvement with the theatre   ☐
    other (please specify)   ☐

    _____

    or
    they are all of equal importance   ☐

The problem with preference questions is that they tend to magnify perceived differences in preference. Just because a respondent has excluded an item from the chosen list doesn't mean that these items are very unimportant, and the extent to which they are less important isn't clear.

Ranking questions take respondents one step further by asking them to prioritize their preferences. The importance of the items in the list given in the example above could have been investigated by asking respondents to rank them in order. This can be a difficult task though, particularly with lists longer than just five or six items. There is a common misconception too that the intervals between ranked items are equal, but in reality this may not be the case (the first feature may be far more important than the second, but the second and third may be seen as having almost equal importance). There is also an in-built assumption that the respondent is equally knowledgeable about all the items on the list and therefore qualified to compare them all with each other. This is unlikely to be the case. Ranking can be useful, but its limitations must be recognized.

Pre-testing questionnaires

This is sometimes known as the pilot stage, when the questionnaire is tested on a very small number of people who are typical of the people to be included in the sample. Every questionnaire should be pre-tested. Questions which seem very straightforward to the researcher may be thoroughly confusing or even offensive to the respondent. It is important to identify questions which are unclear, ambiguous, annoying, difficult to answer or very time consuming, and to make changes before the full launch of the survey. You'll be glad you did – arts audiences usually contain a number of respondents who will make you feel silly if there are ambiguities in the phrasing!

Stage 5   Collect the data

The data collection method has already been identified by this stage, so the survey is ready to be administered. Interviewers need to be briefed and trained for face-to-face and telephone data collection, and administrative systems need to be set up for self-completion and mail surveys. If the preparation work has been competently under-taken, this can be a very straightforward part of the market research process.

Stage 6   Process the data

Data processing is the means by which the raw data (i.e. the responses gathered from the sample) are converted into a form which will enable their underlying meaning to be identified.

Unless the sample size is so small that the results will hold very little statistical significance, the most efficient way of processing data is by using a computer package designed for this purpose. Arts organizations may choose to use a specialist data processing firm to perform the analysis for them, particularly if sample sizes are large and the data quite complex. However, there are several small, user-friendly and relatively inexpensive packages which could be purchased by the organization itself to enable the processing to be undertaken in-house. These are commercially available, and in some cases can be linked to the box office system.

Data processing has three main stages:

Data input   The responses from each questionnaire returned are typed into the computer. This is a laborious process which requires no great skill and can be learned very quickly.

Data summary   The computer will take the raw data and summarize the frequency of responses to each of the questions. This simply summarizes how many people said what. Visual displays of the data (e.g. pie charts, frequency tables and histograms) can then be produced to depict this information more graphically.

As the sample has been designed to be representative of the whole population, it can then be stated with some confidence that the frequency of response observed in the sample will apply to the whole population. Indeed, there is a statistical formula which will indicate how confident one can be that the true figure for the whole population falls within a narrow band around the observed figure for the sample. The table below illustrates how the level of confidence with which the results from a random sample can be treated is related to the size of the sample (though, of course, the quality of the questionnaire, the interviewing, and the coding are all factors which will influence the quality of the results too).

Where appropriate, the computer will also calculate the mean (or arithmetic average) response to scaled questions, and measure the dispersion (or standard deviation) of the result.

The mean does not in itself imply that most people thought something. It simply shows the central tendency of the sample. The standard deviation is calculated to indicate whether the mean was generated as a result of most people having very similar views, or people having wide-ranging views on a subject so that the average is simply a half-way position on a very long scale, rather than a representation of popular opinion. The higher the standard deviation figure, the more wide ranging were the responses from the sample. Sometimes, the responses fall into two extremes and, if this is the case, it may be possible to use the findings to identify two discrete market segments within the population.

Box 3.10

Example: mean and standard deviation

Suppose twenty people were asked the extent to which they agreed or disagreed with the following statements:

Statement 1
'Children under the age of 14 should not be allowed into art galleries unless accompanied by an adult.'
Statement 2
'Museums should never charge entrance fees.'

1 = strongly agree
2 = agree slightly
3 = neither agree nor disagree
4 = disagree slightly
5 = strongly disagree

Twenty people's responses to the two statements might be as follows:

Statement 1
1, 1, 5, 4, 5, 2, 2, 5, 5, 3, 3, 1, 1, 4, 4, 1, 2, 4, 5, 2

Statement 2
2, 2, 4, 4, 3, 3, 4, 1, 2, 4, 4, 3, 3, 1, 5, 4, 2, 2, 3, 4

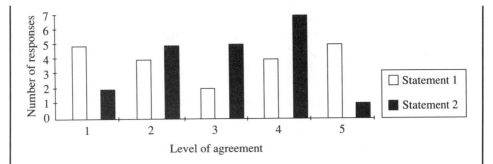

Figure 3.7

Statistically, these results indicate an identical average response to each statement but different dispersions:

Statement 1
mean = 60/20 = 3
standard deviation = 1.59

Statement 2
mean = 60/20 = 3
standard deviation = 1.13

The relatively high standard deviation in the responses to Statement 1 implies that people have strong feeling about the admission of lone children to art galleries, either strongly in favour or strongly against. The mean, in this case, does not imply that the majority of people have neutral feelings on the subject, simply that firmly held attitudes are evenly balanced. There is less divergence in Statement 2, implying that attitudes are less firmly held and more moderate throughout the population.

(Note that this example is given only to illustrate the mean and standard deviation; in reality the sample size would be too small to make judgements about the nature of the population.)

Data analysis   This is performed to identify interrelationships between the answers to different questions and involves the use of statistical techniques.

Cross tabulation is the form of analysis most commonly undertaken. This enables the responses to any question to be compared with the responses to any other question. For example, it would be possible to identify whether there is any perceived difference in the enjoyment of a performance according to whether a visitor sits in the stalls or in the gods. The expectations of tourists from a visit to a gallery could be compared with the expectations of local people, school groups and art students. Any observed differences could then be investigated more closely using quantitative research.

Whilst cross tabulation and other statistical techniques can be performed manually, they are such time-consuming and complex tasks that it is impossible to do a comprehensive analysis. Computer analysis is quick, easy and generates far more valuable information than could be extracted by hand.

Stage 7   Interpreting and reporting findings

At this point in the survey, facts and figures relating to the respondents who participated at the data collection stage have been collected. The final step is to interpret the meaning of these facts and figures, translating them into usable information which can help decisions to be made.

Interpretation

The figures do not speak for themselves. It is their interpretation that renders them useful (or useless!). In interpreting data, a number of key points must be constantly borne in mind:

- The interpretation should relate to the problem identified at the very beginning of the survey process, and the only findings which should be highlighted should be those which help to reach the explicit objectives of the research.
- No survey is absolutely definitive and no figure absolutely correct, and this should be recognized by indicating the approximation of figures.
- Findings should not be exaggerated or dramatized to draw attention to them. Fair weight should be given to all the relevant evidence.
- Small sample sizes should be recognized and generalizations should not be made from samples which are too small to give statistically reliable results.
- Averages should be recognized as merely tendencies and not be thought of as representing a 'Mr and Mrs Average'.
- Recognition should be given to infrequent but significant answers, as there may be new trends emerging.
- There should be clear distinction between fact (what people are, what they do, what they own etc.) and opinion (what people think about issues). Opinions and attitudes do not always translate into behaviour.
- There should be clear distinction between cause and effect. Associated factors are not necessarily causal. Surveys are useful for identifying effects, but conclusions about causes must be drawn very tentatively and sometimes need further investigation.

Reporting

The interpretation is usually presented in the form of a report. If this report is to be used by decision makers, their needs must be taken into account in its preparation. The four main points to bear in mind are:

1 Present only information which is of relevance to the reader
   Too much information is confusing, but there must be enough detail to guide the decision that is to be made. For example, it's important to give information on

sample sizes and details of the research methodology, to enable the reader to estimate the accuracy of the findings. A copy of the questionnaire should also be included to allow the reader to refer back to questions posed. However, when it comes to reporting the responses, some details can be left out. There's no need, for example, to list all the responses to open questions. Also, if a large number of small frequency responses are given to a closed question, some of the categories may be collapsed into one and reported under the heading 'other responses'.

2 Communicate the findings simply

It is useful to report findings visually, with important findings being highlighted and discussed in text. Results are easily produced in the form of tables, where both the actual frequencies and the frequencies as a percentage of the total sample should be reported. Graphical illustration may also be used to highlight important features or trends. Some people cannot or will not interpret the tables or graphs, so their meanings should be discussed in accompanying text. Technical jargon should be kept to a minimum and simple declarative statements used to put the main points across.

3 Don't imply certainty

No survey is absolutely definitive and no figure in a survey is an entirely correct representation of reality. There should be no pretence that you are reporting absolute fact. Findings should therefore be reported as whole percentages rather than to decimal places, both in the tables and in any explanatory text. Unless the sample size is exceptionally large, sampling error alone will make it impossible to calculate percentages with any great precision. If samples or sub-samples are small, readers should be warned that the findings should be treated with caution.

4 Provide an executive summary

Not every reader will want to read the whole report, so a brief summary of the findings, the main conclusions and recommendations should appear at the beginning. Complicated tables, discussion of methodology and analysis should be kept for other sections of the report.

Conclusion

Much of the theory of marketing research applies to arts organizations in exactly the same way as it does to commercial organizations. A desire for more information needs to be formalized by the setting of research objectives, and a structured, methodical process must be followed in the gathering of facts and figures and in their interpretation. The financial constraints facing most arts organizations do not preclude their use of marketing research, but simply require them to be focused in the objectives they set and resourceful in the techniques they use. The more focused a survey is, the more likely it is in reality to be of value to the organization. Vast, all-embracing mega-research tends to lay itself open to challenges on methodology or interpretation of the data. 'Marketing research is like a taxi-cab – it will go anywhere you want (providing you have the fare) but the cab-driver must know how to drive, must have a working knowledge of the Highway Code, and the passenger and the driver must agree at the outset as to the final destination' (Webb, 1993).

Key concepts

ACORN	Marketing research
Ad hoc research	Observation
Causal objectives	Population
Continuous research	Primary research
Data processing	Published data
Depth interviews	Qualitative research
Descriptive objectives	Quantitative research
Experimentation	Questionnaire
Exploratory objectives	Sample
External data	Secondary research
Focus groups	Survey
Internal data	Target Group Index

Discussion questions

1 What is the difference between open-ended and closed questions? Give three examples of open-ended questions that could be used to investigate audience opinions of an exhibition.

2 Distinguish between multiple response questions, scaled questions and ordering questions by writing three different questions, each of which could be used to investigate audience perceptions of ticket prices for a professional performance of a Shakespeare play.

3 How could the ACORN classification system be used to help a dance company plan a national tour?

4 How might an art gallery conduct some qualitative research to help it improve its access and facilities for the disabled? List the practical difficulties of organizing such research.

5 Describe the sample that would be appropriate for collecting quantitative data for a theatre company wishing to conduct some promotional research to assess the effectiveness of the advertising and PR being used to promote its UK tour. Assume that the tour involves eight venues with two matinees and five evening performances per week.

6 What type of primary data could feasibly and usefully be collected by an amateur theatre group to help with the planning of its annual pantomime? What are the main constraints it faces in collecting the data?

7 How would you collect primary data to investigate audience opinions of the catering facilities and bookshop at a major city centre arts venue?

8 What arguments would you put forward to convince the management of an arts complex that it should agree to the appointment of a marketing research agency to investigate audience reactions to the forthcoming season of events and exhibitions?

Action questions

1 Identify the main sources of secondary data available in your locality that could help a touring arts organization to decide on the advisability of including the area in a national tour.

2 Produce a portfolio of secondary data that would be useful for your organization in attempting to attract sponsors.

3 Design a marketing research guide to help community arts organizations conduct their own marketing research.

4 Investigate the extent to which your organization's customer database:
   (a) Is used to produce marketing information.
   (b) Could be used to produce marketing information.

References

Boyden Southwood Associates (1993). *Marketing the Visual Arts*. Commissioned by The Arts Council of Great Britain.

CACI Information Services (1994). *ACORN User Guide*.

Gardiner, C. and Collins, M. (1992). A practical guide to better audience surveys. *Journal of the Market Research Society*, 34, 4, 289–297.

Hinds, N. and Waters, T. (1992). A small arts organization's approach to market research. *Journal of the Market Research Society*, 34, 4, 345–360.

Kent, R. (1993). *Marketing Research in Action*. Routledge.

McCart, M. (1992). Research at the South Bank Centre. *Journal of the Market Research Society*, 34, 4, 361–374.

Macgregor, L.A. (1991). *The role of marketing in galleries*. In the report of the Gallery Marketing Symposium, commissioned by The Arts Council of Great Britain.

Moseley, D. (1992). *Qualitative Research on Schemes to Encourage Attendance at Performing Arts among Irregular Users*, commissioned by The Arts Council of Great Britain.

NOP Consumer Market Research (1991). *Report on Qualitative Research into the Public's Attitudes to 'the Arts'*, commissioned by The Arts Council of Great Britain.

Oakden, J. (1992). *Interpreting Survey Research Results*. The Harris Research Centre, prepared for the Arts Council of Great Britain.

Tomlinson, R. (1992). Finding out more from box office data. *Journal of the Market Research Society*, 34, 4, 389–404.

Walshe, P. (1992). *Guidance Notes on Carrying Out Audience/Visitor Surveys*. Millward Brown, prepared for The Arts Council of Great Britain.
Webb, J. R. (1993). *Understanding and Designing Marketing Research*, Academic Press.

Recommended further reading

National Endowment for the Arts (1985). *Surveying Your Arts Audience*, Publishing Center for Cultural Resources (New York).
Selwood, S. (1991). *Investigating Audiences: Audience Surveys in the Visual Arts*. Art and Society.

4 Product

Introduction

Product is the most fundamental and important element of 'the four Ps' of Product, Price, Promotion and Place which constitute the marketing mix (McCarthy, 1974). It provides the basic building block of any marketing strategy. The product, or (in the case of arts organizations) the service which is provided, has the dominant role in determining the nature of the other marketing variables. In the 1980s it became fashionable to talk about artistic 'product'. As we have seen, the arts industry is 'production-led' in a way which differentiates it profoundly from commercial marketing practice. But what concerns the arts marketer is not so much what is produced by artists, as what is available to audiences as experience. This chapter will address the nature of the experience of art from a customer perspective, concentrating on those aspects of an organization's total offering which the marketing function can hope to optimize. It will cover the following areas:

- Analysing products and services.
- The nature of the artistic experience.
- Managing the product/service mix.
- Innovation.
- Total Quality Management in the arts.

Products and services

Marketing theory has been built largely on the experience of companies (mainly American ones) selling packaged goods in the 1950s and beyond. But there is a good deal of difference between the marketing perspective of organizations like concert halls or galleries, and that of the makers of soap powder or instant coffee. Arts organizations (along with organizations such as banks, doctors and hairdressers) are providing a service, not a physical product. Services have characteristics which such products lack. Four widely recognized ones are as follows (Bateson, 1989):

Intangibility

Unlike products, which can be handled and owned, services are intangible. They are experiences rather than objects. Potential consumers cannot inspect an artistic performance before purchase in the same way as they might, for example, test drive a car. This means that promotion, communicating the benefits of what is on offer in a way which is accurate and relevant, has a crucial role in service marketing generally and in arts marketing in particular. Another marketing consequence of intangibility, as we shall see in Chapter 5, is that prices are generally more difficult to set and justify than they are in product marketing.

The perceived risk of an intangible purchase is much higher than that involved in buying a product (which can always be returned or modified after purchase). Arts promotion needs, therefore, to reassure the potential customer that he or she is making the right decision by providing as full and explicit a proposition as possible. Similarly, distribution patterns in the arts need to focus on being user-friendly and approachable. There is also a sense in which the problem of intangibility in arts marketing can be made into an opportunity. Retailing potential exists for crystallizing the experience of the arts around ancillary products. 'Ancillary' (from the Latin word meaning maidservant) denotes products which have a value from their relationship to the main offering, such as theatre programmes, posters, audio and video recordings, books and memorabilia. In the arts they can also be called 'semi-tangibles' because of the way they link the tangible nature of goods to the intangible values of services. Existing in this hybrid category means that their pricing needs careful consideration (see Chapter 5).

Inseparability of production and consumption

Whereas products are bought and used by consumers some time after manufacture, services are consumed and produced at one and the same time. This is clearly the case in the live performing arts. But even in a gallery or museum, the experience of the art works or display objects is filtered through a controlled and time-restricted environment. The consumer leaves the gallery enriched, but by an experience rather than by a physical possession. As for artworks mediated through sound or video recording, a similar observation can be made. Their value for the consumer lies in the experience of the work rather than its ownership, although Greer (1994) claims that ownership can be seen as more important to male arts consumers than females in the classical CD market. Certainly, for art collectors, the impulse to own is a basic motivation – but it is inseparable from the intangible benefit of aesthetic pleasure. Jenny Houghton, director of a Dublin-based agency which offers a number of Irish artists promotional support, sees this as making the definition of the customer more complex:

Who are the 'customers' of a painting? Either somebody who pays for it, or somebody who is attracted by it. The need to own is important in the visual arts field. Someone's response to a painting – what kind of a value does that have in itself?

It is as participant rather than passive consumer than the customer needs to be envisaged and addressed. Certain modes of presentation make this more obvious than others, e.g. promenade productions, community arts, dance workshops, or small-scale touring drama in intimate venues. But even in an 'arena' environment (such as a stadium rock concert) what distinguishes the experience of live performance for an attender is his or her active participation in the experience of being part of an audience. Ancillary 'products' such as Friends organizations or regular attendance schemes recognize a growing level of involvement in the organization's activities by its customers. Finally, inseparability of production and consumption means that direct forms of distribution tend to be the norm in the arts, although (as we shall see in Chapter 7) there are exceptions to this general principle.

Heterogeneity

No two performances are ever the same. Even art objects which do not involve performance are valued for the variety and depth of experience to which they can give rise in the beholder on different occasions. The archetypal work of art, the Mona Lisa, is famous for this quality. But even the latest in postmodernist art is valued for the many responses it can evoke.

> The postmodern image does not simply and unambiguously represent something in the outside world; it circulates in an endless play of similitude and imitation. Meaning, therefore, is indefinitely deferred. Forg's work explores questions of meaning and the integrity of the art object. It does so, what is more, with striking grace and beauty.
>
> (Hutchinson, 1993)

The quality and essence of an artistic experience can vary according to who is producing it, and even within the same production. To complicate matters further in the performing arts, there are typically a large number of people involved in the delivery of the experience. Not only the members of the performing company itself, but also each member of the front-of-house staff with whom the consumer comes into contact will contribute in some small but important way to the uniqueness of a theatrical experience. This makes like-with-like comparisons practically impossible (although such comparisons are, paradoxically, an important part of the experience for heavy consumers of frequently-performed works within a narrow repertoire, such as different interpretations of the symphonies of Beethoven or the plays of Shakespeare).

Again, this aspect of service delivery confronts the arts marketer with unique difficulties and opportunities. The marketing department cannot hope to have the final say in the choice of artistic product or how it is produced. But it can ensure that the total experience of which it forms a part is fully exploited to maximize the audience benefit.

Secondly, the variability of product which, in a non-arts marketing situation, might be seen as a liability, ought to be considered an asset. The uniqueness and singularity of the artistic experience is a major selling point in a wider environment where so many processes are being reduced to bland standardization. While we will be arguing in this chapter for a more systematic approach to the standards of service surrounding the artistic experience, the individuality of arts experience is itself a core benefit. The service sector is a 'people' business. Just as people are different, so the variety underlying the arts needs to be a constant theme in marketing and promotional strategy.

Because of the need to share an understanding of the needs of the customer throughout the organization, arts marketing departments need to take the lead in fostering internal marketing (as discussed in Chapter 9). This involves the promotion of customer-first attitudes amongst everyone who deals directly, or even indirectly, with the consumer. It also implies the organization's willingness to adopt systems which empower customer-facing staff to take decisions and sort out problems in meeting customer requirements.

Perishability

Like the issue of intangibility, this is a fundamental source of difference between products (which can be stored) and services (which need immediate consumption). Unsold tickets for a performance on a particular date are lost forever as income opportunities, even though the organization will have borne the full cost of providing the service to which they might have gained admittance. Synchronizing supply and demand in a business where what is manufactured cannot be stored is a perennial dilemma for marketers in any service industry.

It presents itself particularly acutely to arts marketers where the size of the audience needs to achieve a critical mass if the experience is to carry credibility (as in the case of a formal theatrical performance), but (as in the case of blockbuster exhibitions) must not be allowed to exceed the available supply. Sometimes arts organizations, because of the pressure from funding authorities to maximize the use of venue facilities, are forced into a position where they may be tempted to do too much. 'Productivity' in these terms is misleading. A clear sense of the organization's mission and capacity is more important than accumulating performance statistics for their own sake. Expansion is not an end in itself.

Much service marketing effort is devoted to trying to cope with fluctuating demand. It underlies, for example, the kind of differential ticket pricing discussed in Chapter 5, where attendance on less popular nights of the week is encouraged by lower pricing than at weekends in most theatres. But it also affects product planning decisions. Many theatres, for example, vary their programmes with other sorts of activity or go dark during the summer months in recognition of the fact that this is a time of the year when attendance patterns are traditionally light.

There are, of course, exceptions to this general rule. In certain locations popular with tourists the pattern is reversed, as is the case at the Theatre Royal York, or the

Stephen Joseph Theatre in the Round in Scarborough. Yet even these theatres, both of whom enjoy summer trade swelled by visitor traffic, tailor their offerings to suit the seasonal audience. They offer production and performance staff patterns of employment which reflect adjustments between demand and capacity to achieve a closer match between the two over an extended period of time.

In summary of this brief examination of the main problems and opportunities created by the fact that service marketing is different from product marketing, here is a checklist of points for arts marketers:

- The experience of the arts cannot be stored: marketing strategy needs therefore to consider the short term as well as the long term.
- The uniqueness of the arts experience, and its human service dimensions, are crucial selling points.
- The consumer is involved as an active participant.
- Developing the consumer usually entails making him or her a more active participant.
- Reducing perceived risk is a high priority in pricing, promotion and distribution strategy.
- High quality is essential in all aspects of the delivery of the experience, but is difficult to control.
- Strategies aimed at predicting demand and managing supply are at a premium.

Analysing products and services

Levels of product

The concept of product or service is a multifaceted idea which repays analysis. Kotler and Andreasen (1991) and Levitt (1969) have provided useful conceptual maps which separate the dimensions of product into distinct levels. This approach can suggest new ways of improving or maintaining an organization's position through refining its offerings. This type of analysis can be transposed to service provision.

Core benefit

At the centre of the offering is the core benefit being purchased. People buying an item of confectionery like a KitKat are not really buying 'four crisp wafer fingers covered in milk chocolate'. As Rowntrees recognizes in their advertising slogan 'Have a Break', they are buying the pretext for a few moments' relaxation. Similarly, a visitor to an exhibition is less concerned with the precise medium in which the pictures or drawings exist, than with their aesthetic or emotional effect. When we define marketing as activity aimed at 'identifying and satisfying customer requirements' it is important to remember that the customer defines the requirement. The organization aims to satisfy it on the customer's terms. So an appreciation of the core benefit being purchased by the arts consumer in a given situation is essential to a

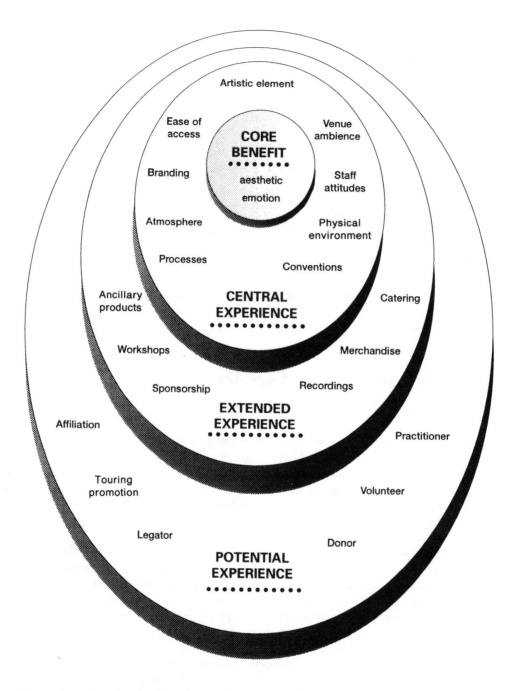

Figure 4.1   Four levels of product in the arts experience

sound marketing strategy. It gives clues to motivation which can then be reflected in promotional copy and imagery, as well as refinements to the presentation of the experience.

The central experience

Surrounding the core benefit, and mediating it to the customer in an acceptable and appropriate way, are the aspects of the central experience of the arts: its actual physical manifestation. This level embraces not only the artistic element itself, but also every aspect of its delivery: venue ambience, front-of-house staff attitudes, ease of access, and so on. Branding (about which we will have more to say later) is also very important at this level for the arts. It is one of the ways in which organizations can respond to the high perceived risk of making an intangible purchase by reassuring their customers with an aura of quality.

As will be clear from our remarks about the core benefit above, the features of the central experience are only important insofar as they are the means to the desired end of the benefit being purchased. One of the pitfalls into which organizations of any kind can fall is to confuse features with benefits. In a sense service providers are at an advantage here. Because their offerings have fewer tangible features than those of product marketers, they are more focused on the delivery of the benefits themselves.

Seeing the offering in terms of its benefits rather than its features is the key to putting the consumer at the centre of the marketing process. Cowell (1984) and Lovelock (1988) both stress the importance of retaining and developing customers in service marketing, and Lovelock particularly stresses the importance of customer data in this process. Computer technology is allowing more and more arts organizations to build the kind of knowledge of their customers which enables this 'customer obsession' to be put into practice. It recognizes the participative nature of service consumption and focuses our attention on the importance of the customer's point of view.

The extended experience

Product aspects at this level tend to merge into other areas of the marketing mix. Delivery is an aspect of distribution, credit is an aspect of pricing, after-sales service can be seen as an aspect of promotion. But they are all directly related to the nature of the product itself, and by enhancing them the organization can extend its offering to specific sectors of the market. Thus, inviting season subscribers to pay by instalment may help lock in existing customers by encouraging them to resubscribe.

Offering an extended level of experience has a special role in arts marketing. As we have seen, the intangible can be rendered less so by surrounding it with various ancillary products. At the Royal Opera House in Covent Garden customers can not only buy tickets to the opera, but also diaries, calendars, recordings and even Barber of Seville Marmalade to make their transient experience of art more memorable. But there is also a sense in which it can open up new possibilities of audience development. Schools workshops are a form of extended experience for a production of a Shakespeare play. Video cassettes are a way of extending the offering of a dance company.

What is appropriate or possible will vary from organization to organization, but this aspect of product development is still relatively underexploited in Britain as compared to America.

The potential experience

This concept results from the way products and services need to change to keep pace with developing needs. Arts organizations need to be focused on the changing external environment in order to keep their provision relevant to new audiences, and to refresh it for their existing ones. We will revisit this theme later in the chapter under the heading of the product life cycle. For an individual arts customer, the potential experience covers a number of forms of deeper involvement: affiliation or membership, becoming a donor or volunteer, or even becoming a more active participant by taking up a particular art form as a practitioner.

Marketing success depends on an organization's ability to 'add value' to its offering. Using a multi-level approach to analysing your product or service allows you to spot opportunities which might otherwise go unconsidered. Like any good model it encourages the marketing strategist to think beyond the immediate situation and anticipate new developments in demand and provision.

The Servuction system model

An original model of service provision which can help arts marketers in analysing their offering has been proposed by John Bateson (1989). This attempts to look at the interface between services and their production, and is known as the 'Servuction' model.

Bateson sees services as produced from a mixture of what he calls 'visible' and 'invisible' sources ('visibility' here meaning what the customer can see). The invisible sources are the organization's own internal systems and processes. In a theatre it might include the backstage operation, the period of rehearsal leading to the play, or the box office staffing rota. These systems are concealed from the customer, and parts of them will probably be concealed from staff not immediately involved in them. They shape and support the visible sources like the unseen mass of an iceberg supporting its visible tip.

The visible sources fall into two types. The first is the inanimate environment: the physical surroundings of the theatre, let us say (including aspects like the shape and spacing of the seats, or the sightlines within the auditorium). The other type of visible source, and possibly the more important from the point of view of marketing management, is the group of people who have contact with the customer and provide the service: whether it be the box office worker who confirms the booking, the actor on stage or the person selling coffee at the interval. As can be seen from the diagram, the model also includes other customers, accurately reflecting how other members of the audience contribute to the experience.

This elegant and inclusive model highlights a number of practical implications:

- Customer involvement: because of the intimate involvement of the customer in the production of the service itself, any changes in how it is produced or mediated will

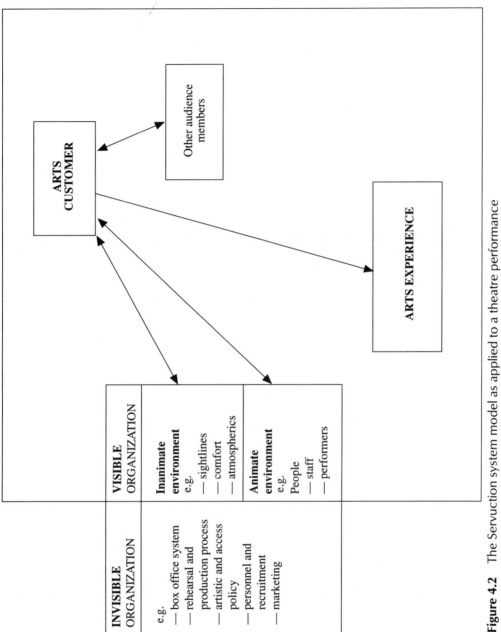

Figure 4.2 The Servuction system model as applied to a theatre performance Adapted from Bateson (1989)

necessitate a change in consumer behaviour. Thus, the introduction of subscription marketing for a concert series or a season of plays will require careful preparation of potential and existing customers, so they can adapt to a new way of creating the service.

- Lack of 'privacy': a new production line in a factory can break down without the consumer knowing about it. But a new departure for an arts organization sinks or swims in the full glare of publicity. Mistakes happen at the point of production, and the arts organization has to have systems which can minimize the damage caused.

- Learning the 'script': customers tend to approach the service experience with a set of expectations. This has been described by some researchers as a 'script'. For example, we all know more or less what is going to happen when we visit the dentist and we behave accordingly. This internalized customer 'script' is related to externalized roles, where we expect certain types of performance from other people. Customers become uncomfortable and have less satisfactory service experiences if these roles are departed from. In the arts environment this places a great deal of responsibility on everyone involved in customer contact to be competent and comfortable in their roles.

- The human factor: everyone and everything which comes into contact with the consumer is delivering the service. So internal marketing and developing staff is at a premium in the arts. The importance of the human factor explains the focus placed in the present book on managing people (see Chapter 9). People are the organization's most important 'product' manifestation, so it pays the marketing manager to have a full appreciation of human resource issues. This is pointed out by Berry (1981) in connection with a case study on internal marketing at Disneyland, but what he says is true of any arts organization:

  > Marketing's scope has traditionally been restricted to the exchange that takes place between customers and organizations. Yet marketing is just as applicable to the exchange that occurs between employees and organizations. Employees are simply internal customers rather than external customers.

- The growing importance of marketing: Servuction recognizes the importance of marketing in a competitive environment. Arts consumers arrive to participate in the process with increased expectations nourished by their experience in other aspects of the leisure industry. The marketing function needs to be able to interpret these changing expectations to the organization as a whole, providing its link to the customer.

- Growth strategies: finally, the model suggests that arts organizations, like any other service providers, face particular difficulty in their strategies for growth. Although research in America has demonstrated the success of certain opera audience development programmes in raising awareness and interest in certain socio-economic groups, it was found that the normal circumstances of its delivery alienated them (Carman and Langeard, 1980). It is difficult, with the emphasis on existing consumers that Servuction implies, to absorb new segments comfortably and permanently.

Service quality

Which dimensions of service do consumers themselves see as relevant? 'Quality' is a popular word in contemporary marketing, but a recalcitrantly subjective issue. One way to understand how consumers perceive quality in service experiences is to establish a list of what they see as its important attributes, and then rate their experiences of the service against their expectations through questionnaire research. The methodology of practical survey research such as this is given in Chapter 3 (although adopting a quantitative approach to an essentially qualitative issue poses knotty questions in question design and ordering).

In its essence this kind of service quality (or 'ServQual') research is a straightforward enough idea. Its original developers (Parasuraman, Zeithaml and Berry, 1988) identified five main areas in which an organization's performance could be measured against expectations. Here we list them as they might be applied to a gallery visit:

- Tangibles: the physical evidence of a service (e.g. what the catalogue looks like).
- Reliability: the fact that the service 'works' (e.g. that the pictures are hung in a way that minimizes unwanted reflected light).
- Responsiveness: the sensitivity of the service to customer approaches (e.g. is there sufficient interpretative material?).
- Assurances: the degree of confidence the service inspires (e.g. is the exhibition well chosen?).
- Empathy: the degree of involvement the service allows (e.g. are the staff friendly?).

But applying ServQual in practice as a diagnostic tool is a difficult proposition. While it might reveal some areas for development or improvement, the essential subjectivity of people's responses is always going to be a problem when trying to interpret numerical data based on the difference between an 'expectation' and the actual experience. Perhaps, too, there may be a clash between the customer's idea of the core benefit and the organization's interpretation of it through the central experience on offer. There is also the danger that people's expectations may themselves be unrealistic. Kotler and Andreasen (1991) suggest that a goal of service providers ought to be to make their users' expectations more reasonable: 'Nonprofits should routinely ask themselves: What are potential customers being led to expect from this organization and what can the organization deliver?'

This question does not let the organization off the hook of providing the best and most relevant service possible. What it does instead is to encourage marketing planning to focus on what is achievable to a high standard, rather than promising what cannot be delivered. Examples of how the question might be answered in arts marketing practice include:

- Clear and relevant promotional activity.
- Helping the customer to be a more active arts consumer by means of pre-performance talks, exhibition tours, workshop events.

- A clear appreciation of the relationship between the core benefit and the central experience on offer.
- A realistic attitude to internal resources, informed by regular audit and monitoring.
- A shared understanding of the mission of the organization.

ServQual can be useful in sorting out priorities in this respect. The set of relevant attributes in the arts will vary according to art form or organizational objectives. A checklist of attributes important to other service areas may be useful as a template from which to develop research into your own organization's performance. Box 4.1 provides such a checklist, annotated appropriately for the arts industry.

Conclusion

Service marketing can add a further three 'Ps' to the '4 Ps' model of the traditional marketing mix (Zikmund and d'Amico, 1993). As we have seen, each of them is worth exploring in depth as a means of optimizing an arts organization's marketing efforts:

- Participants: the importance of the human interface and the co-operative role of the customer are unique to services, and are key aspects of arts experience.
- Physical evidence: the engineering of an appropriate environment for the delivery of the experience (including opportunities for augmented product) from clear booking procedures to explicit signage.
- Process of service delivery: placing the customer at the centre of the sales and marketing systems through which the experience is mediated.

Box 4.1

Determinants of service quality

- Reliability
getting it right first time
honouring promises
  - charging the correct amount
  - keeping records
  - having tickets ready for collection

- Responsiveness
being ready to perform a service
  - answering questions or enquiries
  - following up contacts

- Competence
the skill and knowledge needed to perform the service
  - being able to advise or explain
  - people skills
  - technical knowledge (e.g. emergency procedures, first aiders, etc.)

- Access
approachability
  - telephones not always busy and promptly answered
  - waiting and queuing minimized
  - opening or performance times convenient and consistent

- Courtesy
friendliness and respect from people with whom customers have contact
  - consideration
  - personal appearance
  - willingness to identify oneself on the telephone or by name badge

- Communication
keeping the customer appropriately informed
  - announcements
  - promotional strategy and media chosen
  - clear explanation of options available
  - explicit procedures for handling problems (e.g. lateness, noise, refunds)

- Credibility
honesty and trustworthiness
  - reputation and 'brand image'
  - community involvement

- Security
  freedom from danger or risk in the transaction
  - well-lit car parks
  - confidentiality with bank details for patrons paying by standing order/ direct debit
  - white-lined steps and well-maintained facilities
- Customer empathy
  meeting the customer more than halfway
  - flexibility
  - acknowledging the regular customer
  - making the new customer welcome
- Physical environment
  the physical evidence accompanying the service
  - facilities
  - uniforms
  - signage
  - other customers

Adapted from Parasuraman, et al. (1985)

Box 4.2

Arts customers create their own experience

Research in the USA in the early 1980s suggests a number of ways in which museums can enhance the experience which they and their customers create together.

1 Segment customers on a benefits-sought basis into three main groups:
  Aesthetes: those interested in the artistic merits of particular works.
  Historians: those interested in the works as representative of social or art history.
  Romantics: those interested in the biographical aspect of the artist behind the work.
2 Segment customers on a behavioural basis:
  Those who respond to written information/those who respond to spoken information.
  Brief visitors/lengthy visitors.
  First-time visitors/experienced visitors.
3 Address each visitor segment with a customized itinerary through the museum
4 Augment the offer with a selection of guidebooks, wall-charts, audio-guides and tours reflecting the needs of the different segments.

Adapted from Andreasen (1982)

The nature of the artistic experience

While our discussion of the nature of Product has focused on the entire transaction which takes place between the customer and the organization, the artistic experience itself has the central role in providing benefits. Reflection on how the artistic experience works, and the kinds of needs it satisfies in its customers, can help identify what is unique about the arts marketing process and separate it from the related areas of leisure and hospitality marketing.

Arts events or objects are essentially acts of communication between artists and audiences. We have seen how service models like 'Servuction' stress the co-operative nature of the production of services. Like successful communication it is a two-way process. Ideas from communication theory can help clarify our analysis of the benefits which need to be articulated in promotion as well as our thinking about product enhancement. It also focuses thinking on the relevance of long-term, two-way relationships between artists and audiences, suggesting that the potential contradiction between 'marketing' and 'art' is more apparent than real:

> A customer orientation towards marketing holds that success will come to that organization that best determines the perceptions, needs, and wants of target markets and satisfies them through the design, communication, pricing and delivery of appropriate and competitively viable offerings.
>
> (Kotler and Andreasen, 1991)

Newcomb's ABX model (1961)

Different communication theorists emphasize different aspects of the process. Theodore Newcomb, for example, sees communicative acts as bringing people closer together by sharing their understanding of the external world. His approach differs from more linear models because it involves adjustment and consensus on both sides about the subject of the communication. While his original research emphasized the role of communication in reducing dissonance in personal relationships, his model can be applied to the experience of the live performing arts.

In the case of this application of the model to a performance (X), it is the dialogue created between the performers (A) and the audience (B) that will each time result in a different X. There is a clear link with the kind of process described earlier in our treatment of servuction. But seeing the event in terms of Newcomb's model emphasizes the dynamic nature of the relationship between each audience member and the performance. Both parties have an input to make, both are changed by the experience. This could suggest promotional emphasis on sharing the adventure of art. A possible 'product' response might be to increase the frequency of ancillary events which allow the audience to have a voice (such as discussions or question sessions). Such thinking explains the kind of 'glasnost' which many traditional museums have taken on board in their pursuit of marketing orientation.

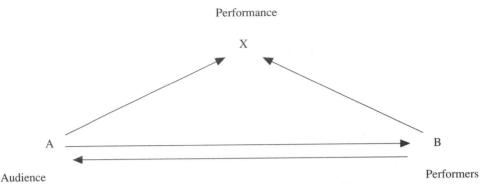

Figure 4.3   Newcomb's ABX model, adapted to a theatre performance

From Reverence to Fun in the V&A

Changing visitor patterns have created new product positioning opportunities for the Victoria and Albert Museum. Central to the museum's 1990s ambiance is a move away from the atmosphere of quasi-religious awe permeating some of the galleries. Instead of feeling intimidated into their best behaviour, families are now made positively welcome. Solemn reverence for the arts has given way to enjoyment and access.

Using communication to come closer to the audience has been a key element of this strategy. Gallery wardens, for example, whose primary function used to be security, now go on regular courses to learn about the objects on display. They can use this knowledge to talk with visitors about the exhibitions. Touch-screen technology is also used to give background information about what is on display, and in the Korean and Chinese galleries labelling of exhibits is not only in English but also in the language of the culture of which they form a part. This is in recognition of the large segment of overseas visitors who are interested in works from their own cultures.

Shannon and Weaver's 'process' model of communication (1949)

A very influential model of communication, Shannon and Weaver's analysis of what goes on in communication was developed in connection with diagnosing problems in telephone systems. It sees communication as travelling from the source to the destination, being encoded and decoded on the way. 'Noise' is seen as anything that interferes with the clear reception of the sender's meaning.

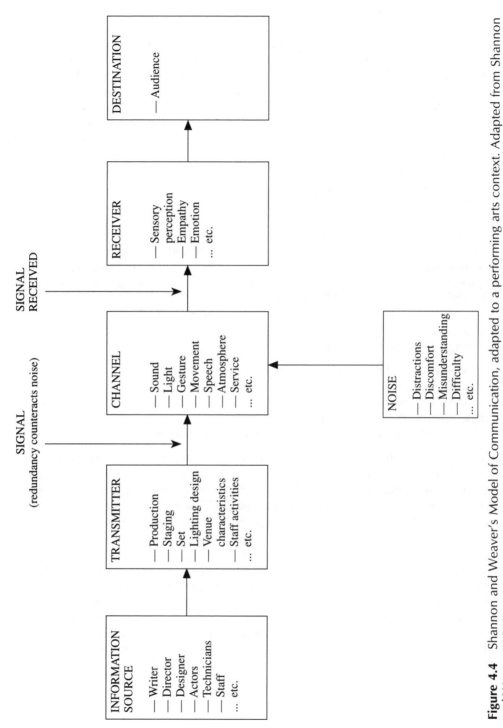

Figure 4.4 Shannon and Weaver's Model of Communication, adapted to a performing arts context. Adapted from Shannon and Weaver (1949)

In spite of its mechanical origins, it has been embraced by marketing theorists as a way of separating communication into manageable steps. Kotler (1991), and many other marketing authors, use it to explain the basics of promotion. Its straightforward, step-by-step approach resembles the AIDA model of advertising discussed in Chapter 6. This reflects its simplistic approach. Later refinements of the model incorporated an element of 'feedback', but the misleading impression of communication as a one-way, linear process remains. In itself the model is not as relevant to the experience of the arts as Newcomb's. But it contains two very useful ideas which are relevant to the arts: noise and redundancy.

'Redundancy' is used here with a specialized meaning. Redundancy can be observed in acts of communication. When the message is complex or new, there will be a considerable amount of repetition, duplication or unnecessary material. This is because of the high level of rejection or confusion experienced by the receiver. The Shannon and Weaver model shows 'noise' as a disturbance in the channel of communication that distorts or masks the signal, interfering with the receiver's ability to pick up the intended meaning. Redundancy compensates for noise by increasing the predictability of the signal for the receiver.

'Noise', interpreting this model for the arts experience, might be all the internal and external barriers to enjoyment of a performance which a customer may have to encounter. They could include:

- Preconceptions of the nature of arts activity.
- The difficulty of the piece.
- Unfamiliarity with a new form or genre.
- Discomfort with the environment of the activity.
- The specialist needs of the audience member him or herself.

The more work that is put into strengthening the signal by the performers in rehearsal and production values, and the more the signal is repeated to the audience through their regular attendance, the more clearly it will be received and a longer term relationship developed. Helpful 'redundancy' comes both from the repeated experience of arts attendance for the audience, and also from programming choice which uses material which in itself has predictable elements. Popular art forms are often criticized precisely for their predictability: stock gags, lots of choruses, stereotypical characters, catch-phrases and foreseeable outcomes. But, controversially, communication theory suggests that such work has a role to play in building new audiences more effectively than more challenging, issue-based work. Francis (1990) in a study of attendance at arts events by black audiences concludes: 'Generally Afro-Caribbeans and Asians have a tendency to dislike attending activities which portray black suffering, poverty and traditional values: "They never seem to portray the pleasant side of Africa or India. It's never cheerful, never entertaining."'

TYPE OF NEED

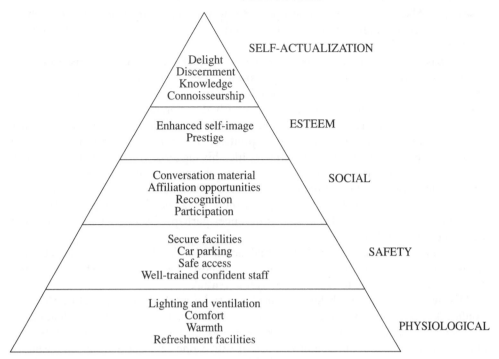

Figure 4.5 Maslow's hierarchy of needs, adapted for the arts experience.

Needs and wants

Communication theory can give us some clues as to what is going on between audience and performers or artists in arts transactions. But our appreciation of the benefits which arts marketing exists to promote can be enhanced by looking at the basic concepts of needs and wants.

Needs are basic human drives that can be allayed for a while, but never go away completely. Hunger, for example, can be satisfied by an evening meal. But the next morning breakfast is still a welcome sight. Wants are the individual expressions of needs. Kotler has defined them elegantly as 'Culturally-defined needs'. Thus, 'I am hungry' is a need. But 'I want a bowl of cornflakes' is a want. Marketing is often accused of creating needs and wants. But what it really does is to recognize needs, and find ways of fulfilling them which consumers find appropriate and attractive. Thus a new brand of breakfast cereal is not creating a need, but will hope to establish itself as a possible 'want', amongst other alternatives, to satisfy the basic need for breakfast.

What kind of needs, then, does the experience of the arts satisfy? Chapter 2 has shown that different needs and wants may be satisfied by the same experience in different market segments. This is known as segmenting by 'benefits sought'. But these needs are clearly not as uncomplicated as hunger or thirst. The American researcher Abraham Maslow came up with a way of analysing needs in 1954 which still has enormous influence on the way marketers think about consumer behaviour: the 'Hierarchy of Needs'.

The base of the pyramid represents the needs that human beings must satisfy to keep going: what Maslow called 'homeostatic' needs (from the Greek word for staying in the same place). Without fulfilling hunger, thirst and warmth needs, the physical condition of the individual would swiftly deteriorate.

The next level features safety needs. Once the immediate business of keeping alive has been sorted out, the issue of security from a predatory environment rears its head. As soon as you have more than the basic essentials of life, this suggests, you need to protect them.

Social needs now rise to the fore, perhaps to compensate for the alienation which the need for safety implies. Humans need a sense of belonging, and involvement.

Humans have a competitive streak, and their social needs develop into the next layer of 'esteem needs'. This is the difference, perhaps, between being loved and being seen to be loved.

The final level is known as 'self-actualization needs'. This level incorporates the ideas of education and self-development. It suggests a need for transformation and transcendence, the need to realize one's full potential.

Maslow insisted that each level of need had to be worked through before the next could take its place. But later theorists have argued that the model is misleading in imposing this sequential hierarchy (beguiling though the notion is). They point out that needs can exist simultaneously on more than one level at a time; that what is important is the structure of the individual's psyche rather than this generalized external map. Be that as it may, Maslow's ideas offer a way of approaching the question of what kind of needs arts experience satisfies. As we have seen in Chapter 1, the arguments for and against subsidizing the arts stand or fall by the extent to which these needs are recognized as serious ones.

It is tempting to see them as exclusively, or predominantly, at the 'self-actualization' level. The fact that the arts are 'educational' allows many arts organizations to be registered as charities. Certainly ideas of education and self-improvement are strong motivators for some audience members. Morison and Dalgleish (1987) see an educational component as an essential component of their evangelistic audience development plan, the 'Strategy to Encourage Lifelong Learning' of 'SELL' system. As in the Servuction model of the service experience examined earlier, the benefits to the consumer include the opportunity to become more adept at receiving the experience, and therefore more satisfied.

But, of course, the arts experience hinges on delighting the audience or the beholder rather than educating or improving them. Where does this sense of enjoyment fit into Maslow's hierarchy? Depending on the art form, it might exist across self-actualization, esteem and social needs. Arguably one might find elements of it on the lower levels too. Re-examining the hierarchy of needs in the context of the spread of benefits available to a visitor to an exhibition, suggests that the arts offer satisfactions at all levels rather than just the obvious one of self-actualization:

Self-actualization:

- Increased knowledge of artist or period.
- Greater enjoyment through widened taste (possible influence on own technique if a painter or student).
- Ability to compare and contrast with previous experience.

Esteem:

- Prestige of gallery surroundings.
- Customer care includes an element of deference.
- Enhanced self-image through being able to discuss the latest exhibition.

Social:

- Pictures provide something to discuss with partner or companion (cf. Newcomb's model discussed earlier).
- Opportunity to join 'Friends' of gallery.
- Possibility of meeting friends and acquaintances at the exhibition.

Safety:

- Cloakroom facilities to store coat and bag.
- Secure car parking.
- Properly trained staff and clear fire exits.

Physiological:

- Adequate lighting and ventilation.
- Warmth.
- Clean refreshment facilities.

The further down the hierarchy we go, the more remote from the actual experience of the art objects themselves the benefits appear to be. But they are all related to the central experience of seeing the art objects in a given environment at a particular time. It is impossible effectively to separate one aspect from any other, although we can recognize that there are priorities at work. For example the customer might be prepared to trade-off inadequate refreshment facilities for ease of parking. We can conclude that the arts experience offers satisfaction to a complex of needs rather than any individual one. While this complicates the task of interpreting the benefits to customers through promotion, it means that there is a virtually inexhaustible number of angles from which they can be approached. It also means that there are an inexhaustible number of ways in which managing the product effectively can introduce small but important improvements to satisfy needs more effectively.

Keeping the product relevant

Product lifecycle

Like the consumers who use them, products and services have lifecycles. In a sense this reflects what has been said earlier about the only relevance of the 'features' of products or services being that they satisfy needs and wants. Because new ways of satisfying needs are constantly emerging, existing ways are superseded. What used to satisfy needs and wants perfectly well a decade ago, is now no longer appropriate. These changes are often driven by developments in the external environment, particularly technology. The wordprocessor, for example, answers a need that used to be answered by the typewriter. But because of the superior facilities offered by computers, the new way of answering the need has superseded the old.

Product lifecycles also exist in the arts. The advent of television, for example, meant that variety theatres faced closure in the 1950s. Sheffield, a city which averaged nightly theatre attendances across four venues in 1950 of nearly 6,000, could only sustain a tenth of that in one theatre (the Crucible) in 1980 (Pick, 1986). Admittedly there has been a revival in the theatrical environment in Sheffield itself, with the reopening of the Lyceum as a high-profile touring house in the early 1990s. But where it exists today, variety entertainment is an acknowledged archaicism. It is presented, for example, at the Leeds City Varieties theatre amidst nostalgic circumstances which often include Edwardian dress by the audience themselves.

New forms come to replace the old, however. Their emergence can be led as much by the socio-cultural imperatives of fashion as by the advance of technology. 'Alternative comedy', for example, has managed to make cult stars out of people who are basically theatrical performers, although their following and ethos seems more like that of rock stars. This phenomenon, as has been suggested in Chapter 2, reflects emerging needs and wants from a generation of young people whose tastes have been educated by the electronic media and who find established forms of theatre too much like hard work.

But lifecycles in the arts, as in other 'cultural' industries such as fashion or broadcasting, can be short-lived. The Early Music 'boom' provided considerable growth in recording and performing in the 1980s but the rate of expansion has now slowed down considerably. This has forced ensembles who were once seen as adventurous into much safer areas of repertoire because of pressures from record companies (Kemp, 1993).

Technology has not only stimulated new forms of artistic expression but introduced new ways of enriching customers' experience of traditional art forms. Music, traditionally an art form concentrating on sound, is broadening into the visual. To some extent this reflects the increasing trend for music to be available on video and laser disc as well as compact disc. In the world of classical music it represents the absorption of product features from live popular music presentation. For example the London Mozart Players have introduced the facility of simultaneous video projection at concerts in the Queen Elizabeth Hall. Live pictures of performers from different angles are relayed on a 12-foot square screen. Louise Honeyman, their managing director, explained the rationale behind an approach, dubbed by one critic 'MTV' (Mozart Television), as being a mixture of enhancement and access.

On the other hand, technology can run the risk of replacing product rather than enhancing it. John Pick (1986) lamented this trend in a typically trenchant aside on

M(ozart) TV

I think there are a lot of people, particularly of my generation, who love music, are absolutely passionate about music, but didn't have the benefit of a musical education. And music's been a bit of a, dare I use the word, elitist thing in that there are those who know about it and can read it, and those who don't know anything. And I think that sometimes the ordinary music lover who doesn't perhaps know a treble clef from a bass clef has been made to feel the odd person out. Now they often don't know the sound an oboe makes. If you asked even musical people what the difference is between flutes, oboes, clarinets, bassoons, usually they can't tell you which is which. So I think this is an interesting exercise because when the oboe has a solo, or the flute, and the camera goes to that instrument, then you know exactly what they are. So you add knowledge. I didn't want it to be exactly educational in the full sense of the word, but intriguing and enlightening and (as we used in the programme) enhancing. Not to take away, and the reason for the screen not being enormously large. It was the right size for that hall. But we wanted people to feel that they needn't look at the screen if they didn't want to.

Louise Honeyman interviewed on Music Matters, BBC Radio 3, November 1994

the excesses of early 1980s West End musicals, which he interprets as a manifestation of the twin demons of high-tech and red tape:

> At certain pinnacles of the contemporary arts, in performance art and most particularly in music theatre, what is celebrated *is* essentially the bureaucracy and the supportive technology. Thus in *Cats*, in *Les Miserables*, in *Starlight Express* or in *Time* the twin attractions are how much it all cost (and what political battles had to be fought in smoke-filled offices) and the dazzling technological display. *Time*, the £4,000,000 epic, has lasers and computerized scenery, a 14-foot high head of Sir Laurence Olivier which 'speaks' his recorded voice, and a plot which is pure baloney. As such it is entirely representative of its genre, and may in due course expect a publicly-funded revival.

The fact that the blockbuster musical now appears to be a genre on the wane is another example of the irresistible march of the product lifecycle.

The implications for the marketing function are as follows:

- Elements of product need to be constantly reviewed for their relevance to the audience.
- Hard decisions have to be made about dropping initiatives (such as Friends organizations in terminal decline) which have been superseded by needs from new segments. Otherwise they will absorb time and resources uselessly which could be better applied elsewhere (as we shall see in the discussion of product portfolio below).

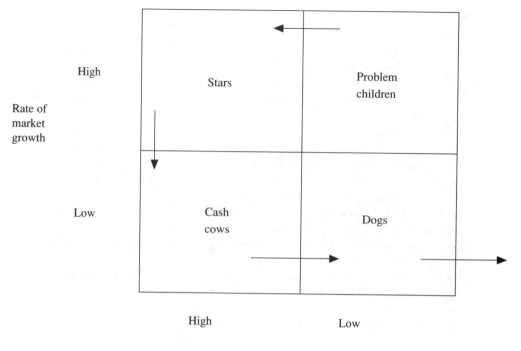

Figure 4.6   The Boston Consulting Group matrix

- The organization must maintain a focus on changes in the external environment (a key feature of marketing orientation).
- In a business that relies so much on its staff to represent the product, their skills and attitudes must be kept relevant to changing circumstances by a genuine commitment to training and development.

Product portfolio management

Few manufacturing organizations can afford to rely on only one product. In spite of the simplicity of such an approach, the risk of having all the organization's eggs in one basket would be too high. Arts organizations are in a similar position. They need to spread the risk involved in producing arts experiences for customers by planning not only a balanced programme of artistic product, but also by maximizing the income they can earn from other activities. For performing arts venues these are often divided into 'performance-related' items like programmes and catering, and 'non-performance-related' like room lettings and costume hire. Some aspects of a venue's service portfolio can have a dual identity. Bars and catering are in one sense performance-related, insofar as takings go up or down in relation to attendance. But they also play a role in non-performance activities like services to business.

The fact that products and services have lifecycles, as we have observed in the previous section, means that at any one time some parts of your total portfolio will be more relevant than others. The need to manage a combination of offerings in a way that optimizes the benefits to the customer as well as the returns to the organization has resulted in the development of a number of 'product portfolio management' models.

The first thing to say about such models is that, even for the packaged goods sector in which they were originally developed, they offer very approximate guides rather than prescriptive rules. With this proviso, however, they can be useful in analysing and planning how your mixture of offerings fits together, and so offer the arts marketer a useful tool. As we have observed elsewhere in this book about models (Chapter 6), what makes them useful is not their accuracy but their flexibility and the insights they can stimulate.

The most famous example of a portfolio model is the Boston Consulting Group's matrix. The model is based on research into the way that packaged goods behaved across a number of companies in the expanding economy of post-war America. The researchers found that not only do individual products have lifecycles, but the markets in which they exist have lifecycles too, expanding and contracting according to broad patterns of demand. They divided markets into those that were growing and those that were declining. Products, on the other hand, were categorized according to whether their share of the market in which they operated was high or low. This led to the picture illustrated in Figure 4.6.

Relating this model back to the products and services offered by an individual organization led to the following categorizations:

High share products in high growth markets: 'stars'

These products are the mainstay of profitability. Their importance to the organization means that they need to be prioritized in terms of management attention and resources. An arts example might be an orchestral 'pop concert' by a big name orchestra, reflecting the current growth in interest for compilation CDs of classical highlights (like the 'Three Tenors') in a programme of extracts from longer works.

High share products in low growth markets: 'cash cows'

These products are the bedrock of many organizations' income, but are not capable of further growth because the market in which they operate is no longer expanding. A municipal choral society's rendition of Handel's Messiah will appeal to a predictable but essentially stable audience. Its familiarity as repertoire will, however, provide some kind of guarantee of its commercial success.

Low share products in high growth markets: 'problem children'

These are the possible 'stars' of the future. Although they need a lot of resources and time, they offer great potential because they provide a foothold in an expanding area. Many arts organizations have identified services to business (conference facilities, promotional services, even training) as ways of accessing a growth area.

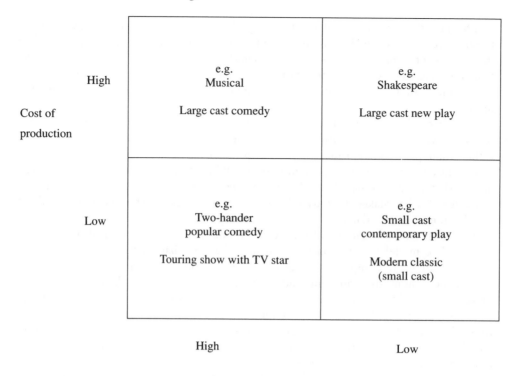

Figure 4.7   A product planning matrix for a theatre season

Low share products in low growth markets: 'dogs'

While still consuming management time and resources, these are products which fail to justify their long-term existence. The markets they are in are not performing as well as others open to the organization, and their share of the available business is low. A theatre group offering community touring productions to a rural area with a declining population might need to reconsider its role.

The Boston Consulting Group saw business strategy as moving resources around an organization so that money and time were not wasted on poorly performing products. Their advice to managers was to 'Polish the Stars, milk the Cows, feed the Problem Children and shoot the Dogs.' In other words, resources should be concentrated on the opportunities most likely to yield returns. Products which are underperforming with no hope of long-term recovery should be jettisoned before they drag the rest of the business under by soaking up its time and money.

Arts organizations need to manage the effective use of time and resources towards their goals through examining their portfolio of offerings. This might involve hard

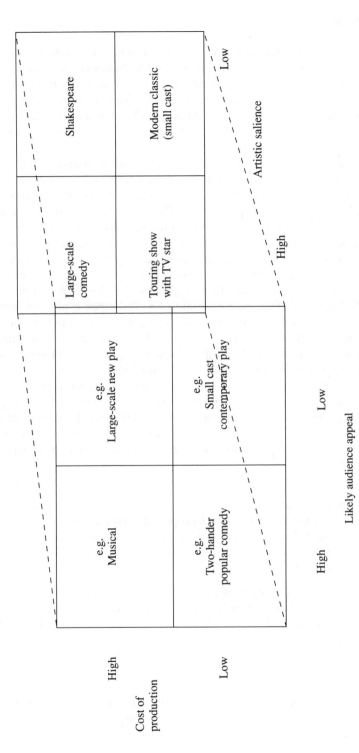

Figure 4.8 A three-dimensional product planning matrix

decisions about dropping some aspects of activity in order to be able to concentrate more effectively on others. Especially in a 'people business' such decisions are difficult to implement. The complicated discounting arrangements to be discovered in some repertory theatres are a case in point. A 'Friends' organization, with its package of discounts and benefits, is often to be found in uneasy co-existence with a more recently introduced subscription scheme because of the personality and power factors involved.

One of the advantages of portfolio models is that they allow simple visual communication of the relationship between a number of complex variables. A modified version of the Boston matrix can be used to model the kind of thinking behind planning a theatre's annual artistic programme. Replacing the axes of 'market growth' and 'market share' with considerations of 'production costs' and 'likely sales appeal' gives a matrix which can help predict the financial effects of programming choice.

Here the offerings are divided into four sectors (see Figure 4.7). As with the Boston matrix there is an implied movement of resources from the 'cash cow' two-hander comedy to the other areas. But rather than suggesting that the 'high cost/low appeal' offering be killed off, the illustrative example of a Shakespeare play or large-scale new work signals that this quadrant is the part of the mix most deserving of subsidy. At the risk of over-complicating what is an essentially simple idea, a third dimension (of artistic salience) might be added to reflect the artistic priorities of the organization, and its claim to support by funding bodies (see Figure 4.8).

Here the Shakespeare and large-scale new work are seen in terms of their relative artistic salience not only to the other quadrants, but to each other. Programme choices could be made accordingly. It may be objected that this kind of diagrammatic approach misrepresents the subtleties which should inform a venue's approach to its programming. But the use of portfolio models as a planning aid can be defended on a number of counts:

- It makes assumptions explicit.
- It encourages quantification.
- It facilitates an appreciation of the way a programme fits together.
- It enables the projected work of the organization to be clearly measured against its mission and priorities.
- It helps identify gaps in provision.

Product opportunities may exist in a number of different areas, depending on the nature of the organization's activities. The following are common types of product in building-based performing arts venues, but aspects of them are equally relevant to touring or the visual arts.

Programmes

Programmes are a 'service adjunct' which should complement the experience of the arts. Apart from their value as souvenirs (research suggests that they are kept well after the performance), they can enrich the experience itself. Normally programmes are produced on a contractual arrangement with publishing companies who sell advertising in them and offer them to the venue at a reduced rate per copy. Predicting likely audience numbers for order quantities thus becomes a very fine art as the relationship between the number of programmes bought and the number sold means profit or loss. Alternatively, organizations can produce their own programmes direct, contracting out advertising sales, or do the whole job themselves (as do amateur companies, for whom income from this part of the operation is crucial).

Arts marketing should aim at enabling customers to be 'better' co-operators in the production of the arts experience, as we have seen. In this sense the performing arts can take some inspiration from the visual arts where the concept of a 'catalogue' to accompany and interpret an exhibition is a well-established service adjunct. But in spite of the audience enrichment opportunity presented by programmes, their quality remains a perceived weakness of many arts organizations. Instead of putting the work in context, like an exhibition catalogue, theatre programmes often major on lengthy lists of names of those involved in the production and venue. They seem designed for internal rather than external consumption.

Time and resources may be indicated as the reason for this deficiency. But, given

Programmes as branding devices

In 1989, programmes at the Royal Opera House were radically revised. The familiar red programme, with contents laid out in a fairly conventional format, gave way to a bigger and thicker publication. The new programmes consciously borrowed elements from glossy magazine design. They were perfect bound (i.e. with a flat glued back) rather than stapled. Their imaginatively laid-out editorial incorporated full-page colour photographs and illustrations, interviews with composers and performers, background articles and other interpretative material. This was in addition to the standard details of performance information, cast biography, venue personnel, and funding credits which are to be found in any programme. The format settled down after some fine-tuning to become a publication which, though more expensive than its predecessor, offered the customer much more value.

There were some complaints that the new format was too large to fit into a pocket or a handbag. But carrying it in the hand meant that Royal Opera House customers on their way home were allowed to be 'conspicuous consumers', and the venue itself got more publicity. The new programme was much more clearly branded as 'Royal Opera House' (featuring a highly visible cover logo as well as running headlines inside), more profitable in terms of sales value, and more attractive to advertisers who responded well to the increased impact offered by the larger page size and enhanced colour opportunities.

our earlier observations about the nature of the needs which the arts experience addresses, giving programmes a customer focus should be a high priority. What is needed is an acceptable quality level which satisfies customer needs without sacrificing resources from other organizational objectives. Perhaps because of their greater perceived need to interpret their art form, opera companies have led the way in producing programmes which look as if they are for customers.

Catering

Catering offers significant income potential. But it is a risky operation. Venues are faced with the decision of whether to run it themselves or to make an agreement with an external contractor who will bring expertise and systems to the opportunity and offer the venue a commission and/or fee for so doing. Whichever route is taken to catering, the image attributes will impact directly on the venue.

> ### New menu at Bolton
> Since the end of 1991 when Lawrence Till took over as chief executive and artistic director at the Bolton Octagon, facilities have been refurbished with the help of donations from the Foundation for the Sports and the Arts, and the Theatres Restoration Fund. Part of the transition has been to a new style of catering. Bacon butties have given place to smoked salmon sandwiches washed down with a glass of 'bubbly': an interval 'special' which costs £3.50:
>
> > It doesn't take an Einstein to realize you don't make much money on chip barns [bread cakes]. That may sound patronizing and cynical but it's not intended to. Theatre has to be about giving audiences a complete experience and the catering and the level of customer care are significant.
>
> *Source:* Murdin, (1994)

Merchandise

Like catering, merchandise can offer a useful source of income as well as enhancing the customer experience. The financial risk of the operation has to be considered. Items related to a particular exhibition or production have a shorter life than venue-related branded items. Long-running shows with high predicted seat occupancy (such as pantomimes) are an excellent merchandising opportunity however. Because of the high proportion of audience members who will not be paying full price (children, family ticket holders, parties, etc.) box office takings are inevitably depressed even though production costs are high. Merchandise allows you to recoup at least some of this. Badges, pens, related books, toys and videos are examples of successful Christmas show merchandise. The back pages of a magazine like *Marketing Week* list suppliers who will be happy to make further suggestions. Minimum order quantities, lead times and arrangements for re-ordering are some of the areas to ascertain.

Venue-specific merchandise (T-shirts, china, tote-bags, etc.) can provide income if there are retailing facilities in the longer term. But such merchandise is also a useful adjunct to sponsorship deals. If a sponsor is negotiating hospitality as part of the package of benefits available from a venue, it is a good idea to suggest that a gift such as a bag or sweatshirt to each guest can make the evening even more memorable at a very small extra cost. For the right kind of quantities, it may be worth conceding a discount on the total price. The quality of the merchandise itself is, of course, paramount. If a sweatshirt is to carry your logo, it will be acting as an organizational ambassador. It is no use if it fades or shrinks. Careful selection and testing of items is very important, as is finding out as much as possible about suppliers (see Chapter 9 on negotiation).

Services to business

Sponsorship (dealt with more fully in Chapter 5) is only one way in which business and the arts can exchange benefits. Building-based organizations can offer room hire and conference facilities, although it must be stressed that competition in this area tends to be fierce. The kind of standards against which your facilities will be judged will be those of commercial meetings venues such as hotels and conference centres. Nevertheless there may be a segment of the local business market who would respond well to a combination of location and price outweighing four-star comfort. Membership of local trade bodies such as tourism associations or chambers of commerce can provide avenues to likely customers.

Skills from within an organization can also be offered as services to business. Drama-based training is a technique used in telesales which can be facilitated by arts venues; small to medium sized enterprises are a potential market for help with writing and producing promotional material; even skills like juggling have been successfully offered to business people to reduce executive stress. Tailor-made entertainment at corporate hospitality events is another possibility, as is a community arts group offering another company banner-making skills. The precise opportunities and resources to match them will vary from organization to organization, but it is worth bearing in mind that services to business can extend far beyond trying to get them to part with money in exchange for publicity benefits. Such relationships can then be built on and developed over time to incorporate other forms of exchange.

Product on the cutting edge

We have seen that the arts involve acts of communication. Arts organizations are therefore very much like media organizations (the press, broadcasting, publishing) in the way that they are constantly innovating. In traditional manufacturing industries the emphasis is on keeping things the same. Thus a can of beans this week should be the same as a can of beans last week. In the media industries, however, the emphasis is on keeping things different. A newspaper today has got to have different news in it from the news it carried yesterday. Innovation is therefore at the heart of the arts offering. Lawrence Till, the chief executive of the Bolton Octagon sees it as essential to the customers of his repertory theatre (both outside and inside the organization):

> You don't provide a diet of what they know they like to eat; you ask them to taste some new flavours as well. It's important you don't pander to the lowest common denominator but try and present work that will challenge people. Sometimes you experiment. Sometimes you hope that the beetroot doesn't bleed on the lettuce: or sometimes that's useful ... A lot of buildings are either doing fewer plays or turning into arts centres and presenting touring work. Everyone could make their job easier sometimes by presenting tours but the people I work with are incredibly creative and they have to have an outlet.
>
> (Murdin, 1994)

Given that arts organizations are trying to extend the experience of their existing customers into new areas, and trying to get their potential customers to try something new, an understanding of the way that new ideas spread in society may yield arts marketers some valuable insights. The American researcher, Everett M. Rogers, has made extensive study of the process he calls 'the diffusion of innovation.' Rogers' research concluded that you can divide society into segments according to their propensity to espouse new ideas or new products (Rogers, 1962).

Innovators

Rogers found that the 'innovation-prone' make up less than 3 per cent of the population. They tend to be younger than average, financially stable, well-educated and confident. Their affluence means they can afford to be 'the first on the block' with new products, although their strong drives lead them to be selective and image-conscious. They can be observed at first nights and private views. They are excited rather than disturbed at the prospect of the unfamiliar.

Early adopters

Following the innovators into the market are the 'early adopters', a larger but less adventurous group. Their receptiveness to new ideas is reflected in high readership of magazines. They are educated and confident. They are usually already keen on the area in which the innovation is being made. So, for example, early adopters of contemporary dance forms will tend to come from within the existing dance audience. Winning early adopters to your innovation is a crucial stage in its success. If they do not take it up, there is no chance of it spreading further through the medium of 'word of mouth'. Rogers found that there was a close correlation between this group and 'opinion leaders', people whose attitudes and behaviours influence those of the members of their social and family groups (this is discussed more under public relations in Chapter 6). Clearly, if you are in the business of innovation you need to understand this powerful collection of trend setters.

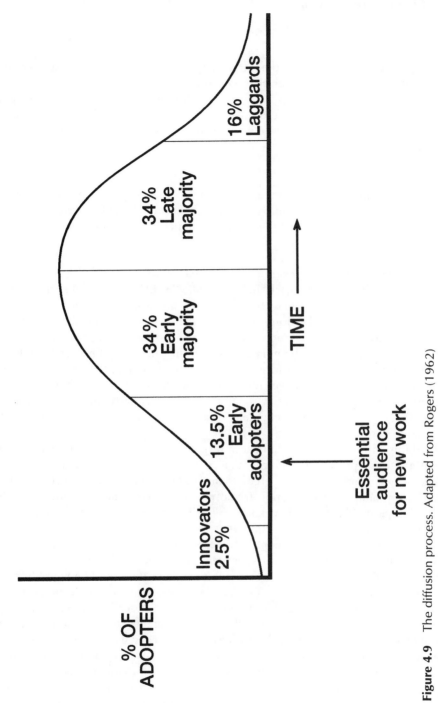

Figure 4.9 The diffusion process. Adapted from Rogers (1962)

Early and late majority

Encouraged by the example of the early adopters, the majority of customers then take the idea on board. Together they constitute more than two thirds of the final total market. The early majority tend to be solid and middle class. Late majority members are older and more traditional in their values, making them naturally conservative. They are reluctant about innovation, but finally come round to it once everyone else has done so.

Laggards

These are the arts marketer's greatest triumphs: the people who are on the far reaches of the arts marketing universe but are eventually led to realize that arts experience has something special to offer them, and climb on board.

Non-adopters

No matter what the product or service under consideration, there will still be a group of people whom it will never reach. In the arts the 'hostile' segment of society are the resolute non-adopters. They may have tried the arts and found them wanting, or their self-image or personal culture has inured them against the prospect. Marketing effort should not ignore this group totally. For the subsidized sector, in particular, arts non-adopters propose a dilemma as discussed in Chapter 1. They still pay for the arts through national and local taxes. It may be, for example, that a theatre's Open Day attracts people who will never return as audience, but have had their experience enriched by that much contact with arts activity. Similarly the bar or catering facilities may attract non-arts clientele, again justifying their investment in the organization.

The diffusion model of how audiences respond to innovation suggests that it is a gradual and risky process. It confirms that, if you can identify it, there is always a market for new work. But it also predicts that at first, at least, it is a very restricted market. Even though the innovation-friendly part of your audience know what they like, the majority like what they know. The importance of a patient approach is underlined by the model's prediction that the total market for any offering will contain less than 20 per cent of people who responded readily to it in the first place.

As we have seen, this scant 20 per cent will tend to be established regular attenders. Marketing terminology would dub them 'heavy users'. The figure brings to mind what is known as the 'Pareto effect', a phenomenon first noted at the turn of the century by the Italian sociologist Vilfredo Pareto who observed that 20 per cent of the people held 80 per cent of the wealth. In many markets 20 per cent of consumers are responsible for 80 per cent of the business. These heavy users need to be jealously maintained, but they are also the best prospects for innovation. What is true for the arts is true for the fashion industry, like the arts a 'production-led' business. It manages to take the mass of clothes buyers with it by concentrating at first on a very small but significant section of its market by presenting the collections of the big designers. Six to nine months later, colours and styles in the high-street shops start to reflect the look that has been unveiled on the catwalk and the ordinary clothes buyer catches up with his or her moneyed counterpart. Your existing users are the best prospects for innovation, and innovations will not stick if your existing heavy users do not take them up.

Arts marketers can take the following pointers for the tricky problem of marketing the unfamiliar, particularly new work:

- Study your heavy consumers and discover cues about new work to which they will respond.
- Think about offering incentives for attendance in smaller groups than your standard discount for groups (this may elicit a response from opinion leaders).
- Be realistic in your expectations, but make sure they are well founded by devoting time and resources to new work.
- Consider the 'unchurched' of the arts, the resolute non-adopters. What kind of activities can you offer them?

Above all be persistent. New and unfamiliar work is essential to internal and external customers of arts organizations. It provides internal customers (staff and performers) with new opportunities to develop, and it provides external customers (audience) with fresh experiences. We have seen how products have lifecycles in the arts as elsewhere. Unless new products are brought on stream on a regular basis, an arts organization can lose touch with its market very quickly.

Total quality management

The kind of marketing approach championed in this book is centred on creating and keeping arts customers by thinking about what needs and wants they are seeking to satisfy and reflecting them in the total offering of the organization. Although we have acknowledged that defining customer expectations is a complex task in the arts, the general principle of 'producing output in conformance to customer requirements' underlies this approach. This phrase is also a very basic definition of 'quality': making sure that the output of an organization is fit for the purpose to which it will be put by the customer (Munroe-Faure and Munro-Faure, 1992).

The models of service provision we have applied to the experience of the arts emphasize how the process depends on the interaction of the customer and everyone with whom he or she comes into contact in the organization. Furthermore, the idea of 'invisible' systems, which enable these first-line personnel to perform their roles more effectively, reveals that even those working behind the scenes have a direct impact on the nature of the experience for the customer. Quality is an issue for everyone in the organization, not just the marketing department.

At the same time, the prioritization of quality does not mean that the balance between benefits for the customer and costs for the organization should tilt disastrously against the organization's interests. Quality also implies increased efficiency in an organization itself, eliminating wastage of time and material by designing ways of working which cut out the uncertainties allowed by less customer-focused systems.

The customer satisfaction at which marketing aims depends on getting things right. In a service environment such as the arts this means getting it right first time. Getting it right first time means that the organization cuts out waste. We have seen that mistakes happen in the service process, as the experience is consumed at the point of its manufacture. The aim should be to prevent problems by anticipating them as far as possible. But by creating reliable systems to deal with problems as they occur, the arts organization not only pacifies the customer more effectively but eliminates a great deal of inconvenience (and expense) for itself.

Getting it right first time also focuses the mind on what is essential about the service and what is irrelevant. This can be called 'doing the right things right': the kind of effectiveness discussed in Chapter 9's treatment of time management. In organizational terms it means a clearer enactment of the mission statement and an increased responsiveness to customers.

The potential benefits of taking quality seriously are as follows:

- Reduced costs through eliminating duplication and wasted time.
- Increased sales or visitor traffic through a better total offering.
- Longer and more fruitful relationships with returning customers.
- The ability to charge more (Peters, 1987).
- A more sustainable organization (thus able to plan more adventurously).

Implementing quality

Management commitment is the first, and essential, step towards establishing a quality culture. But even within a working unit, like a marketing/front of house/box office department, or a gallery press office, useful progress can be made which can then be used as an exemplar to convince the organization at large of the benefits of quality.

The process begins by exploring anew the nature of customers and researching their requirements. The research could be as simple as putting yourself in the customer's shoes and visiting a gallery as if for the first time. Dividing the experience into a sequence of events allows them to be rated as satisfactory or otherwise. Alternatively, a marketing department within a large organization might want to examine the service it provided its internal customers. In this case an interview with a contact in another department (for example, in a theatre, finance or production) would take place to diagnose strengths and weaknesses. There are no shortage of customers, internal or external, for anyone working in a service industry. The selection of those to work on first should be dictated by the organization's own priorities.

Having diagnosed the agenda for improvement, with an idea of the gap between the current situation (base line) and the desired result, the department then finds ways of implementing changes for greater effectiveness. These need to be tried, checked and then refined. Useful techniques in this process include:

- Brainstorming: generating ideas in a non-critical environment which are written down and later evaluated.
- Process flowcharting: mapping out the series of events that constitutes a particular service encounter (e.g. a gallery visit, or arranging a photocall).
- Listing forces 'for' and 'against' a proposed change: this can aid the choice of the most realistic alternative from a number of possible ways of working.
- Diagrams: like the product portfolio model discussed earlier, diagrams of situations (graphs, charts, tables) can force out assumptions and help share an appreciation of the problem.

The process not only has the advantage of improving service to the customer, but the internal communication it generates has an excellent effect on morale and the issues it raises are useful in developing the wider skills of the participants.

Quality circles

This idea, originally from Japan, has been introduced to a wide variety of western companies with great success. Its application is particularly appropriate to the arts because it aims to bring together people from throughout an organization in order to diagnose and remedy quality problems. Arts organizations like producing theatres have a large number of specialist departments who tend to have isolated perspectives. Joining members together in a group forces these perspectives together in a fruitful way. Circles meet at regular intervals to identify problems and chase progress on solutions. Of course their efforts have to be recognized and resourced by the organization as a whole, which is why the commitment of top level management is so important.

Benchmarking

The external focus which characterizes the marketing approach finds its 'quality' expression in this idea. The principle behind it is that organizations can become fixated on their own ideas of what is possible, and thus become complacent. In a competitive environment this will not do. So benchmarks are set with reference to the best organizations in the external environment and performance targets redirected accordingly.

As will be seen in Chapter 5, funding bodies have 'benchmarks' whereby they compare what they see as the value for money offered by the various clients they fund. Customers, too, will have benchmarks of service dimensions like responsiveness, friendliness and flexibility. A useful benchmark for a performing arts venue, following on from the earlier discussion of programme order quantities in this chapter, would be profit per programme in other venues of a similar size. Accessing such data is probably best done by approaching other organizations and offering to share information. This is one of the advantages of networking (of which more in Chapter 9).

Conclusion

'Product' is the foundation of the rest of the marketing mix. But in service industries in general, and the arts in particular, the product has a number of qualities which distinguish it from the physical products with which much marketing literature is concerned. Intangibility, inseparability, heterogeneity and perishability all distinguish services. But to the arts experience we can add the dimension of 'communication'.

This informs our ideas about how to analyse and enhance the experience of the arts. The core benefit is surrounded by layers of features and extensions, each of which can be tailored to enhance the offering in terms of environment or delivery. As to the artistic experience itself, it is co-produced with the customer, making it akin to an act of communication. Communication models, therefore, have a special role in helping us to think about what we are marketing.

Like any other product, arts offerings have lifecycles and are subject to technology and fashion. Planning a balanced portfolio is the key to maximizing audience satisfaction, and adapting product portfolio models to the arts can help understand and communicate the construction of a programme of work.

Ancillary products have a special importance in the service sector, and (depending on art form) they provide useful commercial opportunities. But they should be conceived in the context of enabling arts customers to enjoy the core experience of the arts more fully, and require careful purchasing and specification.

Innovation, while essential to the arts, needs to be skilfully facilitated by marketing. Rogers' model of the diffusion of innovation gives some insights into the nature of the audience's reaction to new work, and points to a tactical response targeting existing users in a special way.

Quality, which begins and ends with the customer, is a marketing issue of direct concern to every member of an arts organization. Each worker is implicated in the customer's experience (directly or indirectly), so practical measures to improve quality need to be as inclusive of the organization as possible. They need, above all else, the commitment not only of marketing but of the rest of senior management.

Keywords

Adoption
Ancillary product
BCG
Benchmarking
Brainstorming
Diffusion
Flowcharting

Heterogeneity
Hierarchy of Needs
Inseparability
Intangibles/Tangibles
Matrix
Need vs want
Newcomb's ABX model

Noise
Pareto effect
Perishability
Physical evidence
Product levels
Product lifecycle
Product portfolio
Quality

Quality circles
Redundancy
Self-actualization
ServQual
Servuction
Shannon and Weaver
Total quality management

Discussion questions

1 Marketing practitioners and theorists make a distinction between products and services. How important do you think this distinction is to customers?
2 List three ways in which the perceived risk of attending a new play can be reduced for a prospective customer.
3 Outline some of the practical problems facing a gallery trying to ascertain customer perceptions of the quality of its service.
4 Compare the role of innovation in a city-centre building-based repertory theatre with a rural community arts project. What might it mean for each organization's workers and customers?
5 Discuss the role of technology in extending the experience of the visual arts.
6 How might the marketing manager of a large touring orchestra approach the issue of total quality management in his or her organization?
7 Outline some methods of making arts attenders into 'better' customers. What mistakes might an organization make in this area?
8 What lessons (if any) might arts marketing learn from the management of innovation in the following areas: (a) fashion, (b) home entertainment, (c) publishing.

Action problems

1 Draw a 'levels of product' diagram for your organization's offering, and select one aspect each from the experienced, extended and potential levels for development.
2 Construct a product portfolio matrix for your organization and identify the flow of resources in the diagram. Are there any changes in policy that you would recommend as a result of this exercise, and why?
3 Establish three appropriate benchmarks for your department's performance. How will you select the best external company to compare your performance against in each area, and how will you access the necessary information?
4 Draw up a membership list for a quality circle in your organization. Is there anyone in the organization who should not be a member (and why)?

References

Andreasen, A. (1982). Non-profits: check your attention to customers. *Harvard Business Review*, May–June, 105–110.

Bateson, J. (1989). *Managing Services Marketing: Text and Readings*. Dryden Press.

Berry, L. (1981). The employee as customer. *Journal of Retail Banking*, **III**, 1, 33–40.

Carman, J. M. and Langeard E. (1980). Growth strategies for service firms. In Bateson, (1989) *Managing Services Marketing*, Dryden Press, 445–459.

Greer, G. (1994). Why don't women buy CDs? *BBC Music Magazine*, September, 35–37.

Fiske, J. (1989). *Introduction to Communication Studies*. Routledge.

Francis, J. (1990). *Attitudes Among Britain's Black Community Towards Attendance at Arts, Cultural and Entertainment Events: A Qualitative Research Study*. Prepared for the Arts Council of Great Britain, London: Networking Public Relations Limited.

Hutchinson, J. (1993). Leaflet accompanying Gunther Förg exhibition, Douglas Hyde Gallery, Dublin, July/August.

Kemp, L. (1993). It's the real thing – or is it? *BBC Music Magazine*, March, 26–30.

Kotler, P. and Andreasen, A. (1991). *Strategic Marketing for Non-Profit Organisations*. Prentice Hall.

Levitt, T. (1969). *The Marketing Mode*. McGraw Hill.

Lingeard, E., Bateson, J., Lovelock, C. and Eiglier, P. (1981). *Marketing of Services: New Insights from Consumers and Managers*. 81–104, Marketing Sciences Institute.

McCarthy, J. E. (1960). *Basic Marketing: A Managerial Approach*. Irwin.

Maslow, A. (1954). *Motivation and Personality*. Harper & Row.

Morison, B. and Dalgleish, J.G. (1987). *Waiting in the Wings: A Larger Audience for the Arts and How to Develop It*. ACA Books.

Munroe-Faure, L. and Munro-Faure, M. (1992). *Implementing Total Quality Management*. Financial Times/Pitman Publishing.

Murdin, L. (1994). It's important you don't pander to the lowest common denominator . . . *Arts Management Weekly*, 1 December, 2–3.

Peters, T. (1987). *Thriving on Chaos*. Knopf.

Parasuraman, A., Zeithaml, V.A. and Berry, L.L. (1985). A conceptual model of service quality and its implications for future research. *Journal of Marketing*, Fall, **49**, 41–50.

Pick, J. (1986). *Managing the Arts? The British Experience*. Rhinegold.

Rogers, E. (1962). *Diffusion of Innovations*. Free Press.

Shannon, C. and Weaver, W. (1949). *The Mathematical Theory of Communication*. University of Illinois Press.

Zikmund, W.G. and D'Amico, M. (1993). *Marketing*. West Publishing.

5 Pricing and income generation

Introduction

Generation of income is an essential function for all arts organizations. There are four main sources for this:

- Box office sales.
- Sales revenues from related activities, catering and merchandising.
- Public subsidy.
- Sponsorship and development income.

The third and fourth, income from funding bodies, sponsors and development (sometimes misleadingly referred to as 'unearned income'), are considered at a later stage in the chapter. It is the first two categories that lend themselves most obviously to marketing strategies in terms of pricing policy. But even the third and fourth sorts of income source involve customers (be they individual or organizational) exchanging value for benefits of one sort or another. So, even in the area of 'unearned' income, the arts organization needs both to examine what is being exchanged, and to determine the appropriate value to be exacted in the marketplace.

Among the issues examined in this chapter are:

- Pricing services.
- Influences on pricing strategy.
- Market position.
- Price competition.
- Break-even analysis.
- Price setting.
- Accessing public subsidy.
- Attracting sponsorship.

Pricing policies will play a major role in determining the level of sales revenue. Prices affect demand. Economic theory suggests a simple trade-off; as prices increase, demand falls. In practice, the relationship between price and demand is much more complex.

Ticket opportunities for new opera audiences

One of the problems facing Nicholas Payne as the new Director of the Royal Opera in 1993 was the widespread perception of Covent Garden as a place for the financially elite. Journalists tend to focus only on the top prices commanded by a limited number of seats on special occasions. The enormous number of reasonably-priced amphitheatre seats, boasting a famous acoustic and clear sight-lines, go unsung. Payne's reaction was to announce a series of 'Saturday specials' when the normal pricing structure (£5–£118) was replaced by tickets ranging from £1.50 to £20. The new prices actively targeted students, UB40 holders, young people and people on income support.

'Saturday specials' can allow the ROH to access a wider range of publics. But its standard pricing policy lets those sections of society who can afford to pay more do so. Also, pricing some productions at higher levels than others can create artistic flexibility.

Why have differences in price?

Prices imply quality levels. In markets where quality is at a premium such as luxury goods or gifts, the normal relationship between price and demand disappears. Cheap champagnes will not necessarily outsell more expensive alternatives. Similarly the cheapest seats in a theatre are not always the first to be sold. What matters in both markets is value as perceived by the customer, and price levels may be a way of communicating this.

Pricing policies can also give arts customers a greater sense of control over their purchases, and a benchmark for comparison with previous experiences. Research on pricing at arts centres in Wales carried out for the Welsh Arts Council (Marplan, 1988) suggests that arts attenders appreciate a range of prices from which to choose. Respondents indicated that they preferred a choice of prices in order to be able to get the 'best value' seats, usually seen as the second-highest or middle price bracket. Only one per cent of respondents cited high prices as a reason for not attending arts events in this survey.

A further fundamental effect of pricing policy is to split the market into different segments; with the possible consequence of denying access to particular groups.

Pricing plays a complex role which links many other marketing mix decisions being made in an organization. In spite of the fact that it is the easiest of the four marketing mix variables with which to tinker in the short term, price should never be dismissed as merely tactical. It is a strategic variable, and getting it wrong not only jeopardizes an organization's income optimization, but also confuses each of the other components of the marketing mix.

The purpose of this chapter is to examine the nature and role of pricing in an arts environment. Key influences on pricing policies are examined, before a more detailed study of tactical pricing decisions is made. The main bases for price setting are considered and the practical implications of pricing strategy are explored. The final section considers non-sales revenues and some of the marketing strategies that can be used to maximize returns from other sources.

The nature of pricing decisions

If price is designed to reflect the value that customers place on something offered for sale, then arts organizations are facing a diverse range of pricing decisions. Their customers place value on a number of tangible and less tangible aspects of what they offer.

Pricing intangibles, e.g. performance

The performance itself is the most obvious part of the product that is for sale, and potential audiences are willing to exchange money for tickets in the expectation of a programme of entertainment. It is a highly intangible benefit that they are buying. This is discussed at greater length in Chapter 4. The audience will have some preconceived ideas as to the likely nature of the experience but it is not until after the performance that they will be in a position to judge the value they gained for their money.

In this way arts organizations are facing the same pricing dilemmas as all service providers who have to price their output to meet customer expectations. They do not enjoy the luxury of being able to prove the quality and reliability of what they offer to their customers in advance of purchase. Therefore, to determine an acceptable price level, service providers must attempt first of all to assess the value customers placed on their previous experience of the service, as this will be a major determinant in customer perception of value.

Pricing semi-tangibles, e.g. programmes

A 'service-adjunct' item such as a programme appears more tangible. It is a piece of print that can be examined by the customer prior to purchase. However, like the performance itself, the quality of the programme cannot be assessed until it has been read, and thus here too the value will be judged retrospectively. The programme also serves as a souvenir of the performance, and will only have a value in that capacity if the performance itself is judged of merit.

Pricing tangibles, e.g. ice-creams

The pricing of tangibles, such as confectionery and drinks, is in this respect an easier exercise. Customers can gauge value for money with these items before purchase and make direct comparisons with the prices of competing products. However, within the confines of a theatre building, usually there are not opportunities to purchase from competitors. Customers are, in truth, a captive audience. Price setting is a matter of ensuring that the product is seen to represent reasonable value for money in the context of its presentation.

Premium price can be justified here by the 'added value' provided by quality, service attributes and convenience. Theatres often provide niche distribution opportunities for small but luxurious ice-cream or confectionery brands which are unavailable elsewhere. This serves to reduce the danger of comparison with much cheaper mass-market brands available in large cinema chains and supermarkets, and heightens the exclusive sense of 'treat' quality available to the consumer.

This, of course, is not the whole story. Whether pricing tangible goods or intangible services, organizations have to look at the financial implications of their decisions. Some segments of their markets will have greater willingness and ability to pay than others. As we have seen the value of some products and services is enhanced by the context in which they are being sold. Price is a major indicator of quality and will itself create expectations amongst customers.

The basic principle of pricing, to reflect the value of the product or service, applies universally. The way in which this value is assessed creates differences between industries. Managers in the arts are faced with the task of creating and implementing pricing policies which will encourage demand for their services, generate revenue to help cover their costs and yet also meet other artistic and social objectives which may not be as explicit in other fields.

Influences on pricing strategy

In a classic account of theatre pricing, Jules Boardman (1978) categorizes five main influences on pricing. He lists:

- The auditorium itself.
- The product on stage.
- The market (existing and potential customer types).
- The box office (the 'human' element of ticket sales).
- The budget (imposed financial targets).

These five factors together he considers as key constraints on pricing decisions. Such an analysis could be adapted for museums or galleries.

A more proactive approach focuses instead not on constraints but on what an organization wants to achieve. Viewed in this light, pricing decisions have to be made at two levels, strategic and tactical. In this section we will concentrate on the strategic level, laying a foundation for implementation and tactics to be discussed later in the chapter.

Arts organizations have to decide upon a general strategic approach to their pricing decisions which is commensurate with their objectives, the position they wish to hold in the market, the composition of that market and the nature and strength of their competitors.

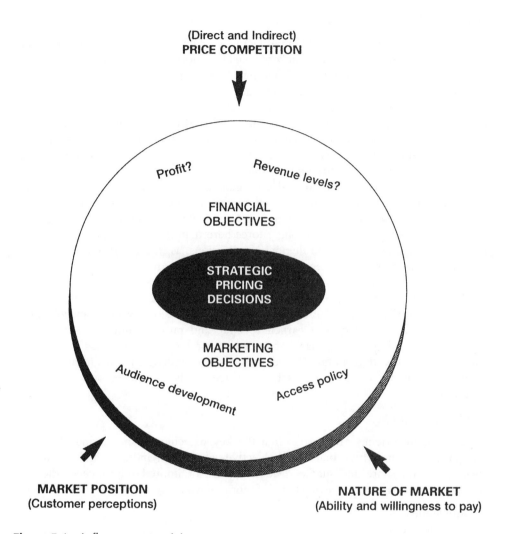

Figure 5.1   Influences on pricing strategy

Objectives

Arts organizations are characterized by diverse objectives. Whilst industry and commerce are driven by their requirement to provide financial returns to shareholders, the mission of many arts organizations is broader than this. A number of potentially conflicting financial and marketing objectives need to be considered in formulating pricing strategies.

Financial objectives

The profit motive may be an influential factor in pricing decisions in some sectors of the arts. In the commercial arts, backers finance performances in anticipation of box office success and financial returns. Therefore West End theatres set prices which are sufficiently high to cover costs and generate a profit margin. Failing to do so may lead to backers withdrawing their support. However, many commercial venues are indirectly in receipt of subsidy by receiving subsidized productions into their theatre. Similarly, commercial production companies benefit by touring to subsidized venues. Therefore, both of these types of profit-driven organizations have to have regard for wider issues than merely return on investment.

Pricing in the amateur arts may also be guided by the profit motive. Any profits generated by a production will be used to finance the next. More commonly in amateur and community arts, the focus is not on profit but simply on covering costs. Internal influences may exert a stronger force here than in professional organizations. All the cast may be involved in democratic decisions, as in a co-operative. This can lead to internal conflict between the desire for short-term returns and the longer-term interests of the company.

The subsidized sector by its very nature does not expect earned income to cover all the costs of the company. Financial objectives will be set by the management to ensure that the combination of earned revenue and public funding is sufficient to cover costs. Funding bodies may even set explicit targets. They may require, for example, that a theatre generates 55 per cent of its revenue itself. This means that the theatre must make a judgement as to the price levels and ticket sales which will achieve this.

Marketing objectives

An appropriate pricing strategy is often the key to achieving marketing objectives. The kinds of competitive marketing objectives evident in industry and commerce, such as market share and market leadership, are of limited relevance to the arts. Specific marketing objectives which are of more relevance relate to:

- Core audiences.
- New audiences.
- Access policy.

Marketing involves developing long-term relationships founded on mutual benefit, and arts marketing is no exception. A core audience needs to be developed, in the hope of gaining repeat business. In order to do this, a company might decide not to maximize profit on a particularly popular event for fear of alienating key audiences in the longer-term. It may also offer incentives for loyalty by making discounts available to regular attenders, the most prevalent of which is based on the idea of subscription (dealt with later in the chapter).

Alongside this core audience focus is the equally urgent need to develop new audiences. This may be to attract new attenders or to recruit existing attenders to a new type of art form, or performance of minority appeal. Under these circumstances the task of the marketing function is to build audiences rather than maximize revenue. From the customer's viewpoint, buying a ticket is a high-risk purchase as there is relatively little evidence upon which to judge its expected value. Therefore ticket prices will have to be relatively low to attract these audiences and lessen the financial risk for them. A range of prices that allows customers to trade up or down according to the perceived risk of the performance is another useful tool for audience development.

In the subsidized sector, one of the purposes of public funding is to offer cultural opportunities as widely as possible in the community. For this reason, prices are set to permit audiences, regardless of their financial status, to participate in the arts. There is, therefore, a latent conflict between access objectives and income optimization which forms a constant ideological backdrop to ticket pricing. Prices of peripherals, such as catering and programmes, may be increased faster than ticket prices as these in themselves do not deny access to the core product.

Market position

Market position relates to the perceptions of an organization held by its customers and potential customers. Price can be a determining factor in creating these perceptions, and conversely, the perceptions held about an organization can limit its pricing flexibility.

High-profile, high-status venues and companies are expected to charge high prices. Part of the pleasure experienced by the audience derives from the exclusivity of the event, and high price is the main factor which creates this exclusivity. To charge lower prices would devalue the experience. To avoid the charge of elitism which might lose them public subsidy, high-cost art forms like opera and dance companies do 'outreach' work which, by segmenting their market, allows them to offer wider access without sacrificing their premium price position.

On the other hand, if an organization is perceived to be offering lower quality, whether in terms of environment or performance, the opportunities for selling high-price tickets are limited. This is particularly problematic for amateur companies. Regardless of their levels of expertise or the costs they incur in staging a performance, there is a relatively low ceiling on the ticket prices that their audiences will be willing to pay.

Nature of the market

When making pricing decisions managers have to assess the importance of price to their target markets. The nature of the target market will determine not only ability but also willingness to pay certain price levels, as in the following situations:

Commercial venues The commercial theatre in London, for example, attracts audiences who are relatively price insensitive. Foreign tourists, who may have spent many

Box 5.1
Legislation increases price sensitivity
The 1988 Education Reform Act prevents schools from continuing to charge parents for ancillary educational activity such as trips or outings to the theatre. Hence the charge falls on the school budget, although parents can make a voluntary contribution. This change has increased the price sensitivity of this particular market. The threat to professional companies offers an opportunity to amateurs to price aggressively, for example, for the annual Christmas pantomime.

hundreds of pounds physically getting to the UK, may consider the price of a ticket to be a relatively small outlay in their total purchasing and accept price levels that may be considered to be quite steep by the average domestic audience. Furthermore, UK ticket prices tend to be considerably less than those in continental Europe or North America, making the arts a bargain for the foreign visitor.

Regional venues   Regional markets may not support the price levels accepted in major cities. Touring companies may provide identical performances in different venues and locations, but pricing will be at different levels to meet the expectations of the local markets.

Amateur events   The market for amateur performances may consist largely of friends and family of the performers. Their primary reason for attending may be quite unrelated to the nature of the performance. They are paying not for the cultural experience, but rather to support the cast. Because the performance itself may have limited value to them, the pricing task involves assessing the value placed on giving this support. Price levels which are set too high may restrict audiences to a loyal core, alienating more peripheral supporters.

Educational market   The market for educational art forms tends to be more price sensitive than the market for arts entertainment. The high costs involved for example in mounting large-cast Shakespearian productions, might suggest the same price per ticket as a musical. However experience shows that the market will not bear that price level. The schools market is an important sub-segment with a particular interest in less popular art forms, but they are one of the most price sensitive segments of all.

Competition

In formulating a pricing strategy it is important to be aware of competitive prices. However, for most arts organizations, competition is difficult to define, so the influence of competitor prices on pricing strategy will be limited.

The situation is complicated by a number of factors:

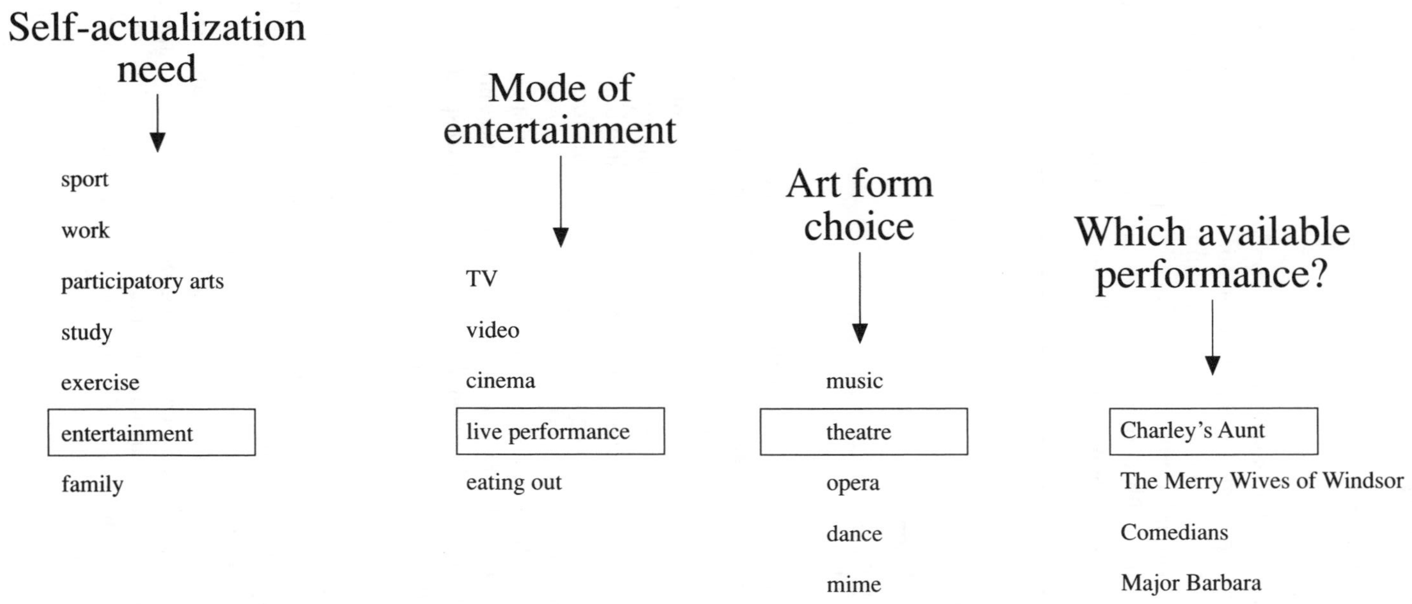

Self-actualization
need

→

sport

work

participatory arts

study

exercise

| entertainment |

family

Mode of
entertainment

→

TV

video

cinema

| live performance |

eating out

Art form
choice

→

music

| theatre |

opera

dance

mime

Which available
performance?

→

| Charley's Aunt |

The Merry Wives of Windsor

Comedians

Major Barbara

Figure 5.2 Competition facing a performing arts venue. Adapted from Kotler and Andreason (1991)

Box 5.2
Rights to perform
In the case of work that is still subject to copyright restrictions, the obtaining of a licence to perform the piece automatically prevents a rival company from performing it simultaneously. There can be both geographical and time restrictions. Amateur companies, as much as professional ones, need to ensure compliance with copyright law. It is always advisable to consult the publishers at an early stage. The usual level of royalties, where they are payable, is 10 per cent of the net box office.

- Similar venues.
- Market segmentation.
- Product differentiation.
- Substitute activities.
- Internal competition.

Museums, for example, may consider the prices charged by other museums in their region. This may be appropriate up to a point, in that the quality of the facilities at the different venues will be a factor influencing customer perceptions of value. There are however factors mitigating against the direct influence of competition between arts organizations, at least in the professional sector. The first is the reluctance of local authority funders to replicate provision. This leads inevitably to a segmenting of the market as neighbouring venues specialize in different art forms.

Secondly, on any given night, the potential audience may be choosing between a performance by the Royal Ballet at one venue and a monologue by a well-known actor at another. Similarly, two adjacent galleries may be showing respectively a multimedia experimental exhibition and a Victorian retrospective. In this respect there is little justification for price comparison.

Only if two similar performances are simultaneously staged by two companies or orchestras of similar artistic status at similar venues in the same region are competitor price levels likely to have a major impact on ticket sales.

Although general price levels within the industry will set a framework for customer price expectations, for the several reasons discussed above, pricing strategy is remarkably free from competitive constraints in the arts.

More importantly, competition takes the form of substitute activities such as watching TV, going to the cinema or going out for a meal. As the price of these substitutes may range from virtually nothing for watching TV, to an indefinable amount for eating out, the practical influence of substitute prices on pricing for arts activities will be limited.

Finally, competition can be found internally, in venues with more than one auditorium. The management may wish to price each performance space equally, if they are considered of equal artistic status. Nevertheless, the public may persist in

> Box 5.3
> **Substitute pricing in crafts marketing**
> When advising clients on pricing policy, we have to look at the competition created by companies like Habitat, and the craft items they sell, and their pricing levels will be one of the influences we consider. But we deal with the artists, who set the prices themselves, and they may not feel this is such a meaningful comparison.
>
> Liza Stevens, Marketing Consultant

valuing one space over another (on a 'Main House'/'Studio' model). Effectively this may force the management to differentiate its product (and price) in a way which the audience demands, thus reducing internal competition.

Implementing a pricing strategy

Implementing an overall pricing strategy requires managers to set prices which will meet the objectives of their organization within the constraints imposed by market and competitive factors.

The performing arts environment poses peculiar problems here. Traditionally, marketing theorists have seen the three elements of competition, demand and cost as the key influences on pricing (Kotler, 1980). As we have seen, competition in the arts is untypical of the wider marketing experience. This is also the case with costs and demand. Yet a balance still needs to be struck between internal (cost-based) and external (demand-based) factors in operational pricing decisions for the arts.

Cost-based pricing

Regardless of their specific financial targets, all organizations will set prices sufficient at least to cover costs. The extent of the costs covered can vary from one type of business to another. Costs can be classified in two ways. Fixed costs do not vary with the volume of activity, and are made up of central overheads and other indirect expenses of the business. Variable, or 'direct', costs relate directly to the activity of the business, and vary according to the volume of sales. Figure 5.3 illustrates the relationship between fixed and variable costs, revenue, and profit or loss.

For much activity in the performing arts, there is no correlation between variable revenues and variable costs. A large musical, that costs a lot to mount, will probably do well at the box office but, as we have seen above, the same will not necessarily be true of a Shakespearian tragedy. Conversely, a 'two-hander' such as Willy Russell's *Educating Rita* has rescued many a repertory season by performing well at the box

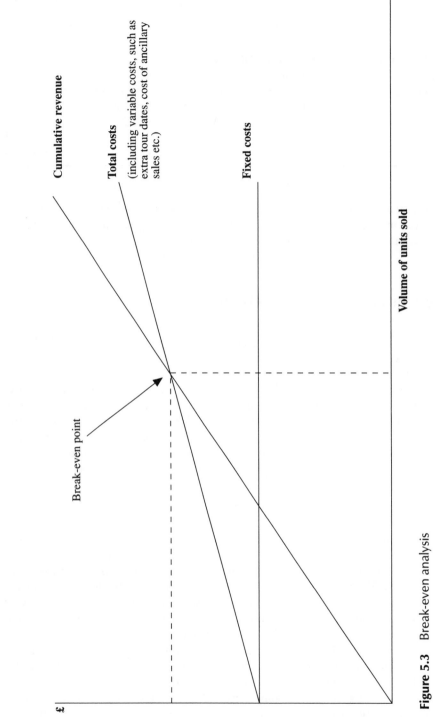

Figure 5.3 Break-even analysis

Box 5.4
Break-even analysis
In a traditional manufacturing industry a technique called 'break-even' analysis can be used to help identify the level at which the price covers the costs. The formula for calculating the break-even point is as follows:

$$\text{Break-even point} = \frac{\text{Fixed cost}}{\text{Price–Variable cost}}$$

In accountancy terms, the lower line of the equation is the gross profit; and the break-even point comes when the gross profit equals, but does not exceed, indirect costs.

Break-even theory assumes a direct relationship between sales and direct costs. If you sell less, then the cost of materials will fall because you will manufacture less. As we shall see, break-even analysis does not generally assist in the costing of arts activity for pricing purposes

office as well as being relatively cheap to mount. Box office ticket prices are usually fixed for a season, so an increase in costs cannot necessarily be recovered in the price charged. The same play can vary enormously in its costs from one production to another, depending on the artistic concept and the lavishness of the sets.

For that reason, performances are rarely costed individually for pricing purposes. Most professional arts companies would tend to budget across a full season. The factors involved in this are considered in Box 5.5.

A cost-based approach to price setting has many limitations. It may be appropriate in industries where customer needs are undifferentiated and competitive activity is intense. In these circumstances, customers will be fickle and consistently look for the best 'deal' in the market, so cost levels will impose a floor on the extent to which businesses can reduce their prices in a competitive battle. Most arts organizations face a very different competitive environment, and whilst break-even analysis may be a useful tool in setting a 'floor' for pricing decisions, it is unlikely to be the best starting point.

Demand-based pricing

Price setting based on customer and market characteristics gives far more scope to managers who are looking to maximize their trading revenues. By assessing the value that the customer places on a product or service, a demand-based approach attempts to set prices according to what the market will bear rather than the costs incurred in providing the product or service. In theory, as the customer is buying benefits which are both tangible and intangible, costs may have little relevance. The price of a painting, for example, is unlikely to be based on the cost of canvas and acrylics.

Box 5.5

Factors in costing repertory productions

Subsidy	Includes all funding from local or regional sources, grants, etc.
Fixed costs	Also called overheads, including administration, marketing, premises and equipment
Contribution	Any shortfall between subsidy and fixed costs will have to be funded from net earnings
Variable income:	
Box office	Estimated income per show after allowing for VAT, royalties, discounts and free tickets. Percentage of total available seats.
Other income	Income from bar, programmes, ices etc. Moves with box office figure – small audiences will buy fewer programmes
Variable costs:	
Company	Actors, directors, designers
Production	Carpenters, paintshop, wardrobe, wigs, props
Staging	Stage crew, lighting, sound, flying, traps
Other	Musicians, fights, choreography, children

Pricing role-play for New York drama company
At New York University Performance Center:

Our price depended on the project brief, and I always knew our bottom-line. More important than the break-even was the customer's willingness to pay. But we managed to negotiate some very profitable deals – like the one with American Express telesales team (a drama-based training project). We didn't make much money on the Irish community play, but it led to a lot of business. We never actually lost money on anything.

Andy Iredale: Marketing Manager, The Creative Arts Team, New York University

The value audiences place on a theatre or concert ticket is likely to be a function of three main elements: the reputation of the performers, expectations of the performance itself and the nature of the venue.

Reputation of the performers   Popular artists and highly regarded companies or orchestras offer greater value to audiences. This may or may not be related to the actual quality of their performance. Higher price levels can be achieved simply on the reputation of the quality of the performers.

Audiences may consist of people ranging from the highly discerning to those with very little knowledge or understanding of the art form. The former group will be willing to pay for the pleasure of appreciating a quality performance whilst the latter may gain value from the fact that others rate the act in question. Their own perceived risk is reduced by the endorsement of others.

Expectations of the performance   Similarly, audiences will have expectations of the quality of a particular show. Whilst the value of a performance of an Oscar Wilde play or a well-known orchestral work can be to some extent assessed before a performance, a new work by a little-known writer is a much higher risk for the potential audience. In this case, price levels need to be set to overcome audience inertia and special incentives may be appropriate, as discussed later in this chapter.

Recent research commissioned by the Arts Council on pricing in the arts (Millward Brown, 1991) has revealed that 'price' ranks tenth in a list of twenty factors which people said they took into consideration when deciding whether to attend an arts event. Product-based attributes such as the level of entertainment expected or the subject matter of the performance weighed far more heavily in the equation than the price of the ticket itself. This general attitude was common to all socio-economic groups surveyed, including young people, unemployed people and infrequent attenders. The few respondents who did see price as a problem tended to be from higher rather than lower income groups.

Expectations of the performance, therefore, need to be well-founded in terms of what is on offer, and enhanced by the arts organization's investment in effective promotion. New work evidently provides a challenge here, which can only be addressed by careful analysis and targeted promotion of the benefits on offer. This approach should always take into account that financial price is only one aspect of a combination of considerations that the customer is offering in exchange for the benefits of live performance.

Nature of the venue   Part of the total experience being purchased by audiences is the ambience, location, comfort, prestige and size of the venue. However well respected an orchestra or touring company, the prices it can command in the market will be governed to some extent by the venue it uses for the performance. The venue can either add to or detract from the perceived value of the event and price levels must take this into account. The extent to which these factors can be related to increasing prices without deterring a disproportionate number of the potential audience is called 'price sensitivity'.

Price elasticity of demand

The price elasticity of demand is an economic concept which attempts to quantify price sensitivity. A market is defined as having elastic demand if a small increase in price leads to a large reduction in sales. This is a characteristic of highly competitive

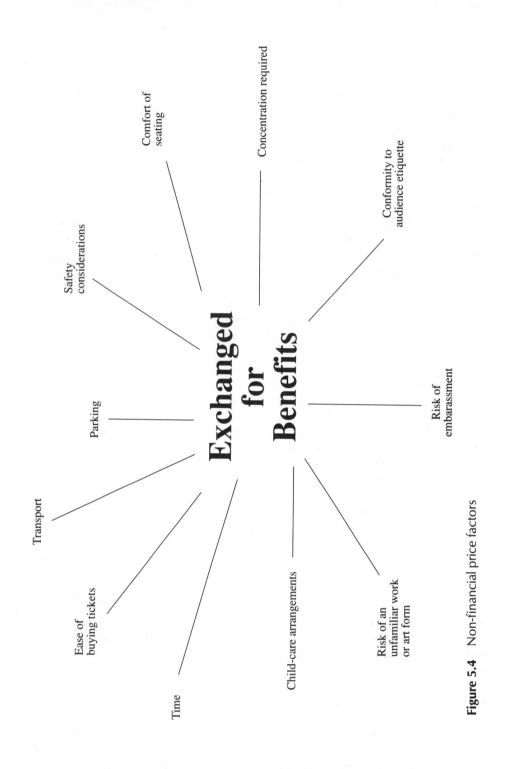

Figure 5.4 Non-financial price factors

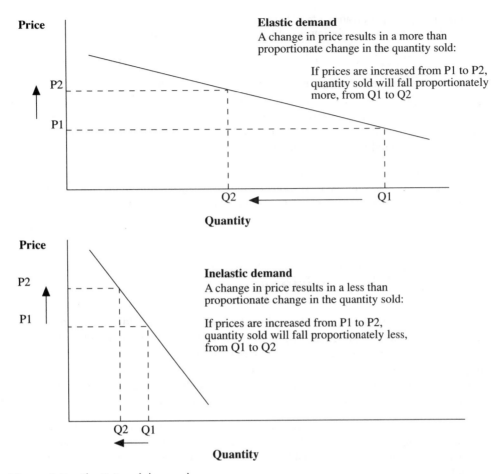

Figure 5.5   Elasticity of demand

markets, where product substitution by customers is common and products themselves have few distinctive features. As discussed earlier, this is not a market condition facing many arts organizations. Direct comparison with competitive offerings is very difficult in most sectors of the performing arts, so ticket prices are sensitive only to a limited extent.

This is even more so in the case of peripherals such as catering. As has been suggested earlier, at the point of wanting a drink or a snack, customers are faced with no alternative suppliers. During an interval they have a choice between consuming or not consuming, but choosing another provider is not an option. In this respect, the market in which price elasticity operates is unique to the arts organization itself.

A lot can be learned by comparing past performance to future expectations. Arts organizations therefore need to maximize their knowledge of the effects of price changes on attendance or peripheral sales in the past. Hugh Davidson, a leading marketing consultant, reflects that:

> Although pricing decisions often have to be taken quickly, the quality of decision making can be enormously improved by taking a hard look at the price dynamics of a market beforehand.
>
> (Davidson, 1984: 232)

A lot can be learned through box office records or sales returns in other areas. A scientific approach is the best guarantee of objectivity in what can frequently be a highly-charged, but not very well-informed debate. Little, however, has changed in the arts since the following observation (about the related area of pricing in local authority sports facilities) was made in the late 1970s:

> There is an urgent need for research into the price elasticity of demand for recreational pursuits, particularly for the recreationally underprivileged. Political decisions are often made at the local level on the basis of certain assumptions about price sensitivity which may or may not be entirely relevant.
>
> (Cowell and Henry, 1977)

Tactical pricing decisions

A number of useful tactics can be employed which recognize additional factors which influence audiences' willingness to pay. In spite of the relative inelasticity of demand which has been observed in pricing research in the arts, these tactics can play an important role in helping to demystify and extend the arts experience. This role has been clearly identified in the National Arts and Media Strategy debate setting out a direction for the arts in Britain towards the end of the century:

> What is needed is a planned programme of offers and concessionary ticket prices, carefully targeted and backed up by programmes of education, outreach, venue development (where appropriate) and marketing, designed to broaden the social and economic mix of audiences and visitors.
>
> (NAMS, 1992: 53)

Among the pricing tactics that can be employed by arts organizations can be included:

- Price structures, to include:
    - seat location.
    - times of opening or performance.
- Unit pricing.
- Concessions and discounts.
- Subscription.
- Psychological pricing.

These tactics are most readily understood in the context of a policy of 'price discrimination' which results in some groups of buyers paying different prices from others. This is based on the principle of market segmentation, as discussed in Chapter

2, which asserts that different parts of a market have different needs and expectations from others, and that service providers can meet the needs of their total market best by concentrating on the needs of the individual segments rather than approaching the market as a single entity. Price discrimination recognizes that different groups of buyers value products and services differently.

Price structures

These create a system whereby different prices are charged according to the characteristics of the performance and other aspects of the service. A number of criteria are commonly used to determine price structures:

Seat location and comfort   Seats with particularly good visibility or legroom are of great value to certain sectors of the audience. Those for whom a visit to a theatre or concert is driven by a need to impress another, such as a corporate client or a new girlfriend or boyfriend, will be happy to pay extra for the privilege. Conversely, those on low incomes whose motivation for attending is a love of a particular art form may be delighted to find a low-price ticket in the gods, or an affordable restricted view seat. Despite a sometimes impeded view, theatre boxes remain popular and can command relatively high prices as they enable a more communal arts experience for small groups of friends and associates.

Time of opening or performance   People value their leisure time more highly at certain times than others. Weekend evenings are traditionally popular times for entertainment and audiences are generally willing to pay more for the privilege of being able to attend a performance and not have to go to work in the morning. Price setters are faced with a relatively price-insensitive market and are able to charge premium prices at peak times without a significant reduction in demand.

This form of price discrimination can be used as a tool for managing demand and encouraging attendance at less popular times. Matinees are a good example of this. Only a limited proportion of the total potential audience is available during the afternoons, so prices are generally set lower than at other times. The aim is to persuade this group to attend at this time, rather than occupy prime-time seats. Some access considerations can be satisfied, without conflict with the organizational aim of maximizing profit. A fuller discussion of this is included in Chapter 7.

Unit pricing

A unit pricing approach makes no concessions and provides very limited pricing structures. A successful recent example is the BBC Symphony Orchestra's season on the South Bank which priced all seats in the house at £9. The theory behind this approach is that audiences will be encouraged to book early to get the best seats. Seats that are left towards the end of a booking period, shortly before a performance, will be those which are poorly positioned or at less desirable times. Indeed, the late booker may be faced with having to pay more than would normally be the case for seats at some distance from the stage.

Unit pricing may be attractive in that it encourages early commitment to tickets, thereby helping cashflow, but in practice it has some drawbacks. It means that the wealthy pay as little as those on low incomes. It may also be that quality of seating is not a sufficiently strong inducement for most people to override the uncertainty attached to early commitment to ticket purchase. Ticket buying in most performing arts situations is becoming later and later, arguably because today's arts consumers are less certain of being free on a specific occasion than their more leisured predecessors. Those members of the audience for whom a well-placed seat is important (whether due to a desire to enjoy a performance at its best or a wish to impress a friend or colleague) may not be the first in the ticket queue. Faced with the prospect of an inferior seat, they may choose not to purchase a ticket at all.

Concessions and discounting

Concession schemes differentiate prices, not on the basis of features of the service, but on the basis of the characteristics of the potential customers. Inevitably this is bound up with the strategic policy on access which arts organizations see as part of their brief. At the same time, this type of scheme is well suited to many service providers whose products are perishable. In the case of the theatre, if the curtain goes up and a seat is not filled, the opportunity for income from that seat for that performance is lost forever.

Concession structures tend to provide reductions for the elderly, for the unwaged, for students and for children. If standard price levels were charged, these groups might be unable to afford tickets, so this practice fits in with a corporate access policy as well as generating income from otherwise empty seats. Concession schemes are not, however, universally popular. It is argued that pricing policy should not be based on the assumption that everyone is hard up:

> The mistake which is sometimes made is to behave as though the whole community cannot afford to pay our prices and so to keep prices far below the level of general public acceptance.
>
> (Diggle, 1984)

In practice, however, it tends to be the case that some 'concessionary' groups such as unemployed people or frail elderly people tend to be less inclined to arts attendance than others such as students. This disinclination may have more to do with social class and physical mobility than with price resistance. If this were so, then the seeming cost of having a thriving access policy expressed in generous concessions might in reality prove an investment. It suggests that the conflict between access objectives and income maximization is less real than apparent. One might even argue that the treatment of students and young people, one of the largest concessionary groups in most theatres' experience, is akin to the use of 'loss leaders' in a supermarket. Present revenue is sacrificed in the expectation of future returns, as they develop a theatre-going habit.

In this respect their treatment is more to do with 'discounting' than with 'concessions'. Concessionary pricing is dictated by strategic considerations of access and equality of opportunity. Discounts, on the other hand, are a mechanism for improving perceived value to potential customers. Discounts can be used tactically to achieve a number of objectives. Popular methods of discounting in the arts are through subscription schemes, group bookings, late availability bargains and previews.

Subscription

As a method of encouraging forward buying of a product or service, subscription schemes have been in existence for hundreds of years. In the arts they grew in popularity in the UK in the 1970s, following a tour of seminars by the American Danny Newman highlighting subscription as an ideal tool for audience building based on his book *Subscribe Now!* (1977).

Subscription works on the principle that the most difficult task for an arts organization is to make an initial contact with a potential buyer. Having made that contact, it is no more difficult to sell a package of tickets for a series of plays or concerts than it is to sell a single ticket. The cash-flow benefits of selling a series of tickets at the start of a season are quite significant but, perhaps more importantly, these schemes encourage attendance at less popular events and can dramatically improve box office takings for lesser known performances.

Discounting is an integral part of a subscription scheme. By offering reduced price tickets for a season arts organizations are providing a financial incentive for potential audiences to commit themselves to attending early on. By attending all the performances they can save amounts of money, so the psychological attractiveness of the discounts are considerable.

In practice, should subscribers fail to attend any performance in a given series, the real value of the discount is reduced. Also, if there are only one or two performances in a season which the subscriber really wants to see, he or she would have undoubtedly been better off paying full price for those particular events. This may account in part for the declining popularity of subscription schemes in UK theatre, though they remain popular with orchestras and concert halls. Subscription is a lifestyle choice. It implies a stability in leisure arrangements which may be increasingly anachronistic in the 1990s.

Group bookings

Arts organizations frequently offer discounts for group bookings in the same way that producers of more tangible products offer discounts for bulk purchases. A theatre or concert seat has no value after the event has taken place, so the prospect of filling a large number of seats at a price which at least contributes to overheads is a very attractive one. The value of a guaranteed audience to the organization is very high, so generous discounts may be offered to groups such as social clubs and school groups. In order not to detract from potential full-price revenue, these discounts may only apply to certain performances.

Special promotional discounts

The concept of 'price bundling' is useful in pricing services realistically (Guiltinian, 1987). This approach offers a package of related services at the same time to certain sorts of customers at a total price which is less than their prices purchased individually. In arts marketing this often takes the form of a combined theatre/meal ticket, in a package to include overnight accommodation in a nearby hotel. This is especially attractive where groups are involved, and can offer increased promotional opportunities to the enterprising organization.

Price promotion to groups can also involve identifying a speciality interest group and trying to attract them with a specific discount. This can be particularly useful for 'issue-based' material involving social or vocation-specific themes.

For limited seasons of mixed programme activity, cumulative discounts can be offered. These can either be based on simple ticket multiples (for example a voucher entitling attenders at the current performance to 'two for the price of one' at the next show), or they can be based on stepped percentage discounts. An example of the latter might be a discount offering 10 per cent on tickets for two shows booked at the same time, but 15 per cent discount on tickets for three shows booked at the same time. Vouchers, a flexible if potentially complex promotional medium, can be used to good effect here to target specific market segments.

Alternatively 'membership' schemes can be used to entitle regular attenders to buy discounted tickets on the strength of a yearly subscription. London's mixed-programme venue the Barbican Centre offers such a scheme to its mailing list members on payment of an annual fee. Similarly, the museums in Lancaster offer joint tickets for several attractions in Williamson Park and for the Maritime Museum.

Late availability discounts

Given the ephemeral value of a ticket, another form of discount offered by arts organizations is 'stand by' tickets. Heavily discounted tickets may be made available hours before a performance to attract the 'marginal' members of a potential audience who, were it not for the discounted ticket price, may be tempted to go to the cinema or the pub instead. Late availability discounts are a good mechanism for filling spare capacity and generating at least some extra revenue with few associated costs. This should be exploited systematically by linking it deliberately to access and audience development schemes. This avoids the danger that such discounts are seen as a form of 'dumping' unsaleable product, and therefore lose their effectiveness.

Previews

Performances in final rehearsal may be opened to the public at discounted rates under the title of 'previews'. The perceived value of a performance may be lower under these circumstances and ticket prices are reduced to recognize this. This too can offer access to targeted groups on lower incomes. For quality reasons, lower prices are deemed acceptable, and the opening night will be improved after the company have performed to a preview audience. For a particular group, however, the idea of seeing a performance before it is generally available will in itself have value of the kind discussed in the next section.

Psychological pricing

Consumer perception of value is not developed on entirely rational criteria. Whilst the attributes of a product or service are major factors in its evaluation, they do not fully explain price acceptability or sensitivity.

Price breaks

Consumer psychology has found that price breaks are very influential in purchase decision making. A price of £9.99 is perceived to be considerably cheaper than £10, whereas there is little perceived difference between, say, £9.44 and £9.45. Tickets could be priced with this principle in mind.

A number of additional factors should be taken into account. Firstly, the practice of pricing marginally below psychological price barriers has been firmly established amongst discount retailers. As a result, it has developed some negative associations in the minds of the public. Arts organizations need to be conscious of the image that this type of pricing practice may evoke. Slightly lower price breaks, such as £9.95 rather than £9.99, are thought to minimize this problem. It may even be possible that a price of £11.95 is more acceptable to the majority of arts consumers than the same ticket offered at £10.99.

On the other hand, there is the view that price points in the leisure/entertainment sector are somehow atypical:

> Pricing policies for leisure facilities are not the same as for most retail businesses. In most cases, the arrival of a customer at the facility means she/he is already committed to a visit . . . you will not lose custom if you charge £1 or £1.50 . . . rather than 99p or £1.49.
>
> (Craig, 1989: 88)

Furthermore, the extent to which price breaks are significant in ticket sales is questionable. Since most tickets are sold in multiples of at least two, the mathematics involved in calculating the final price a customer will have to pay will detract from the spontaneity of response to the psychologically acceptable price. By the time the final bill is added up the cost of an individual ticket may have lost its impact.

Finally, to price traded goods such as ice-creams and drinks in this way requires that all vendors are supplied with copious amounts of change. The more change that has to be given out, the longer the average transaction time. This may lead to longer queues and greater dissatisfaction than would be incurred by having to pay an extra penny.

Price/quality associations

We have already considered in discussing demand-based pricing how the perceived quality of a performance is a benchmark that can be used to help set price levels.

Conversely, having set the prices, we must now consider what effect pricing levels may have in forming new expectations in customers. Reluctance to price at a realistic level from the organization's point of view can lead to a downward spiral in the total quality of an organization's service level.

> There are further disadvantages to an 'across the board' low pricing policy. These revolve around the common (and, often correct) perception that low price equates with low quality. For many authorities and facilities this has been compounded by the ethos that facilities last a long time and have little need of renewing and upgrading ... Low prices and low quality facilities ... have meant low staff morale. This, in turn, leads very easily to low customer expectations.
>
> (Craig, 1989: 18)

There exists here an interesting price dilemma. If the arts venue prices too high it will alienate its market by not being seen to give value for money. On the other hand, if it prices too low it may fail to attract the less price sensitive segments of the market who equate price with quality. And for organizations in receipt of public subsidy, there is also the danger of risking funding from other sources. As we shall see, public subsidy carries with it some inherent contradictions in establishing pricing policies.

Income from other sources

There are a number of different forms of support available to arts organizations. They are included in this chapter because similar marketing decisions apply to these as to the more immediately obvious 'customers' of an arts organization, i.e. those who buy tickets or pay for admission.

To the funding bodies, it is the 'client organization' who is the customer in the relationship, because they exist in part to provide the service of grant allocation. However, any organization in receipt of funding needs to see their funding bodies as important stakeholders in the business, as 'customers' who are buying arts provision for their constituencies, rather than providing it directly.

Marketing exists where there is an exchange of benefits.

> Whether exchange actually takes place depends on whether the two parties can find terms of exchange that will leave them both better off (or at least not worse off) than before the exchange. This is the sense in which exchange is described as a value-creating process; that is, exchange normally leaves both parties with a sense of having gained something of value.
>
> (Kotler, 1980: 20)

This is a useful way of looking at the complex relationships that are developed by subsidized arts organizations with both public and private funders.

The Arts Council of Great Britain, the Crafts Council

Larger arts organizations receive funding from the Arts Council or, if appropriate, the Crafts Council. However, as described in Chapter 1, there have in recent years been moves to devolve funding as much as possible to regional arts boards.

Applications for funding at national level present some problems to a marketing department. Competition becomes a serious threat because funding bodies can draw comparisons with other organizations that might be deemed 'peers.' For example, quality and effectiveness might be measured using such performance indicators as ability to earn income, subsidy per seat and average attendance. As with all evaluation, care should be taken to ensure that data is compiled and interpreted in as consistent and credible a way as possible. Statistical returns, particularly from the box office, are often completed by relatively junior members of staff. It is important that significant variances from the norm are interpreted using techniques of marketing analysis.

National policy directions for the arts are discussed in Chapter 1. There are two particular strands to Arts Council policy that need highlighting with reference to income generation and pricing strategies. The first can best be illustrated by quoting from the ACGB stated objectives in its three-year plan 1990–1992: 'to enable as many people as possible to enjoy the arts; to demand the highest possible creative standards.'

Pricing decisions that restrict access, or programming decisions that consistently prefer a more popular product to a more innovatory one, may jeopardize subsidy. At times, it may seem that these two standards are mutually exclusive. As customer, a funding body will support those organizations that best satisfy its needs. As was suggested in Chapter 1, the potential conflict between excellence and access is best handled with balanced programming over time.

The second strand is concerned with the Arts Council's avowed aim to expand the arts economy:

> If there is to be further growth needed to meet public demand, new sources of funding will have to be found. More emphasis must be given to the principles of efficiency and self-reliance, to the improvement of trading income and to the use of public money to lever private money.
>
> (ACGB, 1989)

This point, about leverage, will be looked at again under the discussion of sponsorship.

The Arts Council is here implying that success in earning income will in itself be a criterion for assessing a successful organization, worth continued support. In practice, the ability to generate income from sources other than the public purse could well, in a climate of public spending cuts and restricted funds, lead to a cut in subsidy. An arts organization could become a victim of its own marketing success.

Furthermore, the pursuit in the public sector of what Gunn (1988) has called the 'five Es' of economy, efficiency, effectiveness, excellence and enterprise, though praiseworthy in themselves, have created an uneasy tension in the subsidized arts world between public-sector regulation and accountability on the one hand, and the new 'business' model on the other. It is from this latter context that the marketing ideas explored in this book are largely derived and, as we have seen with concepts such as competition, a private-sector framework does not always translate successfully.

Anthony Blackstock, who was Finance Director of the Arts Council in the Thatcherite years of the mid-1980s, believed you should 'talk to this government in a language it understands.' Hence the ACGB developed a range of initiatives such as 'Incentive Funding' and 'Percent for Art', which made available funds for very specific purposes and accessed through tightly controlled bidding procedures.

In the arts, as in health or education, the national policy makers support a culture of entrepreneurialism and partnership with the private sector. What is not clear is the extent to which future funding bodies will continue to support arts organizations through subsidy if success in the market economy results either in the generation of substantial profit, or an ideological clash with not-for-profit imperatives like universal access opportunity:

> In practice the public services manager will experience tension and clashes between, on the one hand, taking opportunities to exploit price differences in the economy provided by the ignorance of others, and, on the other, fulfilling the roles of public representative and public servant , offering equity of treatment, keeping the consumer informed, and, generally, proffering conduct tending to the welfare and advantage of the other.
>
> (Willcocks and Harrow, 1992: 63)

On 1 April 1994, the functions and responsibilities of the Arts Council of Great Britain were transferred to three successor bodies: the Arts Council of England, The Scottish Arts Council and the Arts Council of Wales. As the changes to the organizational structure of the funding bodies was not accompanied by any major injection of cash into the sector, it is unlikely that funds will become significantly easier to access. The marketing issue for an organization to address is how best to meet the needs of its funding body, by satisfying its diverse criteria for allocating subsidy.

Local authority funders

Much of the above discussion on the political context in which national funding allocations are made applies also at local government level. Local government arts policies vary according both to party politics and to the importance placed locally on arts provision in relation to other leisure funding, such as sport. A greater knowledge of the arts available locally can help influence change in policy at local level. Lobbying is important as a way of establishing price and value. Arts groups can increase local profile through civic nights and other invitations. This influence can extend beyond securing subsidy into having an input into local cultural policy, planning decisions and matters of civic importance.

Entrance fees or free entrance?

Cllr. Bernard Atha, Chair of Leeds Cultural Services:

> I personally would like to see entrance to all museums free of charge, but we had to introduce a fee some time ago to discourage people who abused the system. People were going into the city's museums on a regular basis and causing damage. However, we are also in the position where we have to raise money to keep the museum service going. We are already starting to draw more tourists to the city, and their numbers will increase once the Royal Armouries opens. This is good for the economy of the city and we need a strategy to make the most of this opportunity. The cultural life of Leeds is not just about the performing or visual arts, but concerns the whole fabric of social, creative and physical identity of the city.
>
> (*Yorkshire Post*, November 1993)

The tendency of local authority funders to segment the arts market has been discussed above (in the section on price competition). This can be complicated by the existence of different levels of local funding, at city and county level. These bodies may have conflicting priorities, and competition for public funds may be offered by a venue too far away to offer any competition for box office customers. Some subsidized theatres, such as York Theatre Royal, have very complex funding arrangements because of their catchment areas, which involve a patchwork of grants from rural councils alongside major contributions from City and County. These relatively small elements in recurrent funding, however, can make the marginal difference between surplus and deficit.

The theatre's part of this exchange process involves attention to promotion, product and, essentially, distribution variables: promotion in its attention to keeping closely in touch with the individuals who make and influence annual grant-making decisions; product in terms of considering the interests of a largely rural community in its programming decisions; and distribution in its tradition of a vigorous policy of community touring which regularly took the actors out of the 300-year-old Theatre Royal building and into remote rural village halls to reach an otherwise isolated audience.

Understanding the organizational equivalent of consumer purchasing behaviour is also an important part of the grant-seeker's analytical equipment when pricing their services to funding bodies. For example conflict can arise between the different funding priorities of separate political bodies at work in the same area. In West Yorkshire, for example, Leeds City Council funds Opera North direct, and also contributes (along with the local authorities in Bradford, Calderdale, Kirklees and Wakefield) to the West Yorkshire Grants Committee, which separately funds Opera North. For the WYGC, on the whole, the Leeds area is a lower priority than others because of its relative wealth, but Leeds can use leverage on the WYGC in order to redirect its priorities back to particular Leeds-based organizations (especially the unique opera company).

An understanding of the particular policies of the funding body helps to frame an appropriate grant application. It may also throw up an alternative source of funds. If, for example, the leisure services budget is fully committed, an application to the local education authority may obtain support for 'outreach' work in schools.

Regional arts boards

Since the Wilding report (1989) first proposed the establishment of regional arts boards there has been considerable change at ministerial level in the Office of Arts and Libraries, now the National Heritage ministry. It is difficult to predict how the relationship with the regional arts boards will develop for the organizations funded by them, until several years have passed and the national scene has stabilized.

Theoretically, the RABs should combine both the policy objectives committed to maintaining and developing arts provision of the ACGB, with the local knowledge and awareness found in local authority funders. There will also, increasingly, be a simplification of the whole maze of grant applications, as anticipated in the report:

> The multiplication of schemes also involves multiplying the processes which arts bodies and artists have to go through ... the burden on the multiple applicant can be out of all proportion to the size of the grants that follow.
>
> (Office of Arts and Libraries, 1989)

An analogy could be struck here with the idea of market segmentation. The segment in question must be large enough to justify the effort of treating it differently to other segments. The multiple grant applicant faces the frequent possibility that the segment of the shrinking or static grant market being targeted is simply not worth the time or resources involved. At best the cost to the organization is exhaustion, at worst distraction from its defined mission, as artistic personnel channel their energies into grant applications. There is the further danger that an organization's policies may begin to be dictated by current funding priorities rather than by its own vision, a sure recipe for eventual disaster.

Arguably the size of an organization should insulate it, to some extent, from this inefficiency trap. However, there is a danger in being among the largest client organizations. A level of subsidy that might appear reasonable among ten similar sized companies at national level can appear excessive at regional level; and it is an easy temptation to slice a few thousand off the largest awards, where resources are limited.

The various forms of public support, national and regional, differ from country to country. There is probably little national difference in the way arts practitioners will seek out funding from multiple sources to maximize their income. Figure 5.6 demonstrates the forms of public funding available in the Republic of Ireland, showing some interesting parallels with the UK system described above.

Box 5.6
New methods of allocating funds to the regions
In future, securing funding will not only depend on the success of the application you write, it may also depend on the success of the application your RAB writes. An RAB which doesn't get its bids approved will have to cut its spending somewhere. It is hard to predict at this stage how each RAB will approach the changes but the room for manoeuvre is limited.
C. King (1993). The acid test. *MAILOUT*, August/September

Business support

Partnership between the public and private sector, to the mutual benefit of each, has been a keynote in central government policy in Britain from the mid-1890s. It has led in the arts sector to some very fruitful relationships, whose benefits extend far beyond the financial returns; but it has also led to financial disaster for those arts organizations who were overconfident in the targets they set for income generation from sponsorship, especially as recession began to bite at the start of the 1990s.

Nevertheless, sponsorship is a growing source of support for the arts. Much of the credit for this must go to the Association for Business Sponsorship of the Arts, a national independent organization which has seen arts sponsorship in Britain grow from £600,000 in the year of its formation (1976) to an estimated £56 million in 1993 (Association for Business Sponsorship of the Arts, 1994). It administers the Business Sponsorship Incentive Scheme which uses money supplied by the government through the Department of National Heritage to match funds put up by approved sponsors. This can double the value of a first-time sponsor's support to an arts project. ABSA also performs an advocacy and training role to advance the idea of 'partnership culture' between business and the arts.

Sponsorship as a term is often used loosely to cover a number of different forms of income generation from the private sector. It is important to classify these separately, and understand the motivation behind them, to ensure that an appropriate marketing strategy is designed to acquire and maintain them.

Donations/gifts in kind

The straightforward gift is the most simple, though probably the most rare, form of sponsorship. It more usually applies to support obtained from trusts. Where companies give donations to arts bodies, it is usually as part of their public relations strategy. Their aim is to improve their image in the local community, especially that subsection of it that makes up their own workforce. Japanese companies, for example, use charitable giving in the local community as a way of establishing themselves as part of that community. An arts organization should be aware of opportunities for

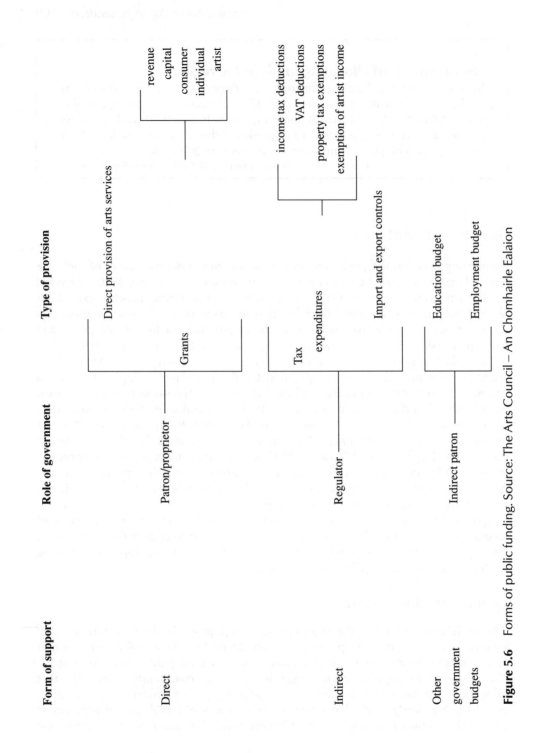

Form of support   **Role of government**   **Type of provision**

Direct — Patron/proprietor — Direct provision of arts services

Grants —
- revenue
- capital
- consumer
- individual
- artist

Indirect — Regulator — Tax expenditures —
- income tax deductions
- VAT deductions
- property tax exemptions
- exemption of artist income

Import and export controls

Other government budgets — Indirect patron —
- Education budget
- Employment budget

Figure 5.6 Forms of public funding. Source: The Arts Council – An Chomhairle Ealaíon

Imaginative Irish transport scheme
Since 1991, the Arts Council and Aer Lingus have collaborated in operating ARTFLIGHT – a scheme that offers opportunities to people working in the arts to travel outside Ireland. Creative artists and performers, managers, and production staff . . . will have satisfied the Arts Council that there is an artistic benefit to them and that their work as a whole will improve as a result of the award.
(The Arts Council – An Chomhairle Ealaion/Aer Lingus, from the scheme leaflet)

obtaining this kind of support from a local company with a particular PR problem with one of its publics.

Sponsorship

Sponsorship proper occurs when a company provides funds to support a particular activity, and in return wants to gain a number of publicity benefits. This is a straightforward exchange of benefits. The sponsorship money is likely to come out of the marketing promotion budget, and the sponsor may well want to make an appropriate tie-up to a particular service or product.

Sometimes this can be a felicitous arrangement. Thorntons, an independent confectionery company with a national network of its own retail outlets, has its headquarters in Belper near Derby. When Derby Playhouse approached it in 1986 for sponsorship of its Christmas show *Charlie and the Chocolate Factory*, a very successful deal was struck. For Thorntons a highly appropriate connection at a time of the year when sales (and competition) are at their most intense. And for Derby Playhouse, not only a sizeable injection of funds, but some excellent photo-opportunities when the cast of 'Oompah Loompahs' visited the factory and tried their hands at chocolate manufacture in the real world.

What may seem an appropriate connection to the arts organization is not always so apparent to the business, however. H.P. Bulmer are contacted as a matter of routine every time a regional repertory theatre mount a production of Laurie Lee's enormously popular play *Cider with Rosie*. They explain patiently that they position their cider brands as contemporary beverages, so the nostalgic atmosphere of the play would be entirely unsuitable.

Corporate entertainment

The third way a company can support a local arts organization is by membership of a corporate entertainment scheme. A premium price is paid for a personalized service that might include use of a private bar, priority booking and a 'free' programme. The money for this sort of activity will usually come out of the 'hospitality' budget, and the company will demand a high quality service, to impress visiting dignitaries, to woo a potential customer or to show an important supplier how she/he is valued. Some arts organizations provide different levels of corporate membership, a neat example of segmentation, although it is often hard to distinguish between the benefits offered.

Obtaining and maintaining corporate support

The same elements of the marketing mix that apply to customers in the box office apply to the corporate market. Price can be a key factor in achieving appropriate sponsorship. Perhaps the most important tactical decision here is the price/quality/value equation.

All forms of sponsorship represent a desire on the part of the sponsor to gain value by association with an activity or organization that is perceived as enjoyable, of cultural merit and highly visible. Therefore, if the arts body prices itself too low, the sponsor will value it accordingly. The association will not feel like a premium product.

In order to ensure that all organizations can find a form of sponsorship appropriate both to their objectives and to their budgets, many arts enterprises have developed a menu of 'products' priced as appropriate. This might include:

- Sponsorship of a series.
- An individual production, or exhibition.
- A single night.
- An educational project.
- A foyer or interval event.
- A full range of corporate memberships with different benefits.

The only limit here is that of the imagination. Derby Playhouse managed to get national tabloid publicity for its cheeky offer of a 'timeshare' in the dungeons of Nottingham Castle for its 1989 pantomime Robin Hood. On a more serious note, the Royal National Theatre launched a highly successful corporate membership package in 1989 aimed at three levels of 'investors'. Using a vocabulary borrowed from the nearby City of London, the RNT capitalized on the recent spate of privatizations by offering 'shares' in its success to companies in a position to benefit from a regular association with the theatre.

Such a scheme enables companies of different sizes and budgets to embark on an appropriate level of sponsorship by offering a number of entry points each with its specific benefit levels. The arts partner in each relationship is thus prevented from having to 'discount' and hence devalue the service provided.

As with all customers, the relationship with a sponsor should be seen as a long-term one. Research shows that sponsors themselves value the relationship over a period longer than that covered by the immediate sponsorship activity. This can be demonstrated by the willingness of many corporate sponsors to trade up or down in their activity in subsequent periods, for example by taking out corporate membership after a successful production sponsorship.

It is therefore important to be clear about the benefits the company is seeking, and to ensure that it receives them. The arts organization should ensure that:

- Unreal expectations (on, for example, the level of likely press coverage) should be discussed before rather than after the event.
- All activity associated with the sponsorship should be of high quality, catering, printed material and media activity.
- A high level of senior personal contact should be evident throughout.

Often the sponsorship will be the 'brainchild' of a particular enthusiast within the company, and he or she should gain personal satisfaction from being associated with a successful initiative. Such opinion leaders may advocate the arts organization not only in their employing organizations but also in their own professional or social networks.

After the event, 'positive stroking' should be maintained through a systematic process of evaluation and review. Regular contacts can take the shape of a sponsors' newsletter, press releases, and occasional invitations to new events.

In a highly sponsored organization there can be a variety of different companies involved in support of the same event. There may, for example, be a one-night sponsorship during the run of a sponsored concert series. The management concerned, using their knowledge of local competition, can address possible conflicts of interest before they arise. Just as the rules of television airtime sales prevent 'break sharing' (so that two beer brands, for example, could not appear in the same commercial break), so too the arts organization can adopt a policy of not allowing sponsorship by competing organizations, such as two national accountancy firms.

When such conflicts of interest arise, an understanding of the different needs of each organization can help the arts enterprise to segment its service, so that the sponsors can be negotiated into a position where they are prepared to co-operate. If, for example, a concert series sponsor is seeking widespread publicity for a product or service by associating its name and logo with all printed materials and posters throughout the season, while the one-night sponsor mainly wishes to host a prestigious evening for key clients, it should be possible to compromise sufficiently to satisfy both sets of objectives. The series sponsor could decide not to take up any seats on the night concerned. Equally, the one-night sponsor could agree to confine his publicity requirements to a programme over-wrap on the night, and a temporary foyer display about his firm.

Types of sponsorship: hidden benefits and hidden costs

The above discussion has assumed that sponsorship will always be available in the form of cash. It can be easier to accept payment 'in kind': the supply of a product that the arts organization wishes to acquire free of charge, or at a considerably reduced rate. This is more likely to be successful if it is a product that is not usually in demand in the charities sector. It is very difficult to get computers, for example, but relatively easier to get trees from a nursery to landscape the venue. So too it will be hard to get sponsorship in kind if the arts organization is a primary customer of the sponsoring company (such as theatres are for lighting equipment manufacturers)

Box 5.7

A price too high?

The value of 'sponsorship in kind' can be hard to fix, particularly in the case of a service that is provided free of charge. The company concerned may estimate the level of service as more useful than the arts organization, and hence set a higher value on it. A further risk of a service that is provided free of charge is that it will not be available at the appropriate time. The print deadline of a paying customer may, for example, override the publication of the 'sponsored' poster that supports the new season launch.

Another aspect of this is the difficulty for the arts organization in setting a value on tickets given free of charge to a sponsor. The arts organization will price them at the box office rate. The company receiving them may well value them less highly, arguing that not all the seats will be sold and therefore they cost nothing. A clear policy needs to be set on this from the start of the sponsorship negotiation. The ticket, the means of attending the performance, is the benefit offered by the arts organization in return for the sponsorship. It must not be devalued in the eyes of either the sponsor or future potential sponsors. Whatever the menu of sponsorship opportunities offered to the public, it should state the number of tickets included at that level; and that should be the number distributed. A discount can be offered for further purchases, but that should equate to the sorts of party booking discounts that are otherwise available.

unless it is perceived as a 'loss leader' gift to bring in a long-term relationship as supplier, for example, of electrical equipment and materials.

The benefit for the sponsor is that the cost of the sponsorship is limited to the cost of the goods. The benefit for the arts organization is the saving on the full price of the equipment.

One of the hidden benefits to sponsorship is the opportunity it offers for new audience development. A big local corporate sponsor will contain, in its workforce, a large number of the local community who form the potential audience of the arts organization for all its activity. A range of opportunities exists to combine new audience development with the generation of a sense of excitement about the sponsorship for the company. These might include:

- Special prices for employees.
- A special staff evening, with particular activities.
- Visits to the workplace by actors.
- Tours of the theatre.
- Attendance at an open rehearsal.

Linking new audience development activity to the human resource management policy of the sponsor company can help to foster a long-term relationship on a number of levels.

A second hidden benefit to sponsorship can be the production of high-quality promotional material, particularly display boards and photographs, that can be used in other contexts at a later date. The photograph of an 'opinion leader' in local industry participating in an event will not only provide publicity for that event, but can also be used to attract further corporate sponsors. The local council also will see such activity as part of the establishing of the area as a good 'business address', a place to which other businesses may wish to relocate because of the 'added value' factors. A report on *the Economic Importance of the Arts in Britain* (Myerscough, 1988) saw artistic activity as a key stimulus to creating employment opportunities and local wealth. Thus a well-managed and high-profile corporate sponsorship scheme can have huge PR benefits for the host organization.

Not the least of these is the leverage which sponsorship brings with it. Funds can often be attracted (or original proposals improved upon) if, by their very exchange, they attract further matching funds from other sources. The knowledge that their decision to embark on a sponsorship may attract further funds from the Business Sponsorship Scheme administered by ABSA to double the value of the arrangement for the arts organization could be the final trigger to a company's assent to a bid for support. So too a charitable trust, albeit for different reasons and on a different footing, may offer funds if it can see that they will be matched from elsewhere.

A final note of care needs to be sounded. Many of the people who work in arts organizations have a very different perspective from their counterparts in commercial life. This needs to be recognized at a basic level in the soliciting and servicing of sponsors. The board of governors and workers in an arts enterprise need to be happy about owning the sponsorship, and there are certain areas of business (tobacco, pharmaceuticals, companies with ethically dubious investments, nuclear power) which may cause difficulties here. Ironically it is often such companies who are in greatest need of the sort of responsible image which sponsorship can provide. Both sides of the exchange need to be comfortable with the transaction for it to be a success, as in any form of marketing process. If not, the whole arrangement becomes enormously vulnerable, and potentially counterproductive.

Trusts and individuals

A final source of 'unearned income' can be found in charitable trusts. The criteria for eligibility for funding are usually clearly laid out in the objectives of the trust, as are the means of application and the timescale for allocation of funds. The particular trust concerned should be researched thoroughly so that the most appropriate application can be made.

As with corporate sponsors, care should be taken to maintain the relationship; particularly by supplying information about the progression of the project and the longer-term benefits gained from the funding investment.

There has been a move in recent years in the trust sector away from supporting on-going activity to a 'pump-priming' approach, that gives start-up funding to activities capable of eventually generating sufficient revenue to become self-supporting. There is also a resistance to providing funding to make good a shortfall from the public purse. Successful applicants to trusts will be those who take care to satisfy the trust's own needs in awarding funds. This is much the same sort of 'exchange of benefits for value' discussed in relation to corporate sponsorship above.

In spite of the emphasis placed on approaches to companies and trusts, it remains a fact for non-arts charities that most donor income comes from individuals. Individuals are enormously important to arts funding in North America, a model which current government policy favours as a future template for the arts in Britain. Certainly, individuals may be a more attractive source of support to many arts organizations than either statutory bodies or trusts, because their support is not tied to policy imperatives. 'Recognized giving' schemes such as individual seat covenants have proved very successful in venues like the West Yorkshire Playhouse where there is either a building project or a major refurbishment to catch the imagination. Other schemes, such as payroll giving, are proving a lot less popular with individual donors than had originally been envisaged.

Capital fund-raising

Applications for funding of capital projects, whether to trusts, sponsoring companies or private individuals, should be carried out in the same way as for revenue programmes.

- Applications should be tailored to the aims and objectives of the donor.
- The level of funds sought ('the price') should be realistic.
- Leverage should be exerted by indicating what other sources of funds may be available.
- The support of a prestigious trust such as the Gulbenkian Foundation or Charity Projects is an excellent lever in itself.
- Particular opportunities, such as 'buy a brick' or 'name a seat' can be offered in a way which suggests a permanent memorial for the donor. However, this kind of benefit needs to be carefully priced with reference to the customer in question. It can be a mistake, for example, to name a room in a building after a particular sponsor in perpetuity. Instead a time-limited association (say five years) should be offered, and then further funding to continue the association should be sought. In this way the arts organization can keep control of its pricing prerogative.

Summary and conclusions

In this chapter we have considered the main areas where 'price' takes centre stage in marketing the arts. Pricing arts services is difficult, even the apparent simplicity of a 'cost-plus' approach is challenged by the sheer complexity of calculating what the arts actually cost to produce. Not only is accurate costing a problematical issue in the arts, but the other two traditional influences on price setting (competition and market demand) are also atypical in this environment.

Box 5.8

Avoid sponsoring the Treasury!

The law relating to VAT differs between gifts and sponsorship. If the sponsor is receiving a tangible benefit in return for the sponsorship money, such as publicity or hospitality, this is considered the same as any other purchase and is liable for VAT. A straightforward gift is not. Some sponsors may not be able to recover the VAT they have suffered and therefore the value you retain of their payment will be reduced. It is worth seeking professional advice on the direct and indirect taxation implications of income-generating activity before final arrangements are made. If you do not have the expertise within your own organization, either your accountants or the local RAB should be able to advise.

Furthermore, the arts have all the usual service-related problems of transience rather than permanence, the need for delivery 'in person' in a specific location, and the subjective values different consumers will recognize in them. Because of the many non-financial costs involved in arts attendance (difficulty of access, availability of free time, venue comfort) it could be argued that many of the significant 'pricing' issues involved in ticket buying have more to do with product, promotion and place than with price as traditionally understood in marketing terms.

But at the heart of these transactions, as in all marketing processes, is a relationship between buyer and seller which needs to be long term if it is to be successful at all. This is most obviously true in the third area where pricing takes precedence, the long-term relationship which arts bodies need to forge with their funders, be they from the private or public sectors. The mutual benefits involved must be carefully considered, and their longevity guaranteed by a genuine attempt by the arts enterprise to identify, anticipate and satisfy its organizational customers' wants and needs in a way which ensures its own success.

Key concepts

Access policy
Audience development
Break-even analysis
Business support
Competition
Concessions and discounts
Corporate entertainment
Cost-based pricing
Demand-based pricing

Elasticity of demand
Financial returns
Gifts in kind
Market position
Price differentiation
Price structures
Psychological pricing
Public funders
Sponsorship

Discussion questions

1 What are the factors that might influence a customer's perceptions of the value-for-money offered by a recent visit to the theatre?
2 The director of a community play wishes all tickets to be free. Put the case for a change in policy, and identify the factors to be taken into account in setting the level of prices.
3 How elastic do you believe the prices in the museums sector to be; and to what extent are these affected by market competition?
4 Imagine you are the director of a newly-formed puppet company. From where can you access the funding to ensure your survival?
5 What are the benefits to a company in engaging in arts sponsorship? What sorts of organizations might best provide these benefits? List the factors which might affect a decision to sponsor.
6 How can you evaluate the success of a pricing strategy?

Action problems

1 Analyse the attendance data for your organization for the last few months. How are the concessions offered allowing you to target particular groups of attenders? Could this be improved?
2 Put together a sponsorship package for a forthcoming event designed to appeal to a multinational company. How can you ensure you have credibility with a large organization?
3 Get hold of a copy of the funding guidelines for your regional arts board, and ensure your organization is maximizing the appeal of its current application.

References

Arts Council of Great Britain (1989). *Three Year Plan 1990–1992*, ACGB, 14 Great Peter Street, London SW1 3NQ.

Association for Business Sponsorship of the Arts (1993). BSIS Business Sponsorship Incentive Scheme Application Form, ABSA, Nutmeg House, 60 Gainsford Street, Butlers Wharf, London SE1 2NY.

Beale, C. (1993). Consumers favour arts sponsorship. *Marketing*, 10 June, 20.

Boardman, J. (1978). Pricing and concessions. In *The C.O.R.T. Marketing Manual Volume 2*, (G.V. Robbins and P. Verwey eds) published by TMA/CORT/ATPM with assistance from the Arts Council of Great Britain.

Cowell, D. and Henry, I. (1977). Marketing of local authority sports centres services – a pilot study. *European Journal of Marketing*, **11**, 445–459.

Craig, S. (1989). *Marketing Leisure Services.* Leisure Futures Ltd.

Davidson, H. (1987). *Offensive Marketing.* Penguin.

Diggle, K. (1984). *Guide to Arts Marketing.* Rhinegold Publishing Ltd.

Guiltinian, J.P. (1989). The price bundling of services: a normative framework. In *Managing Services Marketing Text and Readings* (J.E.G. Bateson ed.), The Dryden Press, 376–392.

Gunn, L. (1988). Public management: a third approach? *Public Money and Management* **8** 21–25.

Howcroft, B. (1990). Evolution of retail banking. In *Managing and Marketing Services in the 1990s.* (R. Teare ed.), Cassell.

King, C. (1993). The acid test. *MAILOUT*, August/September, 21.

Kotler, P. (1980). *Marketing Management Analysis, Planning and Control* (4th ed). Prentice/Hall International.

Kotler, P. and Andreason, *Strategic Marketing for Non-profit Organizations*, Prentice Hall.

Lister, D. (1993). Opera House to launch cut-price performances. The *Independent*, 5 May, 15.

Marplan (1988). *Pricing at Arts Centres in Wales Report.* Marplan Limited, 45 Goswell Road, London EC1V 7DN

Millward Brown (1991) *Pricing in the Arts.* Millward Brown International, Olympus Avenue, Tachbrook Park, Warwick, Warwickshire, CV34 6RJ.

Myerscough, J. (1988). *The Economic Importance of the Arts.* Policy Studies Institute National Arts and Media Strategy Monitoring Group (1992). Towards a National Arts and Media Strategy. NAMS.

Newman, D. (1977). *Subscribe Now! Building Arts Audiences through Dynamic Subscription Promotion.* Theatre Communications Group, 355 Lexington Avenue, New York.

Office of Arts and Libraries (1989). *Supporting the Arts: A Review of the Structure of Arts Funding.* Report by Michael Wilding CB, OAL, Horseguards Road, London SW1P 3AL.

Stoker, R. (1993). 65pc increase in museum fees planned. *Yorkshire Post*, 29 November.

Willcocks, L. and Harrow, J. (1992). Management, innovation and organizational learning. In *Rediscovering Public Sector Management* (L. Willcocks and J. Harrow eds), McGraw-Hill, 50–83.

6 Promotion

Promotion is the element of the marketing mix that communicates the benefits of what is on offer to the target audience. By its very nature it is the most visible aspect of marketing activity. It plays an extremely important part in arts marketing strategy; especially where the aim is to reach not only existing arts customers, but to arouse the interest of new audiences. The costs of such activity need to be carefully weighed. Arts marketing presents them in an especially problematic way because of its frequently 'missionary' intentions on invariably slender resources.

This chapter will look at the following issues in relation to the role of promotion in the arts:

- Promotion in the marketing mix.
- Advertising.
- Sales promotion.
- Copywriting and print.
- Public relations.
- Making presentations.

Promotion in the marketing mix

Because of its visibility, it is tempting to confuse promotion with marketing itself. Artistic directors and board members without a marketing background can fall into this trap. However, promotion is not some kind of veneer whose application to an existing offering can automatically generate high attendances. It can only work as part of a successful marketing mix. If the price is too high, or the product is unattractive, irrelevant or inaccessible, no amount of clever promotion will guarantee success. On the other hand if promotion is not carefully planned and executed the product will not reach as many customers as it ought. While it is an area that demands flair and imagination, it also demands clear thinking and a highly disciplined approach.

Most marketing theorists talk about promotion by subdividing it into four main areas of technique: advertising, public relations, sales promotion and personal selling. Some add 'direct marketing' as a fifth element, but in many ways direct marketing is more like an entire approach to marketing than a subsection of the marketing mix.

Because of its importance to arts organizations in developing long-term relationships with their customers, this book deals with it separately as part of Chapter 7.

Similar industries tend to use broadly similar combinations of techniques in their promotional strategies. For example infrequently-purchased but expensive items like life insurance and encyclopedias rely heavily on personal selling, whereas frequently-purchased goods, like soap powder or baked beans, tend to rely on advertising and sales promotion.

The arts, too, have a 'typical' industry mix of promotional activity. They tend to rely heavily on public relations and a wide distribution of printed material, supplemented by low-cost advertising and an element of sales promotion. The British arts scene has been slow to embrace the advantages of personal selling, although a proactive stance in the box office can both improve income and raise levels of customer satisfaction by improving service (see Chapters 2 and 7).

As we shall see, the emphasis on public relations is understandable because of the intrinsic news interest of the arts. Arts events and activities tend to involve 'firsts' of various sorts, and the news media have an insatiable thirst for novelty. Artists and actors are people in the public eye. They make 'good copy'. Another reason for the popularity of PR is its perceived value-for-money. A growing number of commercial organizations are discovering the cost-effectiveness of PR, making it the fastest-growing area of promotional activity in the early 1990s in the UK (Smith, 1993).

Advertising, on the other hand, is an extremely expensive business. Its use by arts organizations tends to concentrate on the minimum level of exposure deemed necessary for the purposes of information. However, when used in the right context, advertising can offer significant 'image' benefits, particularly for art forms with a strong visual appeal. Although there are a variety of media in which advertising can be placed, the most popular ones for the arts tend to be print and poster advertising. We will examine aspects of the use of these media later in the chapter, but many of the observations to be made about creativity and planning are true of any advertising activity in whatever context.

Sales promotion is used to increase the amount or speed involved in a transaction. It interfaces with the area of price (see Chapter 5) when it offers multiple attendance at a discount through subscription, for example. There is a tendency to regard sales promotion as short-term and shrill. But it can be used effectively across a wide range of demographic segments.

Just as the marketing mix offered by an arts organization needs to be regularly reviewed (because the external environment is always changing), so its promotional mix needs to be constantly checked for its relevance to the audience. The pattern is too often dictated by precedent. There are a number of reasons for this: time, lack of imagination or insufficient experience. Sometimes existing patterns of promotion can be reinforced by arrangements such as standard clauses in contracts between touring companies and managements which will specify responsibility for the cost of printed publicity without questioning whether this is the most appropriate promotional tool in each case.

It is important, then, to be prepared to think laterally when planning promotional activity. If, as suggested by advertising research, one of the ways in which marketing communication registers with its recipients is through 'salience' (that is, standing out from the background) then it makes sense to look for different and fresh ways of getting the message across. (McDonald, 1992). Placing a new angle on a press story from a theatre or gallery can mean that instead of being lost on the arts pages, the item may appear in an unusual editorial environment such as the women's page or the sports section. Here it will be seen by a wider audience. Readers who can be counted among existing attenders will see it in a new light. As with public relations, so with advertising. It is worth thinking about different media, or new uses of existing media, in order to reach your audience in as effective and impactful a way as possible.

Planning promotional activity

The three main influences on the shape of a successful promotional mix are:

- The nature of the audience.
- The nature of the message.
- The size of budget available.

The nature of the audience is the most fundamental of these three factors. All effective communication involves speaking the audience's language, not only in the messages sent but in how they are conveyed. But managing this without preconceptions can be a difficult process. Research and careful observation are important in order to safeguard your approach. One of the signs of an organization's successful espousal of marketing is the consideration of the customer in each decision. Promotional decisions are particularly important in this respect.

The nature of the message content can also have an important effect on choosing the means for its delivery. In order to communicate the important details of price, times, telephone numbers, and access details, the precisely controllable techniques of advertising and printed publicity are essential. Public relations can deal with softer information such as personalities or atmosphere.

Promotion is a cost, so the limits imposed by the promotional budget will be a guiding factor as well. Even in profit-driven marketing there is never enough money to mount the ideal campaign. But sometimes resources can be stretched through negotiation or co-operation. The role of marketing consortia in planning and executing joint promotional activity (for example, inserting a joint season leaflet in a regional colour supplement on behalf of a group of regional theatres) can make available to arts organizations working together what would be impossible to them on an individual basis.

Budgeting for promotion

How much money should be spent on promotional activity is a hotly-debated issue in any organization. Understandably, the excellence of the artistic product itself will have first call on the scarce resources of arts organizations. Yet, to ensure the success of the product, the marketing department has to be able to justify its claim to an adequate budget. Competing for promotional funds in an atmosphere where marketing itself may be misunderstood or distrusted (see Chapter 1) requires very careful argument and planning. There are a number of guidelines in common use to help establish a figure:

Competitive parity   What do other organizations of a similar size and turnover spend? Funding bodies, annual reports and informal contacts with colleagues in other companies can help build a picture of the 'industry average'. Statistics need to be compared on a 'like-with-like' basis (e.g. are salaries included in the figure, or is it a 'spending' figure?). Although there are differences between the environments and tasks of different organizations, any large discrepancies may signal the need to question the size (or lack of size) of the budget.

Percentage of sales   This is another simple, but reductive, technique. Like 'competitive parity' it assumes that there should be an industry average governing the relationship between how much money an organization spends on advertising and promotion, and how much it receives from customers. In most industries the relationship is a stable one, expressed as the 'advertising-to-sales' ratio. Advertising Association figures reveal that 13 per cent of the price of a typical bottle of shampoo goes on advertising, as compared with 8 per cent for coffee and less than 0.5 per cent for petrol (White, 1993). The greater the importance of promotion in building imagery and communicating benefits to a wide range of audiences, the higher the advertising-to-sales ratio is likely to be. In this sense, the arts resemble shampoo more than petrol. Research suggests that advertising to sales ratios for most theatres, for example, are in the region of 12–15 per cent.

Objective and task   This is the most rational method of budget setting, and (predictably) the most popular with marketing theorists. It operates on the principle that you should first decide what you want to do ('objective') and then cost the necessary action ('task'). So, if part of the promotional plan involves reaching 80,000 homes in a particular geodemographic category (see Chapter 2) with a leaflet distribution, then the cost of this will represent an item in the budget. The problem with this technique is that the promotional shopping list can soon exceed the availability of funds. Priorities need to be established, and comprehensive costings should include an allowance for contingency and tactical flexibility.

None of these techniques used on their own offer a watertight solution to the problem of establishing an infallible figure. But used together they can give the marketing department invaluable arguments for defending or developing the promotional budget. It should include not only how much money should be spent on getting the message across in various media like press advertising or mailing, but also how much should be spent on designing and printing the materials themselves: the 'production' figure. Expenditure on the effective delivery of a promotional strategy needs to be planned and controlled like any other form of marketing activity. The techniques outlined in Chapter 9 are particularly relevant to promotion in this respect.

Advertising

Persuasion or information?

Advertising can be defined as paid-for media exposure to inform and/or persuade potential (and existing) customers of the benefits of your offering. The difference between 'inform' and 'persuade' here is an important one. As with the nature of promotion itself, mentioned earlier in this chapter, there is often misunderstanding in the minds of non-marketing managers about how 'persuasive' advertising is. The research suggests that attitude changes as a result of advertising are slight and only take effect in the long term. Nevertheless, the advertising industry has developed a terminology of its own which talks in terms of 'impacts' and 'impressions', as if consumers were easily manipulated into purchase.

Providing 'information' about products and services towards which customers are already reasonably well-disposed is a far more common function for most forms of advertising. An effective advertisement helps your customer decide in your favour by stressing the advantages of choosing your offering over the alternatives. The lesson to be learnt here by arts marketers is to keep their advertising simple and relevant to the product, and to make sure it is effectively targeted. This applies to writing copy for brochures and leaflets as much as it does to the requirements of mailshots, press or poster advertising.

Media research

Concepts like frequency and coverage are not just abstract ideas. British media research is amongst the best in the world. Television advertising, for example, relies upon a sophisticated on-going survey of 4,500 'typical' homes each providing electronically captured viewing data on a daily basis. The resulting information, collected on behalf of the Broadcasters Audience Research Board (BARB), is the currency by which television advertising is traded. Newspaper and magazine readership is calclulated by means of the National Readership Survey (NRS) which is one of the longest established 'random' surveys in the UK. 28,000 respondents are interviewed every year to find out which newspapers or magazines they read. The socio-economic classification of consumers into As, Bs, C1s, C2s etc. (as discussed in Chapter 2) was originally devised by the NRS but has been adopted throughout marketing thinking in the UK.

As we have seen in Chapter 2, consumers' usage of products and services is recorded by a regular survey called the Target Group Index (TGI). It also covers their media usage habits, and (since the late 1980s) their attendance at arts events. This information can be cross-referenced – revealing, for example, that readers of the

Box 6.1

Advertising speak

Advertising, like any other specialist activity, uses terminology which can bemuse the uninitiated. The jargon conceals what are, invariably, very simple ideas. Here are some particularly useful ones when thinking about the whole area of promotional planning in the arts:

Cost per thousand	The cost of reaching 1000 members of your target audience in a particular medium. Although it is a useful statistic when comparing like with like (for example two free newspapers in a specific circulation area) it is not very helpful in making comparisons between media. For example the cost per thousand for a poster is many times less than for a television spot but the two forms of communication are very different.
Coverage	The number of people which an advertisement or campaign reaches at least once. Within this number (usually expressed as a percentage of the target audience) many will have seen the ad more than once in the course of the campaign.
Frequency	The number of times an advertisement is seen. Received advertising wisdom is that most ads need to be seen more than once in order to communicate effectively. The precise number of times ('effective frequency') will differ from case to case. Exceeding it can be wasteful.
Opportunities to see ('OTS')	A similar idea to 'frequency' but used when planning or evaluating advertising to specify the average number of times each member of the audience is exposed to the advertising.
Circulation	The number of copies of a publication sold.
Rating point	One per cent of the targeted audience viewing or hearing your television or radio advertisement. Called 'Gross Rating Points' because the calculation makes no allowance for the number of times any individual has seen or heard the ad. It's a similar calculation to 'man hours'.
Readership	The number of people who read a publication. This varies with the title: it may be from two to four per copy. Total readership rather than circulation is used as the basis of cost per thousand calculations in press advertising.

Observer have a higher predisposition to go to the theatre than readers of any other Sunday newspaper. Such surveys can be of great benefit in planning advertising, or even when targeting publications with editorial matter as part of an organization's PR effort. All of these information sources are examples of the kind of 'secondary research' discussed in Chapter 3.

Not every publication is included in the NRS. Many local papers, particularly free newspapers, provide a different statistic for their advertisers – Audit Bureau of Circulation figures (ABC for short) and Verified Free Distribution (VFD). These figures are not the same as readership, and may overstate the actual numbers of papers which reach the consumer (as opposed to reaching newsagents or distributors). But they offer some kind of yardstick of value when comparing rival promotional opportunities.

Two valuable acronyms: AIDA and USP

Simplicity is the key to effective communication. It can be encouraged by the use of two very straightforward 'templates' in the creation of advertising and other promotional activity: AIDA and USP.

The first, AIDA, is attributed to the American advertising guru E.K. Strong in 1925. AIDA is an acronym standing for:

- Attention.
- Interest.
- Desire.
- Action.

It can be argued that AIDA is over-simplistic in the way it predicts that advertising takes its public through a series of stages to the final goal of purchase. People are not that logical, and they are certainly not as innocent of advertising as the model suggests. But the beauty of a model resides not in its accuracy but in its usefulness and flexibility. From this point of view AIDA is very useful indeed.

It can serve as a checklist for message structure, or as a guide to the layout and design of an advertisement or piece of printed publicity. It concentrates the mind on creating communications which are simple and relevant, and can also help in the evaluation of creative work. It is understandably popular – in fact practically any press advertisement you can find will demonstrate the principle:

- A headline grabs the attention.
- The reader's interest is then captivated by an illustration or a photographic image.
- The words of the ad ('body copy') demonstrate how the product or service on offer will provide a sought-after benefit (thus stimulating desire).
- A coupon, telephone number, or list of stockists will complete the structure, allowing the reader to become a customer by converting interest and desire into the action of purchase.

While AIDA is helpful from the point of view of structuring a piece of communication, what about deciding on its content? Here the ideas of a later American advertising guru, Rosser Reeves, are useful. Reeves coined the phrase 'USP' in the late 1950s, standing for a philosophy of advertising based on what he called the 'unique selling proposition'. This proposes that:

- Every product or service, in order to justify its position in the marketplace, has to have something unique about it.
- This feature has to be strong enough to persuade customers that the product boasting it is more suited to their needs than rival offerings.
- All promotional activity needs to drive home this unique proposition in a simple and single-minded way.

The idea has influenced some classic advertising campaigns because of its over-whelming simplicity. Lines like 'Persil washes whiter', or 'Guinness is good for you' may no longer be current (indeed, present-day regulations would forbid both of them) but they have become part of advertising mythology because of their compel-ling single-mindedness. Volvo cars are not the only 'safe' cars on the road, but by using 'safety' as their unique selling proposition in their advertising, they have carved themselves a niche in our perceptions of the car market.

Arts organizations, too, each have a unique selling proposition. As discussed in the section on arts funding in Chapter 5, funding bodies are not interested in replicating resources. So each arts organization in receipt of public money will need to justify its unique role in the marketplace. The USP of any product or service needs to be reflected in its performance. It is no use claiming that Fairy Liquid is kind to your hands if it isn't. Similarly, the USP you discover for your organization needs to be a recognizable feature of its operation. There may even be more than one feature that is unique to a particular organization in this respect. Possible sources of uniqueness, at least as recognized by funding bodies, are as follows:

- Art form.
- Size.
- Type of audience served.
- Geographical position.
- Physical access.

The challenge is to convert these 'features' into 'benefits' which the potential audience will recognize as uniquely suited to their needs. So, if the unique selling proposition of an arts centre is based on its ability to cater for a less formal audience than a more traditional venue, the USP underlying its promotional messages will stress its friendliness and welcoming atmosphere. Similarly, if a craft gallery is the only outlet for regionally-produced ceramics in a particular area, its USP might emphasize the way its exhibitions reflect local interests and tastes.

This principle of establishing what is unique about an organization can be extended to its individual offerings such as plays or exhibitions, in order to facilitate the clear formulation of relevant messages. By operating in a broad direction like this, the total effect of an organization's promotion is strengthened into an overall 'brand image'. By establishing a consistent personality for your organization, the kind of long-term relationships with customers that are essential to arts marketing can be made easier to build. Tomas Hardiman, involved in maintaining one of Ireland's strongest arts brands the Abbey Theatre, comments on the balance to be struck here:

> The biggest thing in theatre marketing is that you're looking at brand image *and* the individual product. The Abbey has an international reputation, so there's not much of a problem where identity is concerned. Since 1904 it has represented a distinctively Irish personality, it's part of the nation's sense of its own identity. But the heritage is a mixed blessing. There's been a gradual switch from a 'nationalist' appeal to that of 'entertainment'. You have to create a balance, depending on your vision of theatre.

Press advertising

In spite of the steady growth of television advertising since its introduction in 1956 (to over £2 billion in 1994), the press still accounts for the lion's share of advertising expenditure in the UK (White, 1993). Its ability to reach a well-defined target market, with information which can be checked for details of times, dates, prices and telephone numbers, makes it a popular advertising choice with arts organizations. Like any medium, it has its own special terminology and characteristics. Yet, although the minutiae of the techniques used are different, much of what we can say about the planning, creation and evaluation of press advertising is relevant to the way that other advertising media work.

There is a bewildering variety of press media from which to choose. Newspapers alone include national, regional and local press; evening or morning dailies, weeklies, free newspapers (known as 'freesheets'), not to mention trade and consumer magazines which also cover national and regional readerships.

A comprehensive listing of every newspaper and magazine available in the UK (and indeed any other sort of advertising medium) can be found in a publication called BRAD – 'British Rate and Data'. It is usually available in the reference section of larger public libraries. While building-based arts organizations will be aware of the relevant media choices available to them in their catchment areas, BRAD can be very useful when planning advertising for touring productions or exhibitions visiting areas with which the marketing department is not familiar. The kind of information provides brief details of circulation, advertising rates, and the 'mechanical data' specifying the form which the advertisement should take when submitted.

The rate card

BRAD information is summarized from something called a 'rate card'. Every advertising medium has a rate card – which provides a list of 'rates' (the prices for different sizes of advertising). At first glance newspaper rate cards can look confusing and bewildering. But the seemingly impenetrable jargon explains the requirements of the particular publication with complete, if concise, information. We will briefly examine some different types of advertising space available in newspaper rate cards, before moving to the more technical aspects of the paper's requirements.

Display or classified?

Newspaper advertising, and the relevant rates, falls into three distinct groups: display, semi-display and classified.

Display advertising is printed from artwork and thus can feature sophisticated graphics and typefaces. It runs alongside the editorial matter in the paper, the price of the advertisement being relative to its size. The basic unit of display space is called the 'single column centimetre', or s.c.c. for short. Because of the differences in column width from one newspaper to another, the amount of space this actually represents varies amongst publications. Display advertising space is also offered as full pages, or page fractions such as halves or quarters. National newspapers carry almost four times more display advertising than classified (in terms of value).

Classified on the other hand, is more important to the regional press. It features columns of ads, made up purely of words, in a series of categories or 'classifications'. These advertisements are arranged like a simple directory, in alphabetical order. They are called 'lineage' ads because they are charged for by the line. Classified advertising is set off from the rest of the newspaper in a distinct section, although different papers have different policies on where they position 'Entertainment', usually the classification most relevant to arts organizations.

Semi-display is a compromise category of advertising, offering some of the graphic opportunities of display, but appearing within the relevant classified section rather than amongst editorial copy elsewhere in the paper. Touring venues often make use of semi-display to create 'ladder ads', featuring a series of boxes showing forthcoming attractions in chronological order.

As will be clear, classified advertising subscribes to the 'information' model of advertising outlined earlier. It assumes an active consumer searching through the small ads for something he or she already wants. It is naturally of importance to arts organizations who need to keep in regular touch with local or regional audiences looking for entertainment on an ad hoc basis, a reminder of times, prices or telephone numbers. If we accept this function of classified advertising, basic lineage should be sufficient. However, it is in the newspaper's interests to get its clients to 'trade up' to the more expensive semi-display, using the argument of 'added impact' to justify this expenditure. What dictates the optimum advertising pattern, however, is careful consideration of marketing objectives.

Timing, position and discounts

It may be that the objectives demand display advertising rather than classified, appearing on a particular day or in a particular part of the publication. A new season announcement or an exhibition opening are both examples of situations where this kind of precisely-targeted impact may be appropriate. This will involve a rate-card premium, usually a percentage added on to the 'standard' price to guarantee publication on a Friday, for example, or in the books section. The more specific an advertiser's requirements are, the more the newspaper will charge for meeting them. It is worth finding out about variations in circulation (the number of copies sold) of daily papers over the different days of the week. It frequently drops on Saturdays, for example, suggesting that the weekend might not offer very good value for the hard-pressed advertiser.

The rate card will often feature special positions inside the paper (for example the television page, which research suggests will receive repeated attention during the life of the newspaper) or on the front or back pages.

'Title corners'   also known as 'ear-pieces' are available on many newspaper front covers. They are the spaces to either side of the title or 'mast head' of the paper. Some advertisers prize them for their salience, but their ability to carry information is limited by their size.

A **'solus'**   position of any type is an advertisement which stands on its own. (The phrase, from Latin, is used of certain poster sites as well.) Because of the perceived value of having a display advertisement which does not have to compete for the reader's attention with any other advertising in the same field of vision, solus positions are highly sought after. They tend to be booked up months in advance. A 'front-page solus' is a particularly vivid way of announcing a new season or a special event such as the launch of pantomime booking, or the opening of an exhibition. So, assuming the organization's planning schedule is sufficiently long term, it is a good idea to find out from appropriate newspapers when they begin to make such positions available. This enables them to be securely fixed into future advertising plans.

'Run of week' and **'run of paper'**:   an advertiser's flexibility as to date of insertion and position in the paper are rewarded by cheaper rates. Rate-card discounts for 'run of paper' and 'run of week' imply just that: the ad will appear on any page in a particular issue, or in any issue in a given week. In one sense, these discounts represent the laws of supply and demand in the advertising marketplace. However, a canny purchaser of advertising space can use the fact that such discounts are available to negotiate on price even if the advertisement in question does not, strictly speaking, qualify. A salesperson who needs to fill their newspaper may listen sympathetically to an argument along these lines if the alternative is to lose the ad to a rival publication.

Arts advertisers who want to use press advertising to maintain regular contact with their audiences may stand to benefit from 'series' discount. This rewards regular advertisers with lower rates. Again, the test of the wisdom of this pattern of advertising is not the size of the discount, but whether it corresponds to marketing objectives. If they change, or if other media become available to achieve the same contact more effectively, the advertising budget needs to be reviewed accordingly. Many repertory theatres now spend more on direct mail than press advertising

---

Box 6.2

Read the small print

The basic unit of space in a display ad is, as we have seen, the 'single column centimetre'. How much space this actually represents can be gauged by reference to the 'mechanical data' on the rate card – where the width of the column will be given in millimetres. This is important information, especially for anyone promoting a touring event and buying space across a number of different publications.

For example, a common size for a display ad might be 15 cm × 2 columns. So, if the column width of the newspaper in question were 38 mm, the total size of the space booked would be 15 cm × 7.6 cm. If, on the other hand, the column width were 42 mm, the total size of the space would be 15 cm × 8.4 cm. The relevance of this information is that a campaign involving display advertising using a 15 cm × 2 cols space might well require a number of differently-sized artworks if it is being run across a number of titles. If not, the ad may end up surrounded by white space because of varying column widths. Or it might possibly not appear at all because of the need to book additional space. The cost of generating the additional artworks must also be borne in mind at the planning stage. Other useful technical information to be found on the rate card includes:

- The deadline for advertising copy (which may vary between classified and display).
- The 'screen' (which refers to the number of dots per inch used in the way photographic images are reproduced on the printed page).
- The requirements for artwork.
  - The abbreviation 'S/S' means 'same-size. In other words you should supply artwork of exactly the same size as the final printed ad.
  - Another common phrase 'camera ready' means that the artwork itself must be complete – with all its ingredients in position. This is then made into a printing 'plate' by photography during the reproduction process.

(traditionally the largest item on any marketing department expenditure list). Computer power in box office and marketing department has brought accurately-targeted direct marketing within the grasp of more organizations, and promotional patterns have changed accordingly.

Poster advertising

Poster, or 'outdoor', advertising is one of the oldest forms of marketing communication. For the fine arts, posters promoting exhibitions can dramatize the benefits of the experience on offer by reproducing art objects with drama and impact (creating

Posters create controversy at the V&A

Charles Mills, the marketing manager appointed in 1987, put the problem of communicating the museum's benefits as follows:

> The V&A once had the slogan, 'The Nation's Treasure House', and that is still very accurate. We have so many extraordinarily beautiful things for people to see. Our problem is that it is very hard to sum up and define exactly what we have got here.

An answer to this complicated positioning problem came in the first year of Mills's appointment with a poster campaign which solved the problem about which art objects to talk about by ignoring them altogether. Instead it featured the proposition:

> 'V&A – An ace caff with quite a nice museum attached.' One of the posters featured the immortal line 'Where else do they give you £100,000,000 worth of objets d'art free with every egg salad?'

Mills defended the controversial campaign:

> We knew the V&A had a fusty image which was stopping some people visiting us. Trying to shake off this image we produced a campaign that was deliberately controversial. It had to be controversial to get people talking about it. We had a tiny budget.

The then arts minister, David Mellor (himself no stranger to controversy), was impressed. 'It was certainly provocative. While it had some success raising the profile of the museum, and attracting some new visitors, I suspect it alienated those others for whom the museum rather than the support services were a main concern.' Nevertheless, the campaign (as well as a strong exhibition programme for 1988/1989) increased visitor traffic by 10%.

Source: Crofts (1988) and Moyle (1990)

merchandise as well as publicity). London 'blockbuster' exhibitions exploit this strength by extensive use of posters on sites on the London Underground. The deployment of outdoor media was a spearhead of the Victoria & Albert's famous image-building campaign run by Saatchi & Saatchi in the late 1980s. Another aspect of outdoor's long-term association with the arts can be seen in historical 'play bills' – the ornately produced and extravagantly worded posters from the eighteenth and nineteenth centuries which are now collectors' items.

Billing

Posters have given the theatrical profession the concept of 'billing': the practice of heading the poster with the names of the leading actors. Some theatres avoid it altogether as a matter of democratic policy. Others, particularly touring houses featuring familiar names from television, see it as an essential part of their marketing armoury. A pragmatic approach is to be recommended. Some contracts between a venue and a theatrical or literary management will specify aspects of billing, even down to the relative size and order of the artists' or writers' names compared to the title of the piece. These provisions will tend to apply not only to posters, but to all other forms of printed material, including advertising, leaflets and programmes. Clear lines of communication are essential between the marketing department and other areas of the organization in order to avoid misunderstanding.

Economy or effectiveness?

One of the essential attractions of poster advertising to theatrical managements has always been its perceived cheapness. The way that most arts organizations distribute posters has traditionally aimed at maximizing the amount of free display. As well as the essential display work in and near the venue itself, distribution by hand or mail to the following sorts of outlets is a common practice:

- Colleges.
- Community centres.
- Doctors' and dentists' waiting rooms.
- Factories (for display in canteens or rest rooms).
- Libraries.
- Local retail businesses (e.g. hairdressers, smaller shops).
- Other arts venues.
- Restaurants.
- Schools.

Competition in such outlets from other material is fierce. While some venues mobilize staff or volunteers to check and maintain the visibility of displays, there is nevertheless a concern that impact and communication may suffer amidst the visual clutter. For example, while audience surveys reveal that students and education workers are an important part of the customer base, colleges and universities are notorious for overcrowded and out-of-date noticeboards. Furthermore, display in many of the outlets listed above may not be reaching other target audiences effectively, or even at all. Their popularity as outlets seems led not by marketing objectives but by their relative lack of resistance to accepting material (particularly as local authorities crack down on the illegal display of posters on walls and street furniture, known as 'fly posting'). While it is important to have a good 'grass-roots' presence for any arts organization with a local constituency, the wisdom of devoting so much time and energy to this kind of activity (together with the substantial mailing and production costs involved) needs to be kept under review.

Poster contractors

The alternative is to consider using paid-for sites, rented from a poster contractor. Originally a highly regional industry, there has been a recent trend towards concentrating poster power in fewer hands due to mergers and rationalization. At

Box 6.3

Sizing up posters

There is a direct relationship between size and price. The traditional building block of poster display space is the 'sheet' – an area of 30 inches by 20 inches. These are the dimensions of what used to be a very popular size for theatre posters – the 'double crown'. Because of the adoption of international standards in paper size, the double crown has been largely superseded by the slightly smaller A2 size posters. But double crown ('DC') is still used by many touring managements as the basis for their print orders – with smaller variations known as 'hanging cards'.

The most common commercial-size posters, however, are 4-sheets and 48-sheets (the enormous 'bill boards' which dominate roadside advertising). 4-sheets are the kind of posters seen at bus-shelters or in shopping precincts. The last five years have seen the replacement of many 'Adshels', as the bus-shelter sites are called, by a new type of poster called the 'Superlite'. These are larger, (the first metric poster size, in fact, at 1200 mm by 1000 mm) and have the advantage of being back lit. This makes them twice as effective (and as expensive) as their predecessors.

Ordinary 4-sheets are widely available at railway stations – a popular choice with arts advertisers targeting a mobile audience. In fact many larger theatres and galleries will plan posters at railway stations *en route* to their cities, rather than limiting display to the city itself.

present something like three-quarters of all poster sites are owned by the three largest companies (White, 1993). It is still a highly fragmented industry, however, with different companies concentrating on particular sizes and types of poster.

As with newspapers, poster contractors each have a rate card. The price will include putting up and taking down the material (which has to be delivered to the contractor on a central basis) and a period of display which used to be a minimum of one month, but is becoming more flexible. Long-term advertisers are rewarded with better rates than occasional users. The best discounts are to be had if you buy a site on a continuous ('Till countermanded' or 'TC') basis. This usually requires a period of three months before it can be cancelled. Alternatively sites can be bought 'line by line', which means on an ad hoc basis. Poster contractors themselves have become adept at packaging their sites in order to offer advertisers greater convenience. Such packages are aimed at the largest users of the medium, however.

Transport media

Although the majority of the outdoor scene is comprised by 'static' posters, transport media are developing an important role – from taxi doors to liveried lorries! Tactical use of bus-side advertising is an increasingly popular choice for venues promoting major Christmas shows where high rates of coverage and frequency are required. The

TV pulls for Topol

Most arts organizations, if they use media advertising at all, tend not to stray outside press and posters. There are exceptions to this rule, however. The 1900 seater Sunderland Empire believes strongly in the power of television advertising to promote its biggest shows. As a major touring venue the theatre has a lot of seats to fill in a short space of time, and television can generate the kind of coverage needed in a concentrated booking period. The theatre sees such advertising as an investment which leads to a direct return at the box office.

In November 1994 the London-originated musical *Fiddler on the Roof* ran to packed audiences at the Empire on its national tour. Promotion for the show ran in a wide mixture of advertising media, focusing on the visual image of Topol himself – now in his fifties and thus a better age for the star part than when he played it in the classic film at the age of 28. Television was thus an essential part of the mix – using a commercial which the touring management had created, 'topped and tailed' with venue-specific details. Airtime on Tyne Tees Television was booked through one of the theatre's two advertising agencies, the budget for the campaign being jointly resourced by the venue and the touring management under the terms of the performance contract.

sheer size and ubiquity of bus-sides guarantees impact, but the cost of producing the advertising material itself is likely to be disproportionately large for small runs.

Different transport advertising contractors will use slightly different terminology, but the kind of opportunities available on most rate cards for bus advertising will include:

- 'T-Sides' which run along the side of the bus and have a panel going down to form a 'T'.
- 'Supersides' which run along the other side of the bus.
- End panels, which are good for targeting motorists and business travellers.

Periods of display and discounts are structured in a way similar to other outdoor media.

Using an agency

It may be, as in the case of the Sunderland Empire, that the scale of operation suggests the use of an advertising agency rather than negotiating and buying space direct. Services like the preparation of artwork for display advertising will require the expertise of a graphic designer and typesetter. While newspapers can offer to do the 'artwork' for you, the final results are unpredictable. The wider availability of desktop publishing systems has led to many arts organizations handling graphic design in-house. However, advertising agencies can free marketing personnel by reducing the amount of time spent on routine media purchases as well as acting as a filter for the tireless approaches of media salespeople. They can also provide useful input to planning, as well as offering access to better prices for certain marketing services through their buying power.

Agency commissions and mark-ups

Advertising agencies traditionally make their money by receiving a commission from media owners (newspapers, radio and television companies, etc.) of a percentage of the purchase price of the space they buy. Usually this is 15 per cent. So, an advertisement costing £100 will typically yield the agency £15 from the media owner, although the client will be invoiced by the agency for the full amount. This practice dates back to the early days of advertising agencies, when they sold space on behalf of poster contractors and newspapers. On work such as the preparation of printed materials, for which no commission is payable, agencies 'mark up' their expenditure when billing the client. They justify this on the grounds that their bulk-buying power on services such as printing produces savings which cover the mark-up. For work which involves no purchasing (such as consultancy or conference management) a straight fee is negotiated. Often an agency's remuneration will include all three types of payment: commission, mark-up and fee.

Theoretically, using an agency should cost the client no more than if the client were buying the advertising direct. The commission system means that the larger the client's spend, the more money the agency stands to make. While this does not mean that agencies advise unnecessary expenditure, it does have the effect of making their largest clients the ones on which they lavish most care and attention. Arts organizations, with small budgets, may find themselves being left behind as a result.

For a variety of reasons, many arts clients have excellent direct relationships with local media which might not be improved by the intervention of an advertising agency. It may even be the case that discounts enjoyed by a long-established venue have a historical or discretionary basis best left unquestioned. Like any aspect of promotional strategy, however, the decision whether or not to use an agency is best kept under regular review.

Sales promotion

Below the line

Marketing terminology talks about an imaginary 'line' drawn through promotional expenditure. 'Above the line' is expenditure which carries commission (like advertising media as discussed above). Other sorts of expenditure, such as printing or mailing, are deemed 'below the line'. Sales promotion, in its various forms, is often simply referred to as 'below the line' as a result.

Competitive benefits

Derby Playhouse combined competition-based sales promotion with market research into subscribers' attitudes in the mid-1980s. People buying or renewing a subscription were offered the chance to win a weekend in Paris. Respondents were invited to place eight reasons for subscribing to the Playhouse in the order agreed by a panel of independent judges. Not only were the mechanics of the competition easy and familiar from other examples of sales promotion, but by looking at the most often-cited responses the theatre was able to find out more about the motivations of its most regular customers. While the methodology of this exercise as market research can be faulted, it added to the venue's overall knowledge.

Sales promotion is something of a catch-all promotional category. It is any activity that does not fall into the other areas of the promotional mix, but which increases how much a consumer buys, or how quickly the transaction occurs. The kind of 'subscription' marketing advocated by Newman (1977) and Diggle (1984) is a kind of sales promotion which encourages the advance purchase of blocks of tickets rather than ad hoc single ticket consumption. As an arts marketing idea, of course, its pedigree stretches back to the eighteenth century to the kind of 'subscription' concerts at which the symphonies of Haydn and Mozart were first aired. But like any form of sales promotion, it offers direct inducement (such as extra value) to ginger up the process of a sale.

Part of the function of sales promotion is to inject short-term interest and generate publicity. So it is worth considering a number of options beside the kind of discount-based technique on which subscription is built. A selection of techniques are described in the following checklist.

Competitions

Generally the best response levels are achieved by the simplest ideas. Competitions based largely on luck but usually featuring the words 'Using your skill and judgement', are very popular because entrants accept they are very nearly lotteries (see 'Free Mail In').

Coupons

Enormously flexible, these offer some kind of saving to consumers when redeemed against the admission price of a particular event. They are widely used in the museum and stately home markets. The possibility of cross-promotion (joining forces with another attraction or venue) can give access to new audiences. Simplicity, which is a feature of all effective promotion, should be paramount when devising coupon offers. They need to be easy to use and easy for your sales staff to handle. Finally, they need to be accurately costed in terms of expected redemption rates.

Free gifts/trial

As the name implies, this involves giving something away with a purchase. In the 1960s plastic daffodils were all the rage with soap powder. In the arts, experience shows that effective offers are limited to ancillary products which have a direct link to the main experience, such as books, CDs or programmes.

Free draws/free mail ins

These are effectively a raffle. The magic words 'no purchase necessary' absolve them from the legal restrictions attached to lotteries where participants pay for a chance of winning. They can be used to create display interest (centring on the entry-form posting box), or to prompt a visit to a gallery or theatre foyer by positioning the posting-box in-house. Such activity can also result in a list of names and addresses, but only a percentage of these are likely to be good prospects.

Strengths and weaknesses of sales promotion

The strength of sales promotion is that it offers 'something for nothing'. This stimulates a positive attitude to the organization's offering among consumers and intermediaries. It tips customers over the edge of the decision to buy, thus leading to immediate sales increases. It is extremely flexible. Used in tandem with advertising, it can be very effective in increasing the impact of your commercial messages.

Because of the fact that it needs to offer something over and above the basic proposition, however, it is by nature short lived. Most promotions last no longer than 90 days (Stanley, 1984). The technique works best with support from elsewhere. Sales promotions are frequently one-offs, only a few are recurring. There is pressure to be original, which means that you lose the economies of scale achieved in a long-running advertising campaign.

Because of its 'tactical' nature, it is crucial to plan and pace sales promotion across the range of the organization's offerings to maximize its support for the sales effort. This involves looking a year ahead at timing, techniques, geographical areas, co-ordination, synergy with planned advertising and the need to create selling support material.

Copywriting and print

Printed publicity is a major item of expenditure for any arts organization. Audience surveys regularly feature 'season leaflet' as the most frequently-indicated method of finding out about the performance on offer. While the design and printing of this will be the province of a graphic designer (either bought-in or in-house, depending on the organization) the copywriting will tend to be done by the marketing department. The ability to address the audience directly, in literature which can serve as a sales aid by featuring a postal booking form or telephone sales number, justifies the importance with which this task is viewed.

The arts' position as a service industry means that the role of printed material in communicating the benefits of a future experience is a crucial one. The time lapse between preparing promotional material and the delivery of the service itself presents problems. A play, opera or dance event may end up looking very different in performance from the image presented in publicity material designed and written six months beforehand. This is especially a problem with new work as there is no way of telling exactly what will survive in the final version.

One way round this problem is to try to concentrate on selling 'benefits' rather than the more literal 'features' of an arts event in copywriting. At the same time, there is research evidence to suggest that arts attenders expect promotional literature to 'tell us what it is about' in order to help them make an informed decision about what to choose. The acknowledged phenomenon of audiences' preference for familiar repertoire may be less to do with their innate conservatism than with the difficulty that arts consumers face in not getting enough plain information about unfamiliar work.

There is even the perception that copy is sometimes written in a way which deliberately underplays the more challenging aspects of certain sorts of work in order to reduce the risk of potential audiences being scared off. Whatever the truth of this idea, it pays to be explicit about issues like language, nudity and content. Treating potential attenders in any other way is misleading, patronizing and, ultimately, alienating. The philosophy of marketing puts the consumer at the centre of things. This affects copywriting on a fundamental level: the aim should be to talk 'with', rather than 'at', the customer.

This approach can be safeguarded by bearing a number of principles in mind when writing promotional copy:

- Be specific (what's it about?).
- Imagine you are talking to a member of the audience.
- Use short sentences.
- Write to predetermined wordlengths (this concentrates the mind wonderfully).
- Dramatize the benefits in ideas and words that are relevant to the target market.
- Think visually.
- Above all: keep it simple.

Commissioning printed materials

Having decided on the role which mailing and print distribution will play in your promotional strategy, the next step is to determine how many items of print you will require in the course of the year. For a theatre needing to promote two seasons of work in a twelve-month period, this might entail two season leaflets and, say, eight sets of posters and handbills supporting individual shows.

This exercise will indicate what kind of production and design budgets are practicable. They provide a clear idea of financial limits before negotiations with

---

Box 6.4

Going deeper than *Subscribe Now!*

If you spend enough time at it, and push yourself to go deeper than 'Celebrate!' or 'Subscribe Now!' the discipline of writing will force you to organize, isolate and choose priorities about what makes your organization special and what it offers the buyer. That is the key, because people buy and support the specific, the distinctive. Elements of the language you create should refer back to the postitioning statement – indeed, all the way back to the mission statement – and inform the press release, the brochure, the print ad, the telephone solicitation, the public-service announcement, the membership letter, and so on.

Source: Rudman, 1983

---

designers or printers take place. An experienced designer will often see ways of saving money on a job. But it is essential to make the size of the budget clear from the outset to avoid the possibility of wasting valuable design time. Although, like any creative service providers, designers find it difficult to predict their costs accurately, a firm quotation should be obtained before any work is started. This is helpful in setting the paramaters for both sides in the relationship.

Design, copywriting and print production are enormous thieves of time in arts marketing and so every opportunity to streamline the process should be taken. Consolidating production of a whole season's print at the start of the season is a ploy which a number of repertory theatres have used successfully to rationalize the time spent on the project while maximizing the buying power available. This may not always be possible. Different organizations have different planning schedules. But the 'opportunity cost' of time taken away from other essential activities by the fascinating process of print production needs to be recognized by a disciplined approach.

Briefing the designer

Good graphic designers are always in short supply. It may be necessary to talk to several before settling on a final choice. There are various ways of finding out about them:

- Trade directories and yellow pages.
- Phoning the creative directors of local advertising agencies (they often use freelancers themselves).
- Asking colleagues in other organizations.
- Keeping in touch with local colleges and attending leaving shows for design graduates.

Briefing the designer should embrace more than just handing them the copy. They need to understand the background to the job. Explaining the organization's mission statement, outlining the audience (with research evidence where appropriate), and involving the designer in the kind of experience on offer, are all essential steps.

Copy needs to be prepared with an idea of how it fits the format of the leaflet. It is useful to bring along to the meeting with the designer a very rough indication of what you have in mind. Visual references are helpful too. Any picture research you can do will save time and ensure you get what you want. A number of arts organizations now commission photography as opposed to illustration in their publicity material. David Ogilvy (1967), an influential advertising thinker, recommends photography over illustration for its selling power. But it also has the advantage over illustration of allowing you to know exactly how the image will look. Many excellent graphic artists are not necessarily very gifted illustrators, and they find it easier to work with photographs or existing images rather than generate original ones.

Planning schedule for printed materials

Establishing, agreeing and adhering to a timescale is essential in managing the relationship with designer and printer to achieve the desired outcome. It can also be used as the basis for establishing systems and record keeping which will help streamline print production and maximize the scarce resources of time and money. Problems are much more easily avoided than solved, and a schedule helps plan around them. It also imparts a sense of direction to a project. This is crucial when there is a team involved, especially (as is invariably the case with print) if external suppliers are part of the picture.

The schedule for a piece of printed material should include time for conceptualization, copywriting, briefing a designer, commissioning or sourcing visuals, gaining necessary approvals, getting printers' quotations, proofing, printing and delivery. Each of these is potentially a time trap. Sometimes the printing and proofing stages get skimped on because of time wasted earlier in the process, with potentially disastrous effects. Approvals, when required, ought to be straightforward. Artistic directors in arts organizations will inevitably (and justifiably) want to be involved . They can be a useful resource, but it is better to manage their involvement at the early, strategic stages. This will save time later on, particularly when it comes to approving proofs.

So anyone involved in approving (or contributing in any other way, with information, material or pictures) must be clear about:

- The extent of their responsibility.
- When they need to be available (particularly important for approving copy).
- Any changes to copy need to be at an early stage in the process. The nearer the project is to completion, the more expensive alterations become in time and money.

Each organization will have its separate scheduling peculiarities. Touring theatres, for example, are likely to be working on much shorter notice of what they will be presenting than repertory theatres or opera companies who may have the luxury of long-range programme planning. Having said that, repertory theatres can still be subject to unavoidable changes in plans, resulting in late confirmation of season content. The important thing is to communicate the schedule clearly, and keep in touch with each participant. Managing a major print project like a season leaflet requires tact, energy and determination to honour deadlines and make things happen.

Box 6.5

A sample print schedule

A reliable first step is to take the date at which the piece of printed material needs to be in circulation, and then work back through each stage to see how much time there is available. Then a detailed schedule can be constructed as follows:

Week 1: Meeting to discuss content and format with those involved. Agree procedures and schedule.

Week 2: Gather information and brief designer to prepare a rough version (known as a 'Scamp' or 'Rough') for approval of format and overall look. Providing the designer with some kind of model, no matter how rough, can help sort out ambiguities at this stage. A 'flat plan', which gives a page-by-page idea of what is involved, can be a very helpful reference for longer pieces of print. Especially useful is the way they allow you to see 'facing pages' (i.e. left and right page together) – often known as a 'double page spread' or 'DPS'.

Week 3: Agree content. Begin writing copy.

Week 4: Agree format with approval of designer's rough. Begin sourcing images and visuals. Picture libraries, such as the Mary Evans Picture Library in London, can make all the difference in finding the kind of images which will give your publicity material a reassuringly professional look.

Week 5: Finalize copy. Discuss it with frontline staff for their comments on comprehensibility and relevance.

Week 6: First draft of copy complete.

Week 7: Deadline for copy and pictures to be assembled.

Week 8: Copy and pictures approved and sent to the designer. Begin getting quotes from printers. Many will claim that they need to see the artwork itself before they can give an accurate estimate, but they should be able to work from the details of size, numbers of pages, how many folds are involved for a leaflet (or whether it will be stapled), how many colours and photographs will be involved. For detailed guidance see 'Specification' below.

Week 9: Designer marks up copy (i.e. prepares it for the typesetter by indicating size and style of type).

Week 10: Setting comes back from the typesetters in strips known as 'galley proofs' or 'galleys'. Check these and give the OK to commence artwork.

Week 11: Designer does artwork.

Week 12: Designer completes artwork.

Week 13: Artwork checked. The photocopies of artwork at this stage are often called 'page proofs'. Again, they need swift approval.

Week 14: Artwork and all photographs and images to the printer.

Week 15: Prepare to receive 'machine proofs' (sometimes called 'ozalids', depending on the process used).

Week 16: Approve machine proofs. For the first time you will be able to see the copy and the pictures as they will appear in the final printed article – although the colours may well differ from the final effect. Changes made to copy at this stage are very expensive because of the machine time involved – and are known as 'author's corrections' if they emanate from you rather than any mistakes on the printer's part.

Week 17: OK given to printers to print bulk.

Week 18: Await delivery.

Week 19: Receive delivery.

Week 20: Mailing and distribution commence.

Print specification

Being a good customer to external suppliers helps an organization serve its own customers more effectively. This is certainly true when buying print, when an accurate specification can save a lot of time and energy. A specification is a full technical description of what will be required in the printing job. As mentioned in the schedule outline above, some printers will insist that they need to see the artwork before quoting. But a full specification can mean that you are able to access more quotations in advance, and therefore negotiate a better price. By the stage the artwork becomes available, time is likely to be at a premium.

It is a good idea to get at least three quotations. Like the arts, printing is a service business and cannot store capacity. Its machines are either occupied or they lose money. So it may be that, if your print project coincides with a slack period, you get offered very attractive rates. Before making your final decision, it is worth paying the printer a visit. As we shall see in Chapter 9, good supplier relationships are essential to successful marketing, so it pays to find out as much as you can about the printer. Good printers when found are worth cultivating, although the relationship should never become a complacent one.

Box 6.6

A sample print specification

On your specification (one side of A4) include the following information:

- Your name and contact details and the date.
- The title of the project.
- The format (e.g. A4 landscape).
- Description (e.g. 16 pages of text printed in two colours both sides, self-cover, stapled).
- The materials (the heavier the paper the more expensive the print job, as a rule. Ask for samples. Normal typing paper is about 80 g per square metre – or 'gsm'. Do you want a matt or shiny finish – also known as 'art paper'?).
- Artwork (is it to be camera ready, same-size, how many line and photographic illustrations will be involved, will the second colour be marked on an overlay? How complicated will the design be? Will 'bleeds' – colour running to the margin – cost extra?)
- The quantity required (e.g. 10,000 and 2,000 run-on – run-on meaning how much would a small extra quantity be? It can often be minimal once the job is up and running).
- Proofs: details of what proofs you require.
- Delivery: more than one point for delivery will increase the cost, but may save you time if you are using a distribution company.

Public relations

Well-chosen advertising media are powerful but expensive. Arts organizations have traditionally preferred public relations as a cheaper alternative. PR should not be seen as a way of doing advertising on the cheap. Both advertising and PR need a substantial commitment of time and money, although in differing proportions. In spite of what many journalists seem to think, PR is not a case of 'applied conviviality to keep bad news out of the press and free advertising in'. Instead it is the deliberate, planned and sustained effort to establish and maintain mutual understanding between an organization and its public.

Confusing the roles of advertising and public relations can lead to false expectations of what either can do. They are both 'deliberate, planned and sustained'. They operate side by side in the same media. But whereas you can exercise direct control over advertising, public relations relies largely on the good will of third parties. Advertising tends to be a one-way process. Public relations implies dialogue: what the definition calls 'mutual understanding'. Good public relations involves a lot of listening. Mercer (1992) points to the appropriateness of PR as a promotional technique for non-profit and service organizations: 'PR is often a particularly valuable

Box 6.7

Parlez-vous printing?

Like advertising, printing has its own specialized jargon. Here are some commonly used terms and their explanations. If ever you are in doubt about the production process, don't hesitate to ask your printers. They like to work with well-informed clients and will be delighted to explain things and make valuable suggestions:

Airbrush	An instrument producing a very fine spray of ink or paint. Can look great for illustrating metallic effects, but very expensive because of the time involved.
Art paper	Gloss finished paper, coated with china clay.
Bleed	Printing a colour to the edge of the page.
Bromide	A high-definition photographic image on silver bromide paper.
Call-out	A piece of text given special emphasis by separating it from the rest of the copy.
Colour separation	Process of separating the different elements of the primary colours making up a colour image in order to manufacture printing plates for each.
Colours	The cheapest form of printing is black on white ('one colour'). Two colours of ink together cost a little more but open up a number of possibilities (including 'duo-tone' which can look very convincing). If you're strapped for cash, try printing one colour black on a coloured paper. At the other end of the scale, four-colour printing (while expensive) allows you to mix the four 'process' colours to get the full spectrum of effects
Cow gum	Rubber solution used in pasting up artwork.
Cropping	Cutting a picture to size by specifying which areas are not to be reproduced.
Duotone	A two-colour half tone from a single-colour original. Gives an impression of depth and solidity.
Em	A unit of type measurement based on the width of the capital letter 'M'. Unless otherwise specified, an em means a pica (12 point) em. Often called a 'monkey'.
En	Half an em – often called a 'nut'.
Half tone	A photographic reproduction giving the impression of gradations of colour through tiny dots on the page.
Justification	Justified type results in lines of equal length, and straight margins left and right. Unjustified type usually has a straight margin on the left and a ragged margin on the right.

Light box	A light source used for examining photographic transparencies.
Marked-up copy	Copy which has been prepared with instructions from the graphic designer for the typesetter.
PMT	Photo mechanical transfer – a print from an artwork, often used as an intermediary stage or for client approval or artwork.
Point	A measure of the height of a typeface from the top of the tallest letter to the bottom of the lowest. There are 72 points to an inch.
Process colours	Yellow, magenta, cyan and black – from which colour printing can produce the full spectrum.
Progressives	Colour proofs showing each process colour separately, and then their build up ('progression') to the combined effect.
Register	In colour printing, the accuracy with which the over-lays are superimposed.
Retouching	Correcting or improving a visual image. Becoming easier with computer technology.
Reversed out copy	Letters that are white on a coloured background. Impressive, but hard to read in quantity.
Saddle stitched	Stapled, to you and me, but so called because the machine on which the stapling is done looks like a saddle.
Spray mount	An alternative to cow gum – but can be dangerous in enclosed spaces.
Tint	A shade of a colour produced, like a half tone, by tiny dots. A 10 per cent tint means that 10 per cent of the paper is covered by the colour.
Typeface	A style of type. It can impart atmosphere and character to your printed materials.
Vignette	A gradual fading away of colour across a page as a background to an illustration.
White space	The art of leaving things out is as important as includ-ing them in order to avoid clutter in designing printed materials.

promotional device for services; since the "authority" offered by independent recom-mendation in editorial matter can add vital credibility to an intangible service.'

The most important difference between advertising and public relations is choice. An arts organization can choose when and where to advertise – or even choose not to advertise at all. But it has public relations whether it likes it or not. The only choice is whether to manage the process or let things drift along by themselves. Organizations that do not take a proactive approach to PR are still sending out messages about themselves. By their programme choice, pricing, the nature of their buildings or offices, even the way that the telephones are answered (and how long it takes to answer them), they are beaming images to customers, employees, stakeholders, competitors and suppliers.

What can PR do?

Advertising, as has been observed, can be trusted to convey accurate commercial details such as times and prices. Public relations, on the other hand, deals with information which is no less important but is less definite and longer term: atmosphere, excitement, novelty. Furthermore, its advocates claim that public relations, working as it does through editorial, allows your message to reach people who may be averse or desensitized to advertising. Some highly successful commercial organizations such as Marks & Spencer and The Body Shop have achieved leading reputations as companies with a minimum of advertising expenditure, concentrating on establishing and maintaining high profile public relations instead.

'Word of mouth' is the kind of interpersonal publicity at which all promotional activity aims. Public relations recognizes this in the way that it tries to generate 'two-step' communication. This idea, developed as a theory by the American researchers Katz and Lazarfeld (1955), emphasizes the role played in communication by membership of social groups (including families, organizations, circles of friends and colleagues). By conveying the promotional message to dominant members of such groups ('opinion leaders') the message is then passed on to the other members with greater conviction and effectiveness.

This model can be applied to a number of situations to illustrate the way in which an arts organization gets its message across using public relations. In one sense, a features editor on a local newspaper running an interview with a visiting artist is acting as an 'opinion leader' to the readers. In another, people who organize outings for groups of colleagues or associates to the theatre or to exhibitions (the highly-prized 'party bookers') also justify classification as opinion leaders. Invitations to special presentations, inclusion on mailing lists for press releases, active telephone contact, are all ways of nurturing relationships with such key figures in order to reach a wider circle of audience members through this kind of multi-stage contact.

Opinion leaders are one of a number of publics with which an arts organization needs to manage its relations. The chart below (Figure 6.1 'Publics') shows a good way of mapping out your potential audience by dividing them into separate groups or 'publics'. With your organization in the middle, draw a line out to each of the important groups with which you have a relationship. Customers, competitors, suppliers, workforce, agencies, clients, government, media, artists, writers, unions. The list will vary with each organization. This process is another example of the kind of market segmentation discussed in Chapter 2.

The next step in the process is to prioritize the importance of each group. The importance of 'internal publics' (workforce and colleagues) is easy to underestimate in organizations that are focused on surviving in a precarious external environment. But keeping staff informed and consulted is a highly cost-effective policy. They are far more credible to people outside the organization than the slickest piece of

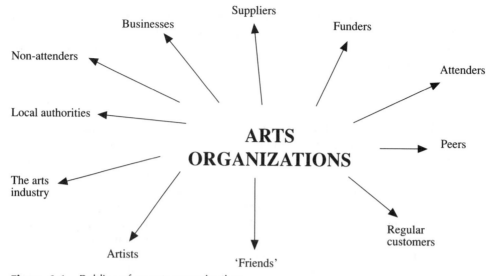

Figure 6.1   Publics of an arts organization

corporate advertising. Chapter 9 looks at the important but too often neglected issue of internal marketing in the arts. Communicating policy clearly and effectively can turn workers into advocates, creating an invaluable promotional resource at minimum cost. External suppliers and dealers are also enormously important. Keeping them in the picture means that you are more likely to get the benefit of whatever discretion they can offer in their dealings with your organization.

Once you have ranked the groups in the order in which their goodwill is important to you, the next step is to consolidate any that are very similar, and to focus attention on the most important groups. What aspects of your organization's message are they most likely to respond to? Do you, in fact, need to tell two or more different stories? Obviously they must be complementary rather than contradictory, but different emphases may be appropriate for different publics.

For example, a theatre funded by a local authority wants to publicize its recent successful record in attracting business sponsorship. The message it directs at its funding body is that sponsorship is helping it reach more people in the local community by attracting employees (and their families) of the businesses concerned. This approach, emphasizing the sponsorship as an outreach marketing activity, should avoid the danger of the local authority feeling that it can safely reduce its funding as a result of the theatre's ability to generate its own income.

To a different public (this time other potential sponsors), the theatre wants to relay the complementary but different message that here is a new promotional opportunity that competitors are using to gain an advantage. The message here is 'be part of our success – like these other leading local companies.'

The basic message is the same – in both cases that the organization is now in the business of successful sponsorship. But the execution of the message, and the way it is

> Box 6.8
> ## What's news?
> News is people. It is people talking and people doing. Committees and Cabinets and courts are people; so are fires, accidents, and planning decisions. They are only news because they involve and affect people.
>
> Harold Evans, former editor of *The Sunday Times*

conveyed, will differ according to the public at which it is aimed. In some cases the best way will be through a direct approach: perhaps organizing a reception or a presentation to selected delegates – business people, journalists or key customers. But more often, because of the size of the publics you need to reach, a third party comes into the equation: the media. How to deal with the media and, in particular, how to write effective press releases, is the subject of the next section.

Media relations and the press release

Journalists are busy people. You can get the best out of them by making their lives as easy as possible. One way of doing this is to be able to spot an 'angle' to a story. And, having done that, to be able to communicate the idea briefly and coherently in a press release. The most important knack to acquire, though, is an appreciation of what makes news.

What makes a story?

The simple answer is 'anything'. But if you take a look at your local or national newspaper, you will see that the stories you are reading hang on some particular hook. Journalists are actually trained to look for what is newsworthy. If you want to get them interested in your story, make sure it contains at least one of the following elements:

- Action.
- Arguments and views.
- Unusualness.
- Community concerns and local interest.
- Human interest.
- Topicality.
- Relevance to a national issue (e.g. a television soap, political crisis, freak weather, Christmas, etc.).

Different papers have different approaches to news. Some are very serious, others mix in the heavyweight stories with quirkier tittle tattle. The same is true for radio programmes and television. The only way to get a measure of the opportunities facing you as a publicist is to make time to read the papers, listen to the radio and watch television. It is part of the necessary groundwork for success. Journalists themselves are avid consumers of other media. In fact a survey revealed that over 80

A good PR story as sponsor coughs up for the Hallé

Coughing at concerts can be a problem. It only takes a couple of afflicted audience members to distract a performer or conductor, or disturb the concentration of other concert-goers. Boarding a plane to the States in 1993 Kent Nagano, music director of Manchester's internationally-acclaimed Hallé Orchestra, asked Dominic Tinner, the orchestra's head of development, to find a cure for the hawkers of the Hallé.

Throat lozenges seemed to be the solution. By a happy coincidence Cedar Health, the sole UK importers of Ricola cough lozenges from Switzerland, are based on the outskirts of Manchester at Hazel Grove. A sponsorship in kind was negotiated whereby the company supplied the Hallé with lozenges for free distribution to its audiences in Manchester and on tour. Complimentary lozenges were offered to all concertgoers in order to facilitate everyone's enjoyment of the music.

The sponsorship formed the basis for an enormous amount of publicity. Tinner later commented:

> We had something like twenty press cuttings from that activity alone. Tabloids, broadsheets, magazines all loved the idea. It even created interest in America. I was interviewed about it on CBC Toronto, and Kent's colleagues at the Berkeley Symphony in California heard news of the story before he came back. The Today Programme on Radio 4 conducted a microphone experiment to see how quietly one of the lozenges could be unwrapped.

Quite apart from the direct benefits of free lozenges for coughers, such wide publicity for both parties to the deal is not to be sniffed at!

per cent of news editors cited articles in other magazines and newspapers as the most important sources for their own work.

Try to get to know a journalist or two. Local publicity clubs are a useful way of establishing contacts, as are events and receptions. Some arts marketers even make a point of attending other people's first nights. Don't be afraid to introduce yourself. Journalists need stories to fill their papers and broadcasts every day of the year. You are doing them a favour, not the other way round (whatever it may feel like). Another thing to learn about your local publications in particular is when deadlines fall. The best story in the world is no good to a journalist if it arrives too late to be used.

Don't try ringing a journalist on an evening paper in the morning – you are likely to get very short shrift from someone struggling to get copy sorted out for his or her next edition. Another point to bear in mind about deadlines is the fact that broadcast media such as television and radio can turn a story round a lot faster than most print media. This means that, if you are not careful about how you release it, you may find that your story is considered old news by a newspaper after it has been run on the local radio.

Box 6.9

A deadline is a deadline

As new technology tightens its grip on the traditional world of the newspaper, deadlines are shortening. But they still need to be honoured. A rough guide to the sort of time you should plan for is as follows:

- Weekly papers: 3 days prior to publication.
- Morning papers: 3 pm the preceding afternoon.
- Evening papers: 11 am day of publication.
- Local radio: an hour before a news bulletin.
- Local TV: 11 am day of broadcast.

The good thing about this, however, is that it forces you to look for new angles. A weekly paper cannot hope to compete with a daily paper for news stories. On the other hand it can afford to cover stories in more depth, and run more 'feature' and 'human interest' material, which does not need to be quite so up to the minute.

A local paper will tend to have one or two people who, as well as doing other things, will specialize in arts coverage. These are, of course, key contacts. But never lose sight of the bigger picture. The business editor, for example, is worth cultivating. Time spent with journalists is a good investment. Staff photographers are another extremely important group whose goodwill and enthusiasm can make all the difference between a routine appearance in the newspaper and a veritable publicity coup. Arts organizations are in the enviable position of being able to offer photographers the opportunity to take pictures which they themselves find interesting and rewarding.

Writing a press release

'Now what I want is Facts ... Facts alone are wanted in life.'
Mr Gradgrind in *Hard Times* by Charles Dickens.

There are five very important facts any press release should contain, preferably in the first one or two sentences (the 'lead' as journalists call it):

- What is happening?
- Who is involved?
- Where is it taking place?
- When is it happening?
- Why is it happening?

The first couple of sentences, answering these questions, are crucial to the success or failure of what follows. They will be scanned by an extremely busy journalist, and whether they end up on the desk for further investigation, or in the wastepaper basket with the rest of the release, depends on what comes across in the first seconds.

Another good reason for getting all the important material into the first paragraph of the release is that sometimes editors print press releases without changing them, except for cutting them. Traditionally editors cut from the bottom. So the supporting details should go into later paragraphs. This practice can be verified by reference to any newspaper. Almost invariably the main point of the story (with the essential information) will lie in the first paragraph of each news item.

It's often a good idea to follow up the release by phone to selected journalists. Persistency pays dividends.

Assuming the press are after you for a change, how do you deal with them? First of all, be honest. If you can't answer a particular question, promise to ring back when you've got the facts. If they are asking questions you would rather not answer, get someone better qualified to deal with them. It helps, if you think you have a crisis on your hands, to get expert advice.

Picture this

There are few things as eloquent as a good photograph. Photocalls are an excellent way of getting to know journalists and giving them a real sense of involvement in what you are doing. Even when there are photographers present from a number of different newspapers, each can go home with a unique interpretation of what you have to offer.

The problem with press releases is that journalists can make of them what they like. This may not always accord with your interests, although it makes a good story. The beauty of pictures is that they are easier to control (in general) and have much more immediate impact than the written word. Best of all, in terms of control, is the ability to supply your own pictures. Here it is worth studying the sort of photographic images that get published in a newspaper. Sometimes what works on stage or in a gallery does not necessarily look good in newsprint. Values to aim at in commissioning photography for reproduction in newspapers include the following:

- Close-ups.
- Upright images rather than sideways ones (i.e. 'portrait' not 'landscape').
- People close together (compact images fit better into newspaper columns).
- People doing something that is easily understood.
- Tonal variety (large patches of black look dramatic on stage but dull in newspapers).
- Upbeat, or unusual, situations (hats, props, costumes, cars and, in spite of W.C. Fields, children and animals . . .).

Organizing photocalls requires a very disciplined approach. The objective is to assemble a number of people together for a very short time, often at a stage (because of the proximity of an opening night) when their preoccupations may be very

Box 6.10

Press releases that impress

In writing or approving a press release, check out the following aspects of style. (It is worth photocopying this list and keeping it in your field of vision when working):

1 Dates should be exact and full: e.g. Tuesday 5 December 1995, not 'this Tuesday'.
2 Addresses, where appropriate, should be given in full. Assume ignorance on the part of the journalist, even if your location is highly familiar.
3 Brevity is the soul of wit, especially in a press release. It's useful to remember that one side of double-spaced A4 fills about 6 column inches in most newspapers.
4 Deal in facts, not opinions. Opinions are for the journalist to form, and you will find that if your press release goes over the top about how wonderful your artistic offering is, it will be dismissed as an attempt to get free advertising.
5 It's often a good idea to include a quote from somebody prominent. This allows the journalist to write as if he or she has interviewed the person concerned, and can inject more life into the final article.
6 Keep it simple and concise. As with any kind of copywriting, complexity puts distance between you and your audience.
7 Check the facts in the release carefully, and get someone else to check them as well. The awful thing about a mistake in a press release is that it is completely impossible to put right. It also makes both you and the journalist look foolish – hardly likely to inspire continuing confidence in your relationship. Now and then ask friendly journalists what they think of your approach to press releases.

The following presentation conventions should be observed:

1 Use good quality A4 paper. Make sure it's clear from whom the release is sent at the top. Headed stationery is best. Many arts organizations use a variation on their standard letterheadings to indicate that it is a press release.
2 Make sure there is a contact name on the release for follow-up from the journalist. It is particularly helpful to specify when the person will be available. Many press releases now carry home and office contact numbers – but journalists tend to work standard hours.
3 Begin the release about a third of the way down the paper, type double spaced and leave wide margins. It is a good idea to indent the beginning of each paragraph five spaces, as it helps the eye down the page as well as giving extra space for editorial marking.
4 If the release runs to more than one page, type MORE at the bottom right hand corner of each page. Do not break a sentence or paragraph between

> two pages. And remember to type your company's name or story caption at the top of each new page. At the end of the last page of the release type END.

different from your own. The following points are worth following – although every situation can be different:

- Phone the photographer first to 'sell' the idea if this is to be an exclusive. Listen to whatever suggestions he or she has to make.
- Write down a schedule with timings for arrivals and departures.
- Make sure everyone concerned in the organization knows about the photocall and is fully briefed on their role.
- Be nice to your subjects. The occasional bacon sandwich has been known to melt a heart or two.
- Ring round the photographer(s) on the morning of the photocall to re-check their availability. Their diary appointments are subject to change at the last moment if a news story breaks elsewhere.

Targeting opportunities in broadcast media

Although this chapter uses the terminology 'press release', what works for printed media does not always apply to broadcast. Success comes from considering what a particular situation might yield for the medium under consideration. It is an extension of the essential marketing principle of putting the customer first, in this case the journalist or producer. Thinking in pictures is essential when targeting television news or magazine programmes. It pays to think carefully about the visual potential of a news story, and to be able to telephone the producer or editor with a very clear idea of what you have in mind. This will enable them to decide quickly on its merits (and resource implications). They will often add ideas of their own – a useful source of experience to the arts marketer.

Similarly, radio can provide a useful and effective public relations outlet. Here it is important to think of aural angles. Even visual art forms like dance and fine arts work well in sound only. Radio is very good for personalities and enthusiasm, so select your speakers carefully. Explaining the history of an art object or the soundscape of a dance piece can open up very exciting possibilities.

When planning for an interview on radio or television, preparation is very important. If you are organizing an interview where two people are involved (for example cast members from a touring production) then think in terms of contrast. A mixture of sexes or ages makes for more interesting listening.

Box 6.11

Survival guide for broadcast interviews

The following checklist can help focus the mind on the important business of communication by reducing the amount of stress that microphones and cameras can create:

- The object of the presenter is to make entertaining programming and look good. He or she will want to sound in control and confident – and therefore your confidence and positive manner will be a real help.
- Focus on the person who is talking to you. Journalists are practised at putting interviewees at their ease. Be natural.
- Check out in advance whether the interview is to be recorded or is going out live. This may affect what you want to say, especially if it might go out of date quickly.
- Make life easier for your presenter by briefing him or her in advance with some written material. A press release, leaflet or other props can be very helpful. For visual arts marketers, bring along some photographs about your product or company.
- If you find it helps your nerves, jot down the main points you want to make on a postcard and keep it with you.
- The presenter will tend to brief you in advance on the shape of the interview. Don't start answering the questions until you are on air, however.
- Finally, enjoy! It's good fun being on the radio or the television.

Making presentations

The ability to stand up in front of an audience and speak persuasively is a great asset in arts marketing. Presentation skills are relevant in a number of areas covered in this book:

- Briefing journalists at a press conference.
- Market research debriefs to other managers or board members.
- Talking to groups about your organization with a view to encouraging their interest.
- Putting proposals to sponsors.
- Motivating and informing colleagues and staff.

Presentations are a personal way of communicating your organization's message. But an effortlessly assured performance does not just happen. It is the result of careful preparation and rehearsal.

Consider your audience

As with all the promotional techniques we have examined in this chapter, this is the starting point. What do you know about the people in the audience?

- They will normally be well disposed to you, but will have high expectations.
- They will listen more closely if you involve them by showing how your subject affects them.
- The only access to their minds is through their senses.
- Seeing things helps them understand and remember them.
- Their concentration fades after 5 or 10 minutes.
- Being human they tend to remember patterns, structures and examples rather than abstract concepts.
- They don't mind meaningful repetition – in fact they like to be reminded that they have understood.

Presentations can fulfil a number of objectives. What is yours? Is the purpose of the presentation to persuade someone of something (e.g. to sponsor your forthcoming exhibition) or is it to provide information (e.g. to announce a new season of opera)? Getting the basic purpose of the exercise clear is the best foundation for making the right decisions later on.

Deciding on content is the first of these:

- Jot down all your ideas.
- Group them.
- Allocate priorities between essential details and support (rather like a press release).
- Prune and select.
- Arrange in the best sequence for your audience's understanding.

Next comes writing the script:

- This can be done in full, beforehand, but it is best to deliver from headings.
- An 'AIDA' type structure can help:
  - introduction to command attention
  - conclusion to review and consolidate content, with an action option.

Deciding on the extent and function of visual aids is the next step. Some may have already suggested themselves. Will you need handouts, and what should their content and role be? Costing and arranging their preparation needs to be taken care of early.

The next stage is to do a 'run through' of the presentation checking the following factors:

- Appropriate visuals.
- Sequence.
- Balance.
- Coherence.
- Answering objectives.

After this it should be possible to amend the package to iron out ambiguities or awkwardness. It should also be possible to decide finally what materials will be necessary and prepare them accordingly. A dress rehearsal in front of a friendly colleague completes this step, and allows you to use feedback to prepare a final version.

At the end of this process you will be well prepared. It may seem an arduous exercise as covered here, but the sequence of suggested actions is meant to minimize the time spent going round in unnecessary circles. Some experienced speakers find it useful to time their presentations to the second. This certainly helps avoid the common, but unforgivable, error of going on too long.

The presentation surroundings

Physical environment, whose general importance to arts marketing is discussed in greater detail in Chapter 7, plays a crucial role in presentations. Equipment needs to be checked. In an unfamiliar venue the kind of technology used may be different from what you are used to. Some practitioners support the idea that handouts should be given out as people arrive. It is hard to follow the logic of this, as handouts can provide a distraction from the presentation itself.

Furniture has its role to play. What kind of seating arrangement should apply? Is it necessary (or desirable) that the audience should have a strong sense of each other (as encouraged by a horseshoe shaped arrangement), or should their attention be focused individually on you as speaker from serried ranks of chairs and desks? If there is a table, which side of it should you be?

Lighting is another important consideration. If you are planning to use 35 mm slides, it is necessary to achieve a good level of blackout in the presentation room. Sometimes this is not possible just by drawing the curtains, so it is necessary to do some advance investigation, and establish a solution to the problem if necessary.

Heating and ventilation are very important. Drowsiness and inattention, even nausea, are possible through a room being too stuffy. Other distractions might include extraneous noise (perhaps it can be planned round) or simply untidiness – other people's material hanging in your audience's field of view, for example. Finally, your own appearance is something which will communicate even before you open your mouth. Make sure it demonstrates respect and consideration to your audience.

Delivery

Now comes the moment of performance. It is important to maintain your audience's good opinion of you by making a good initial impression. Starting in a definite way can help get you off on a good footing. A simple routine conquers butterflies. Here is a tried and tested formula:

- Introduce yourself.
- Say how delighted you are to have the opportunity of speaking to them today.
- Tell them what you are going to tell them.

Box 6.12

Strengths and weaknesses of different styles of visual aids

Flip charts?
–Can be prepared in advance.
–Improvisable.
–Can conceal/reveal.
–Can be used to build up a case.
–Can be retained for future use.
–Can stimulate audience participation.
–Good for smaller meetings.
–Messy.
–Awkward.

Chalkboards
–Readily available.
–OK but unsophisticated.
–Messy and temporary.
–Tricky to do in advance.
–Need artistic ability.

OHPs
–Versatile.
–Advance preparation, using desk top publishing and photocopying the result on to overheads, can look impressive.
–Build up possible (as are crib notes attached to transparencies on Post-It notes).
–Easy to use.
–Avoid visual distraction by concentrating the eye on light.
–Noisy and can be uncomfortable for those sitting near them because of the fan.
–Unwieldy. Even the portable ones are awkward to carry.
–Need to carry spare bulbs and an extension lead for the mains supply.

Slides
–Can be expensive, but look great when done well.
–Hard to prepare (although computers and electronic imaging is making this less of a problem).
–Room needs to be dark.
–Sequence of slides in magazine is inflexible, unlike OHP transparencies which can be referred back to at will.

Film/video/multimedia from a VDU.
–Impressive but needs careful introduction and follow up.
–Can be constraining.
–High production standards expected.

- Tell them.
- Tell them what you have told them.

Eye contact is important. It will help your listeners concentrate and give you useful feedback. Smiling helps (if you can manage it). It puts both the presenter and the audience in a more relaxed and communicative state. As you continue, the contact needs to be maintained and developed. Looking at individuals, avoiding the temptation to talk to your slides or notes, keeping things simple and well structured, are all instrumental in this kind of care for your customers (in this case, your listeners). If things are going well in the presentation, you will find it flows with little effort. All the hard work has been done in the previous weeks. So, speak naturally, and use your notes as support rather than script. This will increase your chances of looking relaxed and comfortable, and help your audience's attention as well.

A little humour can enliven a presentation, but it can also be distracting, embarrassing or simply irritating. So it needs to be approached with care. The focus of the speaker needs to be on communicating first and foremost rather than being amusing or entertaining.

Visual aids

As ever in communication, simplicity, relevance and ease of comprehension make for good visual aids. When designing or using them, the following points are worth bearing in mind:

- Use space imaginatively.
- Clear writing.
- Diagrams can be helpful when sharing information or getting agreement.
- Build up gradually to complexity (if complexity is desirable).
- Allow time for understanding.
- Don't leave visual aids up longer than you need or they become distractions in their own right.

Conclusion

Communicating the benefits of what is on offer from the artistic experience is a fundamentally important part of the activities of the marketing function. While it requires flair and imagination, it also needs determination and a disciplined, evaluative approach. Applying simple structures like AIDA and USP can help reduce the complexity of the task of saying the right things about your offering in the right format.

Arts organizations have a number of promotional techniques at their disposal. Advertising is expensive but can communicate important details to a large number of people very quickly. Print and poster media are traditionally favoured by arts clients, but media possibilities should be subject to constant review.

Sales promotion is most commonly seen in the form of discounts tied to multiple attendance. But, like advertising and publicity, it is capable of a flexible application across a wide range of tactical situations.

Printed publicity, in the form of literature like season brochures, spearheads the marketing activity of most performing and visual arts organizations. Writing or editing copy and overseeing design and production involves tact and determination. Developing good systems and working relationships can minimize the risks involved.

The technique of public relations, internal and external, builds on the strengths of arts organizations and can be used to create background interest in arts activities. It is less good, however, at fulfilling that interest than more specific publicity such as direct marketing.

The formal interpersonal communication involved in making presentations is suited to a number of internal and external arts marketing situations. In common with all the other promotional techniques examined in this chapter, success comes from consideration of the audience, followed by careful preparation and delivery of the message.

Key concepts

AIDA
Brand image
Copywriting
Coupons
Coverage
Free mail-ins
Frequency
Interpersonal communication
Interviews
Media research
News values
Opinion leaders

Outdoor advertising
Press release
Print schedule
Print specification
Printing terminology
Rate card
Rating
Sales promotion
Solus position
Specification
Transport advertising
USP

Discussion questions

1 In a piece of theatre advertising of your choice, discuss the elements of information and persuasion at work in the copy and visuals.
2 Compare and contrast poster and radio as advertising media for a civic museum.
3 How can an arts organization ensure that its unique selling proposition remains unique?
4 What are 'news values'? Do they vary between different media, and how might an arts organization take advantage of them?

5 Public relations is supposed to be about mutual understanding between an organization and its public. How might you recognize this process in a contemporary dance
group?
6 Outline some of the problems facing a recently-appointed marketing manager in a
theatre, who discovers her first task is to produce a season leaflet in two-and-a-half
months. How might she overcome them?

Action problems

1 Prepare a short briefing paper (two sides of A4 maximum) describing, and
justifying with evidence, the USP of your organization to a new board member.
2 Compile a collection of pieces of printed publicity that stand out in some way, and
find out who has produced and designed each one. Compile a list of local graphic
designers and their clients and arrange to have it updated every six months.
3 How might you go about evaluating the success of your organization's public relations programme? What would you do with the insights gained from such an analysis?
4 Outline a 10-minute presentation to a potential sponsor who might be interested in
offering you some help in kind with transport.

References

Bernstein, D. (1974). *Creative Advertising*. Longman.
Bernstein, D. (1984). *Corporate Image and Reality*. Reinhardt.
Broadbent, S. (1990). *The Advertising Budget*. McGraw-Hill.
Burnett, K. (1987). *Charity Annual Reports: The Complete Guide to Planning and Production*.
    Directory of Social Change.
Carnegie, D. (1992 reprint). *How to Win Friends and Influence People*. Cedar Books.
Crofts, A. (1988). Enhancing the past to secure the future. *Marketing Week*, 11 March, 48–56.
Cummins, J. (1993). *Sales Promotion*, 2nd edn. Kogan Page.
Evans, R. (1988). *Production and Creativity in Advertising*. Pitman.
Katz, E. and Lazarfeld, P. (1955). *Personal Influence: The Part Played by People in the Flow of Mass
    Communications*. New York: Free Press.
McDonald, C. (1992). *How Advertising Works*. NTC Publications.
McIntosh, D. and A. (1985). *A Basic PR Guide for Charities*. Directory of Social Change.
Mercer, D. (1992). *Marketing*. Basil Blackwell.
Moyle, F. (1990). Cash cure for art attacks. *Marketing Week*, 30 November. 38–42.
Rudman, W. (1983) Essentials of effective public relations. In *Market the Arts!* (ed. Joseph V.
    Melillo), New York: FEDAPT.
Ogilvy, D. (1983). *Ogilvy on Advertising*. Pan.
Reeves (1977 reprint). *Reality in Advertising*. Knopf.
Smith, P. (1993). *Marketing Communications: An Integrated Approach*. Kogan Page.
White, R. (1993). *Advertising: What It Is and How to Do It*, 3rd edn. McGraw-Hill.

7 Making the arts available

Introduction

The fourth element of the marketing mix 'Place', also known as 'distribution', is concerned with making an organization's offering available to the customer when and where it is required. Practically all the marketing literature dealing with distribution as a subject is about products – moving them about, storing them, displaying them. Yet consideration of the area has much to yield service industries, and arts organizations in particular. The performing arts, for example, use a variety of means to open up the experience on offer to as many consumers as possible. Opera and dance companies, for example, take their work on the road, touring it to audiences nationally and internationally. Ticket agents make buying tickets easier for people living at a distance from a theatre, yet still requiring personal service. Amateur companies will select certain venues over others because of the access they give to established audiences.

In this chapter we will look at the following areas:

- The importance of distribution in the marketing mix.
- The nature and function of marketing channels.
- The physical environment as a factor in marketing artistic experience.
- Time as a distribution variable.
- Direct marketing (where the functions of distribution and promotion are combined in a total approach to marketing).

Distribution in the marketing mix

'The Dark Continent'

Peter Drucker, one of this century's most influential management and marketing thinkers, once described distribution as 'The Economy's Dark Continent'. He was making the point that not only is it widely neglected as a marketing variable, but that it holds rich rewards for those enterprising enough to explore it.

Distribution addresses the issue of how to establish a relationship with the maximum number of customers at the minimum cost to the organization, and with

Wanted: a man in a van

'As a forum for critical debate, small magazines are a symptom of the health of a culture,' says Peter Sirr, one of the editors of *Graph*, a magazine of literary criticism which lasted seven years before ceasing production earlier this year.

Like many others of its kind, *Graph* depended on voluntary labour as well as Arts Council funding to keep going, and its three editors had full-time jobs as well as running the magazine.

'We had no marketing skills to draw on, and no time to develop these skills.' Exhaustion set in, aggravated by the difficulties of distribution in a country which has 'no national distributor for small magazines.' Sirr and his co-editors often wished there was 'a man in a van' who could be employed by several of the small magazines to distribute their wares around the country, but there was never enough money for this dream to bear fruit.'

Source: Donovan (1993)

the best outcome from the point of view of its objectives. Attention to distribution is rewarded by coverage of a wider audience, accessing more customers and enabling existing customers to have a more satisfactory experience. Essentially it deals with managing effective supply. Successful distribution fulfils the opportunities that the rest of the marketing elements create in the market, establishing the all-important final link with the customer. Advertising and publicity can attract the customer, but the sales effort at the box office or the gallery counter is what seals the relationship. Reliable distribution is an absolute requirement of marketing success, whatever your art form.

Traditional definitions tend to connect distribution with moving goods or services from those who produce them to those who consume them. But it should also be remembered that all organizations, whatever their size or role, are involved in purchasing as well as supplying demand. Our examination of distribution will emphasize how arts organizations can improve their position and effectiveness by reviewing their operations at both ends of the process: managing supply both as a customer and a supplier. Increasingly, managers are finding that their ability to satisfy their customers' needs more efficiently and effectively hangs on their relationships with their own suppliers.

Given its importance to effective marketing, why has distribution remained the poor relation of the marketing mix for so long? One reason may be that although distribution channels are in a constant state of development, their rate of changeover time is often very slow. Even long-term relationships can be improved, however, if the status quo is not taken for granted: 'New approaches to distribution are often easier to develop than superior products, yet they can lead to equally large break-throughs in profits' (Davidson, 1987).

Many of the radical changes in mainstream distribution that consumers have witnessed over the last twenty years are directly relevant to the arts. The out-of-town shopping centre, reflecting increased car ownership, is complemented by out-of-town leisure activities such as multiplex cinemas. The combination of telephone, credit card and computer has fuelled the boom of 'direct' marketing. It has changed the way we buy and sell a number of goods and services, including tickets. Data capture at point of sale is becoming the norm at box offices, leading to more efficient and responsive customer care. These are just some facets of the distribution revolution that surrounds the arts marketer.

The fourth 'P'

In marketing tangible goods, the emphasis is on 'physical distribution' – getting the product to the customer in the right condition and at the right price and time. These activities take place in the human context of a 'marketing channel', which adds the functions of selling and transferring goods from manufacturers to consumers. The actions in such channels are performed by organizations and individuals known as 'channel intermediaries'. Each of these concepts is relevant to opening out the experience of the arts to customers, even though (apart from equipment and people) very few tangible products are involved.

Distribution needs to work with, and complement, the other marketing mix elements. The kind of 'Product' you are dealing with has a fundamental influence on distribution decisions. Galleries and museums have to address immediate issues of transport and security for their exhibits. Auction room prices have made the issue of insurance during transport particularly problematical, creating costs which either swallow up large amounts of subsidy or have to be passed on in admission prices. Touring opera and theatre companies, or visiting orchestras, have their own solutions to the physical distribution difficulties of getting from one performance venue to another with equipment and sets. Often the only way to facilitate international touring for a major orchestra is to negotiate sponsorship in kind with an airline.

For the individual artist, the cost of travel may be a barrier to market entry abroad, preventing attendance at exhibitions or meetings with international intermediaries such as galleries or dealers. As we have seen in Chapter 5 (on sponsorship) since 1991 the Irish Arts Council and Aer Lingus have co-operated on a scheme called Artflight which offers opportunities to people working in the creative arts to visit major cities in Europe and North America. The scheme has been highly successful in helping individuals access the market potential that exists outside Ireland itself, with its relatively small population. An Chomhairle Ealaíon, the Irish Arts Council, assists in other ways, as Sarah Finlay, the visual arts officer, explains: 'A lot of our planning is long-term. We aim to have a presence at the Venice Biennale. Being at a curated show attracts the critics' eyes, then we can get them over to Ireland. We aim to build up a network . . . to be in the know.'

Travel and transport activities represent a major investment in resources, and are therefore appropriate operations to keep under review from the point of view of savings or alternative strategies. They offer the closest analogy we can find in the arts industries to the physical distribution strategies covered in standard marketing textbooks – finding the most appropriate methods of transport and storage to ensure that the product is available in the optimum combination of quality and accessibility. Touring companies face the additional complexity of the human factor with performers. But the focus of this chapter will be on the aspect of distribution which all arts organizations have in common, whatever the art form. The marketing channel needs to place the customer at the centre of the process.

As well as Product, Price is a very live issue in distribution. Traditional marketing analysis divides intermediaries into 'merchants' and 'agents'. Merchants take title to the goods (i.e. buy them outright) and thus fix their own resale prices. Agents, on the other hand, operate on a fee or commission basis, and will adhere to their clients' wishes in setting a price to the customer. Pricing decisions in touring drama or music, as we have seen in Chapter 5, need to take local considerations into account.

Specialist forms of distribution can be combined with special pricing in order to appeal to specific segments of the market without devaluing the product for other customers. Major opera companies, for example, approach music societies early on in their campaigns with discounts in order to secure early booking. And, as the experience of the Society of West End Theatres suggests, discounts can also be used to 'dump' unsold tickets on casual ticket buyers.

Finally, Promotion is an important element to reconcile with any distribution pattern. If channel intermediaries are required to play a role in communicating the benefits of what they are making available, this is known as a 'push' strategy. It concentrates promotional effort on each stage of the marketing channel to drive the offering towards the eventual end user. This is usually carried out in tandem with a 'pull' strategy which aims its promotion at the consumer in order to stimulate demand, and 'pull' the offering through the chain.

The nature and function of marketing channels

The role of intermediaries

As we have seen, intermediaries (whether individuals like a literary agent or organizations like a theatre) connect the seller to the buyer. Viewed together in sequence, these intermediaries form distribution chains or 'marketing channels. In the performing arts, especially for the more commercial side of the market such as big musicals or arena rock concerts, ticket agents have become a very important intermediary to potential audiences. Like retailers, they offer a wide selection of different 'products' in one place, saving the arts customer considerable inconvenience. Travel agencies often 'piggyback' ticket sales on their standard business, but there are also dedicated ticket agents, such as the Victoria Centre Box Office in Nottingham's main indoor shopping mall, which turn over enormous quantities of business for both regional and national entertainment.

Brisk business at the booth

In the ten years from its 1980 launch, the half-price ticket booth in London's Leicester Square has filled 3.5 million seats for the Society of West End Theatres which would otherwise have gone unsold. The idea was borrowed from the League of New York Theatres whose willingness to operate a joint marketing venture of this type was one of the reasons for the recovery of Broadway in the late 1970s. Vincent Burke, SWET's first development officer, came back from a visit to New York with three priorities – to do some proper audience research, to increase co-operation with other leisure businesses such as tourism and hotels, and to launch the booth.

In order to protect business from customers paying full price, the Leicester Square booth has certain rules. They almost sound like an attempt at de-marketing, but they ensure that only a very specific market segment is addressed with the opportunity of stand-by tickets through this distribution outlet:

- Customers must pay cash.
- There is a limit of four tickets per transaction.
- Only unsold tickets for that day's performance are available.
- Customers have to queue, sometimes in the rain.
- There is no way of telephoning the booth – you have to turn up to see what is available.

Research suggests that almost 90 per cent of the booth's customers are visitors, half of them from overseas. Most are in the market for a night out, but do not mind what they see. Their commitment to the idea of live theatre, rather than any other form of evening's entertainment, can only be gained by this opportunistic discount distribution channel.

Source: Denford (1990)

The traditional form of remuneration for agencies is to work on a commission basis, whereby the venue remits them a proportion (usually 15 per cent) of the selling price. The price to the customer is the same as it would be at the theatre box office. But recently there has been a growth in the number of agencies who charge a 'booking fee' direct to the customer, such as First Call which specializes in telephone booking. This reflects the cost of distribution (for example, the agency may be providing box office facilities which would otherwise not exist for a one-off event). It appears to be something which customers are happy to pay in return for convenience and speed.

Intermediaries like ticket agents provide an essential service in any distribution chain by reducing contact costs for suppliers in reaching their buyers. We can see this process at work in the way that literary agents place work on behalf of authors and

Creative fusion

In 1993 the award-winning Dublin-based visual arts production company Artsource cut across art-form categories to bring together three contemporary dancers, three jewellers, a film maker and a composer to create an event touring both in Ireland and abroad. The exhibition/performance had a number of themes (body adornment, rhythm, movement, gender, etc.) which guaranteed a wide range of benefits both for spectators and for funding bodies and other sponsors. The Irish Arts Council were pleased to support new music and dance being made accessible to a wide range of people through the tour, and the Irish Trade Board added their support for what they saw as a way to increase the market for contemporary designers both at home and abroad. This kind of innovative, entrepreneurial approach would have been impossible without the contribution of the intermediary organization – here acting as a broker to bring customers and suppliers together in a marketing channel.

playwrights, or gallery owners or exhibition curators provide a 'shop window' to bring the artist or craftworker into contact with collectors. But intermediaries are also worth cultivating because of the entrepreneurial role they can play in presenting opportunities to individuals or organizations in the arts which would be unavailable otherwise. Funding bodies tend to be art-form based in how they allocate money – reinforcing a linear approach where dance, craft and media artists operate in separate categories.

Channel conflict

Marketing channels, as we have seen, are made up of a number of intermediaries connecting the producer to the consumer. While at first sight all the parties involved in a channel have a mutual interest in the success of the process, there are plenty of potential clashes. This is known as 'channel conflict'. A venue's immediate priorities may differ from those of a touring company, especially if the venue has in-house work to market as well as visiting work. Conflict between successive stages in the chain like this is called 'vertical' conflict because it is caused by trouble 'down' the channel (like a manufacturer in dispute with a retailer because a rival manufacturer's goods are being displayed more aggressively). This kind of conflict can knock on to all the other aspects of running a touring company, as Liza Stevens, former administrative director of Phoenix Dance Company recalls: 'We attempted longer term planning of our season's work, in line with our artistic policy. But in the end we found ourselves at the mercy of the venues into which we toured. Their ability to plan ahead varied enormously.'

Conflicts can also arise between venues. An arts centre may be unhappy about the

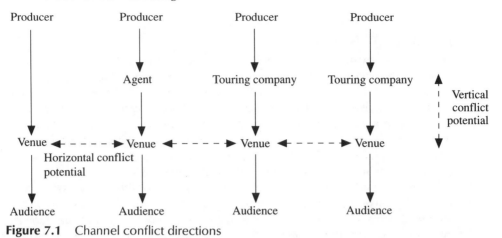

Figure 7.1   Channel conflict directions

fact that a touring company is planning to visit a theatre bordering on its catchment area before it reaches it. This could spoil the potential audience. Or a professional repertory company can get the rights to a show like 'Oliver' for a particular season, thus effectively preventing local amateurs from mounting it. This kind of conflict is 'across' the same stage in two different channels, and is thus called 'horizontal' conflict. An analogy here might be with two rival supermarkets trying to outdo each other on lowering the price of a particular special offer.

Both kinds of channel conflict can be minimized by negotiation and clear lines of communication. But the only sure way to stamp out the possibility of conflict is for one of the members of the chain to assume a dominant role. This can be in one of three ways:

- Through multiple ownership, such as the Apollo group of theatres which has considerable negotiating 'clout' because of the number of major touring venues it operates. A touring company playing at an Apollo venue virtually has to accept the terms offered by the theatre or lose an outlet to a major part of its audience. This is known as 'horizontal integration' because it spreads ownership across the same stage in a number of marketing channels.

- Through buying out an intermediary at an earlier or later stage in the same channel. This is known as 'vertical integration' because it involves ownership 'up' and 'down' the channel. Again, the Apollo group provides an example. At Christmas it effectively becomes a manufacturer as well as a retailer by assembling its own pantomime production team with TV soap star casts. This allows it complete control over an annual production whose success is crucial to financial health throughout the rest of the year.

- Through one of the members of the chain establishing clear legal conditions governing the other members. This is known in marketing speak as a 'contractual vertical marketing system' as it governs relationships up and down the channel. Depending on the attractiveness of the show on offer, a touring management can take this role in its dealings with its venues.

Channel length and control

Chains of distribution are deemed long or short depending on how many intermediaries are involved. While there is no golden rule about the length of a chain, the shorter the chain of distribution, the more control a manufacturer has over the presentation of the final product. Building-based repertory theatre companies thus have complete control over their product and its presentation, compared to the vagaries and conflicting priorities faced by touring venues. The disadvantage, of course, is that the company bears complete responsibility for all the costs and operations involved. At the other end of the scale, the individual craftworker is dependent on galleries and event organizers to reach customers. While this allows craftspeople to concentrate on their core activity, it also means that they are to some extent at the mercy of the intermediaries in terms of support and merchandising (display and sales effort). The writer seeking a market for his or her work often faces marketing channels which seem more like obstacle courses, but determination pays off. Playwright Maureen Lawrence comments: 'If you delve enough and get the right information, it's not difficult to get a play staged . . . there are not enough good plays, it ought to be pointed out in careers advice.'

Distribution and innovation

As well as institutional or personal intermediaries, marketing channels can incorporate new ways of mediating artistic experience, either through innovative organization or new technology. Picture loan schemes, such as those run by many municipal art galleries, allow works of art to be enjoyed in subscribers' homes over a period of time instead of sampled fleetingly in gallery settings. In galleries and museums there is an increasing use of video and other electronic media to explain and interpret material for the visitor.

A good example is the IBM-sponsored installation of multimedia consoles in the National Gallery of Ireland which coincided with the 1993 touring exhibition of forty-four of the gallery's most important canvasses, 'Master European Paintings from the National Gallery of Ireland'. Working in association with the multi-media centre at Trinity College Dublin, the gallery has developed an interactive computer system which allows members of the public to access information and close-ups of the paintings using impressive touch-screen technology. With increasing access to cable technology on a local basis it is likely that this kind of distribution opportunity will play an ever more important role in how the experience of the arts is made available.

Of course the use of new technology threatens existing patterns of employment and provision. Jeremy Isaacs came to the position of general director of the Royal Opera House in 1988 from a broadcasting background at Channel 4. Naturally he grasped the potential of opera for television. This new distribution channel could open up the experience of opera for millions rather than hundreds of thousands. But introducing cameras to Covent Garden on these terms meant that the ROH

Box 7.1

Allowing or enabling?

Merely allowing the public to juxtapose themselves with an artwork, by letting them in to see a picture in a gallery for instance, is not genuine access. Granting someone this kind of access may amount to little more than *allowing* them to look at it. Genuine access would work towards *enabling* them to see it.

From: *Art and the Ordinary*, – An Chomhairle Ealaíon – the Arts Council of Ireland
(1987)

---

management had to spend large sums of money buying out the rights of the heavily-unionized performance staff. However, the demystification of opera as an art form for a wider audience has been helped by the kind of popular access Isaacs' initiative has opened up.

A more traditional way of reaching an extended audience with one piece of work is to tour it. Promoting touring work, whether performance or exhibitions, relies on a close co-operation between the originating organization and the various venues visited. The marketing channels here need to be nurtured. If the venues are not properly motivated and equipped with information and promotional materials from the originating organization their efforts to sell the experience to their local audiences will be seriously hampered. On the other hand, if the touring venues are not committed to putting energy and effort behind publicizing the visiting artists, the source organization may well reconsider its options for the future.

The physical environment

Tangible aspects of service delivery

While the experience of the arts, as we have argued in Chapter 4, is an intangible service rather than a tangible product, it takes place within an environment whose physical characteristics have an important effect on the quality of the experience for the consumer. The way in which the customer is brought into contact with an art form is a distribution issue.

A good example would be the promenade productions which the Dukes Theatre started mounting in Lancaster's Williamson Park in the late 1980s and which have now become a popular regular feature of the theatrical calendar. The productions make use of the remarkable Ashton Memorial as backdrop, but the real hero of the setting is the park itself, as the audience follow the cast from location to location. Sensible shoes and warm clothing are recommended so that the audience can enjoy the unique physical environment in comfort.

Opera in the open air is another way of representing what might be dismissed as

Box 7.2
Fancy footwork: promotion through a marketing channel
In recent years touring contemporary dance companies have set high standards in using marketing channels to the maximum advantage. Perhaps because of the perceived specialization of their art forms they appear particularly motivated in seeking new and effective ways of generating audience figures. Rambert Dance Company, based in London, mounts two national tours each year. Their procedure for involving venues in the promotional campaign includes the following key elements leading up to the visit of the company:

Long term

An initial planning meeting takes place at the venue to discuss promotional strategy, local needs and opportunities, and allocation of responsibilities between the company marketing department and the venue. An example of this is the way that national media coverage will be handled by the company, freeing the venue to concentrate on the all-important local media. Promotional print such as posters and leaflets will need to be printed in advance of the tour for all the dates, so now is also the time to check on the information supplied by the venue at the time of the initial contract. This is also an opportunity to determine final print quantities.

The visit will include the company marketing officer making personal contact not only with the marketing people at the venue, but also with the box office staff and administrative director. In a venue which will be dealing with a number of different managements, this personal touch makes an enormous difference. Rambert Dance Company's approach recognizes that marketing channels are made up of people, and personal relationships repay the time spent forming them.

Medium term

Briefing box office staff in detail about the performances, and supplying marketing departments with photographs and reviews (when available) of earlier performances on the tour, plus material for the programme and display support. It is important to communicate enthusiasm as well as information.

Regular contact by telephone with the marketing department and box office to review booking figures. These are compared in detail with previous years' figures to diagnose any performances which are moving more slowly than the norm. The resultant troubleshooting may include placing extra printed publicity with potential customers through mailings or leaflet drops, or spending more advertising money. The venue's judgement from its own experience of general booking patterns can prove invaluable here.

Short term

Liaising with the venue marketing department and dancers/choreographers to arrange media activity. The experience gained during the tour at other venues can often suggest original and effective ways of generating local coverage. Radio, for example, is a surprisingly rewarding medium for promoting such a visual art form. The ancillary activities that contemporary dance companies now make a regular part of their 'product', such as workshops or pre-performance talks, can also make useful and original publicity platforms.

Attending the first night in order to help with the entertainment and briefing of the local media. This is also an opportunity to continue to develop contacts within the venue in order to understand its needs and capabilities further.

Rambert Dance Company's approach demonstrates how careful attention to its marketing channel can yield dividends in promotion. Information flow, for example, is two way. The company provides information and material to the venue, and in return gathers sales figures and an appreciation of local conditions and opportunities which increase its ability to be effective in future.

an elitist or unsuitably heavy arts experience in a form which will access a larger audience. Opera North, in co-operation with Leeds City Council and the national commercial radio station Classic FM, have played to audiences of 50,000 in the surroundings of Temple Newsam Park on the outskirts of Leeds. By selecting a programme combining popular extracts with highlights from less well-known works from the forthcoming season, the company turn this mass picnic into a valuable sampling exercise for potential local customers.

Of course an outdoor environment can be difficult to control in some respects, but the popularity of promenade and al fresco productions suggests that this form of delivery offers benefits which outweigh the risks. There is evidence to suggest, moreover, that taking theatre and music out of traditional settings can actually reach audiences who would normally feel uncomfortable in the formal surroundings of an established venue.

A surprising feature of many audience surveys is how many of the attenders at any performance are either first-time or very infrequent theatre-goers. Their unfamiliarity with the conventions of the theatre needs to be addressed through high standards of customer care, and a welcoming environment featuring elements like clear signage. Another possible way to 'warm up' hesitant theatre-goers is to take the product to them, either in a small venue in their immediate locality, or in a venue which has more comfortable associations like a social club, village hall or public house.

Community tours: refreshing the parts other theatre can't reach?

'Community touring' formed a notable feature of the work of theatres like Derby Playhouse's Studio Company and York Theatre Royal's 'In Your Neighbourhood' company in the 1980s. In spite of the many differences between Derby and York as cities, they have roughly similar populations and are surrounded by large rural catchment areas. With changes in public transport provision and demographic trends in rural areas, community touring into isolated rural areas was seen as a vital way of keeping in touch with audiences who otherwise might be deterred from making a lengthy journey to and from the theatre. There was also the sense, from the programming point of view, that the interests and tastes of a predominantly rural audience might differ from those of the urban population.

The fact that neither venue now mounts community tours with the regularity they once did reflects the costs of the exercise. Distribution needs to balance effective coverage of the market, or audience in this case, with a reasonable financial out-turn for the arts organization. Subsidy per seat in a village hall with a capacity of 80 has to be considerably higher for a professional company on tour than for the same company in an auditorium seating 500. The system of selling a performance to a local organization, such as a parish council, for a fixed fee (thus allowing the organization to set its own ticket price and possibly make money on the deal) guaranteed local 'ownership' of the production and high levels of attendance. But the amount of money they could expect to take at the box office was limited by what people would expect to pay at a local venue, even for professional theatre. This kept the fee chargeable by the company for a performance at a fraction of the real cost, which had to be made up by subsidy.

Quite apart from the economic constraints (which were soluble for a time through the specific funding such dedicated work could attract) there are numerous practical and logistical problems associated with community touring. Changes in fire regulation standards meant that some well-supported venues which had been perfectly acceptable in previous years became unavailable. Also, small-scale promoting organizations such as parish councils were easily put off by show content such as strong language which would pass unremarked in a larger venue. Finally, the suspicion that the community tours were taking theatre to village hall audiences composed mainly of existing theatre-goers was never quite allayed – an example of 'horizontal channel conflict' which was at odds with the laudable aim of reaching new audiences.

Community touring in the 1990s is increasingly the province of very small-scale specialist companies who do not have the overheads of medium-scale repertory theatres and can better adapt to the cost structure of such a distribution policy.

Atmospherics and retail design

Physical environment for the building-based arts organization is a highly influential component of the attender's experience. Audience surveys frequently name 'atmosphere' amongst the most important factors affecting attendance decisions. It is as if the venue, because of its physical attributes, builds a reputation amongst its users for quality, comfort and reliability. This is reflected both in the fabric of the building itself and the kinds of systems established by front-of-house staff. The danger is, as is often the case in marketing issues, that the organization misses opportunities to improve matters by being too familiar with the status quo to notice or question it.

Box office design is a case in point. The old Leeds Playhouse, which occupied a 'temporary' home in a building designed as a university sports hall for the best part of eighteen years, was not gifted with the most propitious environment for a theatre. Yet its crowded foyer was remarkably effective at making its audience (amongst whom were a proportion of younger theatre-goers much higher than the national average) feel very much at home.

One of the key features was an open-plan box office which was in the centre of the foyer rather than tucked away behind glass at the side as it is in so many traditionally-built theatres. Eye contact with staff was unavoidable, and the counter was a natural stopping off place to collect details of the films and plays on offer. The design of the old Leeds Playhouse (which also had a dramatically raked auditorium to fit the available space) was to some extent a virtue made out of a necessity. But it was interesting to note on the opening of the £14 million new home for theatre in Leeds, the West Yorkshire Playhouse in 1990, that both the open-plan box office and the excellent sight lines of the auditorium had been transferred to the design of the new building.

Art galleries are more experienced than most in the dramatic possibilities of space and colour. Exhibition walls are regularly repainted in different colours to enhance the subjects on view. Lighting, too, has a crucial role in the delivery of the artistic experience to exhibition attenders. The marketing name for this kind of ambience control is 'atmospherics' – a developing approach to promotion which seeks to create the most effective combination of colours, textures, and sometimes sound to reinforce certain dispositions in customers. The technique is particularly useful in a service environment such as health care (to reinforce feelings of safety or well-being) or financial services (reassurance and reliability). Some Japanese companies have even explored the use of aromatic effects in this context. More explicitly, 'experience'-type museums, such as Tetley's Brewery Wharf in Leeds and York's Jorvik Centre, use smells as an overt element in their created environments.

Most arts organizations may lack the resources to emulate these approaches to the fullest extent. But even something as simple as a selection of strategically-placed indoor plants (perhaps sponsored and maintained by a local company aiming at the regional business market) can make a considerable impact on the ambience of a gallery or theatre.

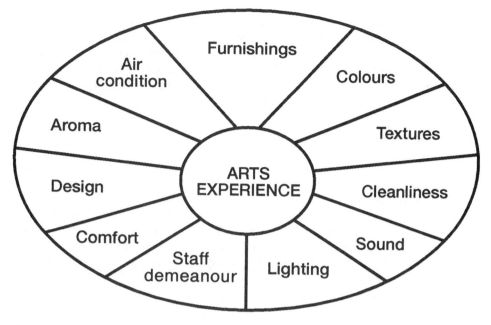

Figure 7.2   Atmospherics

New light on Turner

In October 1994 the Clore Gallery at the Tate (originally opened in 1987 to house paintings by the great English artist J.M.W. Turner) reopened after a £1m refurbishment. It had been plagued by problems from the outset because of inappropriate atmospherics. Andrew Wilton, the keeper of the British Collection at the Tate, commented:

> I'm surprised the public didn't complain more. There was rarely enough natural light and the scale was too small for Turner. The gallery was difficult to maintain and it looked shabby. So there's been a lot of cleaning up. We've removed the carpets – they were thick with dust – and created more wall space so that the paintings can be hung higher. I hope we've sorted out the lighting problem too.
>
> (Christiansen, 1994)

A consciousness of retail design and its techniques can be of great advantage to organizations wishing to increase earnings from trading. In the late 1980s York City Art Gallery decided to raise the amount of money it earned from trading as an alternative to imposing entrance charges. It remodelled its foyer to accommodate a large area dedicated to fine-art related merchandise, including books, guides, postcards and greetings cards, posters and calendars as well as the standard 'tourist' paraphernalia of branded stationery. Many of these items had been available, in a rather understated way, from the attendants' desk at the back of the foyer. This was abolished, and visitor traffic guided through the shop as the obvious way of gaining access to the ground floor galleries. The result is a pleasantly appropriate retail space where visitors can browse in an unpressured environment, but through which they are guided gently but firmly by the signage and layout of the gallery.

Intangible aspects of service delivery: customer care

The issue of staff attitudes and systems is more fundamental, however, than any adjustment in atmospherics or selling. A number of specialist consultancies are now offering training in customer care for service industries, some of the best ones concentrating on arts organizations and their particular needs. An investment in external training like this reaps a number of dividends. Not only is internal morale improved by the interest being shown in staff by management, but customers can expect to receive a new level of consistency and quality surrounding their experience of the particular art form. Roger Tomlinson (1990), the director of a leading training consultancy, sees their role in 'customer care' as making a venue's front line staff its most valuable marketing asset:

> How often are box office, front-of-house, reception, attendants and other staff seen as separate from the marketing function when in practice they are at the centre of customer relations and customer contact? Spending every working day talking to customers, they probably acquire more marketing intelligence than anyone else – and they may understand what brings customers in best of all!

Many large gallery complexes and theatres now number a 'customer services manager' amongst their key staff. This is not lip-service to a trendy new development in management thinking, but a logical recognition of the importance and diversity of audience needs. As venues are driven by artistic or financial imperatives to make fuller use of their facilities for non-performance activities (day-time events, business and conference hire, etc.) the concept of customer service is becoming ever more important. It cannot just be left to the personnel in immediate contact with the customer. A genuinely marketing-oriented organization will imbue all its members with a sense of their contribution to the end-user's experience. As we have seen in Chapter 4, the marketing function needs to take the initiative in this process.

Physical access considerations

Finally in this section about the physical environment, a word about the subject of 'access'. Specialist organizations such as Artlink provide directories of venues offering facilities for wheelchair users and disabled people generally. It is a salutary fact that attendance at arts events still presents an enormous amount of difficulty to disabled patrons, although progress has been made in this aspect of distribution due to the opportunities presented by funding priorities in some areas. New buildings are designed with access for wheelchair users in mind. In 1992 the National Gallery's Sainsbury Wing received an award from Arts Access in recognition of its design achievement in this respect. Interpretation is also a distribution issue. Signed performances for people with hearing difficulties, and taped summaries for visually-impaired customers are becoming increasingly common as part of the distribution strategy of repertory theatres and opera companies.

It is essential to work and plan inclusively when designing access facilities. Working with a variety of agencies will enable an arts organization to meet its target groups' needs and wants effectively. The National Portrait Gallery has recently introduced Braille labels for a selection of paintings, giving information about the artist and the subject. While at first surprising to some visitors (who might not expect people with a visual impairment to be amongst the audience for an art gallery), this move recognizes that many people's sight is not good enough to read text, but sufficient to perceive colour and form. The introduction of Braille labels announces the gallery's commitment to widening access. Yet, of the one million or so people in Britain with a visual impairment, only 20,000 can read Braille. It has been argued that an audio guide would be a more appropriate solution to their needs, although the Braille labels have a wider consciousness-raising effect.

Access in more general terms is an important issue for arts marketers. Quite apart from what is on offer in the theatre or gallery, or the price of admission, ease of physical access can dictate whether customers come or stay away. We will deal with the difficulties presented by the process of ticket purchase in due course. But for many people, the simple issue of transport to and from the venue, and the problem of parking and security, is one of the most important factors in whether their experience is a satisfactory one or not. For those venues who have the advantage of proximate car parking or public transport services, this information needs to be given high priority in publicity leaflets. Venues which are not in such fortunate circumstances (many city-centre theatres, for example) need to adopt creative strategies to address the problems this may cause for their patrons in terms of performance times, information, provision for late arrivals, and lobbying local authorities.

Families with younger children are targeted by most venues at specific times of the year (such as school holidays or the Christmas season). But facilities for pushchairs, baby changing and family areas are usually rudimentary if they exist at all. High-street retailers such as Boots and Mothercare, because of the nature of their business, have led the way in providing such kind of facilities as a matter of course. With increasing daytime use of arts venues, the opportunity presented by family audiences can only be realized by catering for their needs through the right kind of access environment.

The temporal environment

Performance times and opening hours

As we have discussed in Chapter 4, the arts are a perishable commodity. Time is a crucial element in their delivery and consumption. Yet it is remarkable how inconvenient arts attendance still manages to be from the point of view of time utility. The most obvious aspect of this subject is performance starting times, or gallery opening hours. These are often the result of precedent or inertia rather than conscious consideration of the options available with the customer in mind.

As suggested in Chapter 2, segmenting the audience of arts attenders may lead to fresh thinking on performance times or opening hours. The West Yorkshire Playhouse, for example, builds in at least one mid-week early afternoon performance for its repertory productions having considered the needs of its older patrons. They might feel uncomfortable about the prospect of returning home in the dark. Matinees also cater for people living at some distance from the theatre who would prefer to travel during daylight hours.

The National Gallery in London has core weekday opening times from 10 a.m. to 6 p.m., but on Wednesdays from June to August, extends its opening to 8 p.m. This complements the attractions of the centre of London on a summer evening not only for the leisured tourist or holidaymaker, but also for local visitors (such as office workers) who might otherwise have to restrict their enjoyment of the collections to the busy weekend period. These 'summer evening' openings also provide a valuable sponsorship opportunity for a number of companies.

The National Museum of Photography, Film and Television in Bradford is one of a number of museums and art galleries who base their patterns of opening on the convenience of their customers rather than a standard working week, by shutting on Mondays in order to enable Sunday opening.

All of these examples demonstrate ways in which the customer has been included in the thinking behind the organization's temporal distribution strategy. Another way of coping with a time problem is the introduction of booking in advance for attendance at exhibitions at a specific time. Lengthy queues used to be one of the characteristics of blockbuster exhibitions in London and elsewhere – notably the 1971 Tutankhamen exhibition at the British Museum. While these queues provided valuable public relations material in terms of talking points and photo-opportunities, they were a source of some inconvenience to the exhibition-goer and were seen as a deterrent to attendance at some major exhibitions in the 1980s. The press of people at very popular events can also mean that the art objects themselves are more difficult to enjoy because it is impossible to get near to them, or to appreciate them at one's own pace. The distribution solution of an 'appointment' booking system has the advantage of minimizing the waiting time for the customer, and maximizing the quality of the experience by limiting the crowds in the gallery at any particular time.

Time as an obstacle

Ticket purchase itself is often fraught with difficulty for many arts attenders, particularly for theatre-goers. It is instructive to think of the various stages of the purchasing process as a series of barriers for the customer, faced with much easier and cheaper leisure alternatives, to surmount. Booking in person requires a visit to the theatre or booking agent which may be very inconvenient. Telephone booking is an understandably popular alternative, but can be frustrating in terms of busy tones or lengthy ringing before the call is taken. Then the options for performance times and ticket price and position need to be understood. Perhaps the result is for the ticket to be 'reserved' rather than purchased (a common understanding of the idea of 'booking') until the customer collects with payment. This still entails a visit to the box office or agency, or a wait on the night of the performance itself.

Training box office staff to be more systematic in handling calls can make an enormous difference in the efficiency of this potentially circuitous and time wasting procedure.

- The customer can save time, increasing their convenience.
- The organization can save time otherwise wasted in meandering telephone calls and administration.
- Then the next customer can be dealt with more speedily, compounding the benefits all round.

Box office training encourages staff to be more active in their response to customers by imposing a shape to the call and retaining the initiative throughout.

- A greeting, identifying the venue and, ideally, the member of staff personally, begins the call.
- Then, having established a friendly but professional rapport with the customer, questions can be used to get specific answers enabling choices to be made quickly.
- Even calls which appear to be for the purposes of eliciting information are capable of being converted into sales – the customer is phoning because he or she is interested enough in what the venue has to offer to want to know more. Purchase is just another step in fulfilling that interest.
- The key part of the call is to 'close the sale' encouraging payment by credit card: 'Would you like to pay for those tickets now by credit card so I can send them to you immediately?'. The offer to send the tickets on to the purchaser should be made.
- This guarantees the collection of the name and address of the customer, a valuable asset as we shall consider in the direct marketing section to follow. But it also saves the customer the inconvenience of further visits to the box office or waiting on the night to collect the ticket. Naturally this also frees the box office staff from the time required by those further contacts.

Some traditionally-minded members of staff may object here to what they perceive to be a 'pushy' approach to sales. This objection misrepresents the nature of the procedure which aims to standardize the quality of customer service at a uniformly high level. By using a structured approach to answering the telephone, box office staff can actually help their customers far more effectively than if they treat the telephone as an informal, casual medium.

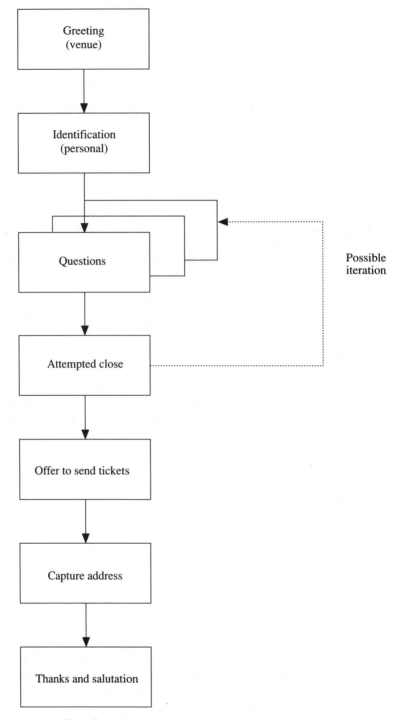

Figure 7.3 Telephone selling flowchart

Selling the Proms

Andrew Stokes, the box office manager for the Proms:

The first morning of Proms telephone booking we have all our operators sitting there. They log in and at nine o'clock, it's like a starting bell. Everyone gets a call and so all of a sudden all the way round the room you hear: 'Royal Albert Hall ticket sales, how can I help you?'. It goes round all the room so you hear 12 or 18 people saying it and then all of a sudden the counter that tells you how many calls are waiting starts flurrying up: one, two, three, four, five, six, seven . . . you get up to twenty calls waiting within seconds.

Virtually on the first day or second morning with dealing with postal applications, there's one that's probably gone or just has restricted view seats left. The staff amongst themselves almost run a little book on it.

The capacity of the hall is over 5000. We sell some of the promenade tickets in advance to season ticket holders but there are large numbers that can be bought on the day. So there are always tickets available for a prom for people who want to come down and book.

Source: Prom News, BBC Radio 3, July 1994

Direct marketing

A total approach to marketing and distribution

Direct marketing is an approach to marketing which aims to create and continue a direct relationship between an organization and its customers on a one-to-one basis. The idea is to treat the customer as an individual. The associated philosophy of 'relationship' marketing sees the customer as an appreciating asset with whom the organization has a mutually beneficial connection, or 'relationship', over a lengthy period of time. This outlook has much to offer arts organizations in terms of developing the tastes of their customers. Because of the uniquely collaborative nature of the arts transaction (see Chapter 4), a continuing and developing relationship with customers is central to the success of arts marketing.

Direct marketing is not just an advertising medium like the post or the television. Nor, in spite of the fact we are dealing with it under the heading of 'distribution', is it just a way of getting goods to the customer. It is a whole way of marketing, of literally creating and keeping a customer in a direct relationship. Ogilvy and Mather Direct, one of Europe's premier direct marketing agencies, describe it as 'a way of doing business' rather than as any particular marketing technique.

The days of the cornershop are long gone – where a shopkeeper knew customers by name, and could anticipate their needs. Perhaps the last widespread survivor of this kind of 'relationship marketing' is when a publican spots a regular customer coming in and asks 'The usual?'. But technology now puts unprecedented computing power in the hands of organizations which could not have dreamed of such things even ten years ago. It is now possible to know our customers as well, in fact better in terms of exact purchasing behaviour, than pub 'regulars.' Box office computers can store information on attendance patterns and frequency of ticket purchase by each customer. This extremely valuable data is preserved reliably and permanently on a 'database'. Arts organizations are turning to direct marketing (also known as 'database' marketing) as a way of being able to treat their customers in this individualistic manner.

It is now cheaper and more feasible than ever before to store information on customers. In the years from 1960 to 1990 the cost of computer storage plummeted roughly 20,000 times – whilst speed of operation increased by a factor of about one million. The early 1990s have seen price wars between major manufacturers, bringing computer hardware within reach of most arts organizations. Computer 'database' power is driving the direct marketing revolution, and the most sophisticated systems, as we have seen in Chapter 2 on Audience, link directly between box office and marketing department for information transfer.

A database is simply a list. But a computer database enables you to store and cross reference complex records of individual purchasing behaviour. Our examination of direct marketing here will focus first on the business of 'creating' a customer, and then look at the mechanics of communicating with that customer through one of the many devices open to the direct marketer – the mailshot.

Direct marketing is not a panacea for all ills, however. The Data Protection Act is a reflection of the growing political concern (more clearly expressed in legislation elsewhere in the EU) that direct marketing can consitute an invasion of privacy. Badly targeted direct mail is not only highly wasteful (because of the expense of production and postage), but can also have a negative, 'junk mail' image. There is a sense, too, that the missionary zeal from which arts marketing derives much of its momentum is not very well served by a technique which focuses on known users rather than searching for converts. Finally, as with any technique associated with high technology, there may be a significant gap between expectations and what is possible. Many computer-generated mailing lists are out of date or irrelevant because of poor maintenance.

Customer acquisition

This is the first stage in creating a customer. It is the most expensive part of the process, but the expense is precisely budgetable – the more potential customers ('prospects') you want to contact, the more it will cost. It may be that an organization is in the happy position of being able to collect the names and addresses of all of its existing customers in the course of its normal business. This would be the case if, as in a theatre box office, the product or service is sold over the telephone to credit card customers or by post.

Alternatively prospect names and addresses can be built up from visitor records or mailing list applicants responding to an advertisement. It may be that some organizations have segmented their market to the point where they feel it is worth doing a blanket approach to a particular area or combination of areas. Or an existing list can be hired or borrowed in order to do an initial mailing. There is a growing number of companies called 'list brokers' who can supply the opportunity of mailing different demographic combinations throughout the country. The respondents to the offer are then retained as the basis of a new list.

Whatever the technique chosen, this is the investment stage of the process. Just as a new product will not go into profit until well into its growth phase, so new customers may take a while to repay the expense of their recruitment. However, research shows that the vast majority of all sorts of sales come from repeat business.

Store account card customers, for example, tend to spend as much as five times more than non-account customers per year. Getting them to take up an account will have required an outlay. But once 'acquired' they are a business's most valuable asset. Direct marketing makes it easier to demonstrate, and protect, this repeat business through allowing an organization to nurture its relationship with its customers.

A customer list itself is a valuable source of other customers. Sociologists observe that people tend to behave in similar ways within peer groups. It follows that existing customers' friends may well be potential customers as well. As a result MGM ('member get member') and FGAF ('friend get a friend') schemes are a frequent component of direct marketing customer acquisition campaigns.

Any organization's customers exist on a continuum ranging from those who don't know anything about it to those who like its products or services so much that they recommend them to others. This is as true of exhibition and theatre-goers as it is of any other group of consumers. MGM and FGAF rely on the fact that most direct marketing operations have extremely well-satisfied customers who have no hesitation in recommending them to their friends. Arts events have the additional advantage that they are often attended in groups. 'Two for the price of one' ticket deals may be a simple way of filling first night seats, but they possibly also represent important sampling opportunities for people who get brought along to the show by a friend.

A related way of prospecting for customers similar to your existing customer base is to identify another group whose members might have similar interests. Care should be taken, however, that your systems are sufficiently sophisticated to detect and eliminate overlap. In the late 1980s Derby Playhouse ran a subscription drive which targeted the local membership of a national charity whose supporters were estimated to fit the profile of existing customers. So accurate was the predicted correlation, however, that many of them turned out to be existing subscribers anyway. In spite of the duplication of contact, extra business resulted from existing members passing on the incentive (an exclusive early booking discount form) to others.

A key characteristic of direct marketing is its capacity to be evaluated. Direct marketers quickly know how successful their marketing activity has been. They can identify the responses to specific pieces of marketing activity by coding the response mechanisms (e.g. marking reply coupons with an identifier). This kind of accountability helps marketing managers plan and justify their budgets for direct marketing campaigns in a way which gives the marketing function credibility in frequently sceptical arts organizations.

Direct marketing is not cheap. Television advertising is measured in terms of hundreds of people seeing it for every pound spent. Mailshots, on the other hand, tend to reach between one and two people per pound (depending on the sophistication of the contents). It has been estimated that using the telephone rather than mailing makes contact about five times more expensive (although its interactive nature can justify this). The costs involved reflect the degree of personalization of the medium.

Experience suggests that as a rough guide you might expect a mailshot to yield a response from between 2 per cent and 5 per cent of those who receive it although the figure will be a great deal higher if you are mailing to the right kind of people. It is a sobering consideration that what really dictates success in direct marketing is not the creative quality of the offer, nor yet the quality or value of the goods being sold, but the quality of the list itself. Research carried out by Saatchi & Saatchi in the 1980s suggests that using direct mail in conjunction with another medium such as press or TV can boost response by up to 40 per cent of what it would be normally. Direct marketing is therefore capable of very good rates of returns, but only after significant investment.

This has led to what is called a 'test mentality' amongst direct marketers. In spite of the popular image of junk mail, direct mail is one of the most rationally driven of all advertising media. Every part of a mailshot is capable of being experimented with. If you look closely at the next piece of direct mail you receive, you will notice that each item in the envelope will have a unique identifying code. This is because the chances are that each part of that mailing is being experimented with. Letter layout, size and position of suggested price points on the order form, even the colour of the ink, are all variables which can be tested to see which pulls the greatest response. As a result, the creative principles which underlie the following advice about creating and writing a mailshot are actually tested against experience.

The variables in an arts campaign may not be as extensive or as sophisticated as in commercial marketing, but much can be learned from experimentation. For example, printed material can be coded uniquely at very little extra cost by the printer in order to identify response on booking forms from various outlets or mailing activities. Or two different sorts of covering letter can accompany a mailed brochure in a 'split' mailing, and the resulting responses compared. The most important marketing experience you can obtain is of your own customers.

Putting together a mailshot

Mail is not the only medium available to the direct marketer. Even posters emphasizing phone numbers are an effective direct response medium. This makes the small size of most box office numbers on theatre posters difficult to understand. Television and radio is a tried and tested method of selling products like Richard Clayderman records, which are, famously, not available in any shops. Newspapers and magazines with reply coupon forms are another popular choice (where the technique is known as 'off-the-page' selling). This technique has been used with some success by orchestras and theatres promoting subscription series who have taken pages in selected colour supplements. In fact direct marketing can use any medium available to traditional advertising so long as it can handle a response mechanism.

But mail is the most popular direct medium. In many ways it is an ideal medium for the arts – as it allows a good deal of information and explanation, as well as the ability to target the offer exactly to the individual concerned. What are the essential components of a good mailshot?

The envelope

An envelope can start selling even before it has been opened. Thinking back to the Attention – Interest – Desire – Action model of communication examined in Chapter 6, the envelope can be used to grab attention. It might be an intriguing line. A famous mailing soliciting subscriptions for the American magazine *Psychology Today* featured the irresistible line 'Do you lock the bathroom door behind you, even when there's no one else in the house?' More elaborate material from companies like Readers Digest, or the Consumers Association promoting *Which?* magazine, often features windows in the envelope through which exciting things like stamps or a 'credit card' or even a key or a coin can be seen. For the arts organization on a limited budget, however, a simple message can be enough. The arts have a positive and cheerful message compared to much of the mundane or tiresome material which usually awaits the householder on the mat in the morning. The cost of having your envelope supplier print it in one colour can be negligible over a large order quantity.

The letter

This is the main selling vehicle. Common sense would suggest that it be kept terse and concise, like a business letter. But, again, research shows that if people are going to read it at all they do not mind length so long as interest is maintained. So the letter should be as long as it needs to be. There seems to be an industry trend towards letters which border on being newsletters, sometimes up to four pages, usually with plenty of verbal and visual variety.

- Keeping paragraphs short is a good idea, as is plenty of space.
- A useful trick is to end each page with a sentence that runs into the next page – the idea being to keep the reader's attention.
- Letters are a personal form of expression, and even though your letter may be going out to many thousands of prospects, it is well to keep this in mind. Give your letters a personal touch which reflects the USP of your business.
- Many arts organizations boast a charismatic individual as a music director or artistic director. This is an asset to be exploited in direct mail – by scripting a letter as if it came from them.

The response device

A card or envelope which allows the reader to respond to the offer is absolutely vital. If the letter has fulfilled the Interest and Desire part of the AIDA equation, then this fulfils the Action element. Modern print and computer technology means that you can partially fill out this card for the respondent with details of name and address. Just as good press relations make life easier for journalists, so good direct marketing makes life easier for customers (in much the same way as structured telephone call handling does in the box office as covered earlier). Pre-printing response forms has the additional benefit of making life easier for the response handler as well, as it insures against indecipherable handwriting and incorrect details.

Other mailing components

Received wisdom in the direct mail world holds that the more gimmicks you can cram into the package, the more opportunities you have to sell. If there are eight things in the envelope, the prospect has to say 'no' eight times. Scratch cards, stickers, stamps, envelopes within envelopes, certificates and letters, all promote involvement. The reason they are there in mailings from the Consumers Association, for example, is that research has proved that they boost response.

The only unbreakable rule about what to put into a mailing is to be consistent. The whole package must have an internal cohesion. So the message on the outside should be carried forward by the content of the letter. The response device should continue the theme rather than going off on a tangent. Any other components should be flowing the same way too. Logic should never be sacrificed to 'creativity', however beguiling the idea might appear in the short term. This is sometimes a difficulty when there are a number of people in an organization whose views contribute to marketing. 'Keep it simple' is a valuable principle.

Always monitor response, as the lessons you learn from your own activity are the most important pieces of marketing information you will be able to bring to bear on your future planning. There is always a temptation to neglect this kind of analysis in the busy world of arts marketing, but it is becoming more and more necessary in maximizing the value to be extracted from scarce resources. Some kind of monitoring ought to be planned into the campaign from the outset, as in any kind of marketing planning (see Chapter 8).

Conclusion

Arts marketing channel decisions have some points of similarity to the sorts of procedures whereby tangible products are distributed. Sometimes services will rely on tangible products as part of their delivery (such as small-press magazines or exhibitions). But the essential element in opening up the experience of the arts to customers is interpersonal contact.

In this chapter we have emphasized how the appropriate forms of distribution are combined strategically with the other elements of the marketing mix, product, price and promotion to maximize the number of arts customers reached in the optimum combination of cost and organizational objectives.

- The role of marketing channels in promotion is often vital in the arts, as they act as conduits of information to and from the customer.
- Intermediaries play a crucial part in this process. Just as retailers in commercial marketing perform functions which manufacturers could not execute unaided, so intermediaries like managements, venues and entrepreneurial agencies open up audiences and opportunities which would otherwise be unavailable to artists and performers.
- The process of distributing the arts relies heavily on physical environment and time. Both of these are strategic issues, careful attention to which can improve an organization's position and effectiveness.
- Direct marketing, which is an approach to marketing which incorporates a form of distribution, is a highly appropriate tool for arts marketers because of its flexibility and individual reach. It emphasizes the importance of relationships in marketing, as does the realization that organizations are not only suppliers but customers of other organizations.

Key concepts

Atmospherics
Broker
Channel intermediary
Contact costs
Contractual VMS
Database
Direct marketing
Horizontal/vertical channel conflict
List broker

Marketing channels
Merchandising
MGM, FGAF
Off the page selling
Piggybacking
Relationship marketing
Retailer
Vertical integration
Wholesaler

Discussion questions

1 Illustrate the influence of the other elements of the marketing mix on distribution for: (a) the Royal Shakespeare Company touring *King Lear* to Newcastle upon Tyne; (b) a major retrospective exhibition of David Hockney at the Hayward Gallery on the South Bank; (c) a craft jeweller with a new collection of work.
2 Give examples of potential channel conflict, both horizontal and vertical, in a tour of a production of *My Fair Lady* visiting a number of venues in Scotland. How might such conflict be resolved or prevented?
3 Discuss the promotional role of marketing channels in the visual arts as opposed to the performing arts.
4 How can atmospherics be used to enhance the experience of arts attenders? How might their role vary with art form?

5 How might audience segmentation inform decisions about time as an element in distribution for the performing arts?
6 'The list is more important than the offer.' What does this mean in the context of direct marketing, and do you agree? Illustrate your answer with examples from arts marketing.

Action problems

1 What are the difficulties awaiting a customer trying to contact your organization by telephone? (You can research this question yourself.) Outline ways of addressing three of them.
2 How can the element of time be better utilized in your distribution strategy? Compare your own performance in this respect with that of a similar venue to create a checklist of positive and negative aspects to work on.
3 Compile a list of customer care training requirements for your front-of-house staff. Research ways of supplying the requirements either from internal resources (members of staff sharing skills), co-operation with other venues, placements, or external training agencies.
4 Create an access information sheet to be used by your box office or information desk, gathering details of public transport, car parking, coach setting-down points, disabled facilities and pedestrian/cyclist access.

References

An Chomhairle Ealaion (1987). *Art and the Ordinary*. The Arts Council of Ireland.
Bird, D. (1993). *Commonsense Direct Marketing*, 3rd edn. Kogan Page.
Bird, D. (1994). *How to Write Sales Letters that Sell*. Kogan Page.
Brann, C. (1984). *Cost Effective Direct Marketing*. Collectors' Books.
Christiansen, R. (1994). Arts notebook: Turner in a new light. *Daily Telegraph*, 1 October, 12.
Davidson, H. (1987). *Offensive Marketing*. Penguin.
Denford, A. (1990). Big booth for ticket sales. *Arts Management Weekly*, 6 December, 2–3.
Donovan, K. (1993). Small, sometimes beautiful – always at risk. *The Irish Times*. 11 August, 8
Horovitz, J. (1990). *How to Win Customers using Customer Service for Competitive Edge*. Pitman.
Kotler, P. and Andreasen, A. (1991). *Strategic Marketing for Non-profit Organizations*. Prentice Hall.
MacDonald, J. (1992). Death of the blockbuster? In *Marketing the Arts*, The International Council of Museums.
McCall, J.B. and Warrington, M.B. (1989). *Marketing by Agreement: A Cross Cultural Approach to Business Negotiations*. John Wiley & Sons.
Mercer, D. (1992). *Marketing*. Basil Blackwell.
Royal Mail (1991). *The Royal Mail Guide to Successful Direct Mail*.
Tomlinson, R. (1990) Great show, shame about the staff. *Arts Management Weekly*, 15 November, 2–3.

8 Marketing planning

Introduction

The purpose of marketing planning is very simple. It aims to help managers identify a range of potential marketing activities, to choose the most effective ones and to work out what they will cost to implement. It is a systematic process which forces an organized approach to marketing decision making, leading to greater effectiveness in meeting the needs of current and future audiences, and greater efficiency in the use of resources in achieving this. Whilst it is not a panacea for all the problems facing the organization, marketing planning can be an invaluable instrument for identifying and responding to emerging issues in uncertain environments and can be a catalyst for constructive and effective marketing activity. It cannot ensure success, but it does improve the chances of success and reduce the risks of failure.

The process of marketing planning is defined quite simply as 'the planned application of marketing resources to achieve marketing objectives' (McDonald, 1989). It is a dynamic process, comprising a series of logical steps which help drive the organization forward by co-ordinating resources and channelling them towards the achievement of predetermined goals.

The aim of this chapter is to examine the key steps in the marketing planning process and to look at the role of the marketing plan itself, and how its implementation can be monitored. This includes sections on:

- Mission statements and organizational objectives.
- The marketing audit and SWOT analysis.
- Marketing objectives and strategies.
- Marketing tactics and budgets.
- Implementing the marketing plan: monitoring and review.

The framework suggested for marketing planning should enable arts organizations to embark on marketing planning in a structured way and to reconcile the aims of their own organizations with the constraints of the environment and the needs and expectations of their markets.

The benefits of marketing planning

The benefits of marketing planning can be seen at both the organizational level and the individual level. Marketing planning takes place within the context of the aims and objectives of the whole organization. It can even help to clarify them, reinforcing the artistic policy and providing a sense of direction and purpose to the activities in which arts organizations are engaged. When the organization is clear about what it is and where it is going, audiences too will be more certain as to the organization's role and position, reducing the likelihood of disappointed expectations.

For the organization, the benefits of marketing planning stem from:

- Better anticipation of change and less vulnerability to the unexpected.
- A long term perspective and proactive responses to environmental changes.
- Acceptance of the need for change and preparedness to meet change.
- Fewer bad decisions when taken by surprise.
- Greater inter-functional co-ordination.
- Better communication and less conflict between individuals.
- Minimum waste and duplication of resources.
- The existence of a structure around which to manage.

Individuals, too, benefit from the planning process, which can create a sense of belonging to and ownership of the organization and increase personal motivation by creating opportunities for achievements to be formally recognized.

Objections to marketing planning

As the benefits of marketing planning are so significant, it is surprising that resistance is often encountered by those who wish to introduce it into arts organizations. Planning is sometimes accepted as a necessary evil, on the basis that sponsors and funding bodies require it, and that budgets are needed to prevent over-spending, but is often treated with suspicion.

Underlying the excuses often given for not planning may lie some quite understandable insecurities. Some people dismiss planning as irrelevant because they don't really know what it is about or where to start, or they believe that it requires a special skill which they do not possess. Others fear that plans are hostages to fortune, and work on the basis that if they don't publish their intentions, no one can turn around and say that they failed to reach their goals! Another objection is that planning time is time that could be spent more productively getting on with the job, though it is likely that their own time-management could be improved by having better direction and focus for their work.

To overcome objections to planning it is important that the process is introduced with maximum communication and minimum mystique, in a constructive rather than critical atmosphere, and with appropriate support, including training, for those who are directly involved in the creation of the plans.

Problems with marketing planning

Marketing planning does not always realize its potential benefits. This can be for a

Inventive incentives

The launch of the Arts Council's Incentive Funding Scheme in 1988 confronted a number of its client organizations with the need to prepare formal business plans for the first time. The scheme encouraged organizations to bid competitively for an award of up to £250,000 to finance a project of their devising which would lead to a permanent improvement in their position. A comprehensive plan, agreed at board level and indicating how the results were to be achieved was an integral part of the application process.

Of the hundreds of organizations who applied in the first year, 48 were successful. Six of them reaped the jackpot of £250,000 – including the Royal Shakespeare Company, the Theatre Royal Plymouth and the Leeds Theatre Trust (West Yorkshire Playhouse). Smaller organizations like the Poetry Book Society also came away with awards appropriate to the scale of their plans.

The scheme aroused a lot of controversy. Some objected to it on the grounds that business planning was an inappropriate model for the way they wanted to operate. Others (some major clients among them) tried to prepare plans which lacked conviction, and were disappointed. Planning is just as relevant to small organizations as it is to large ones – but it needs conviction, commitment and communication if it is to succeed.

Box 8.1

Perceptions of planning

It often is assumed that planning is a restrictive process; that the organization and its creative leadership will be locked into a plan which may well not be good for either, that a plan must be adhered to rigidly once it is formulated and approved, that change is impossible, or at the very best, difficult; that it forces people to do things when they realize from further experience that doing something else would be better, that because one doesn't know what is going to happen in the future, one is precluded by a plan from taking advantage of opportunities which may arise unexpectedly. To put it succinctly, such perceptions of planning are ridiculous. (Crawford, 1985)

---

number of reasons, but arts organizations which are dissatisfied with the results of planning systems may find the following to be the most significant:

Weak support from top management   While chief executives are usually in support of financial planning, they may perceive marketing planning to be in conflict with artistic policy. (Marketing is often taken to mean market-led and giving people what

Box 8.2

Why people don't plan	What to say to people who don't plan
Reasons given:	*Response:*
'Things are changing too quickly.'	'. . . then it's easy to change with them.'
'We're too small to need a plan.'	'. . . then your plan will be short and simple.'
'I've got more important things to do.'	'. . . how do you know which is the best place to start?'
'What's the point of planning?'	'. . . you know which is the best place to start!'
'It's not my job.'	'. . . then whose is it?'
'No one will take any notice even if I do plan.'	'. . . they will if you involve them.'
'I already know which direction we're going.'	'. . . but does everyone else?'
Underlying reasons:	
'I don't like planning.'	'. . . but you'll like the results of planning.'
'Maybe I can't achieve what I'd like to.'	'. . . at least you'll know before you start trying.'
'Where do I start?'	'. . . read this chapter!'
'I'm not qualified.'	'. . . you will be when you've read this chapter.'
'What happens if I don't achieve my plans?'	'. . . you'll be able to give good reasons for it.'
'I've never thought of planning before.'	'. . . there's no time like the present.'
'I hate bureaucracy!'	'. . . the best plans aren't bureaucratic!'

Adapted from: Arts Council Incentive Funding Scheme (1988). *Business Planning Seminar Participants Pack.* The Arts Council of Great Britain.

they want though, in an arts environment, a marketing plan should respond to, rather than lead, artistic policy, which forms part of the mission of the organization.)

Lack of information   A marketing plan is dependent on information to enable sound analysis of markets and the environment. An inadequate commitment to marketing research (or inadequate resources for it) may leave the planner to make assumptions which may be inaccurate, thereby distorting the base on which the plan is constructed, and leading to inappropriate objectives and unrealistic strategies.

Ambiguous purpose   The marketing plan may be used to try to extract funding from sponsors and funding bodies. To accommodate this purpose, targets and objectives may be unrealistically optimistic and ultimately unattainable.

Complexity   The plan does not exist as an end in itself. It needs to be communicated to the board for agreement and to the staff for action. Though the analysis required in the planning process is sometimes complex, the detailed presentation of these complexities in the marketing plan itself simply serves to confuse the readers. Planning terminology can sound like meaningless jargon and detracts from the impact of the report, sometimes leading to otherwise sound plans being rejected by those who would be involved in their agreement or implementation.

Expectations of instant results   Organizations which introduce marketing planning in response to a particular management crisis are often looking for quick solutions to pressing problems. In these situations, managers may hold unrealistic expectations as to the speed at which plans can be implemented and the results observed. Plans may be dismissed as failures before the full process of monitoring and adjustment has been undertaken. It is important therefore, to phrase objectives in terms which allow realistic timescales.

The implication of all this is that marketing planning may be rejected as being unhelpful or a waste of time. By being alert to the reasons why plans fail, arts organizations should be able to avoid the most common planning problems and reap the full benefits of a system which is designed to simplify the task of marketing management and improve its effectiveness.

The marketing planning process

The process of marketing planning involves four key stages, as shown in Figure 8.1:

- Analysis.
- Planning.
- Communication.
- Action and evaluation.

Analysis   This begins by examining the raison d'être of the organization. This may be explicit in the form of a mission statement, a set of organizational objectives and a clearly articulated artistic policy, but it may simply be implicit in the activities that the organization is engaged with, the art forms that it produces and the audiences that it attempts to serve. This understanding serves to create the framework within which the marketing plan should be developed.

After this, an assessment takes place of the readiness of the organization to meet the demands of its changing environment. This evaluation takes the form of a marketing audit which examines the nature of its external environment (especially its existing and potential audiences) and the extent of changes in that environment. The capabilities and constraints of the organization are appraised within this context, and the audit should culminate in a statement of the organization's strengths and weaknesses in the face of the opportunities and threats arising in its environment.

Planning　In possession of this knowledge about the organization's current position, the marketing planner can set objectives and design strategies to help the organization reach its target audiences more effectively and efficiently. Objectives are targets it wishes to reach (usually expressed numerically, perhaps in the form of gate receipts or percentage capacity filled, but also in the form of financial goals) and strategies are the broad approaches to achieving these.

Tactical plans can then be formulated. The term tactics refers to the ways in which the strategy will be implemented; there are usually several possible routes for achieving a goal and a route needs to be chosen which will fall within the organization's capabilities. For this reason, budgets are set to ensure that the planned tactics will not over-stretch the financial resources of the organization.

Communication　The marketing plan is the vehicle for communicating the planned marketing activity, mainly to those who are involved in its implementation, but also to other interested stakeholder groups, such as the board and funding bodies. It should reflect the outcome of analysis and clearly present the strategic and tactical marketing plans along with forecasts of their impact on the market and their implications for the organization.

Action　The quality of a marketing plan will normally be judged by the results of its implementation, so the management of its implementation (which more often than not means the management of change) is fundamental to the outcome of the planning process.

One of the most important management tasks is the monitoring and review of the plan as it is implemented. As the planning process is based on forecasts of an uncertain environment, it is inevitable that at some stage the outcomes of marketing activity will start to diverge from the projections put forward in the plan, with targets either being surpassed or underachieved. The monitoring and review process is one that is essential to enable corrective action to be taken if the planned marketing activity is failing to lead the organizations towards the achievement of its objectives.

The rest of this chapter explores these four critical stages in more detail and provides a blueprint for the introduction and maintenance of an effective marketing planning process in arts organizations.

Mission and objectives

The mission statement

An organization's primary purpose is usually expressed in the form of a mission statement. (As the mission statement is the starting point for marketing planning,

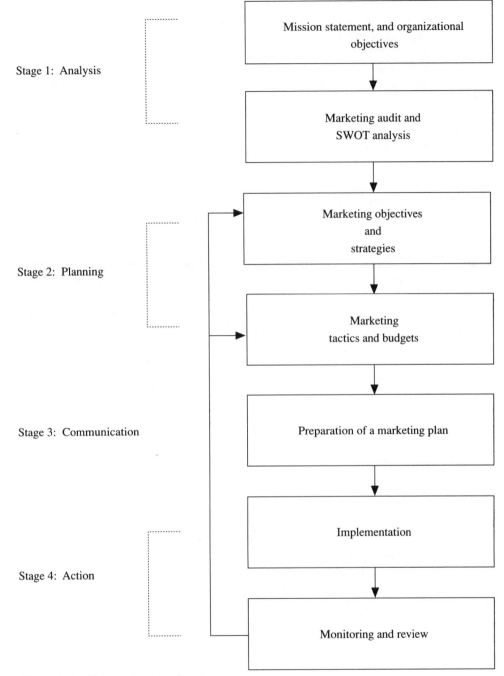

Figure 8.1 The marketing planning process

organizations which do not have one should consider drawing one up.) This will stand as the organization's policy statement in a number of circumstances, including grant applications and sponsorship approaches but, from a marketing point of view, it serves to give direction to marketing strategies.

In organizations where the primary objective is profit making, the mission statement will encourage strategies which lead to the profitable satisfaction of customer needs. In arts organizations, the mission statement will usually be a reflection of the artistic or cultural policy, and will focus on the desired artistic output rather than audience demand. The marketing task is to make links between the artistic work and the potential audiences for that work.

A mission statement is likely to include some or all of the following elements:

- A statement of purpose: this should identify the organization's primary reason for existence. It is likely to describe the artistic or cultural policy and outline the main processes by which these are implemented (including the scope and range of artistic activity).
- A description of target markets: this will outline the types of audience that the organization wishes to attract, but should also recognize a responsibility to sponsors and funding bodies.
- A statement of philosophy: this will establish the values and beliefs that guide the policies and strategies of the organization. It may encompass values relating to audiences (particularly with respect to access policy), artists (perhaps in terms of quality of the artistic product and artistic freedom), and also employees (giving a commitment to staff development).
- A statement of vision: this will explain where the organization is going, and how it sees itself at some future point in time. Its aspirations may relate to both its purpose and its target markets, but may also refer to its assets and resources (for example, the extension of premises).

A few guidelines are useful in creating a mission statement. According to Piercey (1991) it should be:

Succinct: comprise a few words and ideas, not pages that no one will ever read, let alone take any notice of.
Memorable: so that those who are working within it can remember what it is.
Enduring: though not a tablet of stone, it shouldn't need changing on a frequent basis.
Believable: it reflects the reality of the organization and its environment.
Roughly right: giving general directions and core values rather than precise goals and actions.
Energizing to all: it should be exciting and visionary.

Finally, a mission statement must be a statement to which all the stakeholders in the organization can subscribe, whether they be market stakeholders (audiences and target audiences), funding stakeholders (sponsors, trusts and funding bodies) or internal stakeholders (employees and artists).

Examples of organizational missions

Eastern Arts Board

(Eastern Arts is one of the UK's regional arts development and funding agencies.)

Eastern Arts Board's mission is to develop a wide range of arts activities of the highest quality, to stimulate artistic innovation and creativity and to extend involvement in the arts among all sections of the regional community.

Source: EAB (1992)

The Natural History Museum

(The Natural History Museum holds 67 million specimens, a proportion of which are on public display, though others are used only in research by the museum's 300 scientists.)

The Natural History Museum's mission is to promote the understanding and enjoyment of the variety of our natural world through high quality exhibitions, education and science.

Source: The Natural History Museum Corporate Plan (1990–95)

The Mumford Theatre

(The Mumford Theatre is the university theatre of Anglia Polytechnic University, Cambridge.)

The Arts Service of Student Services seeks to provide access for students both as performers and as audience to a wide variety of art forms on all campuses of the University and its environs.

Source: APU student services (1994)

The Scottish National Orchestra

(The Scottish National Orchestra performs and makes records throughout Scotland, the rest of the UK and overseas.)

The Scottish National Orchestra aims to be a leading contributor to the cultural life of Scotland, offering a well balanced programme to the public, a realistic form of sponsorship for supporters and a stable source of employment for players.

Source: Caminer (1989)

The Association for Business Sponsorship of the Arts

(ABSA encourages sponsorship and other links between business and the subsidized arts.)

ABSA exists to promote and encourage partnership between the private sector and the arts, to their mutual benefit, and to that of the community at large.

Source: ABSA (1992/3)

Organizational aims and objectives

The mission statement may be supported by a series of more specific aims and objectives which link a statement of purpose with a statement of vision.

Objectives can be phrased in two ways:

Aims will never finally be achieved as they will always persist. A gallery, for example, may state the following aims:

> 'To broaden the audience base for contemporary fine art by presenting work in an accessible format.'
> 'To ensure that the gallery's work represents a balance across gender and tradition.'
> 'To provide the opportunity for local and regional artists to show their work in a national and international context.'

Objectives are measurable and give time scales within which a particular desired state should be achieved. For example:

> 'Within two years to create in the gallery a welcoming social space in which people from all backgrounds can meet to eat, drink and talk.'
> 'To mount two exhibitions each year which reflect the ethnic and cultural diversity of the region.'
> 'Each year to provide new facilities which improve access for disabled people.'

Both aims and objectives are useful in marketing planning as they give specific direction to marketing activity, though objectives also provide a useful yard-stick against which achievements can be measured.

The marketing audit and SWOT analysis

A marketing audit is the process by which an arts organization gathers relevant information about its environment (an external audit) and itself (an internal audit). The purpose of the marketing audit is to help organizations to answer the question 'where are we now?' It should be a systematic, unbiased and critical review which leads to an evaluation of the organization's strengths and weaknesses in responding to the opportunities and threats in its environment. It is this SWOT analysis that helps the identification of appropriate marketing objectives and strategies.

The external audit (environmental analysis)

This is concerned with the appraisal of those factors which affect the fortunes of the organization but over which it has limited, if any, control. The purpose of the

Aims and objectives: Eastern Arts Board

EAB has published a set of aims and objectives in response to its mission statement. The aims are open statements which are then developed in more detail in the form of objectives giving specific targets:

Aims

1 To co-ordinate a regional vision for arts development, which contributes to both the formulation and the realization of a national arts and media strategy.
2 To facilitate partnership and collaboration among all the individuals and organizations in the private and public sectors with a part to play in translating the vision into reality.
3 To promote quality in the practice and presentation of the arts.
4 To stimulate growth in the Region's cultural economy.
5 To encourage the greatest possible diversity of form, scale and cultural practice.
6 To foster the creation of new and innovative work in the Region.
7 To increase opportunities for enjoyment and education in the arts.
8 To erode barriers to involvement in the arts, whether economic, social, physical or cultural.
9 To provide a range of high quality services in the fields of planning, support and evaluation.

The objectives and targets relating to aim 1, the 'vision' objectives are:

(a) To undertake continuing programmes of research into:
   – The perceptions and requirements of the Region's population in relation to the arts
   Target: Two major market research projects per annum, one in the visual and media arts, one in performing arts; collaboration with clients and others in five other market research projects per annum.
   – Developments in the arts regionally, nationally and internationally.
   Target: All staff at officer level and above to make two research visits outside the Region each year to study developments in their field and to make a formal report to the appropriate department(s) and committee(s). 'Twinning' arrangements developed with regions in three other countries involving one exchange visit each way per annum.
   – The strengths and weaknesses of the current pattern of arts facilities and activities, together with the opportunities for future development, on a district and county basis.
   Target: Five district Arts Plans and one County Plan produced or substantially updated each year.

> (b) To present the key findings of these programmes of research to the national funding bodies and other RABs and to obtain similar information from them.
> *Target:* Two published reports each year. Obtain regular information from NFB/RAB marketing and information officers on current/recent research.
> (c) To formulate a comprehensive strategic plan for:
>   – Raising the quantity and quality of arts activity throughout the Region.
>   – Increasing its accessibility to the widest possible audience.
>   – Co-ordinating the development of strategic networks of provision.
>   – Contributing on a regional basis to the realization of a national arts and media strategy.
> *Target:* Strategic plan published by 30 April 1993, incorporating detailed strategies for the development of the performing arts and the visual and media arts and for the fields of resources and planning and development. Plan reviewed and updated annually.
>
> *Source:* EAB (1992)

external audit is to identify trends in the environment so that actions can be taken to exploit the positive trends and minimize the impact of the negative ones.

Three areas need to be considered – the business, economic and social environment (sometimes known as the macro environment), the market, and the competition.

The business, economic and social environment

Developments in the business and economic environment affect society as a whole, but certain of them will have specific relevance for arts organizations. The STEP factors, described below, are a useful model for identifying the most important trends in this type of environment:

Socio-cultural factors

- The mobility of populations: increased racial integration and a boom in international tourism mean that ethnocentric arts programmes are becoming less relevant and efforts to expand the cultural diversity of work are required if the arts are to remain accessible to the wider community.
- Increase in crime: venues sited in the inner cities may suffer from public fears of rising crime on the streets. This may be compounded by the reduction in public transport services which may restrict access to car owners and require that safe parking facilities close to the venue are available.
- Leisure patterns: an increase in the number of working women can reduce demand for arts events during the day, though a simultaneous increase in the retired population and non-working men may provide a target audience for arts activities at this time and alleviate the pressures on facilities at weekends.

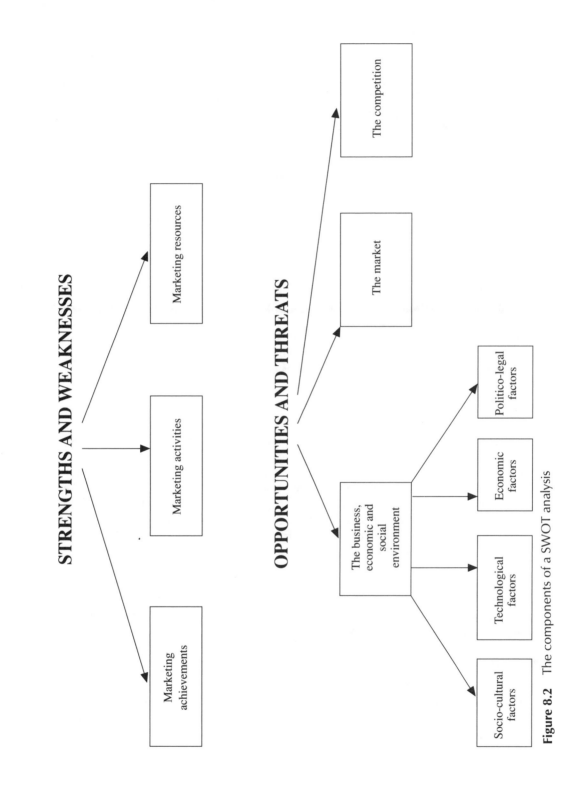

Figure 8.2 The components of a SWOT analysis

Box 8.3

The impact of the recession on business sponsorship of the arts

Business sponsorship of the arts fell considerably during the UK recession of the early 1990s. The overall figure of £57.69m in 1993 was down by 13 per cent in real terms on the 1992 figure, with certain sectors of the arts suffering the loss more than others. Theatre, music and the visual arts saw an increase in sponsorship, though arts festivals lost two thirds of their income and opera sponsorship fell by one third. Literature, photography and heritage continued to attract relatively low levels, being difficult to sell to potential sponsors.

Source: Dunn (1994)

Technological factors

- New applications for computers: far better target marketing can be achieved using computerized box office systems, providing opportunities to reduce mailing costs whilst improving response rates.
- Improved home entertainment: as the arts are in competition with other forms of leisure activity, home entertainment technology such as satellite TV and CD players can potentially threaten attendances at live arts events.

Economic factors

- Unemployment: this may lead to increased demand for arts activities but a reduced ability to pay for them. Pricing structures may need to be redesigned in periods of high unemployment.
- Rising interest rates: house owners experience a reduction in their disposable income when mortgage rates increase. As leisure activities comprise a part of the discretionary expenditure of a household, they may be the first to be cut back in times of economic constraint, and arts organizations may notice that even their most loyal attenders are coming less frequently. Reduced price subscription schemes may be an appropriate measure for encouraging a commitment to attend in these circumstances.
- Recession: businesses often reduce their expenditure on marketing in an attempt to survive a recession. Sponsorship is likely to be one of the first elements of a marketing budget to be cut as it is difficult to measure its results. Arts organizations are one group likely to suffer from reduced funding as a result.

Politico-legal factors

- Arts funding policy: this is likely to change according to the political persuasion of the ruling government. It can change very quickly, leaving arts organizations in the midst of the implementation of long-term plans but without the assurance of long-term income. Relatively fixed forms of financial support such as grants may be replaced by systems dependent on schemes such as lotteries, where the funding

Ethnic minority audiences in the UK
A survey of ethnic minority arts attenders showed some interesting differences from UK arts attenders as a whole. Particularly notable was the socio-economic groupings, with ABC1s being disproportionately represented amongst UK arts attenders while the ethnic minority arts attenders better represented the profile of the UK as a whole, almost half coming from C2DE households. When asked which were the most important factors in choosing entertainment, 52 per cent cited 'a place that makes me feel welcome' as being 'very important'.

Source: Policy Studies Institute (1989)

income and patterns are far less certain. Marketing plans should anticipate and forecast policy change as far as possible, but be sufficiently flexible to react to unexpected developments.

- Health and Safety regulations: legal requirements with regard to visitors and audiences as well as employees may influence venue design and the provision of facilities. Marketing plans must be constructed within these constraints and the finance for any measures to achieve compliance must take priority over other marketing activity.

These Socio-cultural, Technological, Economic and Political factors are inevitably beyond the control of an arts organization. They will produce opportunities for the organization to respond to and threats which it must face up to, but they cannot be ignored. An assessment of the significance of changes in the STEP factors should therefore be the starting point for a marketing audit.

Of much more immediate relevance to the organization, though, are trends which are of specific interest to its own industry, so the next stages of the audit require an assessment of trends amongst target markets and developments in competition. These give an organization a much clearer picture of the more immediate opportunities and threats that it faces. Continuous efforts to obtain current marketing research through both primary and secondary sources can produce the data on which such an assessment can be made (as discussed in Chapter 3).

The Market

The audit needs to search for any changes and trends in the following aspects of the organization's target market (including actual and potential audiences):

- The geographic and demographic characteristics of the primary target market.
- The characteristics of different market segments within the overall target market, e.g. regular attenders as opposed to irregular or infrequent attenders; day-time attenders as opposed to evening attenders; weekday attenders as opposed to weekend attenders; attenders for different types of art form.

- The benefits sought by different market segments, e.g. facilities expected; types of programme or exhibition; quality of artistic product.
- The price sensitivity of different segments.
- Purchasing patterns, e.g. popularity of subscription schemes or group bookings; sources of ticket purchase (agent or direct); preferences for opening hours or performance timings.
- Information sources used to find out about arts events.

This type of knowledge and understanding of the market can enable arts organizations to identify opportunities such as emerging market segments or new means by which they can communicate with their target audiences. It can also help them prepare for eventualities such as increased demand for improved facilities or a decline in the popularity of certain art forms. Market research is the key to this. Information can be pooled with other arts organizations to gain a more complete picture, or funding bodies may be able to provide an overview.

The competition

The audit also needs to recognize changes and trends in competition, i.e. the ways in which the target market is being satisfied. Two important questions need to be answered in building up a picture of the ways in which competition is affecting attendance patterns:

1 What is the nature of the competition? Competition may come from a wide range of sources (Kotler, 1984). An orchestra, for example, will need to recognize:

- Desire competitors (e.g. alternative ways of spending an evening, such as going to the pub or the bowling alley).
- Generic competitors (e.g. other forms of live entertainment, such as a play or a ballet).
- Form competitors (e.g. other types of live music, such as rock music, jazz or chamber music).
- Brand competitors (i.e. other orchestras).

2 How threatening are the different competitors? If audiences are simply deserting one venue for another in the locality, for example, then marketing strategies need to address the impact of a brand competitor, perhaps by identifying a niche in the market that the other venue is not well placed to serve. On the other hand, if audiences are deserting a particular art form, or even the arts per se, marketing communications may need to be enhanced in an attempt to change attitudes. This is likely to require a long-term commitment and more may be achieved by the lobbying of funding bodies and collective action by all the brand competitors than by unilateral strategies.

A perceptual map is a useful tool for evaluating the extent of brand competition (an example is given in Figure 8.3). It is developed by identifying the most important criteria by which audiences judge different arts organizations, placing them on the two axes and plotting the competitors within the framework. Qualita-

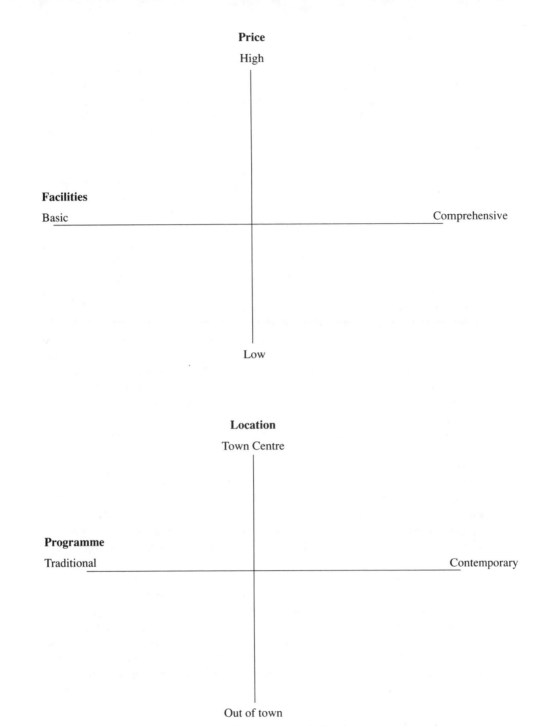

Figure 8.3 Examples of perceptual mapping grids for the assessment of competitive positioning

tive market research is a useful tool for identifying both the criteria and audience perceptions of different organizations. If an organization is positioned well away from its competitors, audiences are likely to perceive the product offerings of the various organizations to be quite different, so the intensity of the competition will be relatively low. However, if a number of organizations fall into the same quartile on the grid, competition is likely to be more fierce, with audiences choosing between broadly similar offerings.

An analysis of the effects of competition on pricing strategy is discussed further in Chapter 5. An understanding of the nature and strength of competition is an important factor in marketing planning, usually leading arts organizations to one of two conclusions (and occasionally a combination of both):

- That marketing strategies must involve collaborating with competitors (for example, through the formation of arts marketing consortia). This is a conclusion often reached in regions well served by arts organizations in the subsidized sector. If a number of different organizations are attempting to serve similar target markets, the extent of the competition may render them individually non-viable. Target audiences will become fragmented if they have to choose between different venues offering broadly similar programmes at the same time, and the cost of reaching these target audiences will be high due to the intensive promotion needed to encourage them to attend one venue rather than another. However, if the arts organizations work together, programme schedules can be designed so that different segments of the overall target market are attracted to different venues at different times. Joint promotional activity becomes possible, bringing economies of scale which reduce costs for each participating organization.

- That marketing strategies must involve proactive competition (attempting to defend oneself against competitors whilst simultaneously trying to attract their audiences). In the commercial arts, this has always been and will no doubt remain the overriding attitude towards competition. 'Angels' will only invest in West End musicals if they can anticipate a financial return, so the objective of the show is to make as much money as possible. In a finite market, this means not only persuading potential audiences to spend money on theatre instead of an evening in the pub or a trip to the cinema, but also persuading them to attend a particular production, rather than any of the others available within a short walking distance of the theatre. The impact of this competitive orientation must not be ignored by the subsidized sector. These commercial competitors are looking for audiences for live entertainment which are very likely to overlap to a large extent with the segments being targeted by the arts organizations with non-commercial objectives.

The internal audit

The purpose of the internal audit is to indicate how prepared the organization is to

TEAM (The Entertainments and Arts Marketers)

TEAM is a regional arts marketing consortium serving both the visual and performing arts in Liverpool and Merseyside. It was established in 1988 in the hope of generating an arts revival similar to the one that had recently been experienced in Glasgow. Whilst a number of established agencies were putting efforts into urban renewal by promoting the area, the arts organizations felt that they were not receiving the prominence they desired, so TEAM was established to plug the gap.

Services provided by TEAM:

- An integrated service for the distribution of promotional literature throughout Merseyside, which includes the provision of leaflet racks to stimulate cross-over of audiences between different art forms and different venues. This is re-stocked fortnightly.
- A computerized mailing database, coded according to interest in performing or visual arts, and used to convert irregular and intermittent attenders to more regular attendance. An 'entertainments and exhibitions' guide is mailed out to the whole list on a quarterly basis.
- Discount purchasing in the local press, achieved through collective buying power which leads to 40 per cent off the normal rate card.
- Bulk purchasing on printing and paper costs.
- Training sessions and a regular forum for the sharing of experiences and information, as well as informal social gatherings.
- Access to marketing research undertaken by other members.

Benefits of membership:

- Cost efficiency (from an initial investment of £3000, each member was able to take advantage of a total operational budget of £70,000).
- Access to new markets and audience development.
- Generation of funding from other public sector organizations (which doubled the amount raised in membership charges).
- Three full-time staff actively promoting the arts on Merseyside on behalf of members.

Drawbacks to membership (according to a visual arts member):

Some visual arts members are concerned that the consortium is dominated by performing arts members, so the initiatives do not always address the needs of museums and galleries. Perhaps too much emphasis is placed on 'bums on seats' and not enough on increasing the awareness of the consortium itself and the individual museums and galleries.

Source: Hope (1990)

Competition in the Canadian arts market

Brenda Gainer gives a good insight into the impact of competition on the Canadian arts market.

> Within the arts sector, two kinds of performing arts companies operate in Canada: profit-making companies whose repertoire is determined solely by popularity and which have a limited 'bottom line' orientation, and non-profit companies which serve multiple constituencies (audiences, corporate donors, individual donors and governments) and have complex goals such as furthering the art form, developing Canadian talent, educating the public, or producing new artistic work. The latter group of companies is that which specializes in what is often termed, for want of a better word, 'high' culture.

She goes on to look at trends in the market for high culture, and speculate on the impact of the profit-making sector on this market.

> We now see in the Toronto market the rapid proliferation of profit-making performing arts companies which can be much more responsive to the market in terms of repertoire choice, driven as they are almost exclusively by financial considerations. Research needs to be done to find out if shows such as *Cats* and *Les Miserables* attract different customers from the 'highbrow' performing arts companies, or if in fact they are now attracting customers away from those companies which have spent years building up audiences for live entertainment in Toronto. Research should also be done to determine what has caused the recent proliferation of privately owned competitors. If a certain 'critical mass' of live arts buyers building up in a city attracts these new competitors, other Canadian cities could expect to see audiences for 'high culture', which may still be expanding, shrink in the future as popular-rep competitors are attracted to previously uninteresting markets.

She concludes by stating that:

> Arts marketers must adopt a long-term strategic marketing perspective, and this must be based on solid empirical data and analytical techniques which incorporate both customer and competitor perspectives in their approach to the market.
>
> As the goal of arts marketing shifts away from expanding the arts market to expanding share within it, attention will be diverted from new advertising tactics in a co-operative industry framework to rigorous competitive analysis at the level of the whole organization ... Increasingly, artistic survival will depend on an overall organizational commitment to developing and sustaining a competitive advantage in the market-place.
>
> *Source:* Gainer (1989)

meet the demands of the changing environment identified in the external audit. The internal audit should look at three broad areas:

- Marketing achievements.
- Marketing activities.
- Marketing resources.

Marketing achievements   Marketing achievements (usually over the past 12 months) are measured by looking at the nature and sources of income generated, including the following:

- Box office income.
- Other earned income (catering, programmes [sales and advertising space], hiring etc.).
- Grants.
- Donations.
- Sponsorship.
- Customer satisfaction (identified through research).
- Audience development.
- New segments accessed.

Organizations with a computerized box office are in a position to obtain more information about the success of different marketing policies with different market segments, by looking at:

- Income for different types of show or exhibition.
- Types of tickets sold (subscription, members, party, corporate, single tickets, concessionary groups [young, OAP, unemployed etc.]).
- Price paid and method of payment.
- Day and time of attendance.
- Seasonal variations.
- Time booked (in advance or on the door).
- Sales channel (box office or agencies, personal, postal or telephone).

This information is particularly helpful if it is collected over many years so that trends can be identified and conclusions drawn as to the effectiveness of previous marketing strategies.

Marketing activities   The marketing mix should be reviewed. This draws attention to the way in which the visitor traffic and income described above is generated.

- Product
  - programming policy
  - range of productions or exhibitions
  - quality of productions or exhibitions, based on peer-group evaluation and reputation
  - nature of venue(s), including location, amenities, ambience etc.

- Price
  - price levels
  - price structures (including concessions)
  - differentials to influence demand (e.g. lower prices for matinees, higher prices at weekends)
  - incentives to promote frequency, including subscription schemes
  - incentives to attract parties and groups
  - sponsorship and other income generation
- Promotion
  - advertising, including the relative success of different media
  - print and its distribution
  - posters
  - PR
  - direct mail, indicating the size and composition of the mailing list.
- Distribution (i.e. availability, especially booking and selling facilities)
  - box office (hours open and staffing levels)
  - other selling points, including ticket agencies
  - range of venues and locations (for touring productions or exhibitions)
  - the proportions of amateur, professional, national or international events (for venues).

Marketing resources   The marketing resources committed to the generation of income and the development of marketing activity must be identified. Not only do they indicate the efficiency with which the marketing function operates, but they also create the constraints within which the marketing function is performed. Four key resources should be examined:

- Staff (including job responsibilities, organizational structure, staff experience, and support from higher levels of management).
- Budgets (including allocation decisions and opportunities for increasing revenues).
- Information technology (including box office systems).
- Other help
  - from public bodies such as local authorities or universities
  - from board members
  - from volunteers
  - from the Arts Council or regional arts boards
  - from venues (for touring productions and exhibitions)
  - from marketing consortia.

SWOT analysis

The most useful way of drawing conclusions from the marketing audit is by conducting a SWOT analysis. From the list of issues identified in the external environment, the specific opportunities and threats facing the organization can be drawn out. The strengths and weaknesses of the marketing function in meeting the

Box 8.4

MAX – a SWOT analysis

'MAX' stands for 'Marketing the Arts in Oxfordshire', which is an arts marketing consortium comprising 11 members. Its primary aims are to work on behalf of consortium members and their associated clients to develop the generic market for the arts in Oxfordshire and its surrounding areas, as well as providing a sound infrastructure for arts marketing in the region and to increase the levels of marketing expertise within the membership. The key points of their SWOT analysis, conducted in 1992, can be summarized as follows:

Strengths
experienced staff with strong marketing skills
commitment from funders, members and staff
high level of technology
well situated rent and service free accommodation
high quality of tactical services offered

Weaknesses
weak 'corporate' identity and lack of clear direction
dependence on public funding (low budgets)
low profile within funding organizations
low status of marketing within member organizations
diverse range of members' priorities and demands
lack of storage space

Opportunities
increasing recognition of consortia work nationally
increasing network of consortia
relationship with Southern Arts
links with non-arts organizations
increasing funding potential from the commercial sector
limited competition

Threats
de-investment in the arts nationally
changes in the arts funding structure
difficult economic climate
poor career structures in the arts generally

Source: Dixon (1993)

opportunities and counteracting the threats can then be developed from the evidence in the internal audit. Although this is a largely subjective process, it is a useful way of summarizing the marketing audit.

Not all the strengths and weaknesses of the organization should be listed; neither should all the opportunities and threats. The SWOT analysis should draw out the major opportunities and threats facing the organization, together with those strengths and weaknesses which affect the way in which the opportunities can be seized and the threats avoided. In doing this, it creates a framework for the formulation of objectives and strategies, helping the organization to decide 'where do we want to go?'

Objectives and strategies

An objective is what you want to achieve, and should be a specific target which can be demonstrably attained. A strategy is how you plan to achieve your objectives. It is a general statement which gives direction to the activities (or tactics) that must be undertaken to achieve the objectives. For the purposes of a marketing plan, these objectives and strategies relate to the arts provision, the related facilities and the audience (or sponsor).

Marketing objectives

Eichten (1983) gives four types of generic objective that an arts organization can set:

- Audience enrichment — objective: to maintain audience satisfaction by paying attention to the total experience offered.
- Audience maintenance — objective: to sell more of existing provision to current audiences.
- Audience expansion — objective: to sell more of existing provision to new audiences.
- Audience development — objective: to sell new types of provision to current audiences.

In addition, arts organizations may need to consider the more radical approach of:

- Innovation — objective: to sell new types of arts provision to new audiences.

According to the strengths, weaknesses, opportunities and threats identified in the marketing audit, any or all of these generic objectives may be appropriate and will need to be further developed into specific statements of planned achievement. These statements need to be written very carefully, as they are the driving force behind the future marketing activity of the organization. Objectives (as described earlier in this chapter) should be SMART objectives:

Specific (make it quite clear as to what the target is).
Measurable (be capable of evaluation of progress).
Agreed (supported by all who are involved in achieving them).
Realistic (not unattainable dreams).
Time-constrained (to be achieved by a specific deadline).

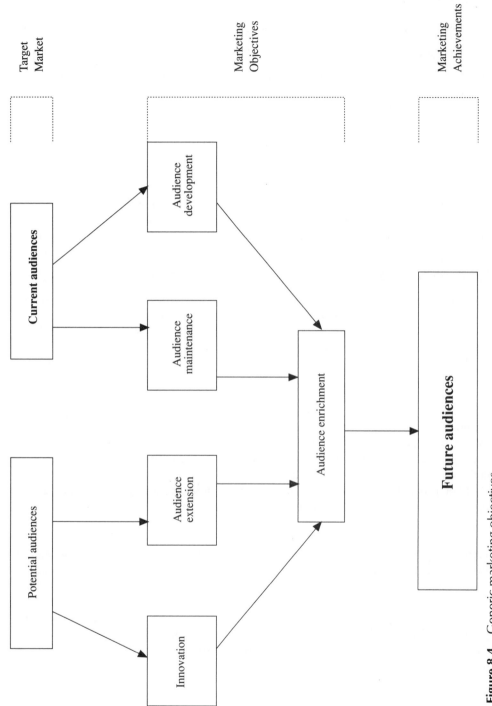

Figure 8.4 Generic marketing objectives

Target
Market

Marketing
Objectives

Marketing
Achievements

Current audiences

Potential audiences

Audience
development

Audience
maintenance

Audience
extension

Innovation

Audience enrichment

Future audiences

Examples of specific marketing objectives relating to each of the generic areas might be:

'To increase the sale of subscription schemes by 10 per cent next season' (audience maintenance).
'To obtain £50,000 of sponsorship income from new sources in 1995' (sponsor expansion).
'To double the number of first-time attenders during the autumn season' (audience expansion).
'To increase audiences for contemporary visual art by 30 per cent over the next 12 months' (audience development).
'Regularly to fill 20 places in an afternoon crèche by 1 September 1995' (audience enrichment).
'To generate £20,000 from the hire of facilities for business conferences' (innovation).

Marketing strategies

Marketing strategies outline the way in which the organization's skills and resources should be used to achieve its marketing objectives. They are inevitably wide in scope, and describe overall routes to achieving objectives rather than giving details of specific 'activities' that must be undertaken.

Marketing strategies are broadly concerned with the four main elements of the marketing mix, and should provide general policy in each area.

Product: the general policy for the scope of arts activity and facilities to be provided. Proposed marketing strategies may state the advisability of either a wider or narrower range of arts activities; this is a controversial area, and often one which causes conflict between the artistic director and the marketing department, though compromises can normally be found.

Other product related strategies may relate to non-core arts activities, such as the role of the catering or retail outlets, perhaps the provision of a crèche, or the improvement of facilities for sponsors.

Price: the general pricing policies to be followed for different audience segments. Pricing strategy determines the way in which revenue is generated. A highly controversial pricing strategy is emerging in a number of institutions in the visual arts and museums sector – namely that of charging an entrance fee.

Other pricing strategies may relate to changes in the basis for concessions; new pricing schemes will often be required to reach new audiences or to develop audiences for new art forms. The role of fund-raising and sponsorship may also be determined at this point.

Promotion: the general policies for communicating with a range of target audiences. The objectives may suggest that a change in the balance between the use of

The Boston Symphony Orchestra

In 1970, the Boston Symphony Orchestra was facing a problem of declining ticket sales. A concert activities committee was set up by the trustees to consider the problem, and subsequent discussions brought forth a number of suggestions as to the cause of the problem, ranging from parking to ease of ticket purchase and concert timing. However, the major objective of attracting new subscribers seemed to require a strategy of changing the actual content of the symphony programs.

The associate conductor at the BSO at the time was 26 year old Michael Tilson Thomas. He took the view that the role of management in relation to programming was to aid and carry out the plans of the music director, recognizing the abilities of both the music director and the orchestra and thinking of ways to capitalize on these abilities. Nonetheless he was a realist. 'In programming concerts for an entire season, you are constrained by the relative poverty of the orchestra. One big thing must be paid for by doing less at many other concerts. One big-name soloist will be a sure-fire success, but then you cannot do as much the rest of the season.'[1]

Therefore, when the issue of changing the program arose, he presented a radical proposal which he saw as satisfying the need of both the musicians and the trustees. His suggestion was for a new series of concerts that 'would consist of music of all periods in unusual juxtaposition', to be presented informally with the conductor talking to the audience. The series would be lower priced and intended to attract an entirely new audience.

> I feel it is possible to present a program which will appeal to a different kind of audience, different from our regular subscribers. I think that we can reach the people who don't normally come, people who aren't attracted to our traditional programming. In short, I think we can reach the music freaks.
>
> The series should be lower priced so that it will not exceed the budget of young people. It should be completely outside the regular subscription series so that we will attract an entirely new audience. These new concerts can be done in a number of different ways. Each year they should become progressively more experimental.
>
> At the end of one of these concerts the audience might sit in a state of shock. According to my ideal, it should be impossible for the audience to return to thinking of things in the same way after one of these concerts.[2]

Malcolm S. Salter, Thomas D. Steiner and Jeanne Deschamps, *The Boston Symphony Orchestra*, 375–340. Boston, Massachusetts: Harvard Business School, 1975.

[1] p. 8
[2] p. 12

Pricing policy at the V&A

Following the success of a 1987 policy decision to request voluntary admissions donations, the Victoria and Albert Museum first considered charging a compulsory admission charge in 1990 when it appeared that its annual grant would only rise by 2.5 per cent. The alternative strategy under consideration was to close one day a week, probably a Monday, to cut costs. From 1977 to 1987, the museum had closed on a Friday, but seven-day opening had been reinstated when revenue from donations started to rise.

Source: Tait (1990)

A community ticketing scheme at Nottingham Playhouse

With the objective of audience development firmly in mind, the Nottingham Playhouse collaborated with sponsors, the Hamlyn Foundation, to make tickets (and ticket prices) accessible to groups of non-traditional theatre attenders. Hamlyn, at a cost of £90,000 over three years, buys tickets for a night at each Playhouse production, which are then re-sold for a couple of pounds to local people through Nottingham's pubs or through local groups.

Source: Dunn (1994)

advertising and direct marketing may be appropriate, so a strategy related to this could involve the commissioning of a new database system. Alternatively, if the objectives are to reposition the organization to attract different types of audiences, the strategic emphasis may be on PR and advertising, and lead to the appointment of agencies. Whilst the details of the promotional campaign should not be raised at this stage, an account should be given of the promotional tools that will be used.

Distribution: the general venue policy (especially for touring organizations) and/or ticket distribution systems. Ticket distribution strategies will indicate the best ways of making tickets available to target audiences. A change in the role of ticket agencies may be suggested, or perhaps increased distribution through schools and clubs. The use of telephone selling may be proposed, and touring organizations may advocate a change in the proportion of performances or exhibitions held in rural venues.

These are just a few examples of marketing strategies. They will set the boundaries for the design of more specific tactical marketing plans.

Marketing tactics and budgets

Marketing tactics

A set of overall marketing objectives and strategies should subsequently be translated into a detailed statement of planned marketing activities indicating exactly what actions need to be taken.

There has already been a lot of discussion in this book about tactical marketing activity. Chapters 4 to 7 explain the use of the marketing tools of product, price, promotion and place in an arts environment. For the purposes of planning this type of activity, a useful device is a tactical marketing planning grid, which takes each marketing objective and recommends a series of activities to lead to its achievement. Figure 8.5 gives schemes of a possible activity linked to two of the example objectives given in the previous section.

Cost and revenue forecasts should be generated for each of the activities on each of the grids, and the activities should be prioritized in the event of financial constraints curtailing some of the plans. These calculations can then be used to prepare a marketing budget. The timing of the activities should also be indicated and, if possible, the name of the person responsible for implementing the planned activity. Clear performance indicators should be put in place to measure success.

The marketing budget

A marketing budget details the planned expenditure on marketing activity to take place in the time period of the plan. It summarizes the expenditures associated with specific activities on each of the tactical marketing planning grids, and will include projected marketing overheads, such as staff costs, photography and telephone.

It has a very important role to play in convincing the rest of the management team that the marketing plans are sufficiently stretching without being over ambitious, that the expenditure required is within the constraints of the organization and that the risks involved are calculated risks. (The whole issue of budgeting is developed further in Chapter 9.) Marketing budgets are usually submitted to financial managers to be considered in conjunction with other budgets from different departments. Their job is to ensure that an organization as a whole will be able to meet its financial commitments.

Writing the marketing plan

The next stage in the marketing planning process is to communicate the plan to all those who will have an interest in its implementation. It is easy to underestimate the importance of this stage. Having done all the hard work of analysis, objective setting

Target audience: Marketing tactics:	Current subscribers	Lapsed subscribers	Regular attenders	Friends and members
Product				
Pre-show 'Meet the Cast' events	x	x	x	x
Seat upgrading facility	x	x	x	x
Priority booking arrangements				x
Price				
Discount for early subscription	x			
Refund for usage below stated levels		x	x	
Discount voucher for bookshop		x	x	
Promotion				
Direct mail	x	x	x	x
Updated subscription leaflet	x	x	x	x
Advertisement in programmes		x	x	
Place				
Telephone sales	x	x		

x indicates the target audiences which the proposed marketing tactics are primarily designed to attract

Figure 8.5 (a)   Tactical planning grid: 'To increase the sale of subscription schemes by 10 per cent'

Target audience: Marketing tactics:	Lapsed sponsors	Sponsors of other arts organizations	Local businesses
Product			
Executive dining facility			x
Corporate membership scheme	x	x	x
Price			
Discount for sponsor's employees			x
Promotion			
PR	x	x	x
Direct mail		x	
Priority ticket scheme			x
Place			
Contacts by board members			
Personal selling	x	x	x

Figure 8.5 (b) Tactical planning grid: 'To obtain £50,000 sponsorship income from new sources'

and designing tactical solutions, it is tempting to cut corners when it comes to writing it all down. The best approach, therefore, is to think first about the people who will want to read your plan and the influence they have. For reasons of commercial sensitivity, external bodies may receive an edited version of the plan. The detailed marketing plan is likely to have a restricted readership.

Target readership for all or part of the plan will include:

- Staff in the marketing department: responsible for the tasks involved in implementing the plan.
- Top management: with the power to veto, postpone or curtail any part of the plan of whose effectiveness they are not fully convinced.
- Other departments: whose co-operation is vital if customer focus is to permeate the organization.
- Board of governors: looking for evidence that the plan will enhance and build on the mission of the organization.
- Funding bodies: evaluating the proposals alongside those from competitors.
- Sponsors: seeking reassurance that links with your organization will enhance their reputations and offer good value for money.
- Advertising and marketing research agencies: needing firm direction to help them create appropriate campaigns.

The clarity with which the marketing plan is written and presented is likely to have a major impact on the willingness of these diverse parties to embrace it and help to make it work.

The structure of a marketing plan

It is likely that the marketing plan will be a subsection of a strategic plan, so its structure may be dictated by those conventions. Normally though, the marketing plan should basically consist of a document which gives a summary of the findings from stages one and two of the planning process, given in Figure 8.1, that is:

- A brief statement of the organization's mission and objectives.
- The key findings of marketing audit, summarized at the end in the form of a SWOT analysis.
- A statement of marketing objectives and related strategies.
- A set of tactical marketing plans and their related costs and projected benefits.
- A marketing budget, indicating the allocation of expenditure.

There are three golden rules for writing the plan:

1 Start with a summary of your main conclusions and recommendations (for those who find the details either uninteresting or unnecessary).
2 Tell the readers what they need to know, not everything that you know (your main findings and conclusions are relevant, but the statistical details of how they were obtained are not).

3 Write in English, not in marketing-speak! (note the very diverse backgrounds of your readers, whose understanding of marketing theory is likely to range from 'a considerable amount' to 'none at all'. If the readers don't understand what you're talking about, they're more likely to reject the plan altogether!).

Implementing the marketing plan

There's no point designing clever marketing strategies and detailed plans if they can't be implemented to enable the organization to reach its objectives. Marketing implementation, therefore, is ultimately far more important than the plan itself, and the central role of the marketing department is to apply its marketing skills to the organization's resources to execute the tactical marketing plans.

Implementation can prove difficult for a number of reasons, and can be considered to have failed if nothing happens as a result of the marketing plan. If this occurs, it is generally for one of three reasons:

1 The plans are incomplete, incoherent or unrealistic. Some plans are never implemented because they are either so vague or so optimistic that they give no real guidance as to what should be done. In the absence of clear and realistic guidelines, marketing staff will, with some justification, ignore the plan altogether and rely on their own experience and judgement when making marketing decisions.
   Lesson: if plans aren't crystal clear they will be ignored!
2 The marketing resources are inadequate. Unless adequate resources are available for the implementation of the plans, lip-service may be paid to them but no real progress can be made in their implementation. This may be due to financial priorities, but in under-resourced arts organizations it is often due to a lack of staff – and those who are available may be inadequately qualified or experienced to tackle the implementation issues that arise.
   Lesson: fight for your budgets and get your staff trained!
3 The organization resists the proposed change. This problem is discussed further in Chapter 9. It is one which can be a greater problem in arts organizations than in commerce or industry, due to the suspicion with which marketing is sometimes viewed by artistic directors. If influential members of an organization, particularly those in other management and board positions, are concerned about the potential impact of the plans they may use counter-implementation tactics. These may range from delaying decisions (in the hope that the deadlines for implementation will pass) to destroying the credibility of the plans and their writers or diverting essential resources to other parts of the organization (Piercey, 1991).
   Lesson: gain the commitment of colleagues early in the planning process to encourage them to feel ownership of the final plan.

If the marketing plan is designed with its implementation in mind, then constraints and resistance can be anticipated and avoided, and barriers to implementation should be minimal.

Monitoring the marketing plan

Assuming that the plans are implemented, it is important to ensure that they are achieving their objectives and that nothing is going drastically wrong. This is best achieved by 'comparing actual results against the desired results given in the plans, and taking appropriate corrective measures to ensure that the desired results are achieved' (Greenley, 1986) – this is known as controlling (or monitoring) the marketing plan.

Effective control requires that mechanisms are put in place before the plan is implemented to enable performance to be monitored, measured, evaluated, and corrective action taken if necessary. In this way, marketing successes and failures can be identified at an early stage and actions taken to cash in on successes and make good any failures.

The monitoring process offers a wide range of benefits (Shaw, 1993):

- It assists decision making.
- It gives staff and the board the opportunity to learn by experience and improve their performance.
- It provides an opportunity to acknowledge the results achieved in a given period of time.
- It provides a framework for training.
- It motivates staff and encourages co-operation between them.
- It provides a structure within which to report on progress to the funding bodies.
- It facilitates the early detection of problem areas and provides a chance to avert disaster.

Monitoring techniques are dealt with in more detail in Chapter 9. What is of critical importance to the marketing function is the way in which the findings from the process will affect the marketing plans.

Corrective action

There are a range of conclusions which can be drawn if it is found that the planned marketing activity is not meeting the marketing objectives, and these will determine the type of corrective action that is needed. These conclusions will fall into one of three broad categories:

1 The marketing objectives and strategies are inappropriate. The objectives set may have been too ambitious considering the organization's environment, or the environment may have changed unexpectedly and made the objectives unrealistic (for

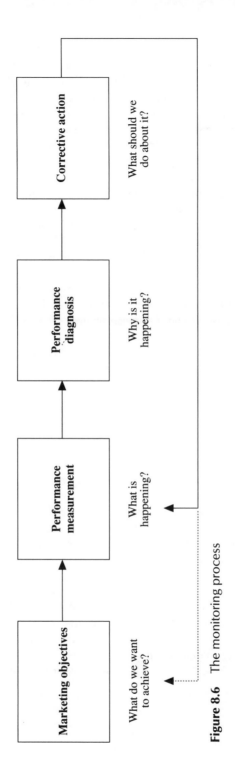

Figure 8.6 The monitoring process

example, if a new and very popular competitor emerged). Alternatively, the organization's resources may have been insufficient to enable such objectives to be met (particularly if there has been an unexpected reduction in income, say from funding sources). It may be impossible, under new financial constraints, for the planned level of marketing activity to be sustained.

2 The marketing tactics are inappropriate. The planned marketing mix may not have the desired impact on its target audiences. It may be that the pricing levels set were too high and deterred attendance, or the message of an advertising campaign may have been wrongly perceived, and the wrong audience profile was attracted. Perhaps audiences had difficulties getting hold of tickets or sponsors were unimpressed with the levels of corporate hospitality available.

3 The marketing budget is insufficient. A plan should be budgeted at the outset and tied in to resource availability. If this is not done carefully, cash constraints may arise to hinder the success of the marketing tactics. This could reduce the impact of advertising, for example, if corners have to be cut in the creative process. The installation of a new box office system may have to be delayed, thereby affecting the response rate to a direct marketing campaign.

Before corrective action can be taken, the cause of the discrepancy between planned results and actual results must be identified. Only then can new proposals be put forward with confidence.

Conclusion

Marketing planning is a process which can lead an arts organization to the most effective and efficient use of its limited marketing resources, helping to direct it towards its artistic goals as well as its financial and market objectives. This structured and rational approach to marketing planning is more likely to gain the support of others in the organization than an ad hoc, piecemeal approach, as it clearly demonstrates the logic behind the marketing recommendations through its thorough analysis, its specific objectives and its explanations of marketing solutions.

The plan itself should not be thought of as a tablet of stone, but as a living document which communicates intentions, guides and moulds marketing decision making, and gives direction and support to the day-to-day marketing activities, as well as the more fundamental and underlying strategic issues. The purpose of marketing planning is to maintain a match between what we can offer and what our audiences want and, at the end of the day, it is their satisfaction that will be the judge of our efforts.

Key concepts

Environmental analysis
External audit
Internal audit
Macro environment
Marketing audit
Marketing budget
Marketing objectives

Marketing strategy
Marketing tactics
Mission statement
Perceptual map
Organizational objectives
STEP factors
SWOT analysis

Discussion questions

1 In what ways is the marketing planning process likely to differ in a commercial theatre from in a subsidized repertory theatre?
2 Explain the difference between a mission statement and organizational objectives. What do you think might be the aims or objectives of the organizations whose mission statements are given in this chapter? (The Natural History Museum, The Mumford Theatre, The Scottish National Orchestra and ABSA.)
3 What is the nature of competition facing contemporary visual art galleries? How might an understanding of this lead to marketing decisions related to gallery opening hours?
4 Now that box office systems enable venues to run closely-targeted direct mail campaigns of their own, do arts marketing consortia still have a useful role to play in the development of arts marketing? If so, what should it be?
5 Explain the difference between marketing objectives, marketing strategies and marketing tactics, giving examples from an arts organization of your choice.
6 In which aspects of the marketing planning process do you feel it is important to involve the board, and why?
7 Where would the marketing manager of a visual arts venue find information to help with the preparation of an external audit? List the publications available in the public domain that would be useful for such an exercise.
8 'Marketing planning is a barrier to imaginative marketing'. Discuss.

Action questions

1 Evaluate the marketing activities of your own organization, indicating your view as to the strengths and weaknesses of different elements of the marketing mix. Then

run a focus group consisting of six to eight of your regular attenders, and investigate their opinions. To what extent do the two views differ?

2 Describe your organization's current marketing planning processes. What is good about them and what is bad about them? How would you improve them?

3 Select two arts organizations, one in the performing arts sector and one in the visual arts. Draw up a statement for each which you believe summarizes its mission and aims. Then ask each organization for a copy of its mission statement and organizational objectives. How similar are your perceptions of the mission of those organizations with their own perceptions? Do any differences matter?

4 Prepare a four page leaflet that could be distributed to amateur arts organizations to help them plan their marketing activity for the next 12 months.

References

ABSA (1992/3). *Annual Report.*

Arts Council Incentive Funding Scheme (1988). *Business Planning Seminar Participants Pack.* The Arts Council of Great Britain.

Boyden Southwood Associates (1993). *Marketing the Visual Arts.* Commissioned by The Arts Council of Great Britain.

Eastern Arts Board (1992). *Bulletin 5.*

Caminer, M.J.T. (1989). The Scottish National Orchestra. In *Cases in Marketing Management* (L. Moutinho, ed.), 308–319, Addison Wesley.

Crawford, R.W. (1985). The overall structure and process of planning. In *No Quick Fix.* (F. Vogel, ed.), 12–30, Foundation for the Extension and Development of the American Professional Theatre.

Dixon, C. (1993). *Draft Business Plan.* Marketing the Arts in Oxfordshire.

Dunn, E. (1994). What women do best. *The Daily Telegraph* (Arts supplement), 21 May, 12.

Eichten, D. (1983). The marketing plan. In *Market the Arts!* (J.V. Mello, ed.) 55–64, Foundation for the Extension and Development of American Professional Theatre.

Gainer, B. (1989). The business of high culture: marketing the performing arts in Canada. *Service Industries Journal,* October 1989, 143–161.

Greenley, G.E. (1986). *The Strategic and Operational Planning of Marketing.* McGraw-Hill.

Hope, B. (1990). *Membership of Arts Marketing Consortia: Report of the Gallery Marketing Symposium.* Commissioned by The Arts Council of Great Britain.

Kotler, P. (1984). *Marketing Management: Analysis, Planning and Control.* Prentice Hall. CIM study text. (1991). *Marketing Planning and Control.* BPP Publishing.

McDonald, M.H.B. (1989). *Marketing Plans. How to Prepare Them: How to Use Them.* Butterworth-Heinemann.

McDonald, M.H.B. (1992). *The Marketing Planner.* Butterworth-Heinemann.

Macgregor, E.A. (1990). *The Role of Marketing in Galleries: Report of the Gallery Marketing Symposium.* Commissioned by The Arts Council of Great Britain.

Piercey, N. (1991). *Market led Strategic Change.* Thorsons.

Policy Studies Institute (1989). *Cultural Trends.*

Stapleton, J. (1982). *How to prepare a marketing plan.* 3rd edn. Gower.

Salter, M.S., Steiner, T.D. and Deschamps, J. (1975) *The Boston Symphony Orchestra*, 375–340. The Harvard Business School: Boston, Massachusetts.

Shaw, P. (1993). *Board Member Manual*. The Arts Council of Great Britain.

Tait, S. (1990). V&A considers fee and Monday closing. *The Times*, 12 October, 3.

Thompson, J.L. (1991). The Natural History Museum corporate plan 1990–95. In *The Natural History Museum*. European Case Clearing House.

Verwey, P. (1987). *Marketing Planning*. The Arts Council of Great Britain.

Recommended further reading

McDonald, M.H.B. (1989). *Marketing Plans. How to Prepare Them: How to Use Them*. Butterworth-Heinemann.

9 Managing the marketing function

Introduction

The focus of this book, as outlined in the preface, is on the practice of marketing within the arts world. For that reason, we are including a chapter that looks at general management principles within the context of arts organizations. This is not intended only for those who manage a department of a particular size, with several members of staff, but is intended to be of benefit also to people who work with a variety of organizations, alone, or in a community or amateur environment. The sections included in this chapter are:

- Budget setting and monitoring.
- Organizational structures.
- Team building and management.
- Liaison with external organizations, particularly with reference to touring.
- Working with creative people.
- Communications.
- Internal PR.
- Personal development and management.

The reference section at the end of the chapter will direct anyone interested in further reading to some of the classic management books on the different subjects. The purpose of this chapter is to help the practitioner in marketing to operate more effectively in the working environment.

Overview of the management function

There are many definitions of management. The common sense view is that it is the process of making things actually happen, to a plan and on time. As a result, there are a number of different resources that can be called upon to assist this process. The two most important resources are people and money. Thus much of the attention of management training is on finance, and human resource management.

Other resources to be harnessed include yourself – the facilitator and leader of the marketing function; the resources of modern technology – which have contributed an enormous amount to marketing (think of database applications, and desk top publishing); volunteers; suppliers and external contractors; and physical resources such as offices, mini-buses and franking machines.

Good management begins with good planning. Marketing planning is discussed fully in Chapter 8. The principles of good planning discussed there, including monitoring and evaluation, apply equally to all management planning. In looking at resource management, it is important to make plans as solid and specific as possible, e.g. to set deadlines, to quantify expected outcomes and to define the measures by which you will gauge whether or not the plan is being achieved.

An invaluable means of firming up the strategic marketing plan is the setting of the budget.

Financial resource management

Probably more anxiety is expressed about this aspect of management than any other. This is surprising, as money is far easier to manage than people. Part of the reason for the anxiety is probably the seeming mystique of accountancy language – balance sheets, cash flow statements and working capital.

It is unlikely that the marketing team in any arts organization will have to worry about the precise meaning of these terms. However your organization is structured, there will be accountants (either internally or externally) to turn the financial transactions for the year into financial statements that can be audited as the 'true and fair' view of what happened within your organization in financial terms in the last twelve months. This is important to the organization, because it represents an account of good or bad stewardship of the resources you received from either the public purse or shareholders. As such, there is a great marketing opportunity to celebrate good financial results, or plead for greater resources on the back of your organization's excellent management.

The reason that the accountancy profession has developed very structured ways of reporting financial data is because of a need for accuracy in this information. Financial data is used to inform many important decisions, including lending money and employing staff. Where the consequences of errors and misrepresentation can include widescale unemployment, it is important that the meaning of figures is precise and credible.

The best way for a marketing manager to understand financial resource planning is to work closely with the person who manages the overall finances of the institution. Both have a strong common interest – the box office receipts are a key measure of both the financial and the marketing success of the organization. In addition, the head of finance will have a vested interest in helping the marketing team stay within budget; neither party will wish to cope with an overspend.

Depending on the size of the organization, at some point there is likely to be a dialogue between finance and marketing about the financial resource needed to manage the marketing effort. This may be a more or less formal process, depending on the complexity of the organization, and whether or not the budget is for a specific project or an annual spend. This is the process called 'budgeting'.

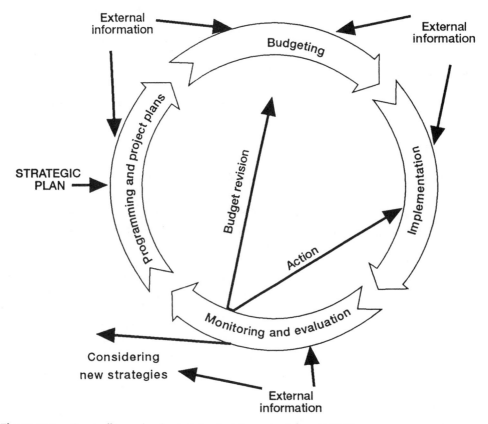

Figure 9.1   Controlling a budget. Adapted from Anthony (1988)

Budget setting

The process of setting the budget is an integral part of strategic planning.

> A budget is a plan, usually expressed in monetary terms and usually for one future year. Almost all organizations have a budget. If the organization has a formal long-range plan, the budget is prepared within its constraints. Budget preparation essentially consists of fine-tuning the first year of the long-range plan.

(Anthony, 1988, p. 15)

This is represented diagramatically in Figure 9.1.

The notion of 'fine-tuning' the strategic plan is a useful way to look at the budgeting process. The manager demonstrates a commitment to the overall plans, and looks at the practical obstacles to achieving that plan, by considering the detailed financial implications of actually putting it into practice.

A budget normally consists of revenue expenditure. By that is meant recurrent spending of the type that is normal for that department. A decision to buy, for example, an in-house desktop publishing system for the department would normally be treated separately, as a 'capital' project. The costs of such a project would include not only the cost of the equipment, but also staff costs for training, inputting all the initial data and developing the pro-forma house styles. These costs would be distinct from the normal day-to-day activity of the department, and thus would not be included as part of the 'revenue' or 'recurrent' budget.

Some budgets may include income also. It is unlikely that the marketing department would retain all the box office income (as several other functional areas would lay claim to having generated such income!). However, income from the sale of pro-grammes, merchandise, mailing lists or other activity relating very directly to the marketing effort will probably be included in the budget for that department. A checklist of items to consider is included in Table 9.1.

Some general principles in preparing a budget include:

- Be conservative. If in doubt, understate your income and overstate your expenditure – to avoid nasty surprises.
- Use historical data. Last year's actual spending is a useful starting point, but remember the differences. If the venue had six exhibitions last year, and intends to have nine in the next year, the budget will have to be adjusted accordingly.
- Remember to include inflation, but check price rises with key suppliers – they may be increasing at a different rate.
- Match the income and expenditure to the financial year to which it relates – for example, the autumn season brochure will probably come out of next year's budget even though the work starts this year. However, make sure the problem is not just transferred to next year.
- Phase the budget as best you can over time – i.e. work out how much you will be spending each month or quarter. This will help with budget monitoring, but also can add some leeway for changes in the course of the year.
- Be consistent. If you are assuming 5 per cent inflation in setting the new price of merchandise, you will need to assume the same figure in the cost to you of purchasing the materials for sale. You should also be consistent from year to year, unless you have made changes in your activity that are impacting on the budget.

It is rare for a budget to balance (i.e. for the planned expenditure to equal the available money) right at the start. There are a number of techniques available for dealing with this. All assumptions should be looked at critically, to ensure they are sound. It is possible that there is a mismatch between income and expenditure, e.g. an extra member of staff has been recruited to do sponsorship and development work but no extra income has been projected. However, care should be taken to ensure that unrealistic changes are not made in an attempt to balance the budget.

The next possibility is to reduce planned expenditure. It is preferable to cut something out entirely than to reduce the budget for a given head of expenditure. For example, the photography budget may have been calculated on the basis of six

Box 9.1

Checklist for budget preparation: what to include:

Income

Programmes	Multiply the number of copies you expect to sell by the sales price, e.g. 20 performances with average expected attendance of 60 per cent, with 50 per cent attending to buy programmes
Advertising space	One full page ad; two half-pages and four boxes at £x each. Check that the space is not sold on your behalf by the printers or another agency who retain the profit

Expenditure

Salaries	The annual gross pay of each employee (not what they take home) plus National Insurance (check current rates with finance staff or DSS) plus any benefits like pension or performance related pay. Remember to include annual pay rises, if appropriate. Don't forget overtime, or sickness and holiday cover if appropriate
Staff-related costs	This includes mileage allowance, training, cost of recruitment (e.g. the press advert)
Publicity design	Usually a set fee agreed in advance, but check implications of corrections and delays
Printing	Seek at least three quotes and look at differences in price involving changes in paper or in number of colours
Print distribution	Number to be mailed plus cost of envelope and stamp, and envelope stuffers (if not in-house or volunteers)
Photography	Set fee, by number of events
Press nights	An amount, by number of events
Cost of programmes	Cost of all programmes purchased from the printer – not just all those sold to the audience. It will usually be better to have some left than run out – but waste is a cost
Advertising	This is very expensive. It may pay you to use an external media buyer. The cost of advertising needs to be compared with direct marketing
Miscellaneous	This includes everything else, e.g. flowers, subscriptions
Contingency	A wise precaution – to allow for overspends and new opportunities (e.g. a cheap promotion jointly with another venue). Try using a fixed percentage of the entire budget

> **Management decision-making improved by financial understanding**
> I have worked for more than ten years in the arts, firstly with the Welsh National Opera and for the last seven years at Covent Garden with the two ballet and the Royal Opera companies. Over that time I have been amazed at the increased financial awareness of non-financial managers. An understanding of cost constraints is now found at all levels in creative teams.
> Lisa Williams, Chief Accountant, The Royal Opera House

events in the year, and some photographs of the facilities for a conference leaflet. It might be possible to produce the conference leaflet with a diagram of the spaces rather than a photograph, and use existing event photographs for visual interest.

That is a real saving, because the planned expenditure will now not happen. Savings that depend on reducing the fee with an external supplier may not happen in practice. To keep the contract the photographer may well offer a 'deal', but travelling and other incidental expenses may go up in proportion. Combining pieces of print, reducing the size or frequency of advertisements, increasing programme prices (but see the pricing chapter for the marketing implications of this) or delaying the appointment of a member of staff are all ways of bridging the shortfall in the budget. Strategic and tactical variables are defined in Chapter 8.

The final thing to do is to talk to other people. If the cost of marketing has increased because of increased activity in the overall organization, there may be further resources available for the department. There may be the opportunity to combine forces with other local organizations to share the costs of promotion or distribution. Most importantly, if the marketing manager believes it is not possible to carry out the strategic marketing plan within the available resources, this needs to be communicated to the rest of the management team.

At the end of this process, a sensible plan for the year's marketing activity will have emerged, expressed in the form of monetary targets.

Monitoring the budget

As with all plans, it is an essential part of the planning process that the plan is monitored as it is implemented; and corrective action is taken where necessary. The exact way that the budget is monitored depends on the type of organization concerned. The use of computers makes it likely that most people will have access to some sort of computerized financial information, and may even have some responsibility for generating it.

As money is actually spent within an organization, a chain of evidence is produced about the financial transactions that are taking place. An order is raised for goods to be supplied, which will later result in an invoice being sent and finally paid. Staff these days are generally paid directly into their bank accounts. Cash is received from the sale of tickets and banked. Grants from local funding bodies will probably be paid monthly directly into the bank. This data is then sorted and processed; and a report is produced for the benefit of the marketing department to show their share of income and expenditure. It is common practice for this information to be produced in the form of a monthly management report, which compares the 'actual' performance for the period against the 'budget' that was originally set. There may be all sorts of reasons for what are usually called 'variances' from the original budget:

- Timing differences. These can occur when, for example, goods have been received into the building but the invoice has not yet come. These sorts of differences can be adjusted in the management reports.
- Accounting treatment. You will need to discuss this in more detail in your own organization, but might include such things as the treatment of VAT or the grossing up of income and expenditure (e.g. you have budgeted for the profit on the sale of programmes, but the reports show the income and expenditure separately).
- Planned variations. In the course of the year, all sorts of changes will happen in the day-to-day running of the organization, and the budget may be adjusted accordingly. For example, a local company may sponsor a minicom for hearing impaired customers; so the income and expenditure budgets both change. Some organizations prefer to leave the original budget presentation unchanged, but explain the seeming 'actual' overspend in terms of planned, and therefore legitimized, variations.
- Over/underspends. These are the important things for the operational manager to consider, as they represent unplanned changes to the budget. Examples of these may include under achievement on income (e.g. a dip in programme sales attributed to the poor box office because of bad weather) or an overspend (reprinting of a leaflet because the incorrect dates were supplied). The first step is to identify the variance, and the reason for it. This may not be as straightforward as it seems. In the above example, for instance, it may turn out that, despite the weather, the box office target was met. One can only surmise that perhaps patrons, arriving late for the performance because of the weather, may not have had time to buy the programme. Perhaps the box office target was met because of a large block booking to a local company, and programmes were included free as part of the package.

Having identified the reason for the variance from budget, corrective action should be taken to ensure the overall budget remains balanced. An underspend in one area may compensate for an overspend elsewhere. Another department may be able to help – front of house staff hours may be underspent as a result of the poor box office. It may be possible to cut some planned activity later in the year. Finally, this may be the point at which the budget manager remembers with relief the contingency set aside within the overall budget.

In addition to monitoring the budget for the current period, the process of planning next year's budget is already beginning as the marketing staff evaluate the success with which the financial resource is being used.

The concept of 'value for money' is of importance here. Value-for-money strategies seek to deliver the most efficient and effective outcomes, in the most economic way. For example, the effectiveness of the marketing strategy might be measured in the number of attenders at a given event. In efficiency terms, the most straightforward way to promote that event might seem to be to place a large advertisement in the local paper. However, the cost of such an advertisement may be very high. Setting up a database of attenders for a direct marketing campaign may cost more first time, but will allow greater development and further campaigns in the future. Direct marketing may sometimes deliver better value for money than advertising.

Other areas to consider include:

- Use of own staff versus sub-contract labour.
- Volunteers who need managing and supporting versus machines.
- Staff productivity.
- Posters versus other forms of media.
- Promotions such as 'two-for-one' offers or early booking discounts.

It can be difficult to quantify the value of many marketing activities, as the long-term payback of some initiatives may not be visible immediately. However, the more that the marketing department can develop their own performance indicators, the better they can develop effective strategies for future years.

Financial performance will always be one of the key indicators for evaluation. Marketing teams generally tend to be viewed as high spenders in their organizations, and this charge can best be countered in value-for-money terms, e.g. our radio campaign cost £5000 but generated extra ticket sales of £250,000. The evidence for this would need to convince sceptics at all levels in the establishment. Other performance indicators would be attendance figures, against budgets and against previous years; customer perception surveys, which might include visibility of corporate design; and audience development data, such as party bookings or subscribers. The practical effect of this sort of evaluation will be seen in the next cycle of planning and budgeting.

One other practical aspect of monitoring the financial resource available to the marketing department concerns cash flow management. This means ensuring that money comes into the organization before it has to go out. For the marketing team, promoting ticket sales in advance of the performance represents an important contribution to the overall cash flow. Interest can be earned on the money, if it is in the bank. Conversely, expenditure should be incurred as late as possible and the maximum credit period negotiated. This is a factor to take into account in agreeing fees with designers or photographers, for example, who may require payment in advance.

Some of these concepts may seem foreign or daunting when approached for the first time. However, as with all management, the best way to approach having responsibility for a budget for the first time is to learn by doing it. The principles are the same as managing domestic finances; and there will be others in the organization to help you with explanations or advice.

Human resource management

Marketing people tend to be outgoing and articulate. They may thus approach the people management side of their role with greater confidence than the money side, only to find a year or two into the job that they have underestimated the diversity and sometimes sheer perversity of the human factor. The marketing team, be it one person or a unit, will be a smaller part of the larger whole. It is necessary therefore to examine organizational structures and cultures, before focusing in more detail on the management of the marketing team itself. The role of the marketing manager as team leader will be considered in this section; and some aspects of personal development and management are included separately in the last section of this chapter. As well as the people with whom the manager has a line relationship, there will be a number of other people who relate closely to the marketing department. These relationships will also need to be managed. In the arts industry, there may be particular issues to address concerning, for example, liaison between the venue and a touring company, or working with creative artists. These are therefore considered in more detail below.

Organizations and organizational culture

The huge and fascinating field of organizational behaviour has attracted many eminent writers. Foremost among these is Professor Charles Handy, whose highly readable book *Understanding Organizations* looks at a number of different aspects of this subject. In the introduction to that book, Professor Handy explains why it is so difficult to generalize about organizational behaviour. He represents this diagramatically, in listing over sixty variables which can differ from organization to organization (adapted in Figure 9.2).

For these reasons, any observations about arts organizations will have similar limitations. Nonetheless, it is valuable to spend time considering the following aspects of the individual organization in which you work:

- Organizational structure. What is the structure in which you work? Is it an autocracy or a co-operative? Who takes decisions? How are decisions taken?
- Politics. How is the power divided in your institution? Who are the people with influence, and from where is that influence derived?
- Groups. How do you and your team fit into the wider structure? How are you regarded?

An understanding of the structure and organizational culture of your institution will enable you to do your job better, and help you to work with, rather than at cross-purposes to, your colleagues.

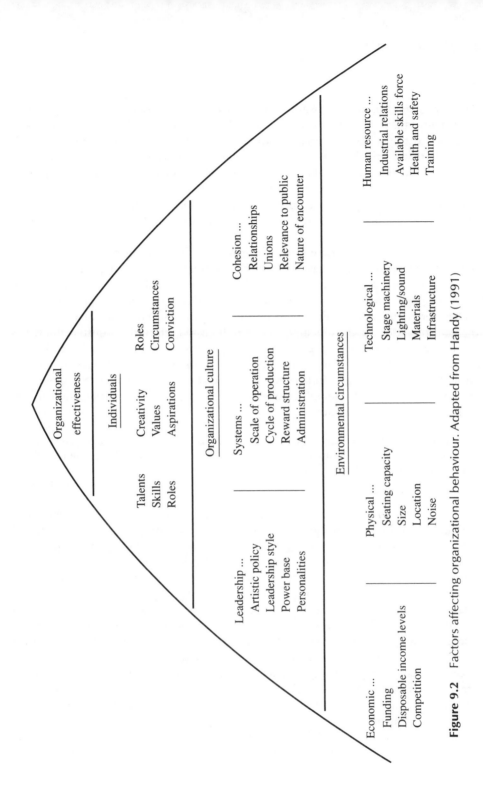

Figure 9.2 Factors affecting organizational behaviour. Adapted from Handy (1991)

Structure

There are many different possible structures and, in themselves, probably no one kind is better than another. It is common in the arts, for example, for a dynamic and visionary artist to gather a company of disciples and supporters around him or herself to further that particular art form. It is equally common to find highly successful companies with a structure akin to a private sector organization, headed up with someone called a chief executive. It is also common to have co-operatives or democratic groups of paid and unpaid workers, where all have an equal voice on policy. All of these models are discussed in another of Handy's books, *Gods of Management* (1986).

The study of the appropriate form of organization is a current concern of many of today's management gurus. It has received critical attention because of the failure rate of so many once successful companies, because of the opportunities and threats posed by the technological revolution, and because of increased competition in a shrinking world.

These preoccupations, which focus on organizational survival, are of value to the arts industry also. As the opening chapter discussed, the arts industry flourishes somewhere in the middle of the larger leisure and broadcast industries. The changes that threaten the wider community offer opportunities and challenges as well as threats to the arts. As larger organizations break down, smaller and more flexible ones can move in. Increased unemployment may lead to growth in participation in the community and amateur sectors.

> I find it sadly ironic that 'arts in the coal fields' seems recently to have been termed an area of work or funding. With approximately 100 pits closed in the last decade it could be argued that the funding has come too late.
>
> (J. Alston, *MAILOUT*, April/May, 1994)

It is, however, those organizations who are able to work in new ways who will continue to develop. Part of the mission of many community arts groups is to rebuild pride, and confidence, in groups who have been disenfranchised or marginalized. That sort of energy and vision is one of the great strengths of arts organizations, which are determined to continue their work whatever the practical obstacles.

These are now fashionable objectives for the largest private sector companies. Rosabeth Moss Kanter, for example, advocates opening up management to new types of people, including positive strategies for women; moving to flatter organizational structures, with less hierarchy; challenging established practice; and placing great importance on shared values. Her vision of a flexible and empowered workforce, which can adapt to rapid change, has had enormous influence on the development of corporate cultures in large industrial companies. Her ideas translate particularly well to the arts environment, where adaptability for survival and individual empowerment are a feature of many organizations.

There is no one answer to the question of what is an appropriate organizational structure – the justification or otherwise is found in how well that organization achieves its goals.

Managing organizational change in a dance company

Phoenix, as a small-scale company, was very much dancer-led. Growth caused change, and though some of the changes were welcomed by the dancers, like the opportunities offered by external choreographers and so on, nonetheless growth is painful. All sorts of issues surfaced. Talking in a neutral environment, and taking enough time, and using external people, showed us that we all believed in, wanted, the same things.

Liza Stevens, formerly Administrative Director, Phoenix Dance

Power

An understanding of the structure can help an individual manager implement plans or manage change. It certainly helps to have clear lines of communication and accountability, and defined spheres of influence. However, such definitions are not always explicit, yet it is still possible to be effective by working within the real power structures of the organization. (Power, in this context, means the people with authority to take decisions and make things happen.)

Handy describes a number of different types of power:

- Resource power – influence derived from the control of key resources.
- Position power – also sometimes called 'legitimate' power, being that derived by virtue of being, for example, chief executive.
- Expert power – this might well be 'artistic' or 'creative' power, and is considered further in this section.
- Personal power – or 'charisma', but this is often more tied to position than the powerful individual would wish to admit.
- Negative power – the power to delay or prevent things from happening, which can often be wielded by quite junior people in the organization.

In the complex ways organizations function, many people will derive their authority for action from a number of these sources, and may use them both to further and to impede organizational progress. Group dynamics may affect the way individuals use their power, through the formation of alliances or factions.

As with the structure itself, the operation of power within the structure is in itself morally neutral. It is only in the way that individuals use their own or others' power – to achieve great things through combined efforts, to manipulate others to force through change, or to delay a decision until it has been fully considered – that the organization can be deemed to have or not to have appropriate management processes.

Culture

Structure and power are components of the wider issue called 'corporate culture'. Much of the thinking on culture in the workplace started with Edgar Schein, who describes the sorts of assumptions about an organization's values and practices which are commonly held by its members. Difficult as the culture is to pin down and describe, it is what makes one company different to another, and makes one employee fit in one place and not another.

In a small museum, for example, the culture would embrace such diverse issues – implicit or explicit – as the mission, the goals; the dress codes and office layout; the values and perceptions of the nature of history, contemporary culture and local society; the organizational ethic, which might include frequent references to the museum's founder and the original collection; and underlying assumptions, concerning behaviour in the workplace, the expected visitors, and strategies for coping when things go wrong.

The organizational leader has an important role in managing the corporate culture, but does not set it, may not understand it and may not be able to change it in time to learn a new culture for new circumstances. The marketing department is likely to have its own culture, which may or may not be at odds with the wider organizational culture. However, understanding the wider corporate culture will be a key to the success of internal marketing, which is discussed in more detail later in this section.

Managing the marketing team

For most arts organizations, good practice in employment is centred on the equal opportunities policy. Some examples of these from a variety of service organizations are included in Box 9.2.

A commitment to equal opportunities is less about providing the exhaustive list of those individuals or groups that must not suffer discrimination, than about having a positive policy to develop individuals to their full potential and address disadvantage.

The extent to which equal opportunity policies are fully integrated into the staff development practice of any individual institution depends on the degree of understanding and ownership of the real meaning of human resource development. Many organizations lack the funding to implement their genuine commitment to the principles of developing individual potential; and still others pay lip service to trendy policies while continuing to employ friends and people they know, with whom they feel at ease.

> A greater degree of organizational participation by itself is no guarantee that equal treatment of women and minorities, for example, will automatically follow. 'Participation' alone will not wipe out sexism and racism.
>
> (Kanter, 1983)

Implementing a staff equal opportunities policy will help the organization foster a wider empathy with the audiences it is hoping to develop. The competent line

Box 9.2
Examples of equal opportunities statements in service industries

The Metropolitan Police is committed to a policy of equal opportunity for all staff regardless of sex, marital status, colour, race, nationality, ethnic or natural origins, sexual orientation, religion or disability.

We are committed to providing equality of opportunity to employees and customers.

(Hampshire TEC)

Committed to Equal Opportunities.
Applicants MUST BE British Nationals.

(GCHQ)

Committed to equal opportunities, job sharing and flexible working. A no smoking employer.

(Southampton University Hospitals NHS Trust)

The Arts Council is committed to an equal opportunities recruitment policy. Registered disabled people are currently under-represented within our work-force and their applications will be considered first.

(The Arts Council of Great Britain)

Working for Equality of Opportunity

(BBC)

Applicants must be able to demonstrate a personal and professional commitment to equality of opportunity.

(West London Health Promotion Agency)

Among the advertisements which did not include an equal opportunities employment statement in *The Guardian*, November 5 1994, were: Channel One Television, Penguin Books, the Australian Museums, the Barbican Centre and Sadlers Wells Theatre.

Internal promotion builds on experience
I worked in the shop, and in the box office, before I moved into the marketing department. The box office taught me a lot about targeting – the focus of marketing is on the customer; and on the non-customer.
Deborah Hindley, formerly of The National Museum of Photography, Film and Television

manager will have sufficient understanding and knowledge of the staff individually to play to their strengths and help them overcome weaknesses in order to develop their full potential. At the same time, however, he or she will need to manage them as a team which balances individual skills to produce something greater than the sum of the individual parts. That is that mysterious process called 'synergy'.

Recruitment and selection

If the cost of a member of staff over three years, including National Insurance and any allowances, is calculated, it can be seen that the appointment of any individual staff member represents a significant investment of the company resources over that period. For that reason alone, it is worth putting considerable effort into making the right appointment.

Over and above the financial cost, the management time needed to sort out problems and the lost opportunities that result from under performance make the selection of the right candidate a key skill of any manager. In the arts, as in all service organizations, it is the attitude of the people that makes the difference to the quality offered to customers.

The recruitment process should be planned in advance, and should accord with any personnel policies on appointments that have been developed within the organization. A job description should be drawn up that identifies the key areas of the role, rather than one that seeks to include every possible task that the new employee might be asked to perform. At this point, a list of desired characteristics in the applicants should be identified. Great care must be taken to ensure that this will not preclude certain candidates from applying. For example, an insistence on formal qualifications may deter women or black people from applying, as there is evidence to suggest that such groups have less access to formal education than some others.

Getting this part of the process right is of great importance, as employers may be taken to an industrial tribunal for sex or race discrimination if their employment practices can be held to exclude certain sections of the community. If there is no personnel expert within the organization, as is likely in most smaller organizations, it is well worth seeking specialist advice on good recruitment practice. This can be obtained from ACAS, the Advisory, Conciliation and Arbitration Service, which is a government organization with a number of regional offices, whose purpose is to provide advice to employers and employees.

At this point, the advertisement can be placed in relevant papers, which should include a closing date and number to which to send for information. The job description and employee specification will normally be sent to candidates, with other supporting material as appropriate. A checklist of these is included in Box 9.3.

The next stage is to design the selection procedure. The normal process is an interview. However, increasingly, employers are extending the process to include a number of different interviews, a practical test, or psychometric testing of some kind. The latter test can take a number of forms, but aims to get candidates to produce a self-evaluation against a number of criteria. Most tests can identify those candidates who select the answer that they think is required, rather than give an honest

---

Box 9.3

Appointments checklist

Job description	Include post title, main responsibilities, to whom the employee reports, for whom the employee is responsible, salary
Employee specification	Often split into 'essential' and 'desirable' characteristics
Application form	A good way of ensuring that the same information is sought from, and sent by, all candidates
Equal opportunities policy	No point in having one if you don't tell people that you do
Background material	This might contain information on the history of the organization, some examples of your work, something about the department, and a map – anything to help candidates make an intelligent application
Advertisement	Ensure as wide a readership as can be afforded
Interview	Do not disadvantage candidates by the constitution of the interviewing panel, room choice or layout, or timing. Prepare questions based around the job description and ask them of all candidates
Other exercises	Practical tests might include writing a press release, preparing a brief for a designer or working out a marketing plan for the next subscription series. Identify desired outcomes in advance. Consider asking candidates to give a formal presentation
Selection	Consider all the candidates equally on the basis of application and supporting letter, interviews, presentation, references. Be able to evidence reasons for choice
On appointment	Offer the position formally in writing. Prepare contract and induction programme. Contact unsuccessful candidates and offer debrief

---

assessment. People tend to have strong views about these tests, but research demonstrates that they result in about the same level of good appointments as do interviews – which is not very high! The best appointment procedures include a range of different inputs into the final choice (and these, of course, include the letter of application and references). Whatever the advantages of psychometric testing, the cost of it may well preclude smaller organizations from selecting it as an interview tool.

An interview, or interviews, is likely to remain the main selection method for most appointments. Decisions need to be taken about the constitution of the panel (which might include someone from another department or, for a senior marketing appointment, a member of the Board); the questions to be asked; the location of the room (will it set candidates at ease); and the duration of the interview. Pre-set questions relating to the job description which are asked of all candidates are a fundamental feature of equal opportunities recruitment practice. This does not preclude different follow-up questions to ensure all candidates have an opportunity to shine. It is also acceptable to reassure candidates who cannot evidence experience or competence in a certain area that you expect that the person you appoint may lack experience in some aspect of the job and that training can be offered to compensate for this, if appropriate. However, it is worth remembering that you may be called upon to justify why one person was appointed, and another was not, so you need yourself to be clear about what you want in the candidate. The individual appointed should have the necessary skills to contribute to the marketing function and should complement the others in the marketing team. Having designed in advance the interview process, a shortlist can be drawn up, matching individual applications to the job description and employee specification. Candidates may be informed in advance of the format that the selection process will take.

After the interview, and any other exercise that the candidates may undergo, the panel should meet to assess each applicant against the same criteria. A job offer should be made and a formal acceptance sought, which confirms salary and start date. A written contract will need to be issued subsequently. It is important to keep up to date with current legislation on employment contracts, as this is an area that does change frequently. Unsuccessful candidates may be offered a 'debrief' on their interview.

On the morning the new employee starts, it is good practice to offer an induction. This can be as formal or informal as the organization wishes, but represents the welcome of the employer to a new member of the team. It can also include a short tour of the premises, introduction to other staff, explanations of how to get a cup of coffee or where the photocopier is, and a copy of all relevant employment policies. Above all, it offers the manager the opportunity to sell the organization solidly to the now successful candidate. It is important that they are made to feel that they have made the right decision in taking the job; and that they are a highly valued member of the team.

Team building

A marketing team, like any other, will not come together without effort. A systematic effort must be made to harmonize the individual's own objectives and goals, which are based around their career development, with the requirements of the organization. The better this harmonization the greater the contribution of the individual. Team building goes beyond this, as it seeks to create a unit to support and encourage each member, so that together their achievements amount to more than the work of each member in isolation. This must be based on a mutual recognition that they have more in common than a shared office or line manager; they have a common purpose

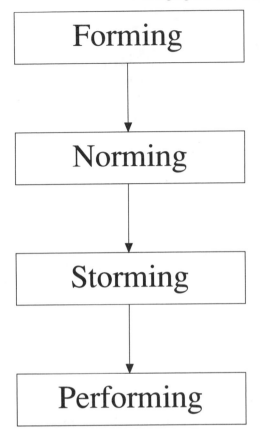

Figure 9.3   Stages in team development. Adapted from Handy (1991)

which needs the efforts of each individual member to achieve fulfilment. Figure 9.3 represents the stages in team development.

A team learns to work together by clarifying underlying assumptions and values; listening to one another; challenging compromises; supporting and reinforcing each other's work; sharing information and developing consensus decision making. All members of the team should contribute. In a team situation, it is best to leave decisions until all can agree – a majority vote does not represent the optimum outcome, as it splits the team.

Leadership

The team leader is one of the team, but with a special role. John Adair is one well-known commentator on leadership styles, who promotes 'action-centred leadership', which holds in balance the task, the team, and the needs of individuals (Figure 9.4). Although these are separate, there are areas of overlap – and a failure in any one area impacts on them all.

Figure 9.4   The motivation and management of an arts marketing department. Adapted from Adair (1973)

There are many styles of leadership, and a good leader will adopt different styles in different situations, and with different people. Among other definitions, the following types of leadership style can be identified within arts organizations:

- Authoritarian: statement rather than confrontation is preferred mode of operation; opposition is disabled or ignored. Commitment to status quo. Might be the original founder of department, or organization.
- Managerial: operates systems and has documented policies and procedures. Leader works with senior management team, or through line structure. Has meetings and committees.
- Interpersonal: high visibility and mobility; has preference for individual leader negotiations and compromises; avoids formal situations; may have problems taking decisions.
- Adversarial: encourages and participates in debate; assumes competing leader interests in department; uses public arena to get messages across, persuade and gain commitment.

All of these styles have advantages and disadvantages; and all managers will tend to adopt a mixture of approaches. Handy (1991) suggests that the best leadership style is the one that 'best fits' the leader's own preference, the preferred styles of the subordinates, the particular task and the environment in which all are operating.

A team will operate most successfully when there is clarity about both the roles of members and the tasks to be done. Within that, a good leader encourages the team to operate in the way that maximizes performance, even though that may not be the preferred approach of the team leader.

The leader needs to possess an impressive list of attributes, ranging from consistency to flexibility, the ability to take decisions and the ability to delegate to staff empowered to take them, the ability to provide inspirational vision and the ability to operate invisibly so that the team are self-motivating, and, perhaps most importantly, resilience and bags of energy.

One tried and tested way of developing leadership skills is to adopt as a 'mentor' an older person, preferably not the direct line manager, whose own leadership style and the weight of whose experience can be an example of good practice. This sort of mentorship can also be extended downwards, to develop the leadership skills of the rest of the team.

Motivation, training and staff development

Motivation in the workplace was analysed by Frederick Herzberg (1959) as compromising two different sorts of factors (see Box 9.4). His much misunderstood theory does not say that it does not matter how much or how little a member of staff is paid; but says that individuals are most motivated by growth and self-realization through their work. It is a necessary pre-condition of such self-realization that the environment factors (the hygiene factors) surrounding the job should be satisfactory. This sort of thinking can be paralleled by Maslow's hierarchy of needs, which is discussed in Chapter 4. Herzberg thus advocates 'job enrichment' which might consist of additional responsibility or new projects.

Many organizations will choose to consider individual self-development within the framework of a staff appraisal or review scheme. There are benefits to undergoing a formal process; it establishes that progression is a right, and it demonstrates the institutional commitment to developing staff to their full potential. Unfortunately, many arts organizations have insufficient resources to be able to invest in staff development; and therefore feel a formal appraisal scheme can lead to expectations that cannot be satisfied.

However, there are many forms of staff development other than expensive external courses.

- Mentoring – as mentioned above, an 'apprenticeship' to an admired senior can be a very effective form of learning.
- On-the-job training – which used to be called 'sitting next to Nelly' but is now being formalized through National Vocational Qualifications. The marketing NVQs will cover five levels from foundation to degree level, and can take account of previous learning as well as the competencies that are displayed in the current job. The disadvantage of these qualifications is the labour involved for senior staff in becoming an accredited assessor or verifier, and the cost.
- Team training – various individuals can deliver a training session or practical workshop to their colleagues. Inputs might be sought from the press officer, the

Box 9.4

Factors affecting staff motivation

Motivating factors	**Hygiene factors**
Achievement	Company policy
Recognition	Working conditions
Satisfaction in the work	Salary
Responsibility	Status
Progress	Job security
Personal growth	

head of finance, the artistic director, heads of the different production departments or special collections etc. Anything that widens the team's appreciation of their organization, and their understanding of the interdependency of the different sectors, will help them in their role of promoting and marketing all aspects of the artistic work.

- Shared training – the arts industry is good at working collaboratively with similar organizations. The opportunities for shared training are a good example of this.
- Funding bodies – funding bodies may well be willing to promote training activity, if the need is made clear. They often have the contacts to persuade other organizations to participate, or offer secondments.

Managing volunteers

Although unpaid, the principles of working well with volunteers are akin to those of managing employees. Among points to bear in mind are:

- They will not be with you forever – two years is a reasonable commitment to expect.
- As with sponsors (Chapter 5) positive stroking should reinforce their value to you – keep in touch by, say, a regular newsletter or with press releases.
- The 'motivators' and 'hygiene' factors (Box 9.4) need to be right. Refund reasonable expenses. Offer tickets, invitations to previews, include them in first night parties.
- Include them as part of the marketing team, so make sure they understand why they are doing things, and how their actions contribute to the wider marketing effort.
- Give them work to do which is within their abilities, and with which they feel comfortable.
- Make sure someone is looking after them, and ask a senior member of staff outside the department to thank them for their efforts.

Problems with staff

Appraisal should be a positive development opportunity. Inevitably however there will come a time when even the best manager has to deal with a staff discipline issue.

All organizations should have a disciplinary policy, and it is important to follow this exactly. If the policy is not clear, ACAS publish a number of helpful booklets that give not only the legal framework for disciplinary procedures, including employment rights and the grounds for fair and unfair dismissal, but also offer practical advice on ways to address the issue before it needs to be taken up formally.

Because a disciplinary matter may end in dismissal, it is important to be clear and to document all stages beyond the most informal preliminary ones. This will also satisfy the equal opportunities principle of offering people positive opportunities, and treating individuals equitably. More pragmatically, an arts organization with scarce resources does not want the unnecessary expense of a fine from an industrial tribunal.

Whatever the precise framework adopted by a particular institution, there are likely to be the following stages:

- Informal period of dissatisfaction, culminating in some sort of meeting to discuss the problem.
- First warning, which may be verbal, which should be recorded in written form as a safeguard. This should identify the problem and set clear targets for improvement, with a time scale. Training and support may be offered. The employer may wish to consider mitigating circumstances.
- Second warning/final warning – must be recorded in writing and be as clear as possible. The employee should be informed for how long the warning will remain on the personnel file. It should be clear what the implications of a failure to improve will be.
- Dismissal. It is likely that only a senior member of staff will have the authority to dismiss an employee. There may be a procedure for suspension, followed by an investigation and disciplinary hearing. There should be the right of representation at the hearing for the employee by a friend or trade union representative. There should be an appeals procedure, probably to the board (and the final appeal for employees with the relevant service is to an industrial tribunal, and the law courts).

For cases of serious or gross misconduct, it is possible to start at any stage in the above procedure.

However, the majority of disciplinary cases will never get past the informal stage. That does not mean it is easy to sit down with a colleague and discuss their underachievement or unacceptable attitude. The employee should be made aware of the exact nature of the problem and what is expected in the way of improvement, but the tone of the interview needs to be positive and supportive. It can be helpful to talk over the intended interview with a trusted colleague in advance.

External relationships

The marketing staff of an arts organization will spend a considerable amount of time dealing with external organizations, individuals, companies and public agencies.

Negotiating with suppliers

Among the suppliers that marketing teams deal with frequently are designers, printers, newspapers and other forms of media, consultants, photographers, distribution companies and sales promotion agencies. It is refreshing for a marketing manager to be in the position of customer, because it reinforces from the other side the principles of marketing. Price may well prove to be a more important factor in making a final decision than the quality of the promotional material, which can be a salutary fact for the manager to remember.

As discussed in the preface and throughout this book, marketing is about forging long-term relationships between suppliers and customers. This is the sort of relationship that you will ideally seek with your own suppliers, because it will make your life easier if you can have continuity and reliability in the service you get.

The negotiations between you and your supplier depend on your mutual needs being satisfied – you get the service you require at the price you can afford and they get the contract.

The problem for arts organizations often arises from the financial constraints in which they operate. If, for example, the advertising budget is being cut, it can be very difficult to negotiate acceptable future volume discounts from a large newspaper. The larger the newspaper, the greater the split between editorial – who may be very interested in your work – and advertising, who are not very interested in your small budget.

Wherever possible, you need to strengthen your negotiating position by trying to find something that they want from you. Money is, of course, the main consideration; but arts organizations can sometimes offer sponsorship opportunities, corporate hospitality, workplace arts activity or (especially good for circus skills performers) stress management for senior executives. In offering any sort of non-standard deal, it is important to negotiate with someone with sufficient standing to take non-standard decisions.

In other cases, the marketing manager may find themselves the side with greater bargaining power; for example, in dealing with a freelance designer who is just setting up. It is important in these sorts of negotiations to maintain the same high standards in coming to an agreement, because a reputation for sharp practice can easily get round, and may be very destructive of other supplier relationships.

The principles of good negotiations include:

- Preparation: define your ideal outcome, your realistic target, and the minimum for which you would settle. Work out what you can offer, and what the other party's needs and expectations are.
- Opening stance: both parties reveal their negotiating stance. This is a time to listen carefully. It is important to close no doors, but at the same time make no concessions at this stage.
- Hard bargaining: identify the weakness in the other's position. Try to shift them

> ### Negotiating the provision of drama-based training
> Everything was subject to negotiation – as long as I didn't go below my bottom line. I found that our most interesting drama workshop projects were won by personal contacts; mailshots were not an effective way of reaching organizations to tell them what we could offer them. But with a personal visit, and face-to-face negotiation ... well, that's what worked for us. We usually managed to persuade the other party to take what we were able to provide, and we made sure that we met their needs.
> Andy Iredale; Marketing Manager, The Creative Arts Team, New York University.

nearer your own. Make conditional offers – 'I'll consider this if you are able to move on something else'. Try not to allow the other party to define the deal – you are negotiating the package you require.

- Handshake: judgement on whether there is scope for further negotiation. Agree trade-offs, and make sure both parties know exactly what has been agreed (confirm in writing). Settle practical details.

Whether or not an agreement is reached, it is good practice always to be courteous and appreciative. Although in this relationship you are the customer, you will get better service by being magnanimous in victory. It represents a failure in both parties when a customer–supplier relationship breaks down to the extent that the contract is invoked in court.

Touring venues

The relationship between the marketing teams of a venue and a touring company should be positive and fruitful. There is a common interest in the success of the piece. Unfortunately, in practice, all too often the relationship is strained. This may be because of the disparity between the two organizations, e.g. between the volunteer marketing officer of an amateur company and the local civic theatre; or between the overstretched marketing officer of a regional concert hall and the 'large national orchestra' coming in for one night.

As with all relationships, the secret is effective communications. This begins at the planning stage with the marketing requirements being made clear in the contract, or in a supporting document. Who pays for what, the time scales, the funding credits and other acknowledgements; all of this detail should be covered alongside the main items of product, date and price.

Nearer the time, a personal contact between the two marketing teams will tend to give disproportionate benefits. Both have expertise to offer – the venue has local knowledge, and the touring company has specialist interest groups. Whether there is a visit or a phone call, contact has been made between two individuals who may have to work closely together if there is a problem at a late stage. The venue staff may be able to visit the show at an earlier stage on the tour, which would help them to know exactly what they are marketing. An example of a touring dance company optimizing promotional opportunities offered by the venues in its distribution channels is given in Chapter 7.

When the appropriate deadlines arrive, both parties should try to fulfil their side of the agreement exactly. Because of the lack of a close working relationship, the delivery of desired outcomes will be the primary way in which the success or otherwise of the other team's marketing effort will be judged. Where both sides have delivered, accurately and on time, they are able to share success or failure – knowing that the marketing staff, at least, have conducted themselves with professionalism.

Working with artistic and creative people

The marketing team in an arts organization will work with two different groups of creative workers – the practitioners of the art forms which are the product of their own organization, and the 'creatives' associated with the design and advertising side of the marketing work.

Definitions of creativity are not very helpful: the fact is that most people can recognize a distinction between certain sorts of work, and will define 'creative' work as something that is original, beautiful, challenging or non-rational. Bertrand Russell described the experience of creativity as follows:

> Having, by a time of very intense concentration, planted the problem in my subconscious, it would germinate underground until, suddenly, the solution emerged with blinding clarity, so that it only remained to write down what had happened as if in a revelation.

> (cited Fletcher, 1988)

Research work carried out by psychologists and behavioural scientists, starting with Freud, have described some characteristics found in creative individuals. Like all generalizations, these need to be challenged in the case of any particular individual. Among these characteristics, one might include:

- Non-conformity – creativity is often associated with challenging received ideas and perceptions.
- Frustration – Freud argued that all creativity involves fantasy and 'a happy person never fantasizes, only an unsatisfied one.'
- Seeking appreciation – requiring admiration of their creative output.
- Sensitivity – to criticism.
- Visibility – more than most other workers, creative individuals are personally identified with their work, and its success or failure.
- Independence – perhaps by virtue of this visibility, artistic people are autonomous and derive their standards from within themselves, and from excellence in their peers.

- Intelligent – although intelligent people may not be creative, creative people generally are intelligent (see Professor Frank Barron's work in this field).
- The ability to work hard – because driven by their standards of excellence.
- Poor timekeeping – because meeting a deadline may be perceived as less important than getting things right.

While being very wary of applying a stereotypical view of creativity to the artists with whom the marketing staff work, some understanding of their perspectives may help facilitate the relationship. For example, attending a photo call in some inconvenient location to attract publicity for the venue's forthcoming season may not be high on the priorities of an artist currently exhibiting there. Good communication skills – about what is required and how it is to be arranged; listening skills – about how that individual feels about what is being asked of him or her; and appreciation for what is being done, will minimize friction.

With the creative staff who work for the marketing team, the situation may appear more straightforward, as they are working for you. This will not necessarily be so. Particularly at the start of the working relationship, their interpretation of the brief may be very different to yours. It may be necessary to be firm, as your responsibility is to have work appropriate for the house style of your organization; brilliant though you may feel the alternative to be. Problems at a later stage may be largely avoided if care is taken at the planning stage to be very clear about the brief, the deadlines and the design standards. Briefs should be in written form, and should contain accurate information about time and money. There may be other parameters also to be defined (see Chapter 6).

If a piece of creative work has to be rejected, and possible amendments have already been explored, then the rejection should be clear and definite. As far as possible, the explanation given should be rational, and not subjective ('I don't like it'). You will be aiming to retain the relationship in the longer term. It is also important to be honest about your own contribution to the lack of success of the project; and to pay accordingly.

Communications

Managing all the above relationships requires high level communication skills, both verbal and non-verbal. The most important of all these is the skill of listening – as the saying goes, two ears to one mouth. Nonetheless, the marketing team are likely to find themselves responsible for a lot of formal communication, and this requires experience and training. Formal presentations are covered in Chapter 6. In addition to the communication skills required both to manage and to carry out the marketing function, this department may well have an internal role in communications.

Internal organizational communications

Charles Handy suggests that: 'poor communications are a reliable symptom of an underlying disorder in the organization or in the relationship between the people concerned' (Handy, 1991). This is disconcerting, as many in arts organizations are highly critical about their internal communications. This may be compounded by the difficulties of communicating with guest artists and companies, touring, multiplicity of projects and roles. Amateur companies may meet relatively infrequently, around the pressure of their other activities. This means that importance has to be given collectively to improve communications. All communications – written and verbal – imply dialogue: there is a sender and a receiver.

Handy identifies the following reasons for communication problems:

- Perceptual bias by the receiver – ignoring unpalatable information.
- Omission or distortion by the sender – either consciously or unconsciously.
- Lack of trust – on either side.
- Non-verbal obliterates the verbal – confusing signals between what is said, and the emotional content conveyed by the way that it is said.
- Overload – too much information.
- Distance – physical or hierarchical.
- Lack of clarity – jargon, woolliness, ambiguity and imprecise thinking.

The marketing team has a role to play in facilitating both formal and informal communications. Rumours are less likely to take root where all staff feel involved, and have access to information.

Formal communications may include briefing sheets, a staff bulletin, staff meetings, focus groups, upward information such as the show reports, box office printouts, management reports. Informal communications include the famous meetings in corridors, the grapevine, gossip and rumour.

The importance of informal communication should not be underestimated. One commentator on management practice, Henry Mintzberg, found that managers spend most of their time responding to external stimuli; and cherish 'soft' information, in the belief that today's gossip is tomorrow's fact. Keeping an ear to the grapevine and analysing what is heard can help identify early problems and issues that are surfacing both internally and externally. People operating daily in a particular environment know a lot about what is going on. Rumour, on the other hand, may be a symptom of unrest, fear or hostility that needs to be addressed; even if the actual rumour is without foundation.

Internal marketing

A specialized application of the marketing department's involvement in organizational communication comes with internal marketing. This broadly means involving all staff in marketing, so that a market-centred culture pervades the organization.

> ### Artistic director as impresario
> A good artistic director has a gut feeling about what shows will work. That's how the good ones get to the top. It is a fundamental requirement that they are marketing orientated, then it is for others in the organisation to use the more formal marketing techniques. Not everything will succeed, but a lot will.
> Tomas Hardiman; formerly Marketing Director, the Abbey Theatre, Dublin

The first way of achieving this is to give everyone information about the organization – its success, its plans, and a few quick memorable details ('did you know we have exhibited more new developing world sculpture than any other UK gallery – we are a known centre of excellence, according to the British Council'). Feeling proud of your organization, as we have seen above, is a powerful motivator, and this information will be widely spread. Secondly, the importance of marketing needs to be explained to everybody in terms of the organization's ability to survive and develop its work. Practical ways of helping can be identified, from taking leaflets to distribution outlets near where an employee lives, to coming up with an exciting angle for a press story.

Thirdly, the potential damage that can be done by inappropriate publicity or marketing needs to be carefully explained, so that all the organization are working with the marketing department to ensure a certain consistency in approach. Feedback, particularly of the benefits received from others' help, should be given frequently. For example, if a friend of the maintenance manager who happens to work on local radio plugs the new show – everyone should know about it, and know where the contact came from.

Finally, in case of a major disaster, be open with all employees. If a potential scandal is lurking which could cause serious adverse publicity, share the facts with all staff and trust them to understand the necessity for a common approach to the crisis.

> A well-managed crisis develops a sense of togetherness among employees – in the spirit of 'all for one, and one for all'. This can be an enormous gain for the company, affecting the working climate long after the crisis has ended.
>
> (Ten Berge, 1988)

The board of governors

A particular internal communications relationship to be considered in the arts environment is that which exists between the marketing department and the board of governors, or management committee. These unpaid volunteers can act as superb ambassadors for the organization, as they are often pre-eminent in their own sphere, or can be a distraction or irrelevance if the relationship is not managed successfully.

Different boards manage their affairs differently, and may adopt a more or a less hands-on approach. In a sense, they represent the apex of the upside down triangle in Figure 9.5. Their role therefore is to support the management in supporting the

ARTS CUSTOMERS

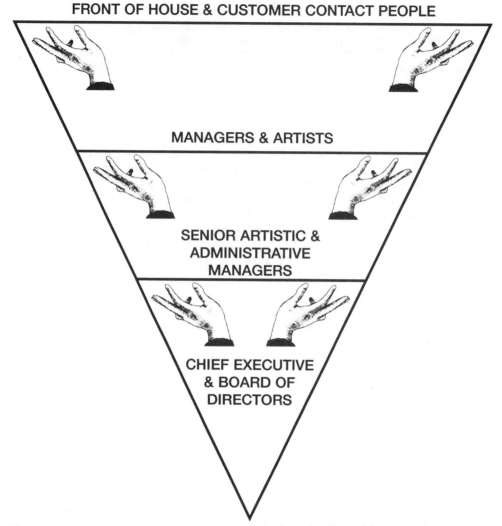

FRONT OF HOUSE & CUSTOMER CONTACT PEOPLE

MANAGERS & ARTISTS

SENIOR ARTISTIC & ADMINISTRATIVE MANAGERS

CHIEF EXECUTIVE & BOARD OF DIRECTORS

Figure 9.5   Supporting customers starts with the board. Adapted from Nordstrom Organization Chart (Peters, 1987)

artists who create or perform for their various attenders and audiences. This support can best be exercised by the board confining their role to long-term policy making.

> Trustees are the guardians and interpreters of the values and purposes of an organization. Their primary concern is to clarify principles, to develop insight, to maintain standards and chart a direction which will further the purpose of the organization. Trustees are distinguished not so much by what they do but by the way they see.
>
> (B. Spiegal and D. P. Turner, *MAILOUT*, June/July 1994)

Good communications with the board will facilitate their thinking, and help them in their long-term planning. At the same time, a greater knowledge of the way the organization is run may help preclude helpfully-meant but inappropriate suggestions ('Your new leaflet must have cost a lot of money, surely you could get someone to sponsor it?'). Governors can be a great asset in publicity terms for the marketing team and, with a good brief, can be persuasive advocates with people of influence.

Networks

Staff, governors, suppliers, the marketing team themselves – all the individuals who encounter your arts organization are themselves involved in hundreds of other relationships throughout the region, their local community and their work. By forming formal and informal links with as many organizations as is possible, partnerships and collaborative ways of working may evolve at a later date. A joint funding application between two disparate organizations working for some shared purpose may have a greater chance of success than one on its own. Mailing lists, staff training, transport or premises may be shared.

It is part of the marketing function therefore to foster a creative attitude in all staff to building up such networks, to encourage them to develop community links and to go out and talk to community groups, and to follow potential leads and make contacts.

Personal development and self-management

Grappling with the challenges of the budget, the team and the external environment, and while attempting to apply the marketing mix, product, price, place and promotion, the beleaguered arts marketer might start to have serious doubts about his or her chosen career path. Better resourced companies probably have more staff carrying out the marketing function, and may well be able to offer greater training and support. Most people who work in the arts find compensations in the excitement and variety of the work they do, and the satisfaction of being associated with a product that brings so much richness into people's lives: 'the importance of the customer is not how much they spend on the arts but how much they participate in the arts, and how much they benefit from art' (John Pick, *MAILOUT*, June/July 94).

However, the work can at times be highly pressured, and it is necessary to develop techniques for coping with this. Box 9.5 gives ten maxims for developing yourself as a manager:

Box 9.5

Ten principles of good management practice

1 Accept that you are the one person you can actually change.
2 If you haven't got enough time, blame yourself.
3 Respect other people's views – yours may be wrong.
4 Don't appoint people because they remind you of yourself.
5 Never assume they heard what you said, or understood what you meant.
6 Catch people doing things well – and tell them so.
7 Learn from mistakes and problems.
8 Persuade yourself, before you try to persuade others.
9 Make it easy for people to give you what you want.
10 Don't live in the past – it's gone, and was never really like that.

Adapted from Nicholson (1992)

Time management

Probably the most useful guides to time management are the 'One Minute Manager' series. This is a series of books of snappy and practical tips on managing time. Often individuals have developed their own ways of coping, and if it works, don't fix it!

For those others who, while competent in other spheres of management practice, have problems with time, it might help to reflect on the following:

- Time is a unique resource.
- The supply of time is totally inelastic.
- Time is perishable and cannot be stored.
- Time is in short supply.

(Drucker, 1968)

Thinking about time in this way, as a valuable resource, can allow the same sorts of resource management techniques as have been described above for finance and human resources. Good planning is the key.

Most people use lists and diaries as the key planning tools. Lists can then be prioritized:

A – must be done today
B – could be done, if time
C – might be done, if time

It is important to use your analytical powers on this exercise, as it is necessary to distinguish between 'important' and 'urgent' tasks. Urgent tasks may need to be done first, but should only be allowed to take up time if they are also important – which may well not be the case.

If there are too many 'A' tasks to manage, other resources can be substituted – i.e.

Box 9.6
Avoid time-wasters
– Poor meetings.
– Long telephone calls.
– Unwanted visitors.
– Crisis management.
– Panic.
– Background reading.
– Other people's paperwork.

people or money. In other words, tasks can be delegated or farmed out to an external agency. Learning to say 'no' is an important time management technique; and this may mean saying no to yourself, i.e. not becoming involved in a fascinating project that is not your job.

Meetings

Everybody who attends a meeting, whether or not they are the chair, needs to work at making the meeting effective. This includes:

- Setting an agenda.
- Starting on time.
- Allowing everybody who needs to contribute to do so.
- Keeping to the point.
- Not interrupting.
- Summing up.
- Not going round in circles.
- Being willing to defer a decision.
- Recording agreements.

The co-operative style of working adopted by many arts organizations may make it harder to chair a meeting in a firm way. The best method of obtaining everybody's consent is to get their agreement in advance on the length of the meeting, and the approximate time that should be devoted to each item. Everybody should then stick to this.

Stress management

Very often, the first time people consider stress management is when they are already suffering some of the warning signs. Take action if:

- You are weepy, depressed, irritable, forgetful, find it hard to concentrate, dislike yourself or feel others dislike you (or a combination of these factors, or increase in their level).

- You lose your appetite, cannot sleep, have headaches or muscular pain, sweat, clench your teeth, have butterflies.
- You avoid certain situations or people, rely on alcohol or tobacco, become violent, lose your skills, start being late or absent from work.

The more often these and similar signs recur, and the more strongly they are felt, the greater likelihood that you have a stress-related problem.

The best remedy is prevention. Working in an arts organization ought to offer you opportunities to find other outlets for your energies – an arts activity is a great stress reliever, when part of your leisure or recreational life.

Other tried and tested stress-relieving techniques include:

- Humour.
- Distancing – draw an imaginary circle around the problem and step outside it.
- Exercise – we know it's good for us.
- Cut off – leave it behind you and go home.
- Deep breathing and meditation.
- Learn to accept the stressful situation.
- Whinge session – have a good moan to a friend and stop after a certain length of time.
- Medical help – but you are likely to be advised to try one of the above techniques.

Management diary

A helpful way of maximizing personal development is to keep a management diary which allows you to analyse your performance in your working life. If you are doing any reading, you can relate your own experience to the theoretical material being suggested in the books.

The real value of a management diary is that it allows you to reflect on your practice over time. This can help you both to see how you are developing, and to identify any particular issues or problems that surface again and again.

Entries need only be short, and occasional. They should concern things that immediately rise into your mind, because they are the issues that are really concerning you – a missed deadline, a meeting that went wrong, a wasted opportunity, or unexpected tribute.

All workers need to learn for themselves the difference between being 'efficient' and being 'effective'. Being efficient involves doing things right; being effective means doing the right thing. A management diary can help you to identify the difference between the two in your own work.

Summary

The focus of this chapter has been on the different management functions and processes which are aspects of working life as a marketing practitioner in an arts environment. Suggestions for further reading in all the above areas are included in the reference section.

The preface defined marketing as being the development of long-term relationships with customers: audiences, attenders, funders and a complex web of other people and organizations who interact with an arts practitioner or organization. An effective marketing professional will have this definition in mind when managing human and financial resources; and in dealing with internal and external customers and suppliers. The source of the energy and commitment which distinguishes a good marketer is fed by an ability to continue to learn, both from your own experience and from the good practice of others.

Key concepts

Board of governors	Negotiation
Budget setting	Networks
Communications	Organizational structure
Culture in organizations	Personal development
Disciplinary procedures	Power
Equal opportunities	Recruitment
Evaluation	Stress management
Internal marketing	Team building
Leadership	Time management
Management	Touring venues
Management diary	Training and staff development
Monitoring spending	Value for money
Motivation	Working with artists

Discussion questions

1 Imagine you are managing the marketing budget for an amateur production of the *The Pirates of Penzance*. How would you quantify the resources you need; and how would you ensure you operated within those resources?
2 It is six months into the financial year of your organization. How can you satisfy the administrative director that the marketing budget is being controlled effectively?

3 What steps should the newly-formed management committee take to ensure they appoint appropriate personnel to work in several local prisons on a multi-disciplinary project to be called 'Take heART'?

4 What sorts of external professional management advice might be of value to a museum of ten staff, turnover £500,000 p.a.?

5 As press officer of a national touring orchestra, how might you facilitate internal communications?

6 What are the most important characteristics of a good manager in the arts? Can these be learnt?

7 'I'm the marketing manager, this is nothing to do with me!' Is this an appropriate response to a senior colleague in an arts organization?

Action problems

1 Draw an organizational chart for your company. To what extent does this reflect the way people work together?

2 Draw up a budget for your ideal press launch. Now halve the budget. Work out a plan to achieve the same ends with half the resource.

3 List all the external contacts with whom the marketing department comes into contact each week. Work out a strategy to involve them in supporting the marketing effort of the department.

4 Think about a meeting you have recently attended. What worked and what didn't? How might you help improve the next one?

References

Adair, J. (1973). *Action Centred Leadership*. McGraw Hill.
Adair, J. (1983). *Effective Leadership*. Pan.
Alston, J. (1994). A change of mine. *MAILOUT*, April/May, 19.
Anthony, R.N. (1988). *The Management Control Function*. Harvard Business School Press.
Barron, F. (1969). *Creative Person and Creative Process*. Holt, Rinehart and Winston.
Ten Berge, D. (1990). *The First 24 Hours*. Basil Blackwell.
Blanchard, K. and Johnson, S. (1984). *The One Minute Manager*. Fontana.
Blanchard, K. and Lorber, R. (1985) *Putting the One Minute Manager to Work*. Fontana.
Blanchard, K., Oncken, W. and Burrows, H. (1989). *The One Minute Manager Meets the Monkey*. Fontana.
Drucker, P.F. (1968). *The Practice of Management*. Pan.
Fisher, R. and Ury W. (1990). *Getting to Yes*. Business Books.
Fletcher, W. (1988). *Creative People*. Hutchinson Business Books.
Freud, S. (1959). *Creative Writers and Daydreaming*. Hogarth Press.
Handy, C. (1986). *Gods of Management*. Business Books.
Handy, C. (1991). *Understanding Organisations*, Penguin.

Herzberg, F. (1966). *Work and the Nature of Man.* World Publishing.

Kanter, R.M. (1977). *Men and Women of the Corporation.* Basic Books.

Kanter, R.M. (1984). *The Change Masters.* Allen & Unwin.

Kanter, R.M. (1989). *When Giants Learn to Dance.* Simon and Schuster.

Mintzberg, H. (1989). *Mintzberg on Management.* Collier Macmillan.

Paton, R., Brown, S., Spear, R., Chapman, J., Floyd, M. and Hanwee, J. (1984). *Organisations.* Paul Chapman.

Peters, T. (1987) *Thriving on Chaos.* Knopf.

Schein, E.H. (1985). *Organisational Culture and Leadership.* Jossey-Bass.

Spiegal, B. and Turner, D.P. (1994). Common knowledge, common ground. *MAILOUT*, December/January, 4.

Cases

Temple Bar Properties Ltd

Introduction

This case looks at the role arts activity can play as a marketing tool for economic activity of a non-arts nature. This particular example examines the use of street art in an urban development and regeneration context and considers the efficacy of the arts as a promotional tool, as well as issues of artistic integrity and external control.

Background

The Temple Bar area of Dublin borders the River Liffey, starting at the O'Connell Bridge, and links the two principal retail and business areas of the city – Mary/ Henry Street to the north and Grafton Street to the south. It is part of the original historic city of Trinity College and Christchurch. Like many areas in the heart of old cities, it has been in decline, but still consists of a mixture of retail, residential and cultural activity. The Temple Bar Renewal and Development Act 1991 established Temple Bar Properties Ltd as the development agency for the area, with a mission:

> To develop Dublin's Cultural Quarter in Temple Bar, building on what has already taken place spontaneously in the area. The project has a five-year implementation period. The aim is to develop a bustling cultural, residential and small-business precinct that will attract visitors in significant numbers.

Aims arising from this mission include job creation and economic growth. The total value of developments with which Temple Bar Properties will be associated, directly or in partnership, is anticipated to be £100m.

Temple Bar marketing strategy

During 1991, approximately 4 million people (12,000 pedestrians daily) walked along the main north–south route, by Crown Alley. Temple Bar Properties expects by the end of 1994 to increase significantly this movement of people into the entire area, by providing alternative routes for pedestrians to traverse, and by drawing people westwards. The planned development initiatives will provide an alternative to what is currently available in the city centre, and will entice greater numbers back into the city from the outer areas of Dublin.

These are some of the key messages which Temple Bar Properties will communicate about Temple Bar:

- It is unique, in national and international terms.
- It is a community, of artists, small businesses, residents, retailers, restaurants – a highly individual mix.
- It has a leading *role* in terms of artistic quality and experiment, new forms of making and promoting art and creating employment in new cultural industries.
- It is an area of economic growth in terms of increased revenue and job creation potential.

The ways in which these messages are communicated will reflect the nature of the messages themselves; Temple Bar will be promoted in national and international markets in distinctive and even 'alternative' ways through a programme of events, the publication of literature and the dissemination of information about the area and its attractions.

The role of public art in Temple Bar

Temple Bar Properties identified the opportunity for artists to be involved in many aspects of the development, including having design inputs into features such as gates, windows and signage. In addition, the '1% for art' scheme offered opportunities for temporary and permanent artworks and site specific pieces. This scheme, under the auspices of the Department of the Environment, encourages local authorities to apply 1 per cent of the budget on all major capital building projects towards 'some appropriate artistic features'.

The Temple Bar Development plan, in creating the concept of a cultural quarter, wishes to go beyond simply the creation and presentation of art. It wishes to develop a mix of cultural activities to include an arts infrastructure of production facilities, rehearsal and storage spaces and small cultural businesses which will offer potential for job creation.

The development of a cultural community is an organic process. How was this to be facilitated on what was in effect to be a building site surrounded by hoardings for five years?

A marketing solution

A small company called Artsource articulated this dilemma for Temple Bar Properties and proposed a possible solution. They set up a project called 'Street Art'. Its aims were to:

- Offer commission opportunities to existing artists and thus alert them to the Temple Bar development.
- Encourage people to walk through the area and look at what was happening while it was being developed.
- Draw attention to specific watersheds in the development.
- Be integrated into the wider marketing strategy of Temple Bar Properties.

Artsource have been used to create several different programmes of visual and multi-media arts activity over the years of development. 'Street Art', for example, treated Temple Bar as an open-air gallery with temporary installations of artworks along the east–west pedestrian route, including hoarding art which used the hoardings both for artistic treatment and to draw attention to the fact that something was being built.

On another occasion, when the Irish Film Centre was opened in the middle of the quarter, images were projected onto a screen suspended high over the narrow street in which the centre is located; while a sound/slide show focused attention on the influence of artists on film.

In working with Artsource, Temple Bar Properties accepted their advice to allow artists to criticize the development. Such criticism should be viewed as an input into the marketing programme of the development company, as artists are both customers of, and agents for, the communication of that very strategy.

David Kinnane, for example, produced a piece entitled *Street Traffic Sign*, made from cans of coke. His work was a comment on the quality of the environment and the priorities of the Temple Bar development. Another piece (*Beacon* by John Moore) was made of bread, suggesting the area was rotting. 'If the bread attracts rats' said Moore to the *Irish Times* 'that's fine. It reflects the dangers of property development in a area like this.' Other images were more positive, including Eoin Byrne's *Something from Nothing*, of colourful papier mache flowers which sprang from every window of an old dark building.

Artsource

Artsource's directors are Emer McNamara and Jobst Grieve. Both have worked for a long time in the arts in Ireland, including working in arts centres, for the Arts Council and on other projects, most notably 'In a State', an exhibition on national identity curatored by Grieve in Dublin's historic Kilmainham Gaol.

They describe their company as a visual arts production company, but also provide other curatorial, marketing and PR services. They are non-profit making and receive project funding from a variety of sources, including the Gulbenkian Foundation, the Crafts Council of Ireland and The British Council. The company was runner-up for the best new business award 1993 of the Irish Enterprise Development Programme.

I wanted to turn the whole place into a gallery, to use derelict sites to enable artists to engage in a dialogue with developers. It's impossible to say exactly what will come of it, whether architects may ever be influenced, but it's a unique opportunity which will never happen again.

(Jobst Grieve, on the Temple Bar project, July 1992)

Questions

1 Why have Temple Bar Properties continued to work with Artsource? What are the benefits to them of using an external agency?
2 How are the objectives of the marketing strategy being met by Artsource's work? How should this be developed?
3 What measures of success can be used to assess the impact of such projects?
4 What possible conflicts could arise between Artsource and Temple Bar Properties? Which aspects of the Temple Bar marketing strategy are most likely to cause problems for creative artists? How should they be dealt with by Artsource?

Song for a Sanctuary: promoting Asian new writing on tour

Introduction

This case study looks at some of the marketing issues involved in promoting Asian theatre; and, in this context, it looks at all elements of the marketing mix. It concludes with an evaluation of the adopted strategy, drawing on audience research carried out after three performances.

Background

The visit of Kali Theatre Company to the West Yorkshire Playhouse in June 1991 with Rukshana Ahmed's *Song for a Sanctuary* was the first time an Asian Company had played there. The theatre's regional constituency houses nearly eight per cent of Britain's Asian population. The marketing team at the Playhouse felt it appropriate to concentrate a special effort on targeting new theatre-goers for this show; and, to this end, employed a freelance consultant to do extra work. He returned with some second-year marketing students from Trinity and All Saints' College in Leeds to carry out the audience survey.

In addition to the specialist marketing opportunities offered by an Asian play, it was also a piece of new writing. New writing in box office terms, while an important element in the West Yorkshire Playhouse's artistic policy, can be problematical to sell, especially if the piece is issue-based (i.e. dealing with issues of social relevance). *Song for a Sanctuary* was set in a women's refuge, and told the true story of an Indian woman fleeing from her violent husband and his traditionally-minded family.

The marketing campaign

The potential audience for *Song for a Sanctuary* was segmented on a 'benefits sought' basis, working from an outline of the play's content and casting. The following key targets were identified:

Target	*Benefits sought*
Playhouse theatre-goers (female bias)	Variety of entertainment in venue
Women occasional theatre-goers	Drama/strong women characters
British Asian people	Drama/Asian subject matter, director and cast members
Social work professionals	Drama/social work theme
New writing group members/West Yorkshire Playwrights	Technical interest in original production of new play

Each of these target groups were tackled individually, in addition to the theatre's usual distribution of the season leaflet.

The Playhouse theatre-goers received a direct mailshot, which included an early booking/multiple ticket offer. The purpose of this was to encourage regular attenders to try something different. In addition, there was a foyer display for several weeks preceding the opening, and programme advertising in the two preceding productions.

Women occasional theatre-goers were targeted through the Playhouse list of women's groups. A particular initiative was made in the region through the Kirklees Equal Opportunities Unit. Social workers were contacted via the directors of Social Services. The departments in Bradford, Halifax and York undertook to distribute promotional material through their own internal distribution channels.

Because of the West Yorkshire Playhouse commitment to new writing, the marketing department already had a well-developed database of interested writers, who were targeted for this campaign with a special mailing.

The particular focus of the consultant's work was British/Asian people. Invaluable advice was obtained from Bradford-based Oriental Arts, an organization which promotes highly successful Asian cultural events locally. This provided the following key points for targeted activity:

1 Although the 'Asian' market consists of a number of distinct sub-groups, separate approaches were not a practical option for this sort of promotion.
2 60 per cent of British Asians were under 30, in contrast to only 38 per cent of their white fellow citizens. Oriental Arts recommended that an approach via the young people (especially students) might be effective, as they often acted as opinion leaders and 'gatekeepers' of information to their families.
3 Distribution outlets were suggested that ranged from the Bombay Stores (which attracts sari buyers from all over West Yorkshire) to businesses concerned with home entertainment.
4 PR contacts were also offered, including Bradford's licensed commercial radio station, Sunrise North; *Ravi*, an Urdu language weekly; and a Manchester-based Asian radio magazine show, as well as BBC Radio Leeds ethnic programming.

As well as Oriental Arts, distribution networks were sourced from Bradford Alhambra and Major Road Theatre Company, both organizations with a track record of promoting Asian theatre in West Yorkshire.

The campaign

All specialist PR activity was in addition to the usual mainstream media routinely addressed by the theatre's press officer. Particular editorial material of relevance to Asian audiences was placed to appear in the week leading up to performance. Print was distributed through the mailing list researched by the consultant, who found a lot of duplication and out-of-date material in the lists he had been given. His view was that theatres develop a 'missionary' approach to building lists, and neglect maintenance and cleaning. A regional approach to specialized list building was one of the recommendations of his final report.

Posters were personally distributed and sited to ensure all major community centres and colleges were covered. In other cases, material was posted out (after a telephone call to establish contact). All new distribution outlets were added to the theatre's marketing database to ensure future mailings.

The evaluation

Song for a Sanctuary opened to well over 50 per cent capacity – a good result for a new play. A self-completion questionnaire was administered at three of the performances, with a 25 per cent response rate from attenders. The findings of the questionnaire were then correlated with box office information to give some indication of the extent to which it was representative of the total population; and the data patterns were consistent with those of the overall audience.

Almost one quarter of all respondents were visiting the theatre for the first time (and box office data confirmed that only 15 per cent of the tickets went to subscribers or to people taking advantage of the targeted two-for-one promotion). The audience were young and predominantly female. Over 80 per cent of respondents were women, and over half aged under 35. 16 per cent were social workers. Ten per cent of the respondents described themselves as Indian or Pakistani, and a further four per cent as black. The Playhouse had no base data with which to compare this, but it was felt that there were a higher number of non-white audience members than was usually the case at that time. The other findings of the survey can be summarized under the four elements of the marketing mix.

Product

'Subject matter' was given as the single highest motivator for attendance, followed by 'it makes you think'. Product is therefore seen as very important. This factor was considered valuable in helping the West Yorkshire Playhouse decide on how explicit the description of contents should be in promotional material. Although for issue-based plays there may be a temptation to tone down the subject matter in the copy, the findings of this survey indicated that it is important to audiences to know 'what it's about'. 'Entertaining night out' and the venue's atmosphere were also indicated as important motivators. Box office data demonstrated that almost 20 per cent of tickets were sold at the party rate. This suggested that organized groups are a good target for issue-based material.

Price

Over half the tickets sold were subject to some form of discount. The Saturday night box office data showed a steep drop in attendance when concessionary discounts were not available. Without eroding the perceived quality of new writing, the pricing clearly needed to encourage the risk taken by both new and existing audiences.

Promotion

The most frequently indicated ways of finding out about the production were 'word of mouth' and 'picking up a leaflet.' Mailing activity lagged some way behind that, and 'magazine' got more responses than 'newspaper' – because of one particular cover-story in a regional listings magazine. The lack of a great deal of newspaper editorial can be common with a touring show, which only performs a few times. In this particular instance, the active distribution of print was seen to be a factor in the show's success.

Place

The importance of the venue atmosphere to the experience of live theatre was borne out by the evaluation. Telephone and credit card purchasing patterns for this particular show emphasized the value of that route, both in terms of accessibility for traditional non-attenders and for a geographically dispersed regional audience. Fewer tickets were bought in person at the box office than was the theatre norm, confirming the trend away from regular patrons for this piece.

In summary, the evaluation re-emphasized the long-term nature of any attempt to build new audiences. This particular exercise demonstrated that some inroads were made into the targeted groups, but they were only a portion of the whole audience – which was comprised of various segments with various reasons for attendance.

Questions

1 'We know that tackling issues of religion will be controversial. My only fear is that it may be misinterpreted in the same way as the Rushdie affair.' *Spare Rib* interview with director, Rita Wolf (May, 1991).
   What appropriate marketing strategies can be developed to minimize the misinterpretation of sensitive or controversial issues?

2 What techniques of marketing planning can be applied to the promotion of new work?
3 What particular issues need to be considered in respect to the marketing of a touring play or exhibition?
4 Received arts marketing encourages selling more to existing users. What opportunities are missed by this approach?

The Mumford Theatre

Introduction

This case looks at an audience survey conducted by students at a university theatre. It examines the construction of the questionnaire and the survey results, and raises issues relating to research objectives, research methodology and research interpretation.

Background

The Mumford Theatre is a university theatre, managed by the Arts Services unit of Anglia Polytechnic University. The unit's mission is 'to provide access for students, both as performers and as audience, to a wide variety of art forms on all campuses of the University and its environs'. It also seeks to attract members of the general public to arts events, to provide a service to the local community and raise the profile of the University.

The provision of arts access takes place in a number of ways:

- By organizing events (such as play festivals, photographic competitions, and opera) which encourage active student participation.
- By organizing activities and events which students can attend for their pleasure and enjoyment (such as a film club, visiting theatre groups and performers of all kinds, ranging from concert pianists to stand-up comedians).
- By co-operating with outside agencies (the City Council, local cinemas, the Regional Arts Board etc.) to make joint provision for arts events both inside and outside the University).
- By improving the skills of individuals or groups of students through workshops and other forms of tuition.
- By supporting and encouraging opportunities of student participation in arts activity outside the University.

Initiatives are supported from throughout the University, whether from individual or informal groups of students, the Students' Union, teaching departments or societies and clubs. The Arts Services unit provides advice, facilities and funding for all those with viable arts projects.

To make maximum use of its space and raise external income to contribute to further internal activity, the Mumford Theatre is also promoted commercially as a venue for other arts providers. Those who use the Mumford are almost exclusively local amateur groups producing just one or two productions each year. The theatre is located opposite the library and the refectory at the University's Cambridge campus and seats 250. To visiting companies it offers a full range of technical theatre equipment and support services, and for audiences there is a small entrance lobby where interval refreshments are served.

The survey

The Arts Services unit was in the process of conducting a strategic review of its operation when it identified a lack of information about the profile of its audience for student productions at the Mumford Theatre. It wanted to understand more about the characteristics of its audiences and the perceptions and attitudes they held about the Theatre.

A group of students studying marketing on a Business Administration degree were asked to design and conduct a survey at the summer term student musical production, *Chicago*, which was to take place on five consecutive evenings in June, Tuesday to Saturday. Their main task was to undertake the primary research by constructing and administering a questionnaire, analysing the data and producing a report of the findings, but they were also asked to identify and obtain any additional sources of secondary data that would support their research.

The specific research objectives were set as follows:

1 To identify the audience profile in terms of age, geographic location, socio-economic classification and occupation.
2 To discover how people first heard of the show.
3 To identify audience perceptions of the venue and facilities.
4 To assess levels of price sensitivity for student performances.
5 To identify attitudes towards and expectation of student performances generally.

The questionnaire

The questionnaire shown in Figure C1 was designed and produced, and administered to all attenders over the five evenings. A usable sample of 377 was obtained.

QUESTIONNAIRE.

This questionnaire is part of research being undertaken at Anglia Polytechnic University by a group of final year marketing students, in order to identify the characteristics and motivations of audiences for Anglia student productions. The results will be used to improve the service of the Mumford Theatre.

We would appreciate your cooperation.

(1) How did you first hear of this production?
☐ THROUGH A FRIEND/RELATIVE.   ☐ OTHER.
☐ LEAFLETS/POSTERS.   PLEASE STATE_____
☐ LOCAL NEWSPAPERS.
(You may tick more than one box if appropiate, circling the most important)

(2) How did you obtain tonights ticket?
☐ ON THE DOOR   ☐ OTHER.
☐ IN ADVANCE.   PLEASE STATE_____
☐ THROUGH FRIENDS.

(3) How much did you pay for your ticket? _____

(4) Did you find this:-
VERY CHEAP/ CHEAP/ AVERAGE/ EXPENSIVE/ VERY EXPENSIVE.
Please underline the one you agree with.

(5a) Other than this performance, have you attended a student production in the last
year?   ☐ YES.   ☐ NO.

(5b) If yes, which theatre?
☐ ADC   ☐ OTHER.
☐ CORN EXCHANGE.   PLEASE STATE._____
☐ MUMFORD THEATRE.

(6) Are you happy with the commencement time of the performance?
☐ YES   ☐ NO   If no, please state why._____

(7) How did you get to the theatre tonight?
☐ CAR.   ☐ WALKING.
☐ PRIVATE COACH.   ☐ BICYCLE/MOTORCYCLE.
☐ PUBLIC TRANSPORT.   ☐ TAXI.
☐ TRAIN

(8) Did any of the following hinder your journey to the Mumford Theatre?
☐ TRAFFIC CONGESTION.   ☐ PARKING.
☐ SIGNPOSTING.   ☐ PUBLIC TRANSPORT.

(9) What are your favourite types of production?

☐ MUSICAL. ☐ DRAMA. ☐ PANTOMIME.

☐ OPERA. ☐ COMEDY. ☐ OTHER._____

☐ CABARET. ☐ DANCE. _____

(Tick as many as you want.)

(10) How would you rate the following facilities and features, with the use of the following scale:-

	Very poor	1	2	3	4	5	Very good
COMFORT OF SEATS.		☐	☐	☐	☐	☐	
LIGHTS		☐	☐	☐	☐	☐	
ACCOUSTICS		☐	☐	☐	☐	☐	
TOILETS		☐	☐	☐	☐	☐	
BAR.		☐	☐	☐	☐	☐	
STAFF HELPFULNESS		☐	☐	☐	☐	☐	
ENTRANCE / FOYER		☐	☐	☐	☐	☐	
FACILITIES FOR THE DISABLED.		☐	☐	☐	☐	☐	

(11) How important are the following in affecting your perception of a performance?

	Not Important	1	2	3	4	5	Very Important
STAGING		☐	☐	☐	☐	☐	
SINGING		☐	☐	☐	☐	☐	
DANCING		☐	☐	☐	☐	☐	
COSTUMES/MAKEUP.		☐	☐	☐	☐	☐	

ABOUT YOU

(12) In which age group are you?

☐ LESS THAN 18. ☐ 18-24. ☐ 25-34. ☐ 35-44. ☐ 45-54

☐ 55-64. ☐ 65+

(13) Are you? ☐ MALE. ☐ FEMALE.

(14) What is your occupation?_____

(15) About how far do you live from the Mumford Theatre?

☐ Less than 3 miles. ☐ 3-10 miles. ☐ more than 10 miles.

If more than 10 miles, which town/village?_____

(16) Are you a tourist, visiting Cambridge? ☐ YES ☐ NO

(17) Are you registered disabled? ☐ YES ☐ NO

If yes:-☐ MOBILITY ☐ SIGHT ☐ HEARING

PLEASE, PLACE THE QUESTIONNAIRE IN THE BOX AT THE EXIT

Figure C1 Mumford Theatre audience questionnaire

The findings

The data summaries produced the following frequencies:
(note: * indicates that some respondents gave more than one answer, so the percentages add up to more than 100%)

Question 1
How did you first hear of this production?*

Friend/relative	60%
Leaflets/posters	32%
Local newspapers	6%
Other	14%
No response	0%

Question 2
How did you obtain tonight's tickets?*

On the door	19%
In advance	57%
Through friends	18%
Other	14%
No response	0%

Question 3
How much did you pay for your ticket?

£3.50	29%
£4.00	35%
£5.00	16%
£6.00	13%
Nothing	7%
No response	0%
(Average price paid	£4.009)

Question 4
Did you find this:

Very cheap	8%
Cheap	28%
Average	53%
Expensive	6%
Very expensive	1%
No response	4%

Question 5a
Other than this performance, have you attended a student production in the last year?
Yes   48%   No   51%

Question 5b
If yes, which theatre?
ADC   13%
Corn Exchange   3%
Mumford Theatre   28%
Other   5%
No response   52%

Question 6
Are you happy with the commencement time of the performance?
Yes   91%   No   7%   No response   2%

Question 7
How did you get to the theatre tonight?

Car	52%	Walking	33%
Coach	0%	Bicycle/motorbike	11%
Public transport	2%	Taxi	2%
Train	1%	No response	0%

Question 8
Did any of the following hinder your journey to the Mumford Theatre?
Traffic congestion   9%
Signposting   4%
Parking   8%
Public transport   0%
No response   79%

Question 9
What are your favourite types of production?*

Musical	76%	Drama	59%
Pantomime	24%	Opera	24%
Comedy	60%	Cabaret	18%
Dance	29%	Other	2%
No response	2%		

Question 10
How would you rate the following facilities and features?

	Mean	Very poor 1	2	3	4	Very good 5	No response
Comfort of seats	3.35	4%	12%	36%	30%	11%	7%
Lights	3.66	1%	4%	29%	40%	11%	15%
Acoustics	3.60	0%	10%	25%	32%	14%	19%
Toilets	2.76	12%	22%	28%	16%	5%	17%
Bar	3.02	8%	18%	26%	17%	9%	21%
Staff helpfulness	3.64	2%	9%	26%	32%	19%	11%
Entrance/foyer	3.12	6%	17%	31%	19%	10%	18%
Disabled facilities	2.97	8%	14%	19%	12%	8%	40%

Question 11
How important are the following in affecting your perception of a performance?

	Mean	Not important 1	2	3	4	Very good 5	No response
Staging	4.13	1%	3%	18%	30%	39%	9%
Singing	4.36	1%	2%	9%	31%	49%	8%
Dancing	4.11	1%	3%	19%	33%	36%	9%
Costumes	4.01	1%	5%	20%	32%	33%	9%

Question 12
In which age group are you?

under 18	8%	45–54	15%
18–24	39%	55–64	7%
25–34	12%	65 +	5%
35–44	11%	No response	3%

Question 13
Sex

Male	31%
Female	66%
No response	3%

Question 14
What is your occupation?
(note: occupations were classified into socio-economic categories. Group E consisted of the retired, the unemployed and housewives)

A	5%
B	16%
C1	15%
C2	1%
D	0%
E	9%
Student	54%
No response	0%

Question 15
How far do you live from the Mumford Theatre?

Less than 3 miles	50%
3–10 miles	20%
over 10 miles	28%
No response	2%

Questions

1 To what extent does the questionnaire help to achieve the objectives of the survey? Which are the most relevant and irrelevant questions?
2 Examine each of the questions that you consider to be relevant. What information do you think the question is trying to obtain? Suggest an alternative way of asking the question.
3 Which of the questions would you cross-tabulate to provide further useful information?
4 What conclusions can you draw from findings given and what actions might the Mumford Theatre consider taking as a result of these?

Charivari: touring to rural communities

Introduction

Charivari exists to entertain, stimulate and excite people through performance. To do so, they use many different performance media – acting, music, circus skills, dance, mime, singing, costume, sets and pyrotechnic effects. They place great emphasis on accessibility and participation, and also work with and support other companies in the same field. Their primary, though not their only, focus for touring work is in rural areas.

This case study looks at how the company defines its aims, develops its product, and reaches its audiences.

Background to the organization

Charivari was formed in 1980 by Taffy Thomas and Mike Bettison. They had been working and performing together for a number of years, primarily in organizing barn dances and street theatre. This background provided a basis for the company work, although workshop-based projects, bonfire events and community celebrations were also included.

Charivari was originally based in East Suffolk, with the administrative office in Felixstowe. The company consists of two full-time workers, a part-time administrator and freelance workers employed on a project basis.

The initial funding for the company came from the Arts Council's Community Arts panel. They were thus funded as a national touring community arts company. In 1984/5, following the first phase of ACGB devolution (The Glory of the Garden), they were devolved to the Eastern Arts Association, their nearest RAA. The company rejected this option and, following consultation, were successful in bidding for funding from Yorkshire Arts Association (now the Yorkshire and Humberside Arts Board); being funded first from the community arts budget and later by the drama panel.

Aims of the company

1 To perform street shows in festivals, galas and other outdoor events.
2 To perform touring shows specifically aimed at village hall type venues.
3 To perform shows in schools.
4 To undertake residences in workshop format.
5 To perform outdoor spectacles.

Among the work produced since the company's formation can be included their long-running and constantly developed piece *Vaudeville, Variety and Cabaret* which tours rural village halls; *A Way of Life* – a play accompanied by a photographic exhibition on contemporary rural life; and *Running Down the Line* about the Settle to Carlisle railway, then under threat of closure. Among their street theatre were two international tours to Expo 86 in Vancouver and Expo 88 in Brisbane.

Developing the product

From the aims of the company, appropriate products are developed to achieve their goals. Ideas are there all the time, sometimes taking up to ten years to come to fruition – which can depend on the right moment, or the required funding. The idea is the starting point. The company then tries to find a sponsoring organization to fund it.

Rarely, a piece may be commissioned, as the North Yorkshire Heritage Coast did with *The Salty Tales of Reginald Whelk*. In these cases, where there is input into the artistic content of the show by outside agencies, any difficulties are resolved through dialogue. The company are aware that a failure to produce a piece to meet the needs of the commissioning group will not result in work in the future.

Reaching audiences

In rural areas, there are particular problems of remoteness, isolation and distance. Advance publicity is usually done by the host organization (a local promoter who organizes the tour), with posters and handbills supplied by the company. A street audience is attracted by starting to perform, and allowing a crowd to gather. Sometimes the company takes part in a carnival or event which has been happening for a number of years, but without any professional artistic input. In that sense, the potential participants are already identified – but with no guarantee that they will become involved with Charivari. The organization that is funding the tour may themselves have a particular focus for the audience. In the case, for example, of the Somerset-based Take Arts village circuit, the variety show was toured to a number of new and developing venues where audience size was unpredictable. The very accessibility of the piece being performed made it suitable as an audience development exercise. From the company's perspective, however, it would have been easier to have been sent on the established tour circuit, where full houses would have been the norm, because of the familiarity of the venues involved as places to see drama.

Limitations and frustrations

The first of these is inherent in the art form itself. There are many unpredictables in village hall touring. Firstly, the venue itself may prove unsuitable, being possibly misrepresented in the reported dimensions, with unreliable electrics or with awkwardly placed fire and access doors.

Secondly, the company can fall foul of village politics, or (a problem with a small potential catchment area) the performance can clash with another social or sporting event nearby. Particular sections of the community (for example, adult men) may not wish to be involved in community projects; providing a problem for the company to overcome, if all concerned are to end up feeling the event truly involved all the community.

The third major limitation is attempting an honest evaluation of the success of the event. Using the performance indicator of audience numbers, there are various difficulties in counting associated with rural and community arts. For example, the company estimated that, on a musical walkabout, they were playing to around fifty people every eight bars – three times through the tune was six hundred. Without tickets, there is no way to quantify the numbers concerned with any degree of accuracy.

In another example, the number of workshop participants that could be accurately accounted for was six. This failed to take into account the impact that having professional arts workers around had on the whole project; the audiences for spontaneous performances for a local lunch club, in a nearby canteen, and (one rainy sports day) for the parents and children of the local school; and the cheering audiences for the procession and the performance at the gala.

In qualitative terms, because of the spontaneity and the distances involved, the company finds it hard to get audience feedback. Talking to the audience after the performance is an important part of this and, on some tours, a comments book is kept at the back of the hall for written contributions. The company members stay with various people involved with the tour while it is underway, for example village hall organizers, and their feedback is included in the company review, along with any other comments received.

The most meaningful evaluation is against the original targets set in advance, both by the company as artists and by the host organization. The success or failure of any particular enterprise needs to be matched against expectations, and to take into account any unexpected developments and potential growth in terms of the future.

The final evaluation – and the demonstration that the limitations and frustrations are ultimately creative rather than restricting – comes in the renewed demand for the company's work. As co-founder Mike Bettison explained:

> Originally, we did not set out to be rural based. That is where both the demand for the work and what we perceived were our strengths, took us. Once we were doing it, the real importance became obvious.

Questions

1 What are the difficulties in communicating with rural audiences? To what extent can Charivari's solutions be applied in other contexts?
2 How does the company ensure their product is suitable for a largely unresearched marketplace?
3 What useful evaluation can community arts organizations make of the impact of their work?
4 As a freelance press officer, how would you propose to promote the company's participation in a week-long residency to celebrate the six-hundredth anniversary of a rural village?

Tetley's Brewery Wharf: developing a new venue

Introduction

This case looks at the problems in developing an audience for a new venue, for a type of attraction that differs from both a traditional museum and a theme park. It examines the role market research played before the opening of the venue, and the development work that took place in the opening months of operation to build the customer base.

Background

Tetley's Brewery Wharf is a six million pound development in the centre of Leeds, on the bank of the River Aire. It tells the story of the pub, over the last five hundred years; utilizing live actors, stage machinery and eleven pub sets which range in time from a fourteenth-century monastery to the Star and Crater, the bar at the end of the Universe. In addition, visitors to the venue can see the Tetley shire horses in their stables; watch traditional crafts demonstrated by a farrier and a cooper, among others; visit the museum display of items from the Joshua Tetley pub archive; eat in the waterside restaurant or enjoy a pint in the bar; and spend money in the giftshop. There is an outdoor amphitheatre and an option to purchase tickets for the brewery tour across the way in the (separate) Joshua Tetley and Son Brewery.

Pre-opening market research

Prior to the opening in April 1994, a firm of external consultants identified target markets for potential attenders. These were:

- Groups – sub-dividing into individual groups, and parties organized by tour operators.
- Education.

- Individuals and families.
- Corporate.

Potential problems with these groups

The permanent marketing team were largely appointed across the summer in 1993, with an opening in April 1994. Their detailed work identified some potential pitfalls with the proposed groups.

1   The group market was hard to reach initially. Private groups (Women's Institutes, social clubs and similar loose structures of individuals who meet informally, usually for recreational reasons) are difficult to address through generic print. Once reached and captured on a database, they are then relatively easy to persuade to book as the group organizer is very close to his or her constituents. The tour operator market is easier to identify, but harder to persuade to buy. The operators are looking for a high word-of-mouth satisfaction, as they are themselves in the business of customer satisfaction. They needed to see an established product before they would commit themselves.

2   The education group was not identified by the consultants as being all that large, because of the difficulty in taking time out from the National Curriculum, and problems over charging for schools visits. Nonetheless, there were further problems with that market. The potentially negative impact of the association with drinking had been underestimated, because the attraction was concerned with the social history of the pub. In reality, the title 'Brewery Wharf' suggested a closer link with the product 'beer' than is in fact the case.

3   Individuals and families tended to see the Brewery Wharf as a museum with a consequent potential perception of it being 'worthy' and hence, possibly, dull. In addition, the concept of 'museum' suggested an indoor venue, whereas a key strength of the attraction was supposed to be the extent of the outdoor facilities – the waterfront, the live animals, a children's play area and the amphitheatre.

4   Many of the above perception problems equally well related to corporate groups. The biggest problem for all groups was the short time scale to build business.

Some solutions

The main approach adopted by the marketing team was to exploit the potential of the venue to offer customized programmes. Although the Brewery Wharf is a physical attraction which is to be visited, it leans heavily on the presence of live actors to allow flexibility in the range of offerings. Among the actors who tell the story of the pub through history, for example, is a fourteenth-century monk who brewed his own ale. This character can deliver different scripts to different groups, tailoring the content as appropriate to the needs of the group.

So, for example, in addition to straight visits, the group market was wooed with the offer of themed evenings – such as Christmas packages, murder mystery evenings and quiz nights. Groups were approached through the network of Tetley pubs; ensuring in the timing of events at the Wharf that there was minimal conflict with the pub busy periods, especially Friday and Saturday nights. Schools were offered a range of activities, including a tailored workshop, and these were packaged to match National Curriculum topics:

Primary   Food and Drink
             Transport and Travel
             Games and Pastimes

Secondary Food and Drink
             Social Leisure and Pastimes
             Travel and Communication
             Social History and the Politics of the Inn.

There was less opportunity to tailor for the general public – the focus of the marketing effort here was to maximize the visits of the individuals outside term time, i.e. when school visits by definition are not happening. That placed a clear focus on family groups. The family leaflet addresses the children but makes sure that the parents know that among the attractions is the opportunity to purchase 'the perfect pint'.

In the 'notes to plan the visit', the limitations of the optional brewery tour are made explicit, i.e. that it is for adults only, or for children over fourteen if accompanied by an adult and that, unlike the Brewery Wharf, there is very restricted disabled access, as it is an industrial building.

Corporate groups are similarly offered both a wide range of attractions and a customized service. Among the offerings are meals in the Georgian Gentleman's Club, conferences in the Bar at the End of the Universe (with state-of-the-art technology) and large-scale events in a marquee in the amphitheatre. The actors will tailor entertainment to the client need – including themed cabarets.

Development opportunities assessed before the end of the first year

The early months of the Brewery Wharf were deemed successful, but the missing factor was sufficient time to build relationships with visitors. This problem, by definition, will rectify itself. Other issues to be addressed include extending the restaurant – the Tetley association with hospitality resulted in a higher than anticipated take-up rate; and, possibly, doing something with the name to identify the venue more with the pub than with drink. Opportunities for the future include joint promotions with the Royal Armouries Museum which opens nearby in 1996, and with third-party agencies with fellow Allied Domecq companies.

Questions

1 What sort of market research would be appropriate on an annual basis to ensure marketing objectives are being met?
2 What promotional opportunities are there to extend awareness of the new venue nationally?
3 What are the advantages and disadvantages of association with the Yorkshire firm of Joshua Tetley and Son?
4 In your view, should this venue position itself as a theme park or a museum? What are the pros and cons of each approach? Is there a middle road?

The West Yorkshire Playhouse: developing a corporate image

Introduction

This case study looks at the place of the corporate image in the development of a theatre's overall promotional strategy. It looks at the way the image was developed initially, and how its use has been refined over the first few years of the theatre's life.

Background

The West Yorkshire Playhouse opened in March 1990 on Quarry Hill in the centre of Leeds. It was built with capital raised mainly in the region – over £5m from Leeds City Council and £4m from West Yorkshire County Council. As a condition of funding, the latter body asked that the building was named 'The West Yorkshire' Playhouse, although it replaced the previous Leeds Playhouse. In addition, the maximum possible award was received from the Arts Council Incentive funding scheme, whose assessors commented in their appraisal:

> In many ways we feel that this is the best articulated and most achievable example of the repertory theatre of the 21st century, being not just a play factory for a predisposed audience, but a genuine regional resource, leading into the communities and offering opportunities to enjoy, participate and learn well beyond the scope of a traditional theatre.

Developing the corporate image

The work on the corporate image started in the summer of 1988, many months before the planned opening in March 1990. The management team of the theatre wished the new image to be well established before the opening launch.

Certain things were given – the name, the building (then under construction, but a large model stood in the foyer of the Leeds Playhouse), the mission statement and the artistic policy which had formed the basis of the new theatre's strategic plan.

In the initial stages, one of the two architects of the building was very much involved in the discussions about the concept of the corporate image. He brought some important insights to the project – an awareness of the building as the physical basis of the theatre's work, and a very visual emphasis to that building – centredness. He talked about the internal and external appearance of the building, the patterns of the bricks, the repeated yellow, red and blue of the colours inside and outside. Above all, he helped the marketing manager see that corporate image is a unified concept, something that encapsulates all aspects of an organization and its work, something that goes far beyond the development of the logo.

From these discussions, the marketing manager and executive director took to the board a recommendation that an image was developed that was classic and that wouldn't date easily; but at the same time was fresh, modern and contemporary. The logo should be flexible and able to be developed in a number of ways.

The board gave their approval to the outline brief and three firms of designers were interviewed. Each team provided a portfolio of their current work, and discussed in depth their ideas about theatrical logos. The firms were not asked at this point to submit proposals for the West Yorkshire Playhouse specifically, because of the costs incurred in this (the 'pitch fee'). From this exercise a recommendation was made to the board that a particular firm be asked to produce a number of ideas. The solution was not specified to the designers, who were given an open-ended brief and in fact quite a lot of different ideas were developed and worked through. One in particular stood out.

The chosen solution

The design solution that was ultimately adopted was four-colour: blue, red, yellow and black. It consisted of a pictorial strip in blue and yellow, with the black words 'The West Yorkshire' on one side in helvetica (a sans serif typeface), and 'Playhouse' in red in a drawn serif on the other. Under the 'Playhouse' was a line of blue dots. The image could also be presented vertically.

The images in the strip consisted of different elements of theatrical activity – music, theatre, dance, classical and modern pieces. There were masks from both the Greek theatre and a masquerade, a crown, a rose, a violin: all floating in a fragmented way against the blue background.

The disadvantages with this logo did not become apparent until it was being used. As is often the case with linear logos, it did not reproduce well when it was reduced in size. It lost a lot of its impact in newsprint. The drawn letters in 'Playhouse' did not constitute a full alphabet and did not correspond to a known typeface. Therefore designers who wished to use the same style in other places had to draw the letters individually. This was a problem, for example, in the Annual Report 1989, in which each page started with an illuminated initial capital. The requirements for a 'C', a 'W' and 'B' could not be satisfied from 'PLAYHOUSE' and thus required extra design time.

Developments of the logo

The number of different elements within the overall design offered considerable scope for flexibility and imagination in its use.

Firstly, there was considerable impact to be gained from the colours included in it. An eye-catching press release paper was developed which had the vivid blue and yellow strip as its border. In contrast, the corporate letterhead used the blue and red, which gave a more formal feel to official communications. All of the accounting stationery was produced in blue; which was both reasonable in cost as it was one colour but also extended the corporate image throughout the supplier chain. The annual reports for 1989 and 1990 which were highly finished pieces of corporate print, central to the capital development promotional strategy, used the strip in half tones of red to link the inside pages visually, and in half tones of yellow and blue on the outside cover, to pick up the full four-colour glossy logo prominently displayed front and back. This guaranteed maximum impact and recognition.

In the months before the opening, the logo was generally used in its full form to establish the new entity; and to ensure a clear distinction from the Leeds Playhouse which was still trading. In the months after the opening, various other options were introduced, to give variety within consistency.

Developing the image beyond the logo

The logo, with its typeface, was the cornerstone of the corporate image. It was widely used on all printed material, from promotional leaflets, to generic leaflets aimed, for example, at corporate groups, to all the official stationery of the organization.

This was not without some internal conflict. For many, the old 'owl' logo of the Leeds Playhouse symbolized a very strong tradition. It took some adjusting to the new strip, which symbolized the whole transition to a much larger enterprise. With the new logo came the trappings of a whole new way of doing things – business cards, invoices, computerized cheques, the ephemera of the catering operation such as drip mats, napkins, customized sugar sachets and so on. The staff of the theatre came to see that corporate image was concerned with all aspects of the way the theatre company communicated with the outside world.

Signage in and around the theatre was an important aspect of this and, as in any new building, there were problems initially with signs in the wrong place or with unclear messages. Decisions had even to be made about whether the female toilets were called 'ladies' or 'women'.

The exterior signage hit problems both with the town planners, who had a very strong and city-wide view on signs, and with the architect, who believed that, as with a cathedral, no signs were necessary as the theatre building was its own unmistakable sign. A compromise was reached with an external edifice sporting three banners of the Playhouse logo, but these were given to flying off whenever there were high winds. It was several years before large external signs were erected on the fabric of the building.

A further successful development of the logo was its use on a variety of merchandise – fine china mugs, sweatshirts and T-shirts which used different elements of the strip on various versions of the base colours. The blue version was used by attendants and bar staff initially as their uniform but sales of merchandise to audiences were so successful that the in-house team had to change their own livery to distinguish themselves from their customers. Over the years of its use, the logo has allowed itself to be adapted to suit the needs of different contexts, to emphasize modernity or display a more classical constraint, or to add variety while conforming to the house style encapsulated in the corporate design manual.

Questions

1 Examine an example of a strong corporate identity known to you. How are the various elements within the design used flexibly?
2 What problems do arts organizations specifically present in corporate design terms? How can you distinguish the variety of products offered, to emphasize their unique qualities, while maintaining an organizational identity?
3 As marketing manager of an arts organization, what factors would you take into account in designing a new letterhead?
4 Is it possible to design a logo which will not date? Give some examples of logos that you feel have stood up to the test of time.

Cambridge Arts Theatre

Introduction

This case examines the way in which the Cambridge Arts Theatre embarked on an ambitious plan to raise £3m to enable it to renovate its building and thereby secure its future. The history of the fund-raising activities and their results are described and issues relating to the role of volunteers, the use of consultants and the management of both a community campaign and a major gift campaign are raised.

Background

The Cambridge Arts Theatre was built in 1936, conceived by the economist John Maynard Keynes and paid for entirely from his own pocket. Two years later he established the Arts Theatre Trust which provided both the city of Cambridge and the University with a suitable venue for drama, opera, ballet and music. Keynes was deeply committed to the importance of the arts. He believed that 'a good small theatre, equipped with all the contrivances of modern stagecraft, is as necessary to our understanding of dramatic arts, with their complicated dependence on literature, music and design, as a laboratory is to experimental science.'

Since the early days, the Arts Theatre has held a unique place in the artistic life of the city and is today recognized as a centre of excellence for the arts, attracting audiences from throughout the region. It is closely associated with the Cambridge Footlights Revue, the Cambridge University Marlowe Dramatic Society and the University's other theatre groups. It has proved to be the training ground for many of the country's leading actors, directors and media personalities who benefited from the chance to explore and develop ideas unattainable within a normal student environment. Peter Hall, Trevor Nunn, Stephen Fry, Ian McKellen, Griff Rhys Jones and Emma Thompson are among those who started their careers at the Arts Theatre.

What they say about the Arts Theatre . . .

'I am sure that most people do not realize how much a theatre means . . . until it's gone.'

(Griff Rhys Jones)

'The Arts Theatre is probably the main reason that Cambridge has always taken the lead in producing England's most distinguished actors and directors.'

(Jonathan Miller)

'Is there a better theatre? Is there a friendlier theatre? I think of the Arts with abiding affection.'

(Derek Jacobi)

'Performing on the stage of the Arts was probably the closest I ever came to erotic ecstasy.'

(Stephen Fry)

Plans for restoration

By the late 1980s, after more than fifty years of continuous operation, it was becoming apparent that the theatre was badly in need of modernization.

Improvements were needed in four key areas: the stage, the auditorium, customer care and catering. The fabric of the building was falling into disrepair and its technical limitations, particularly the small, unusually-shaped stage, were increasingly restricting the potential range of performance. Facilities for performers were primitive, with only one shower in the building. Trading opportunities were severely limited by the layout of facilities. The main restaurant was at the top of the building, and its floor was shared with the ceiling of the auditorium, making it impossible to open the restaurant in the evenings when a production was on stage. There were no lifts, only a very steep staircase. This restricted access to the fit and able-bodied. It also meant that food from the kitchens on the first floor had to be carried up the public staircase to the restaurant above. The theatre bar was a converted broom-cupboard, with such a narrow entrance that queues of people trying to get into the bar were faced with queues of people trying to get out of the bar, and the foyer was the only space available for drinks to be consumed. The combination of these factors had led to severe financial difficulties which were becoming critical to the future of the theatre.

An endowment fund had been set up in 1960 in memory of Keynes to support the work of the trust. The income from this, coupled with very small subsidies from the Regional Arts Board, Cambridge City Council and South Cambridgeshire District Council, had been the main source of revenue for many years. Increasingly, though, the capital had to be drawn upon to supplement revenues and, despite a top-up in

1980, it was forecast that the endowment fund would run out in September 1993, at which point the Arts Theatre would become insolvent.

For the new chief executive appointed in April 1990, one of the first tasks was to evaluate the options. At a time when public funding of the arts was starting to be heavily curtailed, it soon became clear that the potential for attracting additional subsidy was very limited and that this would not be a viable means of securing the future of the Arts Theatre. The only alternative was to consider renovating the building so that new facilities could be used to stimulate the revenue generated from both the box office and trading activities.

Corpus Christi College owned a sizeable piece of land near the Arts Theatre, some of which was adjacent to the stage area of the theatre. The College was planning to develop new student accommodation on their site, and had offered a small piece of the land to the theatre at a peppercorn rent. This land would enable the theatre to improve dramatically its stage and backstage areas – one of the most serious problems facing it at that time. Some important synergies would emerge if the Arts Theatre building work was pursued at the same time as the student accommodation. Furthermore, if the Arts Theatre did not take this opportunity, the land needed to extend the theatre would be lost forever, cut off by the new accommodation block. With this in mind, in September 1990 a firm of architects was appointed to undertake a feasibility study. This confirmed that the site was suitable for the proposed alterations and by February 1991 the decision had been made to rebuild the Arts Theatre (see Figure C2).

Planning for fund-raising

From a shortlist of three, an Australian firm of fund-raising consultants was selected to prepare a feasibility study into the fund-raising potential for the project. Their managing director for the northern hemisphere was given responsibility for the study. His research included interviewing some 30 people, both local and national figures, whom the Arts Theatre management believed would be influential in this project. It concluded that £3m could be raised. The majority of this was projected to come from major gifts and the rest from community activities.

Encouraged by this, in September 1991 the Arts Theatre contracted this same firm of consultants to plan a fund-raising campaign on their behalf. The firm supplied a UK based consultant with considerable experience in community campaigns. His role was to create a structure for the campaign and to set up an appropriate committee of volunteers, as well as initiating some early fund-raising activity. He would also install his firm's own hardware and dedicated software to start up a fund-raising database and would organize the fund-raising systems and provide training so that before long the Arts Theatre would be self-sufficient in fund-raising and his role with them would cease.

A local businessman with a strong commitment to the Arts Theatre volunteered to

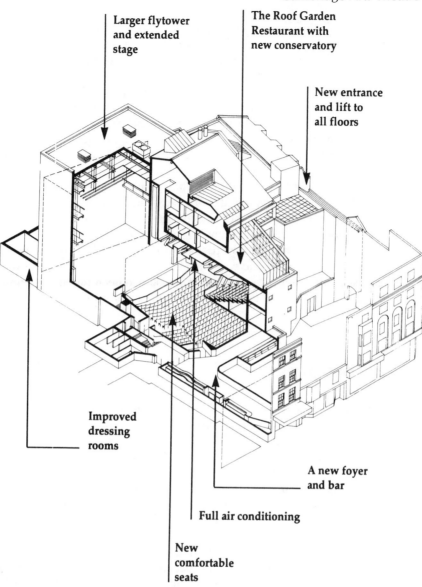

Larger flytower and extended stage

The Roof Garden Restaurant with new conservatory

New entrance and lift to all floors

Improved dressing rooms

A new foyer and bar

Full air conditioning

New comfortable seats

Figure C2   The new interior of the Cambridge Arts Theatre

take the role of campaign chairman, working alongside the consultant. It was their role to put together a committee of volunteers, mainly business people, who would identify key targets, make strategic approaches and ask people for money.

During the autumn of 1991 though, both the chief executive and the campaign chairman felt a growing concern over the performance of the fund-raising consultant. Their expectation was for the development of a coherent and dynamic campaign, but few initiatives were forthcoming, and by January 1992 so little progress had been made that a new consultant was sought. As the fund-raising firm were unable to provide an acceptable replacement, the relationship with them was also ended, which resulted in the removal of the database hardware and software.

It transpired that the manager who had satisfactorily undertaken the original feasibility study had left the firm of consultants in early January. Keen to re-engage his expertise, the Arts Theatre approached him independently in February 1992 and he was offered a six month fixed-term contract with a brief of getting the campaign started, setting up a fund-raising committee and training both staff and volunteers to continue the fund-raising activity. The agreement included the provision for the Arts Theatre to continue to contact him for advice until the end of the campaign. When he left in August 1992, much good ground-work had been completed.

The fund-raising committee, re-motivated on the arrival of the new consultant, had set to work. Their first task was to investigate possible sources of grant-making trusts. Letters were sent off and, thanks partially to some of the acquaintances and contacts that committee members had with members of the boards of trustees of these grant-making trusts, within a few weeks about £50,000 had been raised. A community campaign was subsequently launched in November 1992, and further efforts were put into securing major gifts.

Campaign progress

The autumn of 1992 was a very busy time for the management of the Arts Theatre. It was at this stage that the planned closure of the theatre was announced and redundancies had to be negotiated with the unions. Shortly after this came the Government's announcement that Britain would be launching a National Lottery in 1994, some of the proceeds of which would be allocated to the arts for capital projects. In the light of this, and a failure to reach original income targets, the plans for the rebuilding were revised and extended, meaning that the reopening date, originally set for the Christmas 1994 Pantomime, would have to be put back to spring 1996.

The Arts Theatre closed in April 1993 and the following six months were difficult times for fund-raising. The theatre was dark, yet there was no evidence of building work starting, though in fact a lot of design and archaeological work was being undertaken during this period. The public seemed to lose confidence in the theatre and securing donations became increasingly difficult, not helped by the severity of the recession which was by this time affecting the willingness and ability of corporate donors to give money. The campaign chairman was experiencing personal business difficulties of his own and was not in a position to devote as much time to steering the campaign as he would have liked. By the summer of 1993 it was becoming apparent that a new management structure was needed to drive the campaign forward and in September 1993 the campaign chairman stepped down and his role was taken on by the chairman of the Arts Theatre Trust. The chief executive of the theatre was designated executive in charge of the campaign, and a member of the committee took special responsibility for the community campaign. Things started to look up in the autumn, particularly when the crane arrived on the site and the residents of Cambridge had firm evidence that progress was being made. By Christmas the workload related to the fund-raising activity was sufficient to justify a paid fund-raiser on a part-time basis.

The campaign continued apace. Significant construction work started on the site when the steelwork for the new fly-tower was erected the following February. In the summer of 1994, the part-time fund-raiser resigned to take up a full-time job elsewhere. The opportunity was taken to review the position and a full-timer, responsible for major gifts and corporate support, was appointed. A temporary post was created to manage the lottery application. The committee members, many of whom had been dedicated volunteers for nearly two years, were offered a break. Several, faced with pressures of work, were happy to be replaced by new faces.

By January 1995, The Arts Theatre Campaign has raised a total of £2.4m, £400,000 of which has come from the community campaign. This leaves a fund-raising target of another £600,000 by April 1995, with the balance to come from the National Lottery.

Fund-raising techniques

The Cambridge Arts Theatre fund-raising campaign has relied on two major initiatives – the campaign for major gifts and the community campaign.

The major gift campaign

Right at the start it was identified that major gifts from individuals, businesses and organizations would have the most leverage on the success of the campaign. The committee members were responsible for generating major gifts and they set about identifying and contacting individuals and organizations who could potentially contribute to the campaign.

A lot of effort was put into building relationships with potential donors, familiarizing them with the theatre and the plans for its renewal. Donors needed to be fully convinced that their money would be well spent and that the project was viable.

Two sizeable donations were made at an early stage by the Foundation for Sport and the Arts and Cambridge City Council. It was they who enabled work on the site to get started. The more wealthy of the Cambridge colleges were very generous too, and gifts from these sources sustained the committee through the difficult task of obtaining corporate support during the recession. Even those businesses that could spare some cash for the campaign were reluctant to do so, concerned about bad PR if they were seen to be giving away money at the same time as laying off staff.

One event which was planned to help stimulate major gifts was a reception at 10 Downing Street in July 1993. A number of contacts were made and are still being worked on. It often takes between six months and two-and-a-half years between an initial approach and the realization of a major gift.

The community campaign

The structure of the community campaign was put in place at the very start of the fund-raising planning on the recommendation of the independent consultant.

The theatre's computerized database, set up on the PASS system, was divided up according to the nine post-code areas within a 25 mile radius, and those who had attended four times or more in the past three years were identified. From this list of over 2000 attenders, shortlists were drawn up of those who might be willing and able to either lead or be a member of a small team of fund-raising volunteers in their part of the theatre's catchment area. Each potential recruit was telephoned and interviewed by the chairman of the community campaign. Eventually eight team leaders were recruited. The community campaign chairman led one team himself, on the basis that why should he ask others to do a job if he weren't willing to do it himself. Each team leader was then responsible for recruiting another ten volunteers to spearhead the campaign in his or her area. Each team was set a fund-raising target, anything from £12,000 up to £35,000 depending on the size and location of their territory.

A professional fund-raiser was invited to train the volunteers. She recommended to them that the quickest and most effective way of reaching their targets would simply be to identify individuals who might be sympathetic to the renovation of the Arts Theatre (regular attenders on the database), and then to ask them for a one-off donation or a covenanted gift on a regular basis. Her training focused on the most difficult task of all – that of asking for the money. Some of the teams used this technique almost exclusively, whilst others used a mix of approaches, including the organizing of fund-raising events.

The great benefit of the fund-raising events was the way that they raised the profile of the campaign in the community. The subsequent activities organized by the teams were many and various. They included bridge evenings, coffee mornings, an art exhibition, functions at the Cambridge colleges, a Cole Porter evening and even a duck-race on the river. A prize-draw for a car, bought at cost from a manufacturer, raised over £26,000 net, but the administration required to manage this proved onerous.

Two fund-raising initiatives were undertaken as an extension to the general community campaign. These were the Arts Access Campaign and the Schools Campaign. As the plans for the Arts Theatre have placed a great emphasis on creating appropriate facilities for the disabled, special efforts were put into involving local disabled groups in fund-raising activities. Schools have also been encouraged to raise money for the campaign, and prizes, sponsored by a local bookseller and stationer, have been provided.

Questions

1 Why do you think people make large donations to support the arts? List the different motivations that you think might have influenced individuals and organizations to give money to the Arts Theatre campaign.

2 What are the advantages and disadvantages of using a committee of volunteers to spearhead a major fund-raising programme? What sort of management structure do you think is necessary to support such a committee?

3 What criteria would you use in appointing a fund-raising consultant? How would you evaluate his or her performance? What kind of remuneration arrangements would you put in place?

4 The community campaign has so far brought in about 20 per cent of the total funds raised. Do you think it has been worth the considerable efforts made? What other benefits may stem from the community activities?

5 The Arts Theatre campaign is still £600,000 short of its target. Write down ten fund-raising ideas to help them reach their target, five of which are aimed at attracting major gifts and five of which are community initiatives.

Index